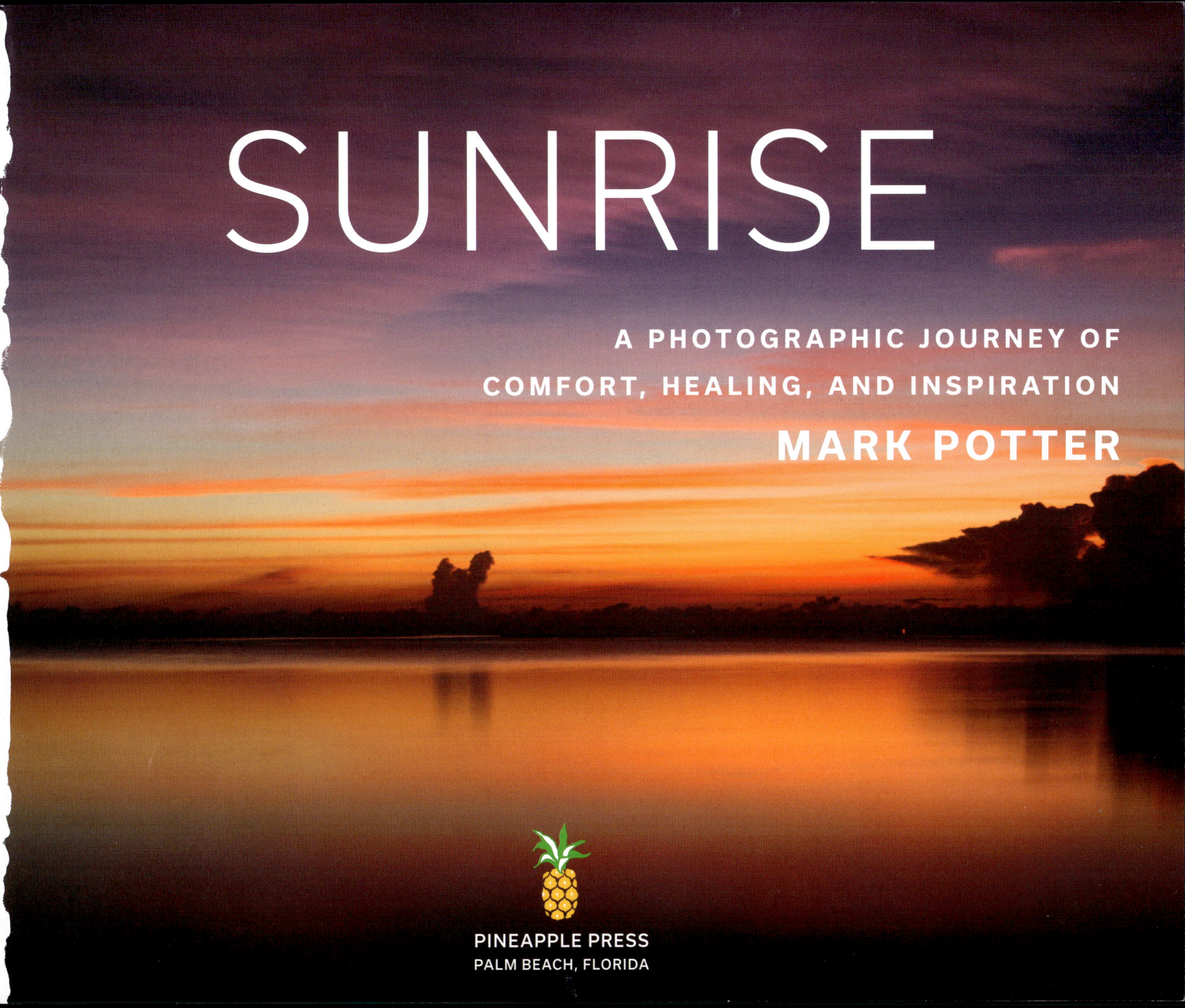

SUNRISE

A PHOTOGRAPHIC JOURNEY OF COMFORT, HEALING, AND INSPIRATION

MARK POTTER

PINEAPPLE PRESS
PALM BEACH, FLORIDA

Pineapple Press

An imprint of Globe Pequot, the trade division of
The Rowman & Littlefield Publishing Group, Inc.
4501 Forbes Blvd., Ste. 200
Lanham, MD 20706
www.rowman.com

Distributed by NATIONAL BOOK NETWORK

Photography by Mark Potter

British Library Cataloguing in Publication Information Available

Library of Congress Cataloging-in-Publication Data

ISBN 978-1-4930-6603-2 (cloth : alk. paper)
ISBN 978-1-4930-6604-9 (electronic)

∞™ The paper used in this publication meets the minimum requirements of American National Standard for Information Sciences—Permanence of Paper for Printed Library Materials, ANSI/NISO Z39.48-1992.

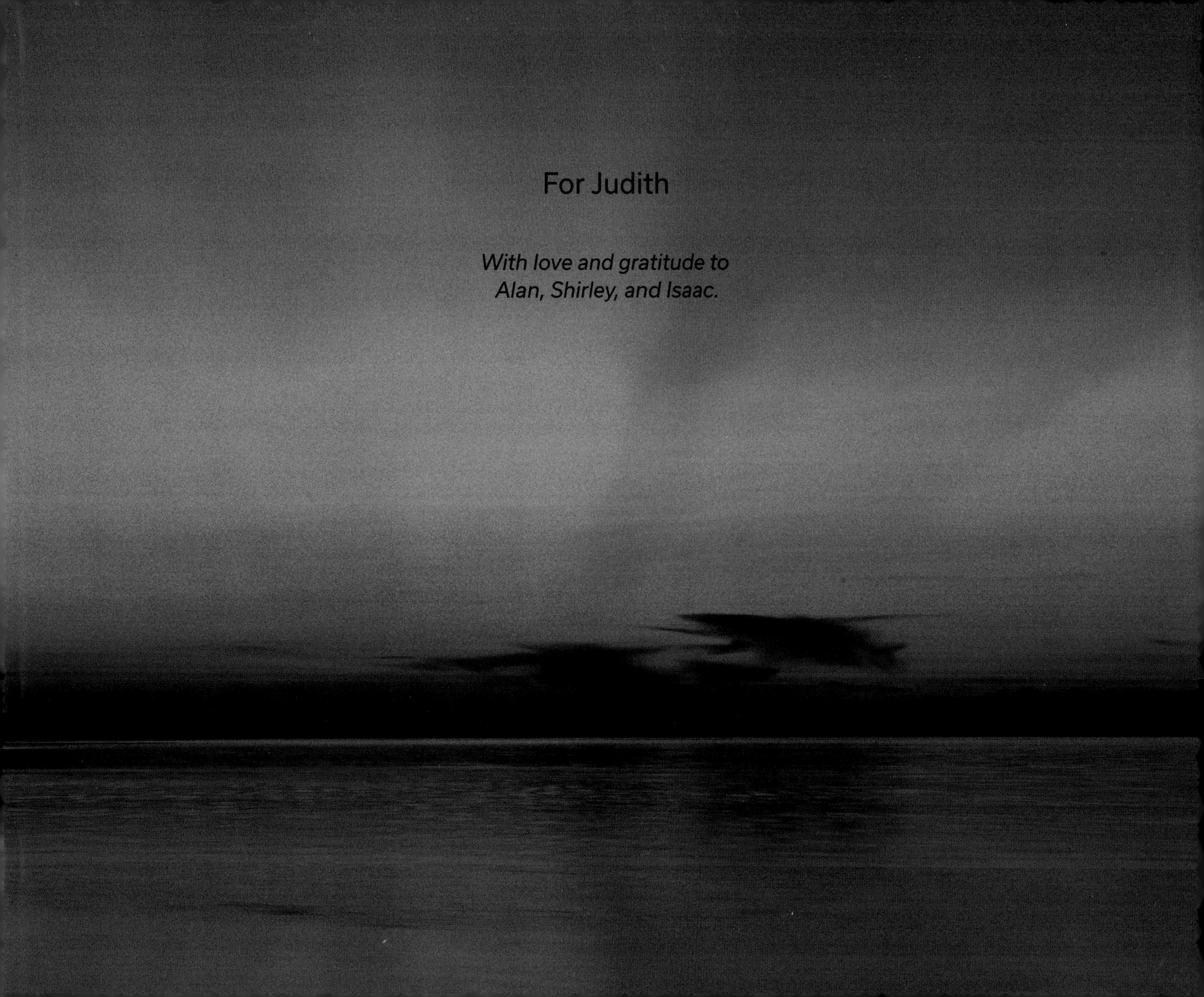

For Judith

With love and gratitude to
Alan, Shirley, and Isaac.

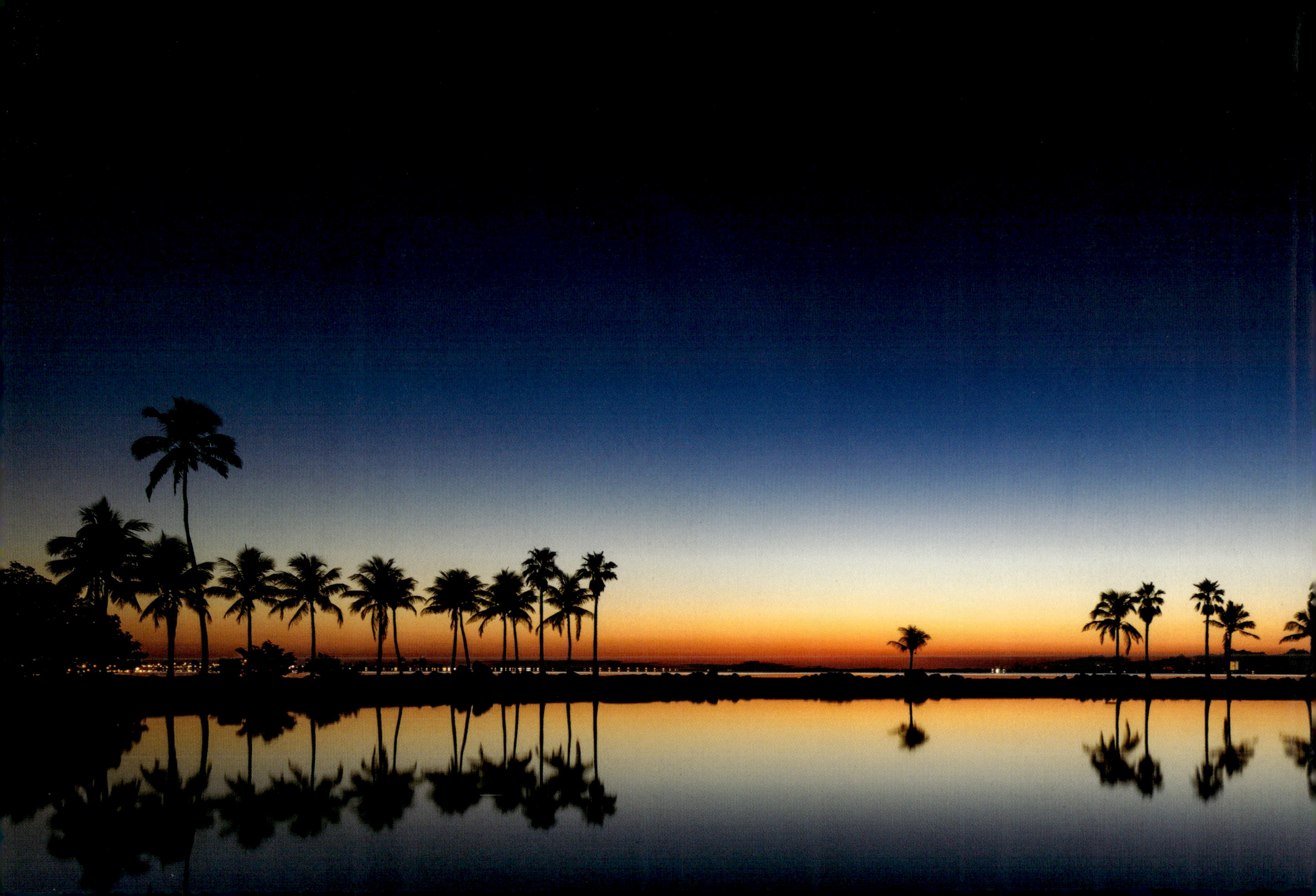

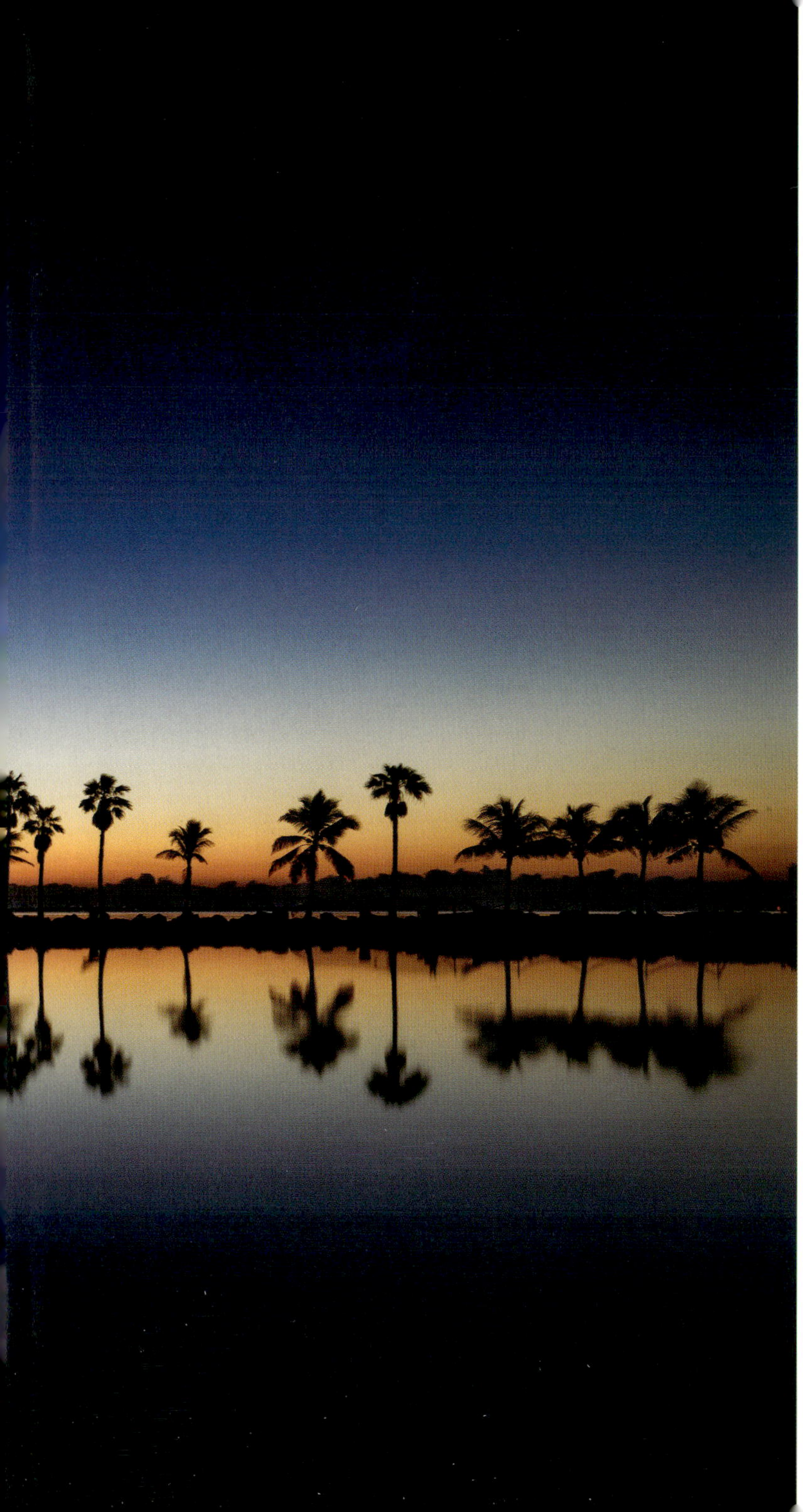

Contents

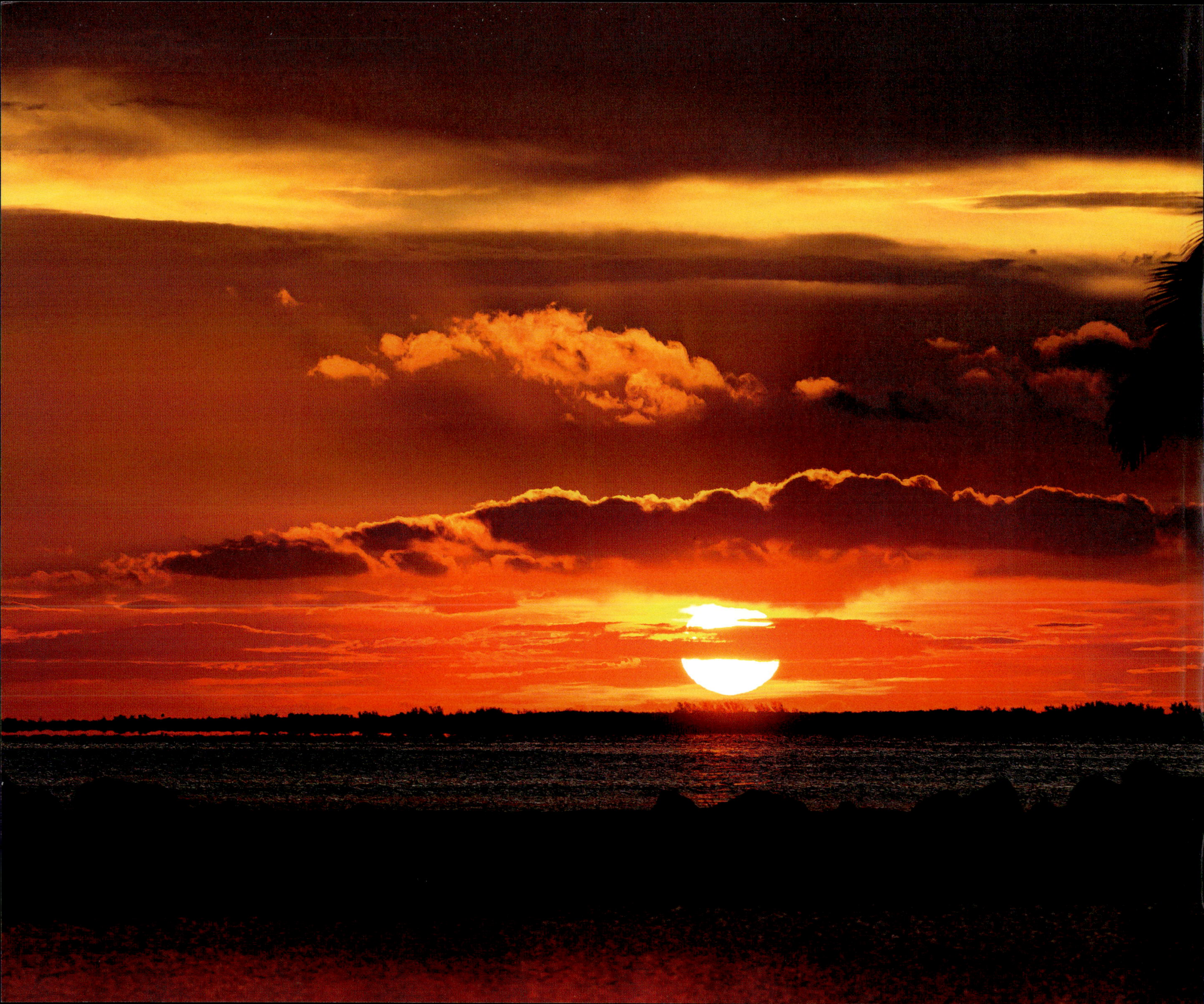

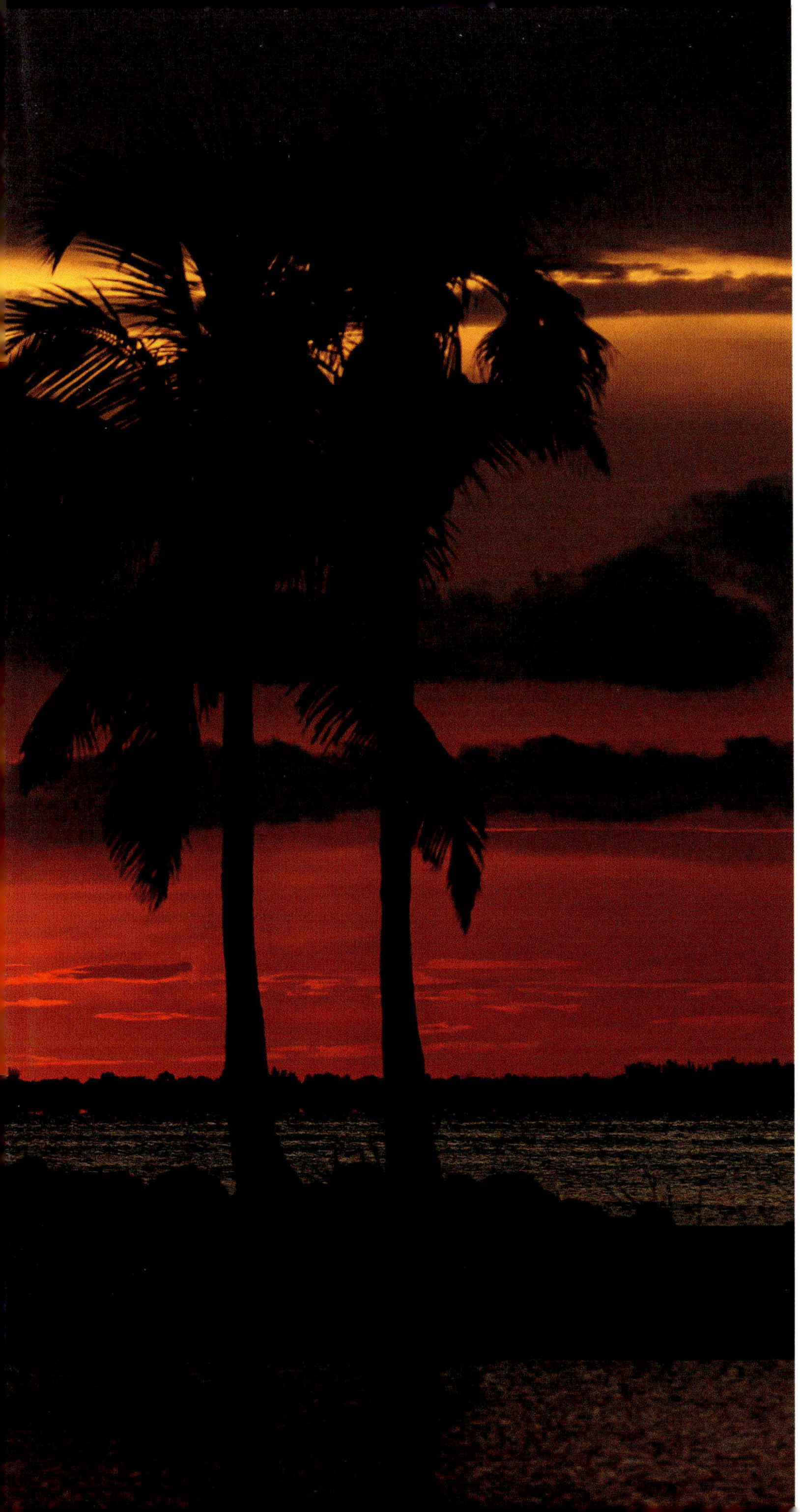

Sunrise for Judith

With a moonless sky this early morning, it is eerily dark out here, and I can feel the weight of the hot and humid South Florida air. As I head toward the sound of the rolling ocean surf ahead of me, the soft beach sand shifts beneath my feet, making it hard for me to walk while balancing my two cameras and a heavy tripod. Even though I go out like this virtually every morning, it never gets old, and once again I am starting to get excited. I am very alert and can even feel my breathing increase as I approach the shoreline. These are welcome signs that I'm fully alive right now and engaged in what I call "magic time." It's that ungodly hour of the day when most normal people here are still safely at home, asleep in their comfortable beds, and blissfully unaware that they are on the verge of missing out on one of the best lightshows on all of planet Earth: The tropical sunrise!

I have been taking lots of pictures of that lightshow, from many different angles, all in loving memory of my beautiful wife, Judith Rodriguez Potter, who slipped away from us on April 12, 2019. As she did in life, she still inspires me now to get up early, go outside, look upward, and capture the arrival of the magnificent and restorative sun. I rarely miss a day, and I can see her face in every sunrise.

If someone ever tells you how the sunrise is going to look tomorrow, make a wager because you're likely to walk away with extra cash in your pocket. I have been photographing sunrises for several years now and I still can't tell you with any accuracy what's going to happen the next morning. You just have to wait and see. That's the beauty of it.

I am always surprised and often amazed by what I am witnessing in front of me. On a few occasions, I've actually found myself just standing there, momentarily forgetting my camera, wondering how in the world could this be happening? At times like these I feel as if I am attending my own church without a roof.

While the morning is still dark, I can actually feel, see, and even hear the atmosphere change as the sunrise starts to slowly build. The black and blue colors of night begin to fade as the first light of day emerges. The stars and planets you marveled at when you arrived are now nearly invisible. The nighttime winds will often quiet down, the waves become gentler, and any overnight fog starts to lift. Not long afterward, flocks of gulls begin to squawk and fly. Ospreys circle widely overhead, and ibises form tight formations as they head for the morning feeding grounds. Snook, snapper, barracuda, and other fish crash into the mangroves and chase their prey in the surf and on the ocean flats. Unfortunately, mosquitos and the dreaded no-see-um bugs also make their appearances. It's as if the entire ecosystem has come awake and is proudly announcing itself.

Sometimes, if the clouds and humidity are just right, and luck is on my side, the darkness is softly replaced by wisps of pastel pink, red, purple, gold, and orange. If that persists, and the colors start to deepen, or better yet explode, I am in for some glorious pyrotechnics—a full-blown Technicolor movie in the sky. And if all this begins before I am where I need to be to set up my camera, I will find myself doing foolish things, such as speeding too fast down quiet beach roads to get there quickly. Or I'll run and trip in the sand and mud to position my tripod for a proper shot. I know all too well how this can happen. It's usually because I tried to be like everyone else for a day and slept in just a little too late. It can be a costly mistake for a dedicated sunrise photographer. We are not like everyone else.

I have experienced all of this now, because of the inspirational woman at the center of my life—my wife and best friend, Judith, who turned me into a chronicler of the morning sun. She did it in the firm belief that she was saving my life, at the same time I was struggling to help save hers from the ravages of ovarian cancer. It is the unvarnished truth that all of my bright and colorful sunrise photographs began from extreme pain, fear, isolation, sadness and loss. But as miracles will sometimes have it, and in a great surprise to me, the images actually turned out to be the exact opposite of the way they began. So many people tell me they find my photos to be upbeat and exciting or comforting and calming. Friends have also said the morning pictures are inspiring and give them hope, which moves me deeply, and of course, propels me to shoot even more of them. My clever wife clearly knew what she was doing.

Judith was a loving, smart, caring, classy, and independent woman who always devoted herself to her family. She doted heavily on me and pursued several careers. She was born Judith Rodriguez in Havana, Cuba, and spent much of her childhood in the tiny town of Los Palos, where her father owned a small sundries business. As she grew older, Judith and her family chafed under the rules and privations of the Cuban revolution. At the insistence of her father, who spent three years as a political prisoner, Judith emigrated to the United States by herself in 1970 at the age of twenty-two.

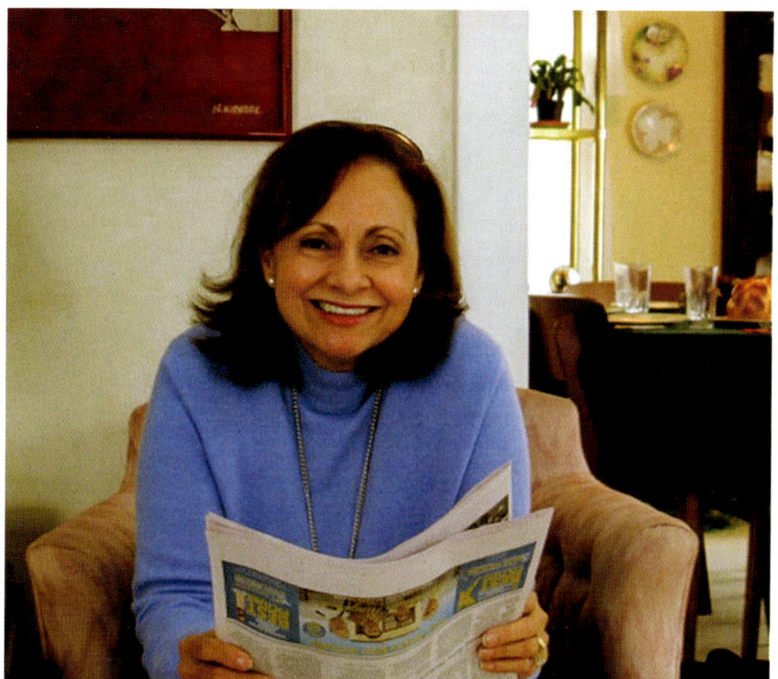

After arriving in Miami, she went to Tampa to stay with her aunt, uncle, and cousin who welcomed and protected her. Judith took English lessons and other classes by day and worked nights in a shrimp processing plant. Two years later she moved to Los Angeles where she earned a literature degree at UCLA. She also took medical courses and worked for several years as a doctor's assistant at the Kaiser Permanente hospital emergency room. Most importantly to her, she proudly became an American citizen.

Judith's biggest regret then—and a source of heavy sorrow—was that she was away from her parents and two brothers in Cuba. She missed them dearly. After her beloved father died in 1977, Judith was alone and in agony. She didn't learn of his passing until two weeks later because her family had been unable to make a call to the United States. Judith was forbidden by the Cuban government to return home.

Shortly afterward, her family decided the time had come for them to also leave Cuba. As fate would have it, dramatic events in 1980 finally made it possible for Judith and her family to reunite.

The Mariel Boatlift was a historic wave of mass emigration that brought 125,000 Cubans to the United States, mostly to South Florida, after Fidel Castro allowed them to leave.

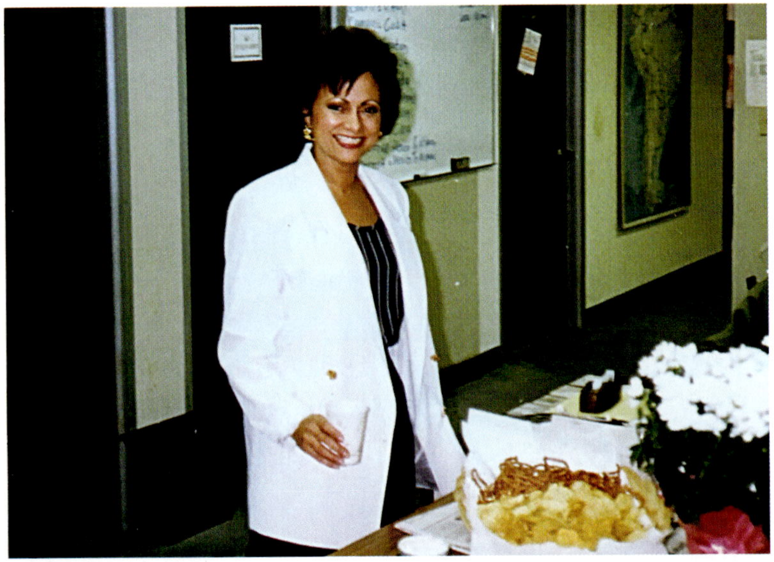

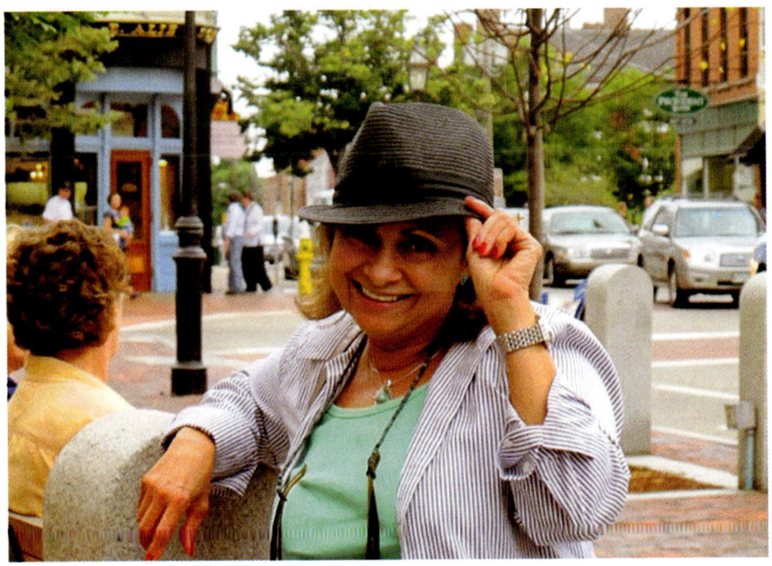

It began in the spring of 1980 and caught Judith's attention in California. Seeing this as her last chance to bring her family to the United States, Judith drove nearly three-thousand miles across the country to Key West, Florida. There she and several other Cuban exiles paid a fishing boat captain for a trip across the treacherous Florida Straits to the Mariel harbor near Havana. On shore, she tried to negotiate the release of her family, but Cuban authorities wouldn't allow it because her youngest brother, Isaac Rodriguez, hadn't served yet in the military as is required by law. Judith was ordered to leave Cuba. Arriving back in Key West broken-hearted and emotionally drained, she then had to make the long trip back to Los Angeles.

Fortunately, there was one last ray of hope. While still in Cuba negotiating for her family, Judith had gotten to know a government official whom she felt she could trust. Right before reboarding the charter boat in Mariel to head back home, she quietly gave him a cash payment and a copy of her family's home address. A short time later, after Judith was gone, the official honored their agreement. In the middle of the night, Isaac and his mother were moved from their apartment and later put on a boat headed for Key West. Judith's second brother, Alfredo, took another boat. Judith had no idea any of this was happening until a United States Navy sailor in Florida called to surprise her with the exciting news: Judith's dream of embracing her family in the United States had finally come true.

Eventually, the whole Rodriguez family settled in South Florida. Judith found a temporary job as a secretary for ABC News at the Miami bureau. The bureau chief liked her so much he promoted her to the position of full-time budget administrator for Latin American news gathering. As part of that job, she traveled alone to Central American war zones hand-carrying cash to pay for coverage expenses.

My life, on the other hand, started out much less dramatically. I grew up in a middle-class family in Sedalia, Missouri and Ann Arbor, Michigan. My father was a newspaper editor and a dedicated birdwatcher. My mother was at various times a teacher, a full-time homemaker, and an office manager at the University of Michigan graduate business school. For years, my only sibling and brother, Alan Potter, and I shared a tiny bedroom on the west side of a two-story house. The brutal Michigan winter winds could easily be felt through the walls because the room had no direct heat. I may have been the only teenager to actually ask for, and receive, a bright-orange electric blanket for Christmas.

Alan still lives in Michigan where he teaches art appreciation at Eastern Michigan University and lives with his wife, Shirley. My thoughts on cold-weather living were much different, though, and as soon as possible, I began moving south. After graduating from Ann Arbor Pioneer High School in 1971, and attending classes for two years at Eastern Michigan, I entered the University of Missouri School of Journalism, determined to become a television reporter. As part of the J-School curriculum, I covered high school sports with a wind-up film camera. My first paying job after graduation in 1975 was at WTVW-TV in Evansville, Indiana. I was mostly an on-air reporter but also shot news reports with film and newly invented video-tape cameras.

A year later, I moved to Miami after being hired by the NBC station, WCKT, where I quickly became a full-time reporter, ending my brief stint as a news photographer. A poignant memory is that in 1980, the assignment editor dispatched me to Key West to cover the momentous Mariel Boatlift with all the Cuban refugees pouring in. During the weeks I was there, I had no idea that my future wife, my future mother-in law and two brothers-in-law might be passing right before me.

After covering the Miami cocaine war, the deadly McDuffie race riot, and the Theodore Bundy murder trial, I joined an investigative-reporting team at WPLG-TV. Two years later, in 1983, I launched a thirty-three-year national network career and joined the ABC News Miami bureau, where I met Judith, the budget administrator. We became co-workers and good friends, and for eight years we would flirtatiously "fight" over my travel spending. When the bureau was dramatically downsized in 1991, Judith moved to the New York news headquarters while I stayed in Miami. Only then did we start to formally date. We fell in love and were married in 1995. By then she had left the network and returned to Miami where she earned

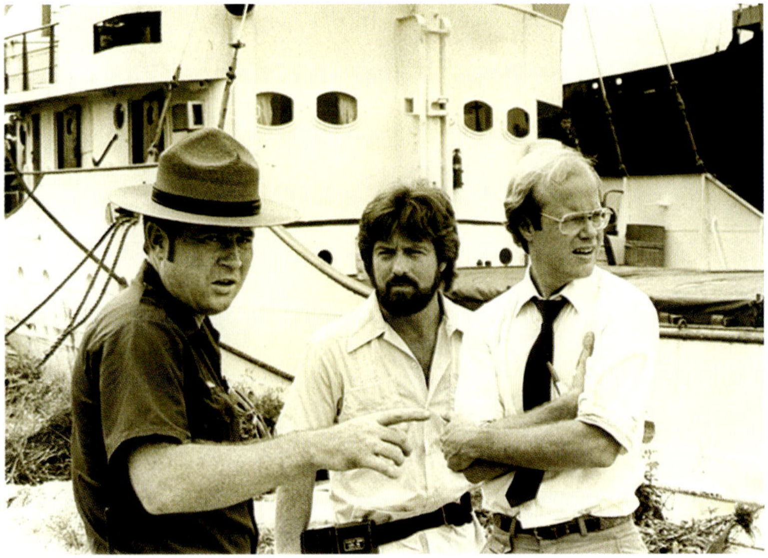

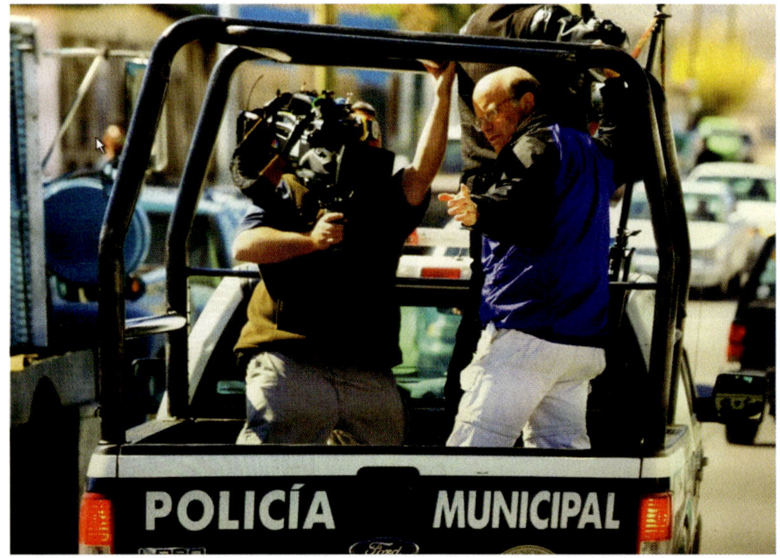

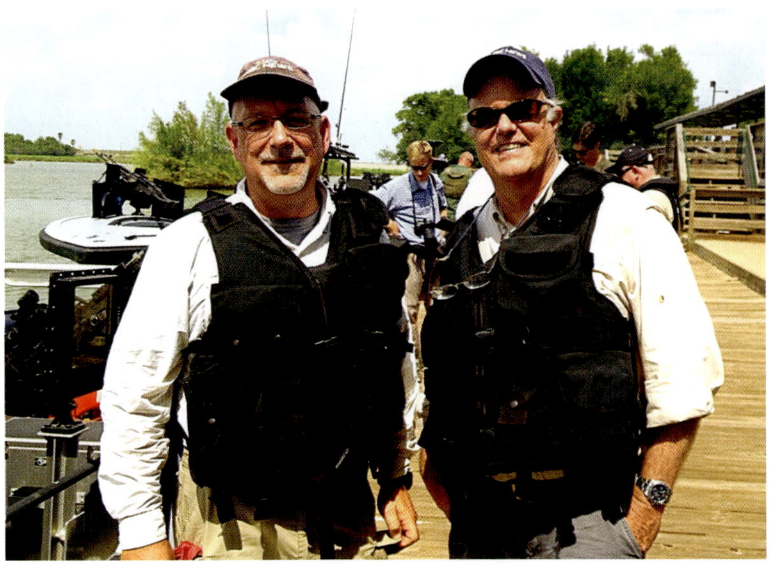

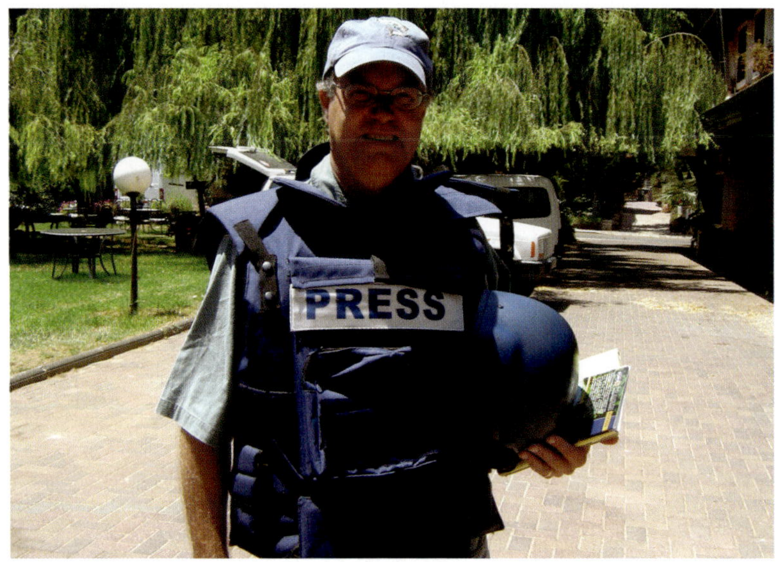

From top left: covering Haitian migrant smugglers in Miami, the Mexican drug war, the Israel-Hezbollah war, and the Southwest border crisis.

two more college degrees and became a teacher of learning-disabled pre-school children.

As the years passed, I also worked as a correspondent for CNN and NBC News in their Miami bureaus. I spent most of my time covering investigative and hard news throughout the United States, Latin America, and other parts of the world. Among the stories I covered were the Grenada invasion, the Colombian drug war, Cuban rafters and Haitian boat people, the southwest border crisis, countless hurricanes, tornados, earthquakes, and the daring prison tunnel escape of Mexican drug kingpin Joaquin Guzman Loera, better known as "El Chapo."

During those years, I was always on call and often on the road. Judith gracefully managed our household, kept me in good health, paid all the bills, and made sure everything else ran smoothly while also working on her own career. As the two of us got older, we began to talk about retirement and how we planned to spend our free time together. Front and center was the hope we would travel at a leisurely pace to interesting places around the world. I also thought I might become a part-time journalism teacher. Judith's dream was to attend college classes and to become more fluent in her third language, French.

In 2016, the prospect of our joint retirement became a reality. Judith had already left teaching, and I was notified that the NBC News front office was not renewing my contract, which finished my career. My NBC colleagues in Miami threw a nice going-away party for me, with guests from around the country. I had a lovely time and enjoyed all the speeches, gifts, and good food. But I also noticed that Judith wasn't feeling well that night and wasn't her usual self. She had been complaining of belly pain and bloating, and we had scheduled an appointment with a gastroenterologist for a CT scan.

For as long as I live, I will never forget the catastrophic shock we both felt when the doctor walked into the exam room, sat down, drew a breath, and collected himself for a few moments before delivering the devastating test results. In a quiet professional tone, he told us that Judith's abdomen was filled with what appeared to be gynecological cancer tumors. Hearing that was as close as I've ever come to being hit with a shotgun blast. Judith and I just looked at each other in frozen terror. Somehow, we made it back to our car, and as I numbly drove us home Judith turned to me and said, "I've just been given a death sentence."

Even though my heart was racing, I tried my best to assure Judith that together we would fight and beat this cancer. I truly meant it. As soon as we arrived home, I called a highly-respected former medical reporter, Diana Gonzalez, for advice. Through her contacts, she quickly put me in touch with Dr. Brian Slomovitz, who was the director of the gynecological cancer unit for the Sylvester Comprehensive Cancer Center at the University of Miami. He was very kind and reassuring, telling me he would gladly take Judith as his patient. Shortly afterward, he confirmed that my wife, who always took good care of herself, exercised, ate a healthy diet, and had never been seriously ill in her life was suffering from high-stage ovarian cancer.

What began then, just one month after we both had finally retired, was a three-year fight for survival in which Judith always amazed me with her dignity, courage, dedication, and endurance in the face of this relentless and deadly disease. She braved two operations, painful procedures, repeated chemotherapy, radiation, several hospitalizations, extreme fatigue, nausea, and emotional upheaval. Through it all, Judith characteristically worried less about herself and more about how I and her two brothers were holding up. In my case, it became a valid concern.

From the moment we received the cancer diagnosis, I became Judith's full-time caregiver, advocate, and protector. All thoughts of retirement or teaching had vanished. For months I believe I did a really good job of helping her prepare for treatment, taking her to appointments, dealing with insurance coverage, going to the grocery store, arranging her prescriptions and just being supportive as she struggled emotionally. At some point, though, it began to take a toll on me, too. I started to despair. I became overtired, extremely anxious, and at times deeply depressed.

On sleepless nights I listened to Judith's shallow breathing and feared I was going to lose her—this was unfathomable to me. As too many problems and losses stacked up I began to feel my world collapsing. I had recently lost my mother, my father was in rapidly declining health, and I was angry about what I believed to be the premature end of an award-winning career that I loved. For almost two years, I withdrew from most of my very active life as I focused only on Judith and me. I isolated myself from my friends and stopped engaging on social media (where I had started posting a few sunrise photos that I'd taken when my job wound down).

I choose not to go any further here with details of my emotional reaction, nor will I lay out any more about Judith's ruinous late-stage cancer. But I will proudly tell you that through all of it, Judith and I always loved and supported each other during the roughest times, and we tackled our problems head on. One day, she insisted that if I were to survive this, I needed to spend more time outdoors away from the hospital, chemotherapy rooms, and even our own home. She said I should either go back to saltwater flyfishing—which I had done for years, but had now abandoned—or I should resume my newer hobby of sunrise photography.

I knew that Judith was absolutely right and I took her words to heart. I worried that fishing would take me too far away from home. On the other hand, I could take early-morning photos at a bayside park right near our house, and if I got an emergency phone call, I could get back home quickly. So, I chose the photography option. From that day forward, I tried to begin each day of cancer care by taking an hour or so to chase the rising sun and soak up its healing warmth.

What began then was a daily pattern that, with only a couple of exceptions, I still follow today. I would usually wake up before our bedside alarm clock sounded at 5:00 a.m., check on Judith to make sure she was all right, get dressed in the dark, and go to the kitchen to make a pot of coffee. After a light breakfast, I would load the car with my cameras and tripod and put a coffee cup next to my seat. Locking the house behind me, I drove a few minutes to nearby Matheson Hammock Park on the western edge of Miami's Biscayne Bay. With its swimming lagoon, marina, rows of palm trees, and eastern views, this Miami-Dade County park is an ideal location for shooting the sunrise.

The challenge for me each day was to find the best location there for the most appealing photographs. The shot was always determined by what was happening in the sky, which changed daily and with the seasons. When I arrived at the park, I would ask myself a few quick questions: where are the colors today, which way is the wind blowing the clouds, will the sun be cresting over the horizon or breaking through the ocean cloud mass I call the "the Miami mountain range?" I also wanted to know if the sky colors or the sun's rays were reflecting on the water. And where were the pelicans diving

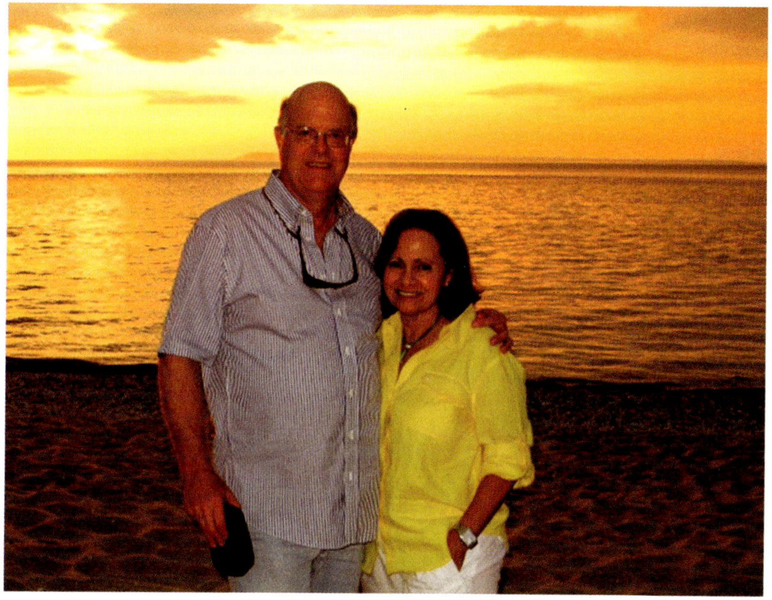

today to catch their fish? If I went there with my eyes open, tried new photography angles, and experimented with the camera settings, I could always shoot pictures that were different from the ones I had taken before.

I also discovered that sunrises have several distinct phases. If I got there really early when it was still dark, I would marvel at the celestial beauty of all the stars, planets and the moon. I learned how to photograph them with a slow shutter speed and loved how the black and blue color tones made for dramatic images. I watched as the sky turned gray, then lighter shades of blue before the brighter tropical colors emerged and the real magic began.

Usually, the most beautiful and dramatic colors of the morning appear during the half hour or so before the actual sunrise. If the sky is going to put on a show that day, and to erupt in a blast of exquisite color, that is the time. Yes, the sunrise, itself, is often spectacular, especially if the sky is clear and the sun makes a dramatic entrance by peeping over the horizon. Or it may throw bright white or yellow rays upward through the clouds. But the show everyone usually talks about, and features in most of their photographs of sunrises, takes place in those glorious moments when the sun still has not yet reached the horizon.

When I finished my daily sunrise shoot, I would put my gear back in the car and drive home to check on Judith. Later, I'd select a few photos for editing on my computer and picked one for posting on my Facebook page (in time, I also opened an Instagram account). I felt really good when Judith told me she loved the colorful images and was thrilled I was getting out of the house for a while. Usually around 8:00 a.m., I would put the photography aside and begin a full day of cancer care for as many as fourteen hours a day.

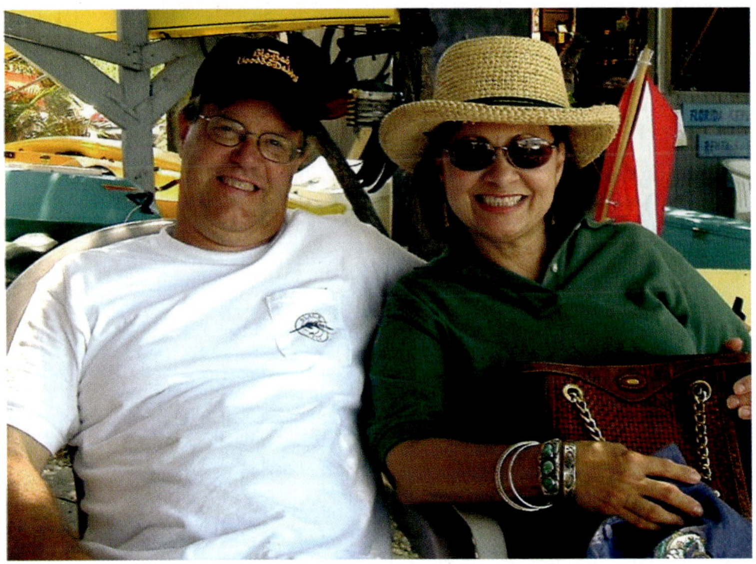

My initial goal in doing this was to clear my head and help myself cope with the strains and emotional weight of cancer care, as Judith had suggested. And over time it began to work. Walking and shooting in the warm ocean air under the rising sun, and meeting and talking with other photographers and new friends, helped ease my exhaustion and isolation. To my pleasant surprise, I also started to reconnect and received nice notes from old friends and colleagues who said they enjoyed my photos and were glad to see me back on social media. I also found a doctor who understood what I was going through and put me on a medication and treatment plan to get me fully back on my feet. That worked, too, and I started to feel much better.

The best result of this was that I became a much stronger and better caregiver, and frankly, a better husband. It happened at an important time, because, unfortunately, Judith's health was getting worse. We had been warned that even after successful surgery and follow-up chemotherapy treatment, ovarian cancer can often recur. For a while after her initial treatments, Judith felt great, and the cancer seemed to have gone away. But then an abdominal scan revealed new tumors, indicating the wretched cancer had returned.

Once again, Judith gracefully endured chemotherapy and other treatments. Her doctors and nurses were both aggressive and compassionate in their efforts, but the medical science for recovery from her particular level of the disease just wasn't there. In early 2019, with no more viable chemotherapy options, Judith's doctors placed her in hospice care, first at a hospital and then at our home where we set up a special bed and an oxygen machine. My brother-in law, Isaac, and I went into hyperdrive around the clock doing everything we could to keep Judith comfortable, clean, and properly fed (with guidance from a hospice doctor and a few nurses). On paper, Isaac and I were brothers-in-law. But in those critical months working extremely well together for Judith, I truly believe we became brothers.

Even during this most demanding and difficult time, I still tried to take my morning hour to shoot the sunrises, so I could stay focused and strong. The only difference is that I took less time away from the house than before, and while I was gone, someone was always watching over Judith—either Isaac or a nurse. While outside waiting for the sun to rise, I often prayed, wept, planned, and hoped that somehow my wife would survive this. But in my heart, I just knew it wasn't going to happen. With guidance from a hospice counselor, I reluctantly made end-of-life arrangements and began to learn about all the finances and other parts of our homelife that Judith had managed.

On a warm and partly cloudy afternoon in the spring of 2019, my courageous and sweet Judith drew her last breath in bed at home, just as a Catholic priest we had called walked in the door. I don't remember much about the next few days leading up to the family graveside service, except that I was broken, lost, and inconsolably sad, especially while alone at night. Repeatedly, I felt a powerful urge to reach out and plead with her to please come back to us. I had already prepared an obituary for the newspaper, and on the day after she died, I also posted a more personal tribute to her on my Facebook page. Among other things, I finally answered the question I had been asked so many times before by well-meaning friends: why do you only photograph sunrises, and why as a retiree don't you sleep in and relax in the mornings and shoot sunsets, instead?

Most of my social media friends didn't know Judith was battling cancer. She was extremely private and had asked me not to say anything publicly about her condition and desperate struggle. I firmly honored her request and deflected the questions until after her passing. The answer to why I only shot in the morning, of course, is that it was the only time I had to leave the house to take pictures. The rest of the day was consumed by the demands of cancer care. In my online

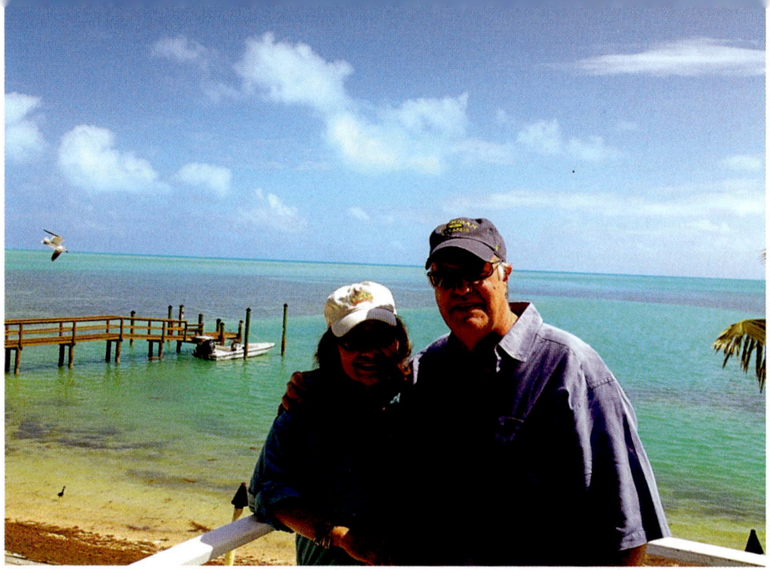

tribute I also wrote: "Now, all those bright and colorful images are dedicated to Judith—lovingly and publicly." Since then, I have taken thousands more sunrise photos, and those, too, are dedicated to her.

During the long days, and weeks, then months after Judith died, I began to feel and understand some things I'd been too consumed by caregiving and sadness to appreciate earlier. I realized that as I became overwhelmed, I had made a most critical mistake when I turned deeply inward and isolated from my friends and even my family. By doing that, I had turned off a wellspring of loving support that could have eased me through the rougher times. I first came to see this when I once again started shooting and posting photographs on social media. The public response was immediate, wholly positive, and at times emotionally overwhelming. I was very surprised. The outpouring grew as time went on. So many friends—and people I didn't even know—offered their support and consoled me. All I needed to do to receive all this was to simply unlock the door I had previously closed.

Among those stepping in to help, after I first started shooting and had so much to learn, were three wonderful photographers. Bev Armstrong showed me how to best take sunrises photos at Matheson. Oscar Lopez taught me a lot about camera settings and mechanics. The late Steve Lipson, a fifty-year commercial photographer who tragically died just two months after Judith's passing, showed me some of the finer points of photography. And then, NBC News video editor Vincent Genova set up my computer and patiently taught me photo editing skills. I was most grateful to them and applied everything they taught me.

I was also truly stunned to learn that the photographs I was initially taking and posting just for me, to clear my own head and calm my soul, were beginning to take on meaning for other people, too. That became especially apparent after I revealed why I was only taking sunrise images and how they were dedicated to Judith. I never expected the level of goodwill, positive messages, and thoughtful and caring comments that I received then and continue today. I couldn't be more grateful.

Many people would tell me the photographs helped them start their day, eased difficult and sleepless nights, and softened their anxieties. Some of my northern friends, especially in Michigan where I was raised, told me repeatedly that the bright, tropical photos were a warm and welcome respite from their frigid winters. And then, after I began to post my photographs regularly, viewers said they looked forward to them and waited for them every morning. I am certain these warm and wonderful people had no idea just how much their kind words meant to me, nor could they feel just how deeply moved I was and how all of them together were actually helping me begin to heal.

The constant support and feedback also taught me a lot about the true meaning of the sunrise, itself, and steered me toward a new purpose in my life. From the earliest days of going to the park, I had come to welcome the warmth and beauty of the rising sun. But, with the insightful and sensitive responses I received from friends and colleagues, I began to learn much more. In time I would come to see that the sunrise symbolizes a new beginning, an opportunity to start over, a new shot at redemption and a chance to do better today than we did yesterday.

The sunrise also represents strength, energy, and hope. It is a constant presence upon which we can always rely. On the cloudiest days, the sun is still going to pop over the horizon. Even if we can't see it, we know it's there. The sun will always rise, no matter how we feel or what we have done the night before. And when it does, the darkness becomes light. Most personally for me, the emerging sun is a daily confirmation that Judith now lives in my heart. She is the one who sent me out here to record the morning magic show, and I can always feel her warmth when the sun makes its appearance.

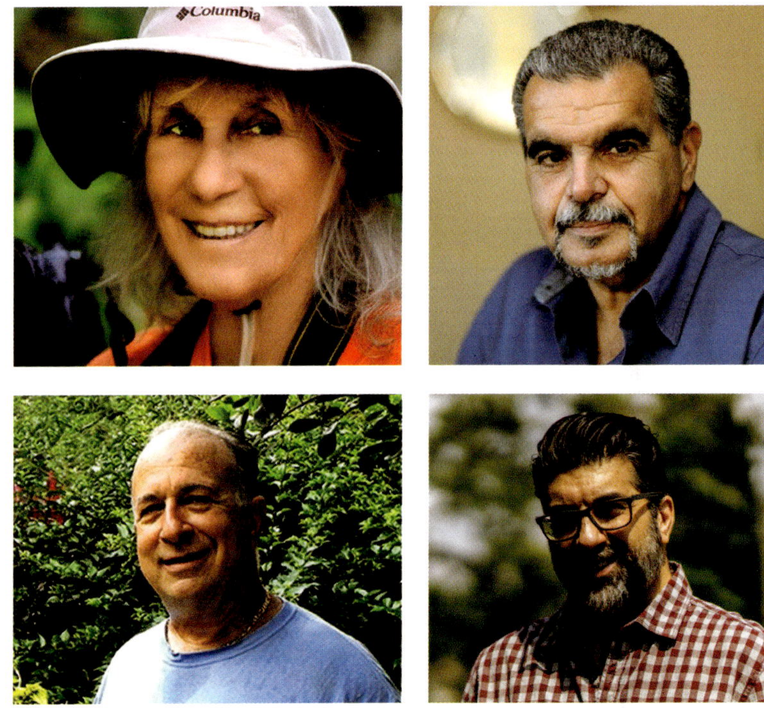

Clockwise from top left: Bev Armstrong, Oscar Lopez, Vincent Genova, and Steve Lipson.

Photographing the sunrise everyday has also given me a new purpose—something constructive I can do while healing and moving forward. Just as the sunrise helped me, it can also be used to help others, and that's my new life plan—to share my morning photographs with anyone who wants or needs them, especially cancer patients, caregivers and those who work to heal and support them.

The comments I get on Facebook, Instagram and in personal conversations assure me I am on the right track. One former colleague wrote, "Your photos have been a comfort to me during a tough time." Others wrote, "What a lovely way to start the day," and, "The beauty you have shared with so many of us every morning is a lasting tribute to Judith. Now every time I see one of your photos it will mean something so much deeper and more meaningful." President Joe Biden, who suffered the horrible tragedies of losing his wife, daughter, and oldest son, has written and talked a lot about this. During his 2020 convention speech, he said, "I found that the best way through pain and loss and grief is to find purpose."

I was very moved at the beginning of 2020, when twenty-five of my sunrise photographs appeared on the walls of the Lennar Foundation Medical Center at the University of Miami. I donated them in Judith's memory, and the Center framed and placed them in a large-sized format throughout the fourth floor cancer-treatment area where Judith received her care. My gift of sunrise beauty was meant to support and comfort the many cancer patients and caregivers who are now experiencing what Judith and I went through. I also wanted to honor and thank the doctors, staffers and nurses who have made it their life's work to help these patients, and who treated Judith and me with tremendous love and kindness. I will never forget how the nurses, in particular, were so compassionate with Judith.

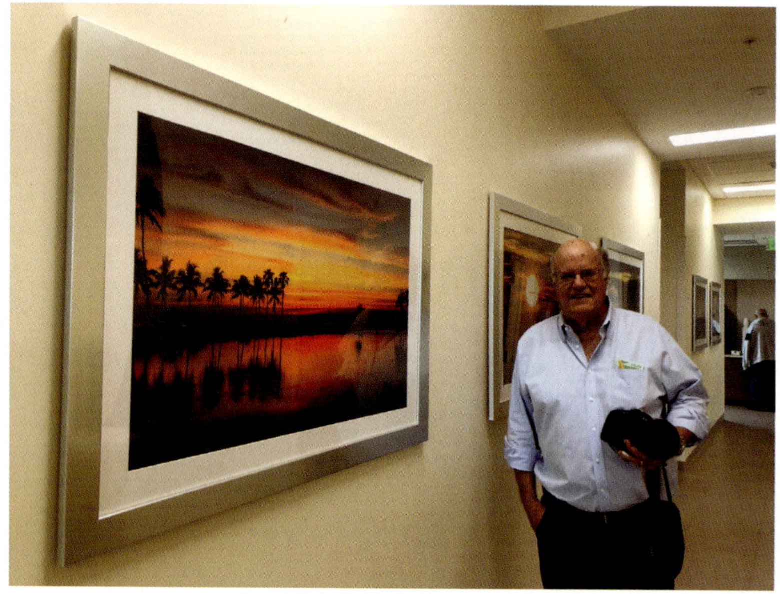

Moving forward now, I'm no longer restricted to taking pictures near the house and am expanding my photography. I still visit Matheson Hammock Park, but I also photograph the tropical sun from other places in South Florida—including the Everglades National Park, the Big Cypress National Preserve, Fakahatchee Strand, Key Biscayne, Miami Beach, Coconut Grove, the Deering Estate, Palm Beach, Broward County, the Florida Keys, Naples, and Marco Island. In addition to the sunrises, I am also shooting sunsets, moonrises, and even the Milky Way. I am always adding other subject matter such as boats, paddleboarders, runners, tai chi and yoga practitioners, and lots of wildlife. I particularly like photographing the big hawks, eagles, owls, and waterbirds. I hope one day to find a Florida panther in the wild! I have a special fondness for photographing alligators and crocodiles which is, perhaps, a vestige of my decades as a newsman on the hunt.

I often marvel at how my life is so different now from the four decades when I was an active correspondent living in the high-pressure world of broadcast journalism where I often delivered bad news to millions of viewers. I joke with my friends that I've gone from chasing narcos and natural disasters to joyfully chasing pelicans and gorgeous sunrises. When I think about it, though, I can actually see some similarities between them.

As in news coverage, you must always be on time to capture the rising sun. It's also true that it takes the same skill set to surreptitiously photograph drug smugglers on the border as it takes to routinely snap photos of flying pelicans! They each require preparation, positioning and patience. A big difference is that pelicans are actually quite lovely and honorable. And with them, there is also no pressure. If I miss a pelican, or if I photograph one out of focus, only I know it, and I don't have to worry about getting a rocket e-mail from a New York editor wondering why I flubbed the shot. Plus, being a former investigative reporter, I will carefully remember what the pelican did today and will get him tomorrow. Bet on it.

Meantime, it is early morning again, and I am back on the road, coffee cup in hand, listening to news and music as I comfortably drive to my next destination. This has become my favorite time of day, when it is still pitch-dark and only a few drivers are out here with me. Soon it will be "magic time." I'll be back on a shoreline, or maybe this time in the Everglades river of grass, waiting with my cameras to be surprised and amazed by the brilliant scene before me. It is always an exhilarating and welcome sight, a daily friend now—the arrival of yet another beautiful and healing Sunrise for Judith.

In loving memory, I am most happy to share it with you.

—Mark Potter

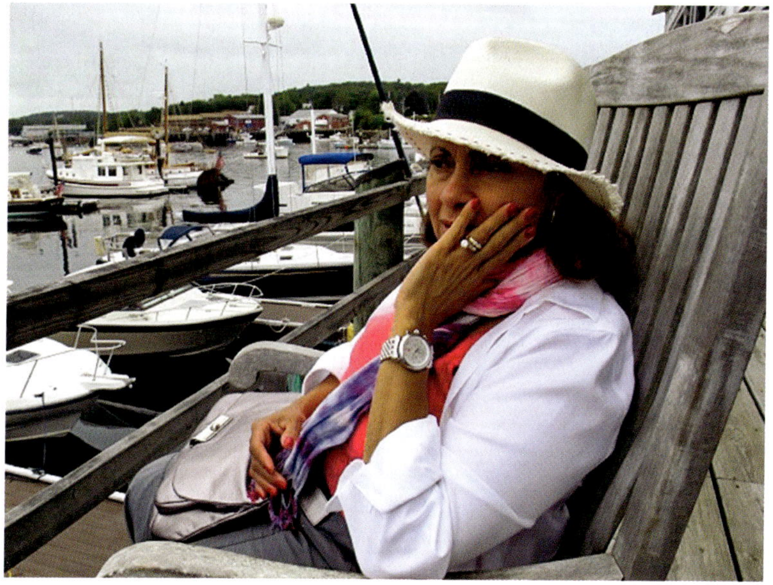

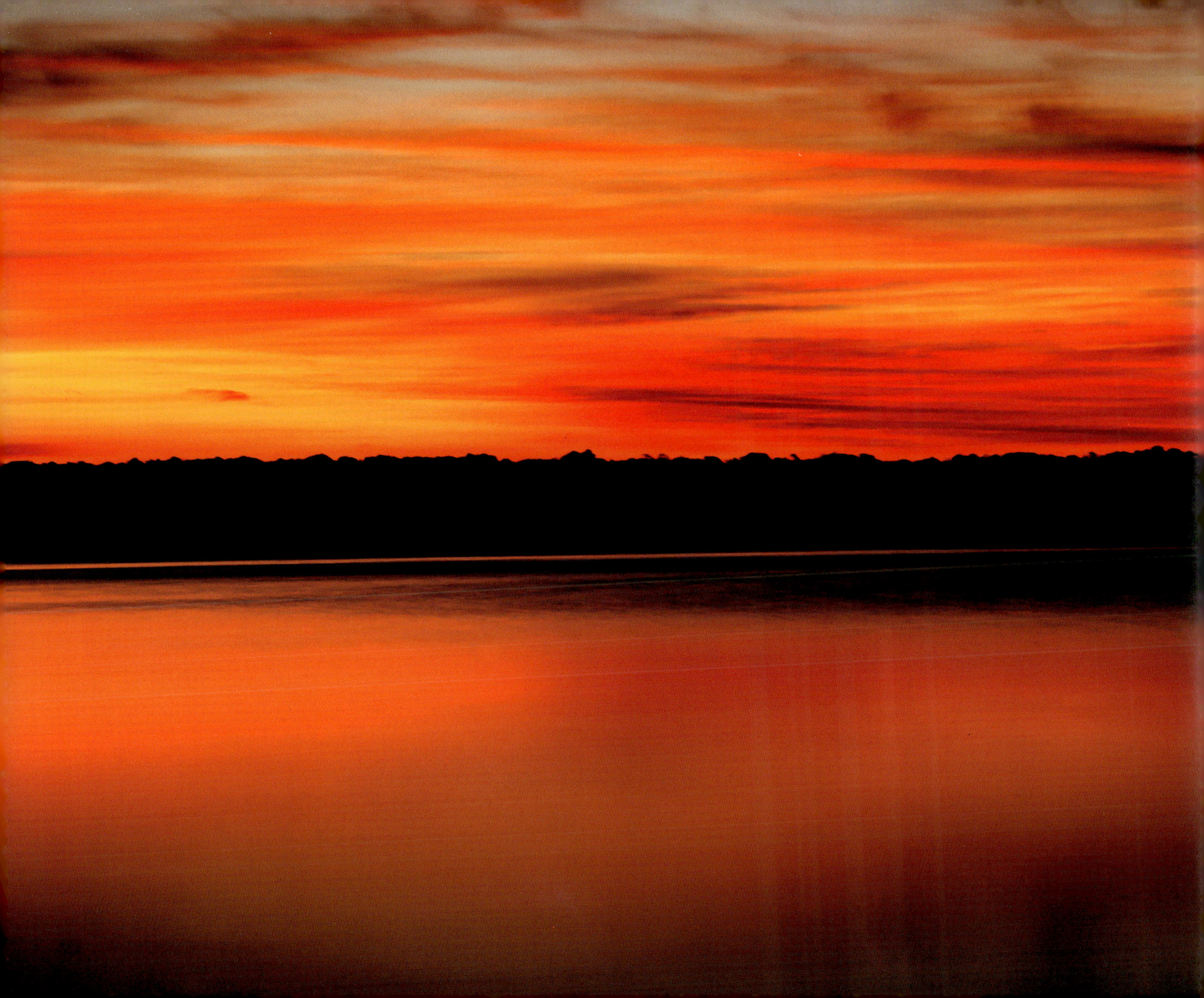

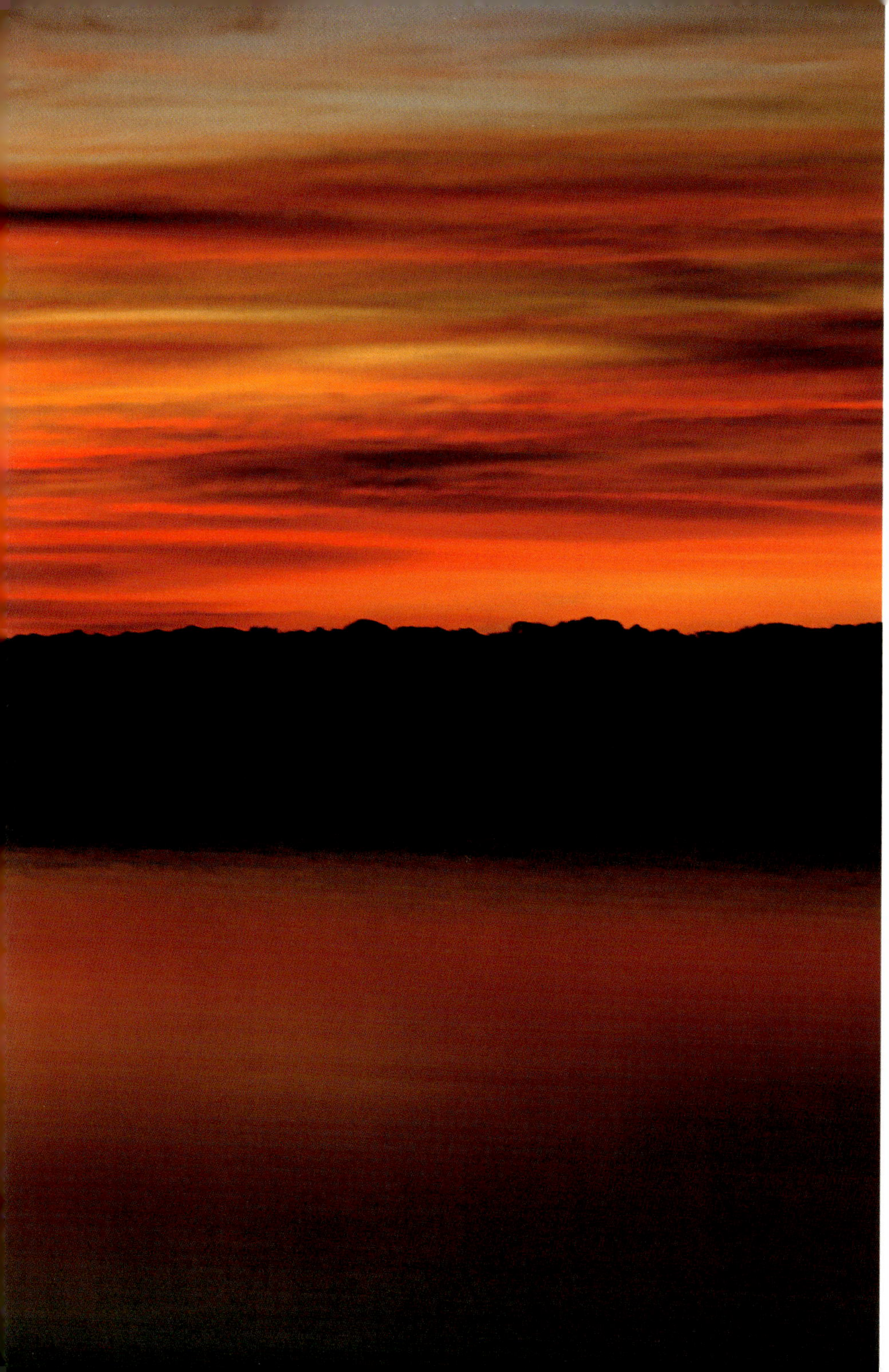

Magic Time

The early-morning hour leading from darkness to dawn, from brilliant skies to a blazing sunrise is what I call "magic time." It is that daily transition when the world around us re-emerges and refreshes itself. Darkness becomes light, the ecosystem comes alive again and the sky often explodes into a kaleidoscope of exotic shapes and breathtaking colors. Why would anyone ever want to sleep late and miss seeing one of the best light shows on earth?

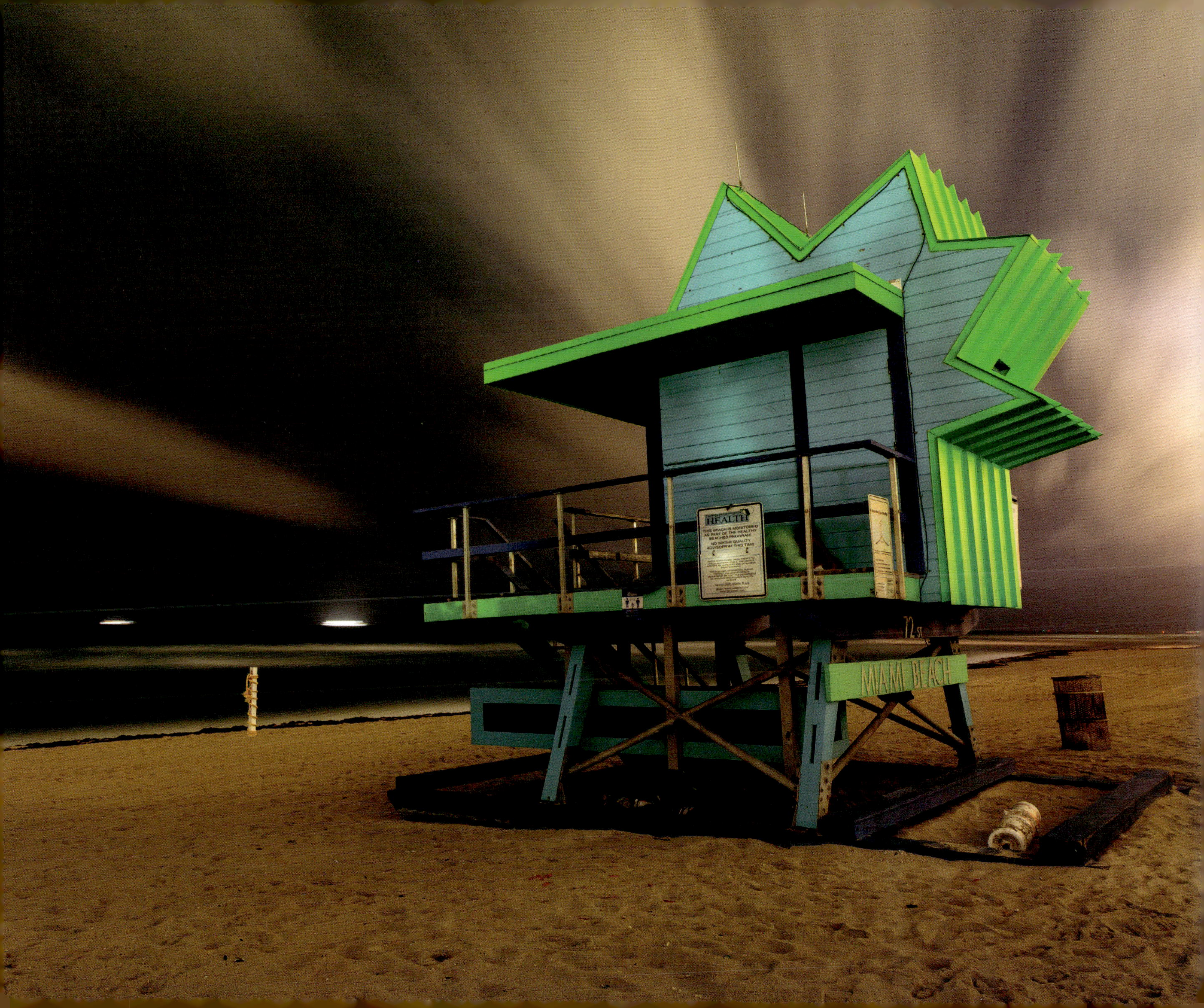
HEALTH
MIAMI BEACH

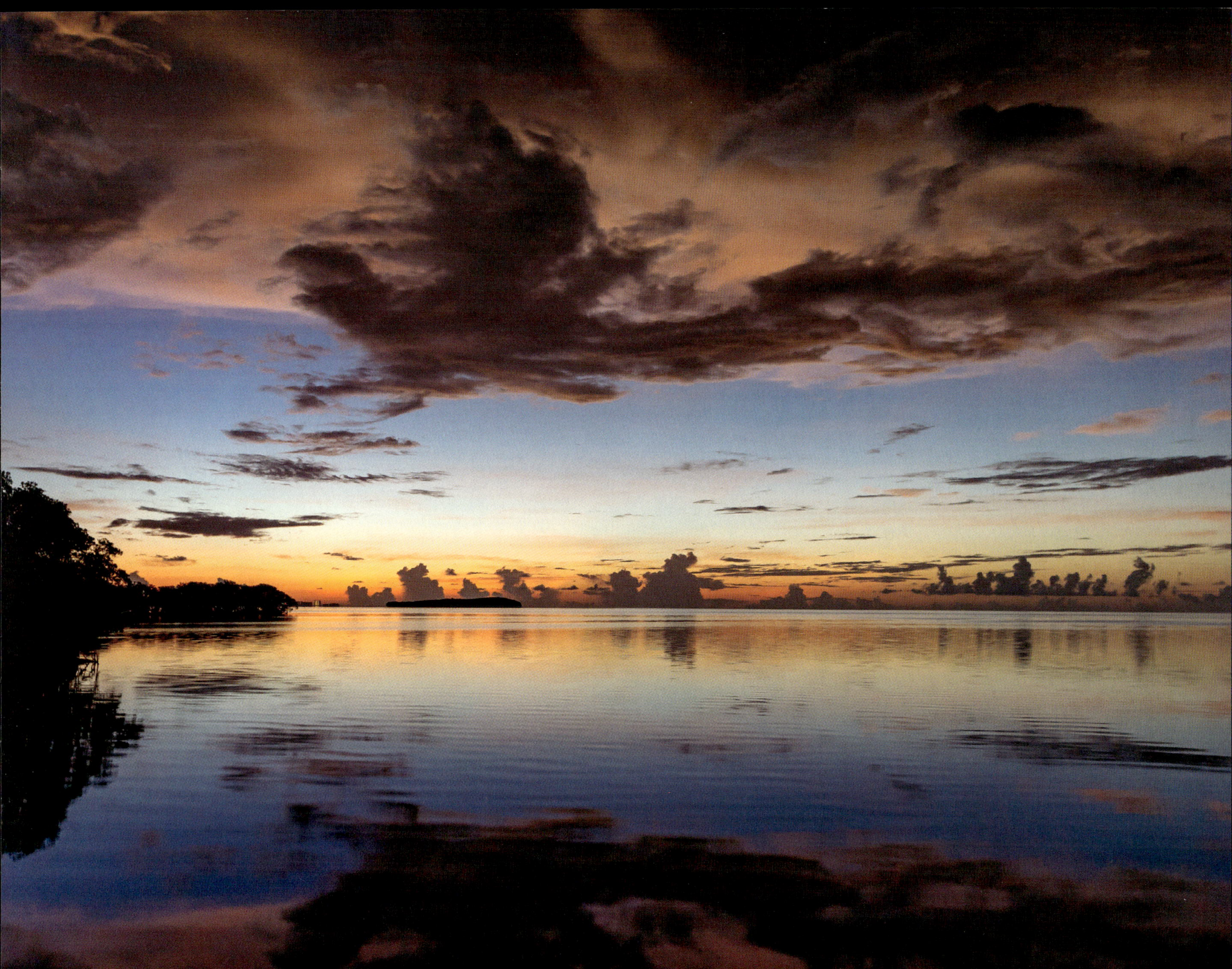

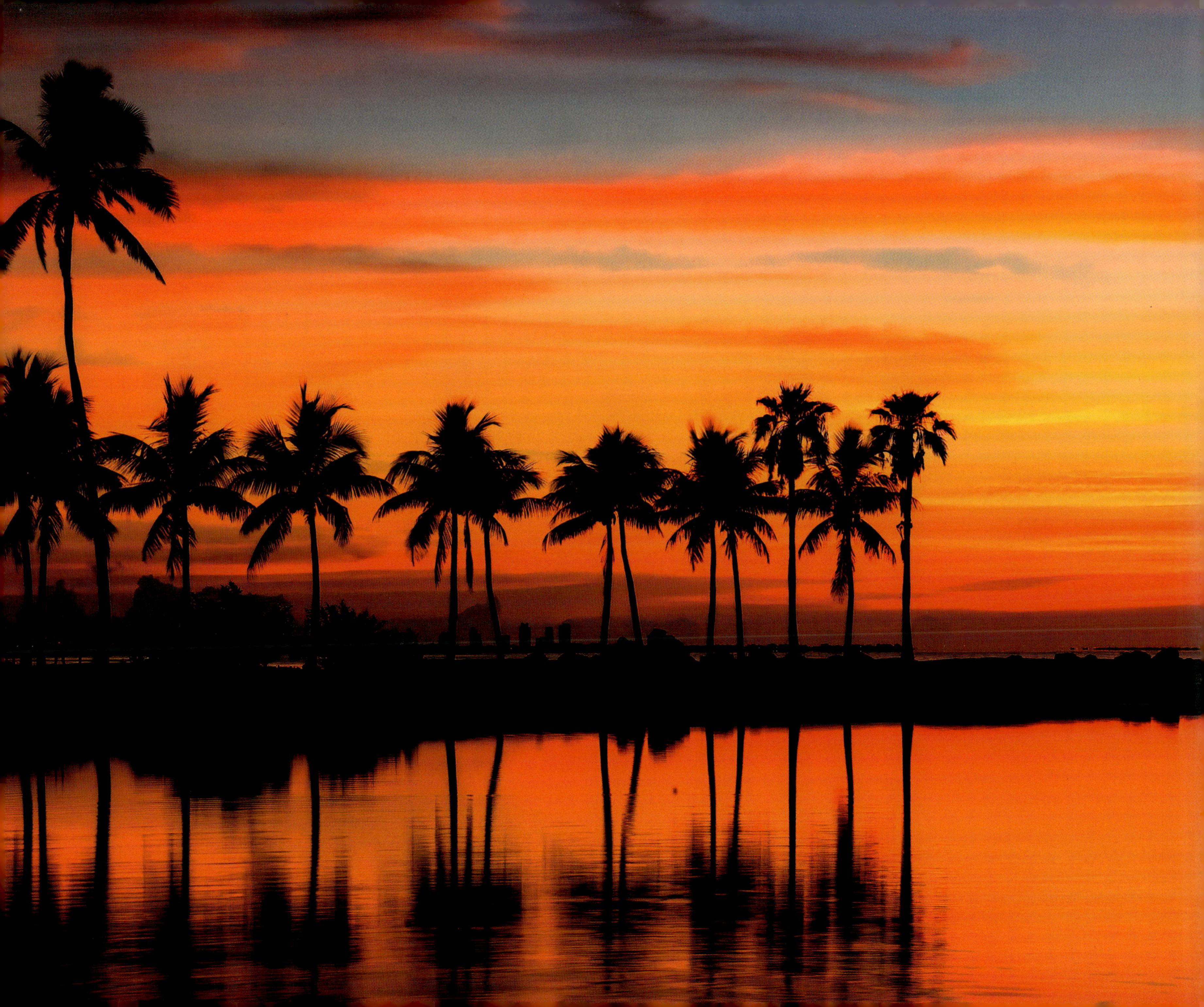

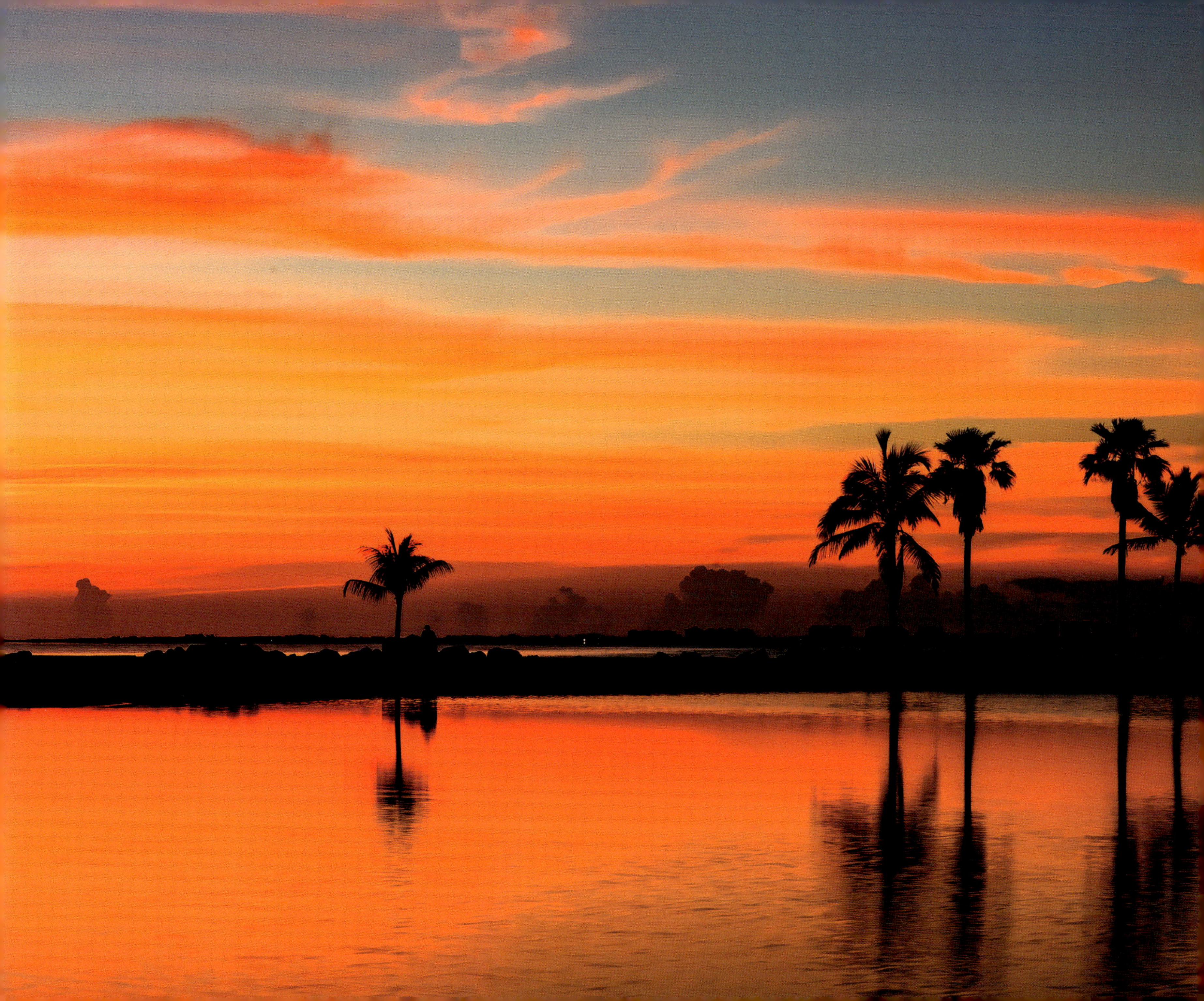

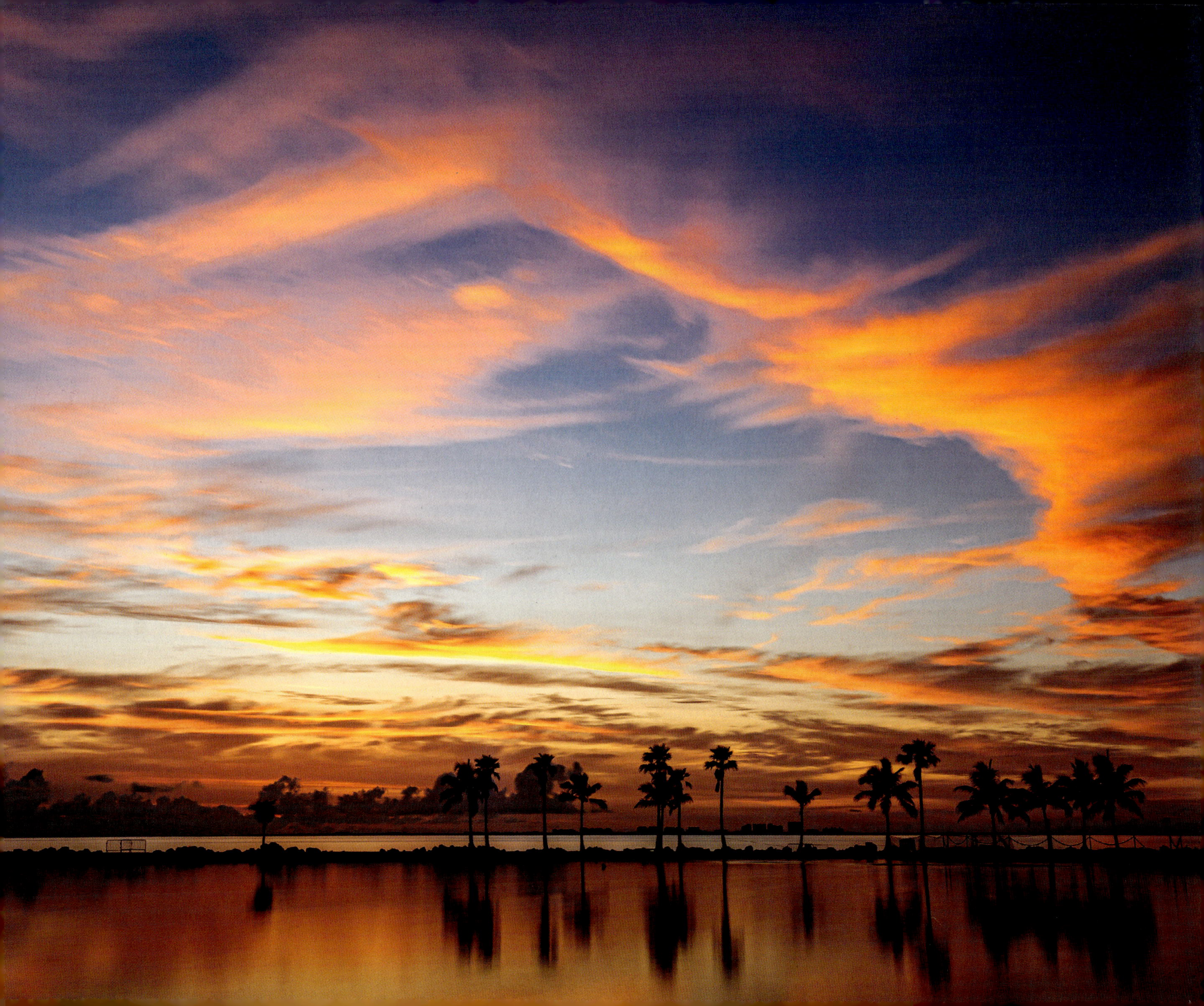

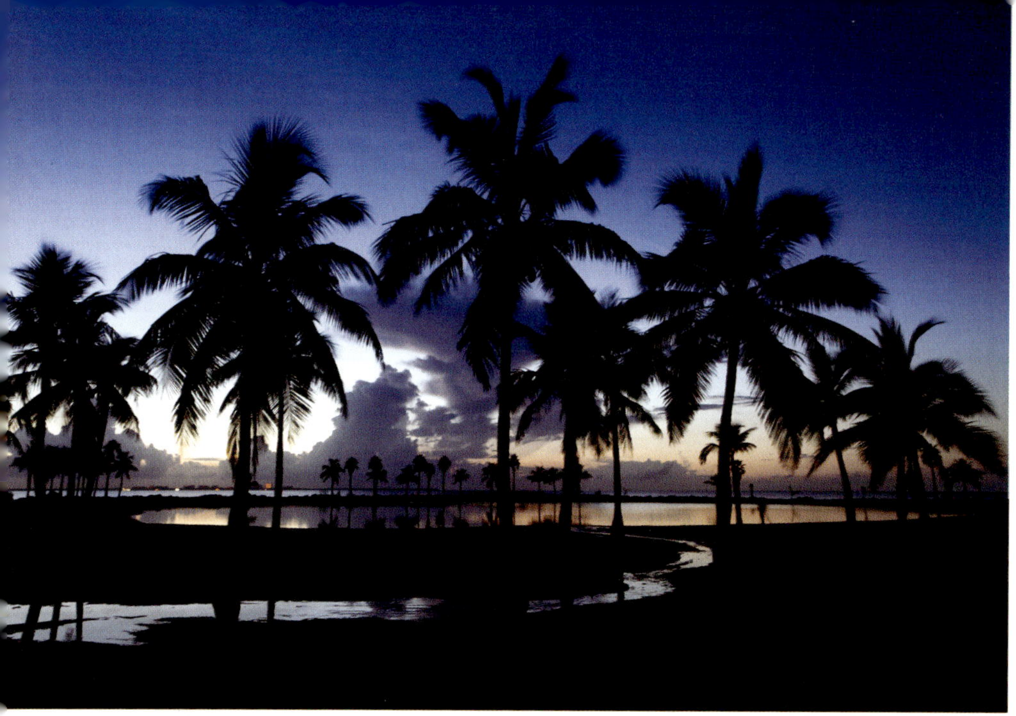

Glorious morning colors at Matheson Hammock Park near Miami. This is where my photo journey began.

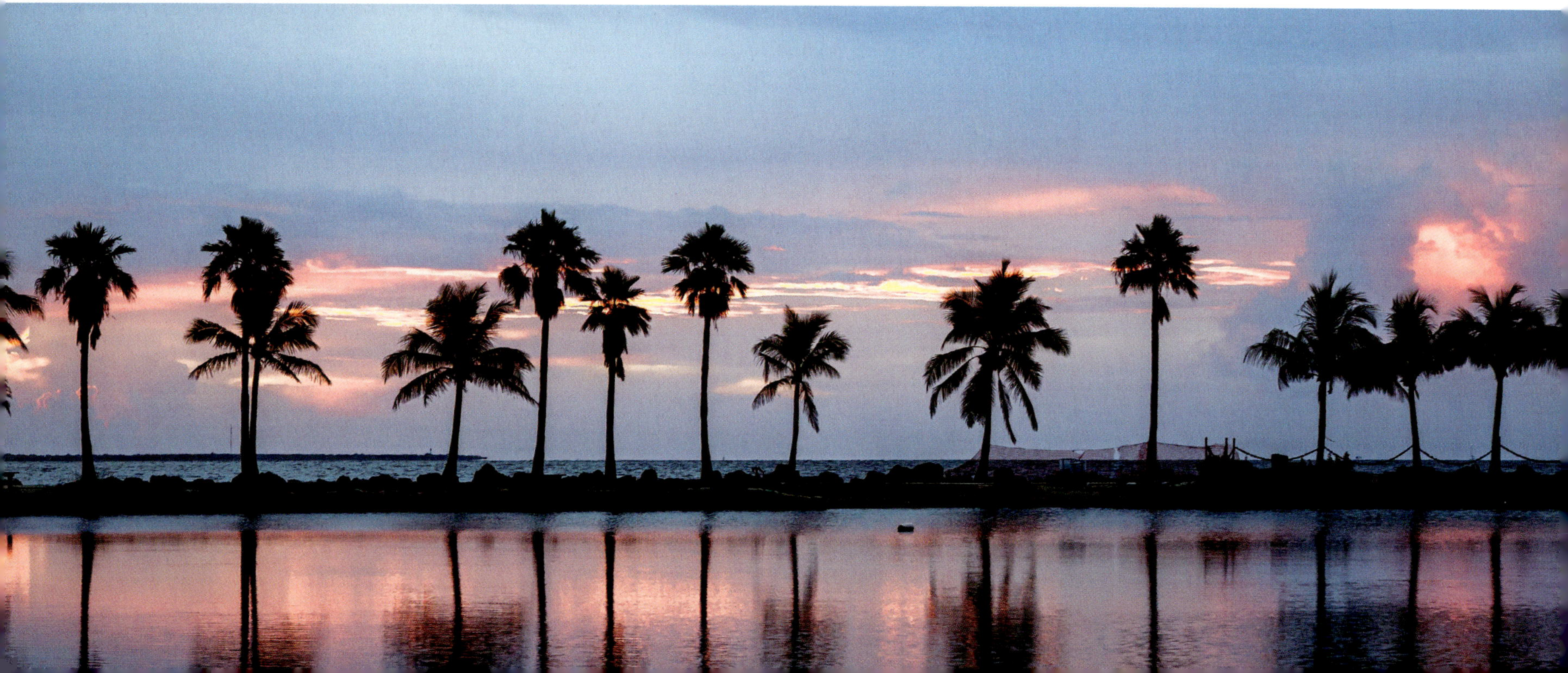

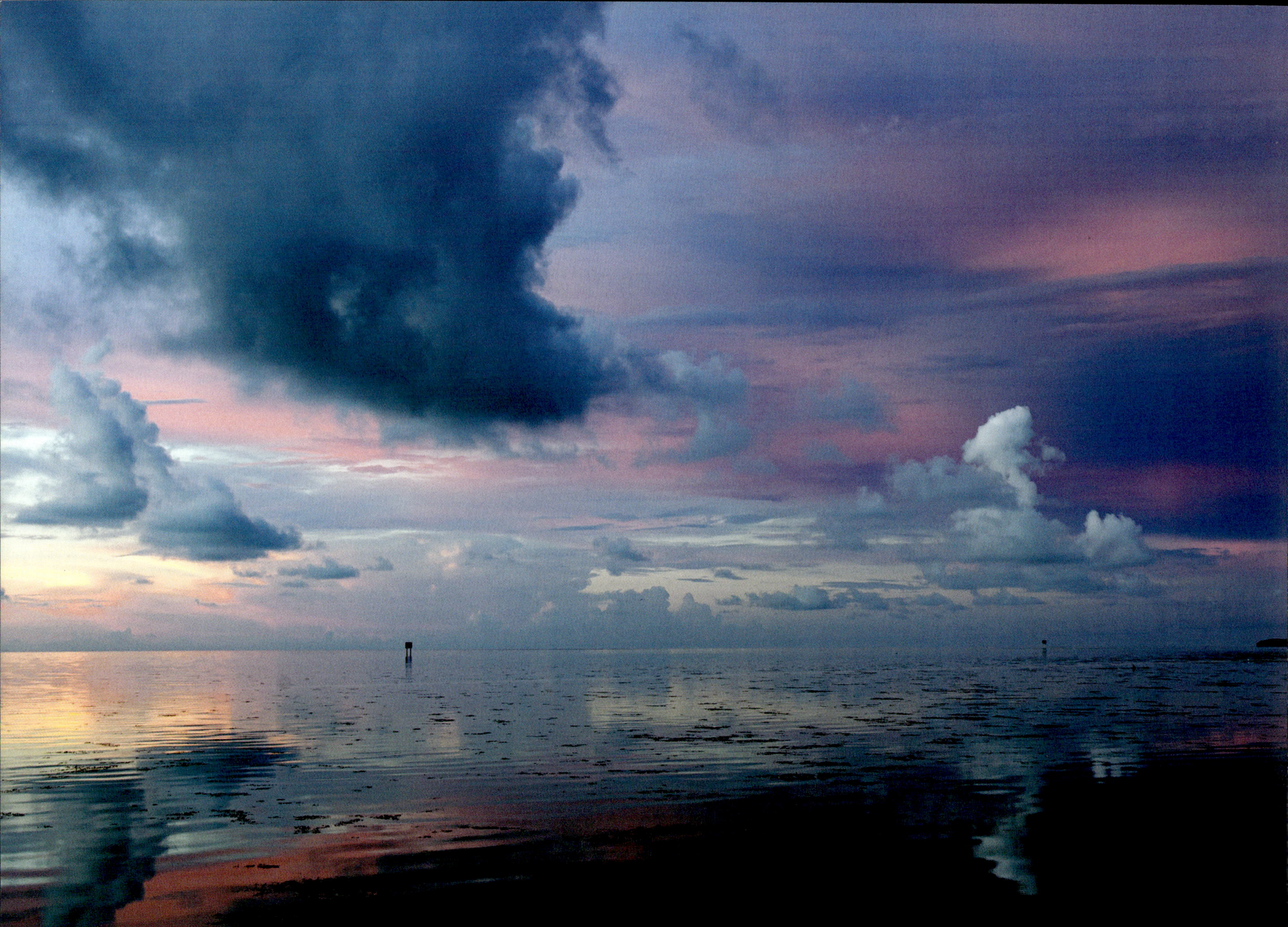

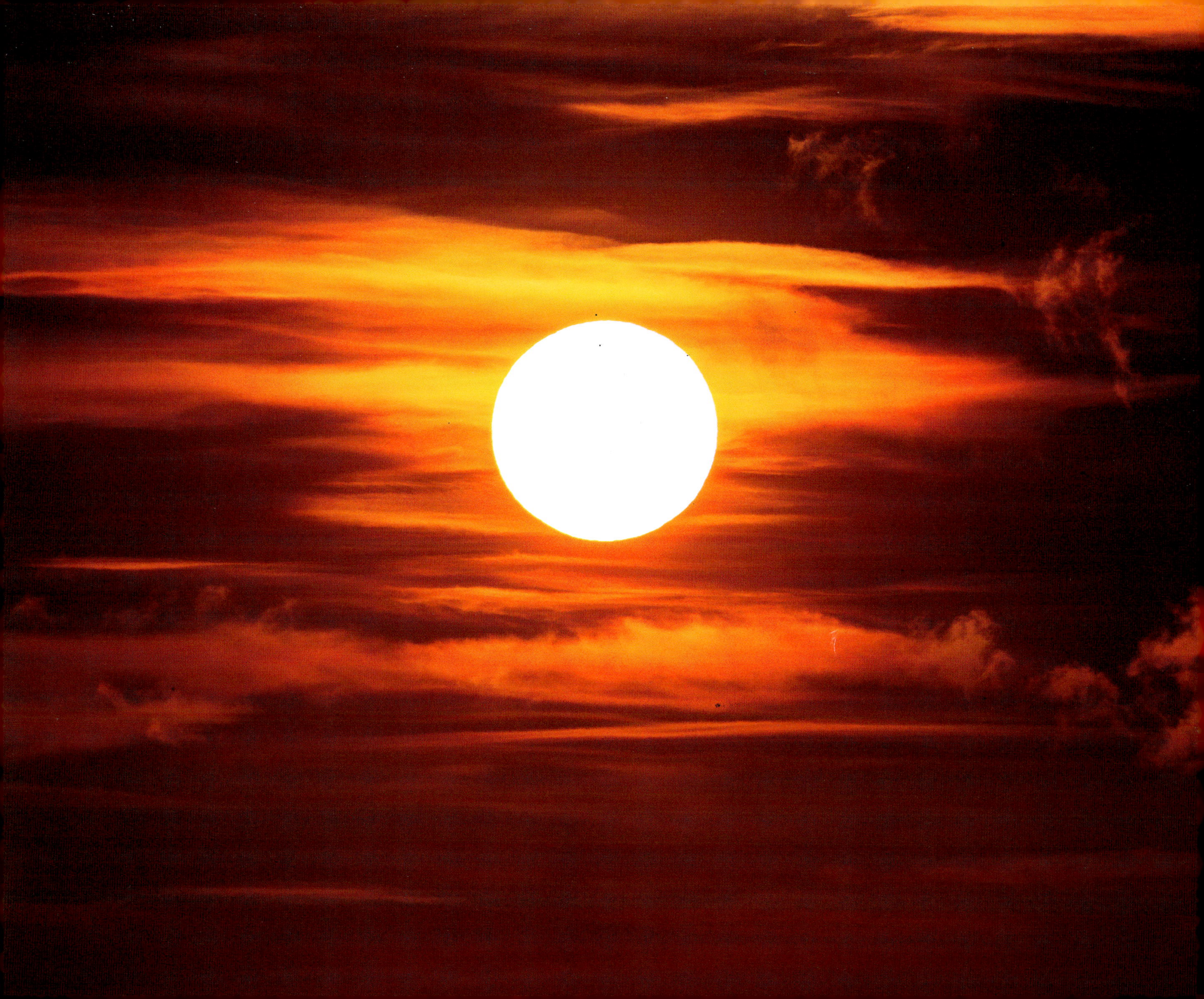

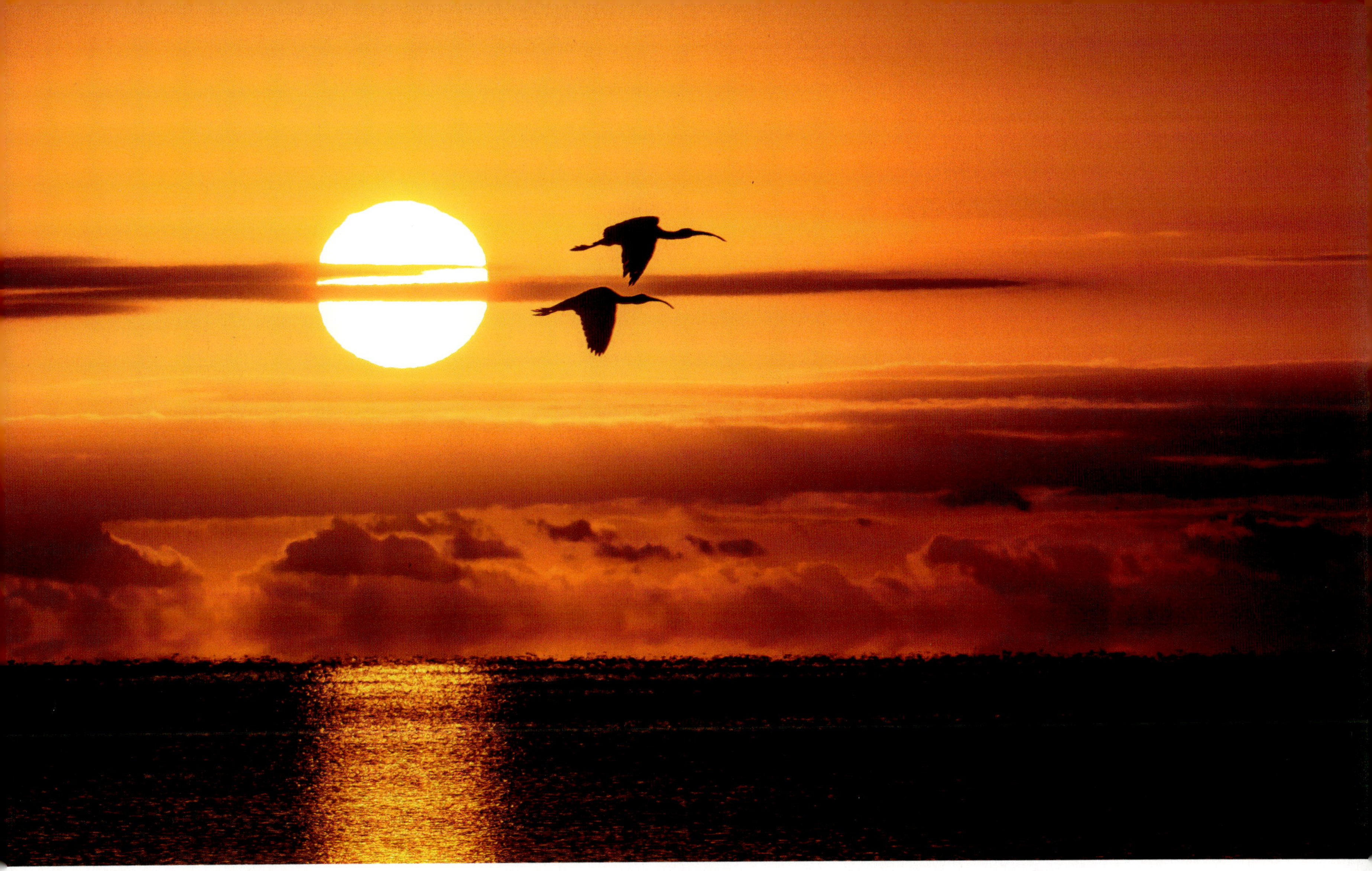

I love this photograph above, but it is also bittersweet. To me, it will always symbolize Judith and me together.

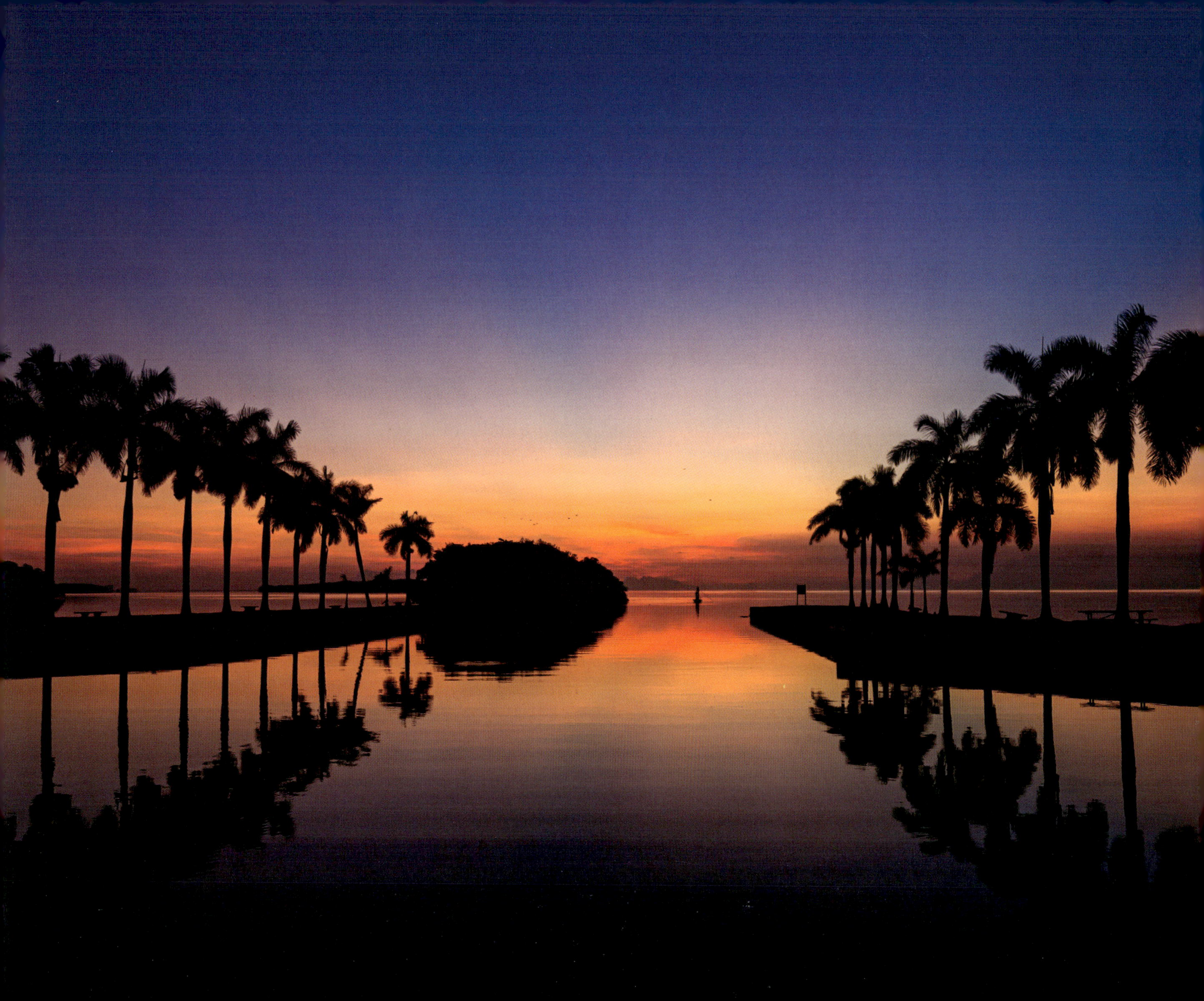

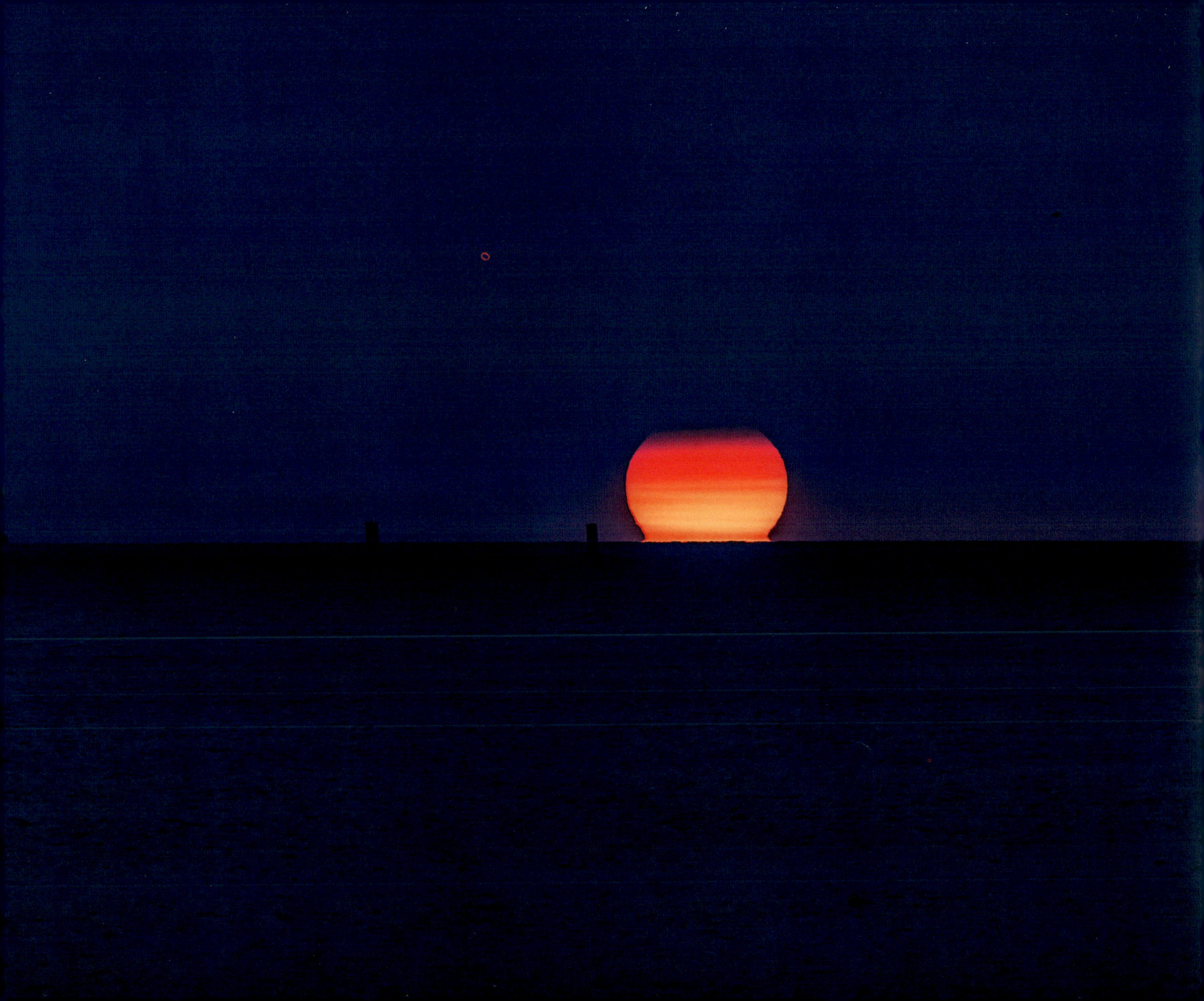

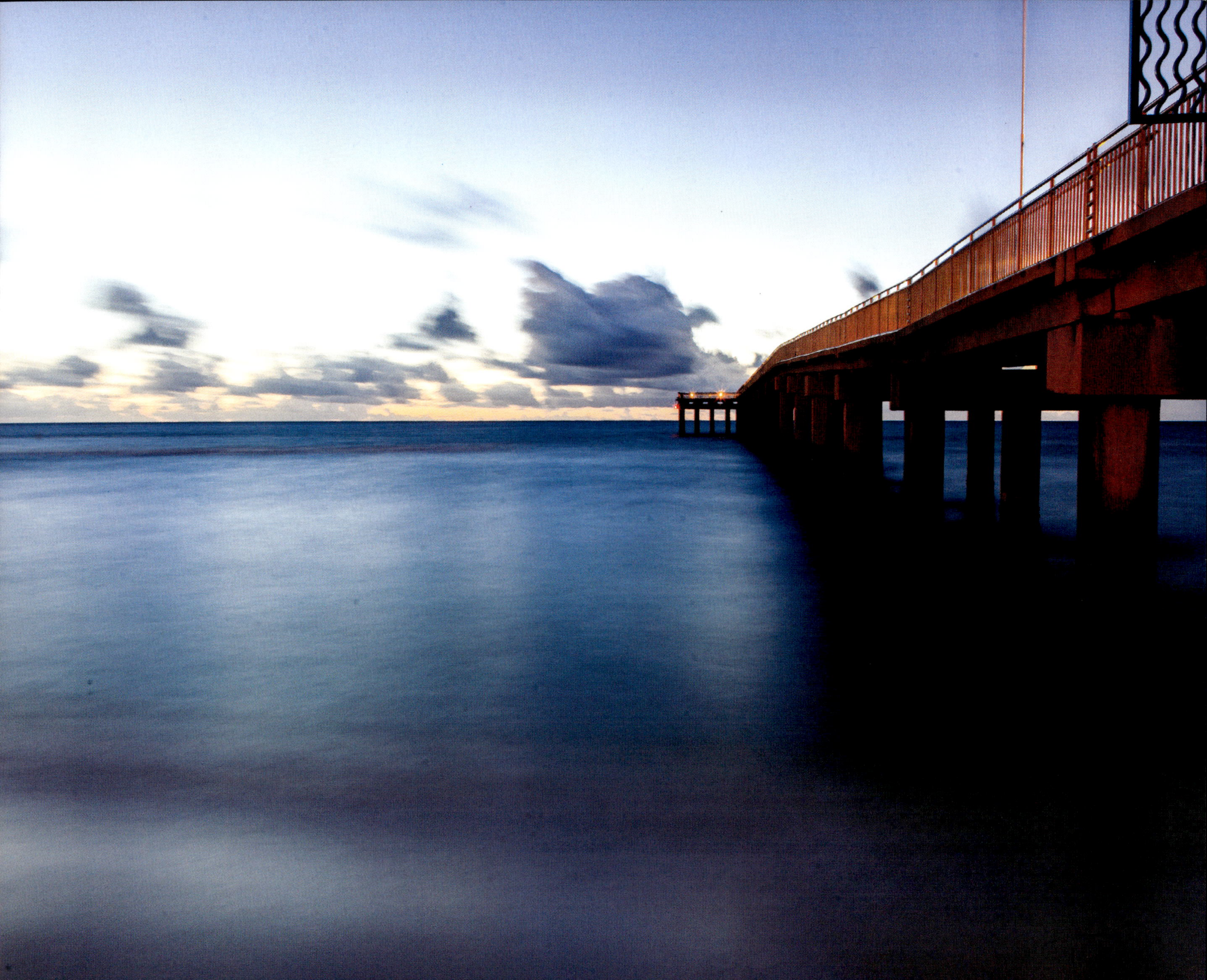

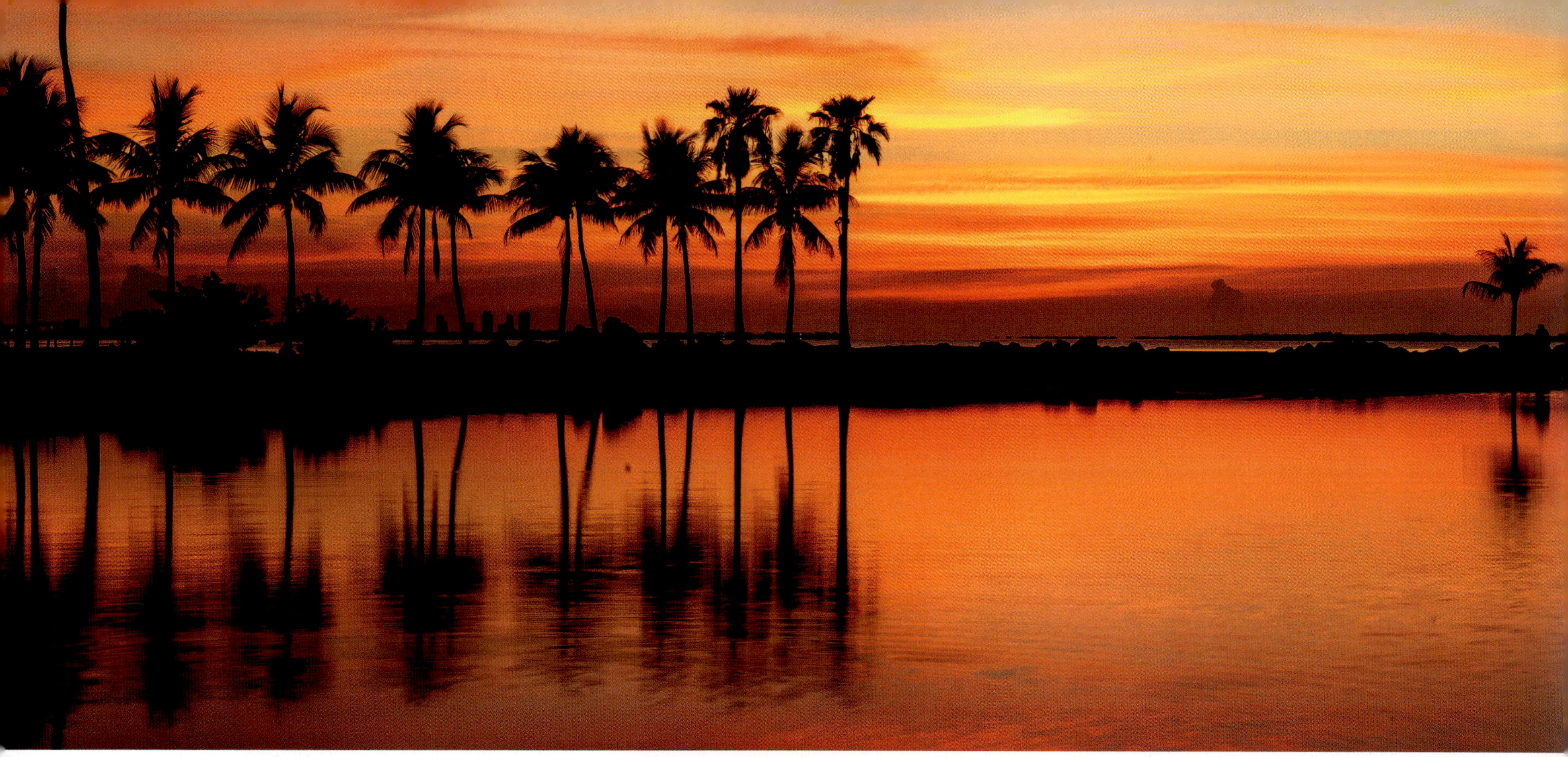

These spectacular views are our just rewards for getting up early and turning toward the rising sun.

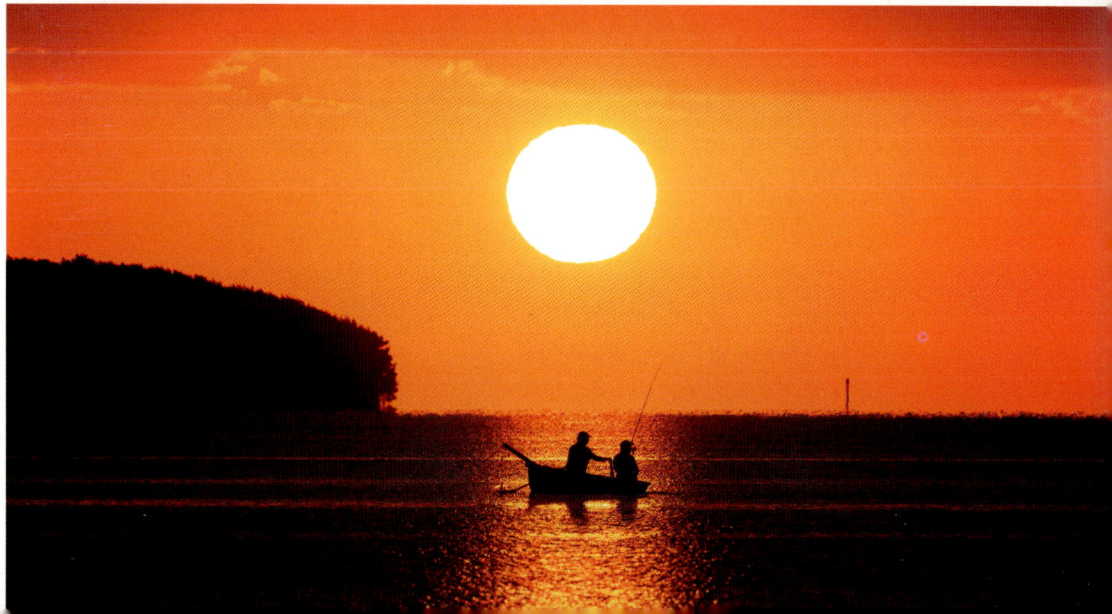

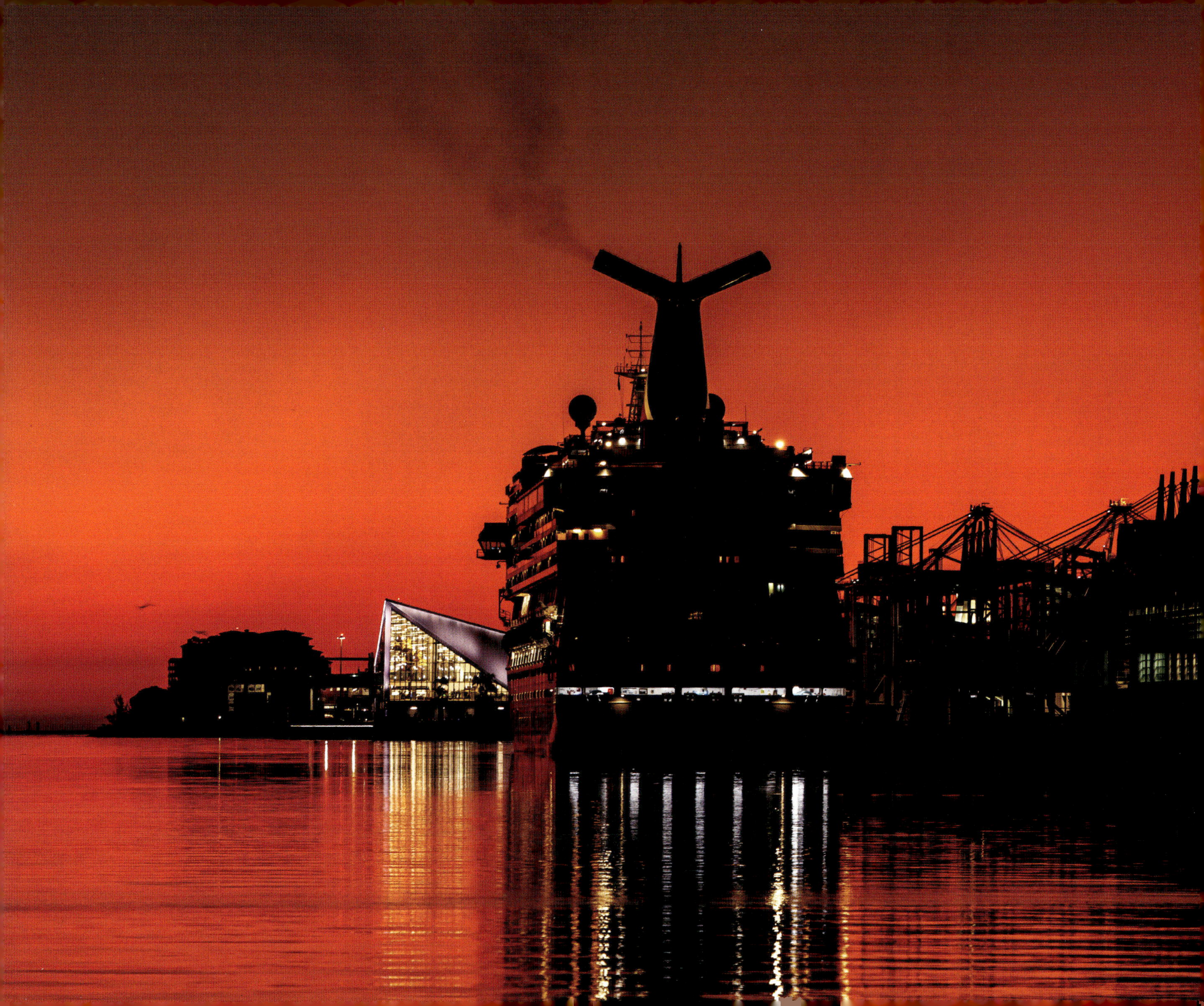

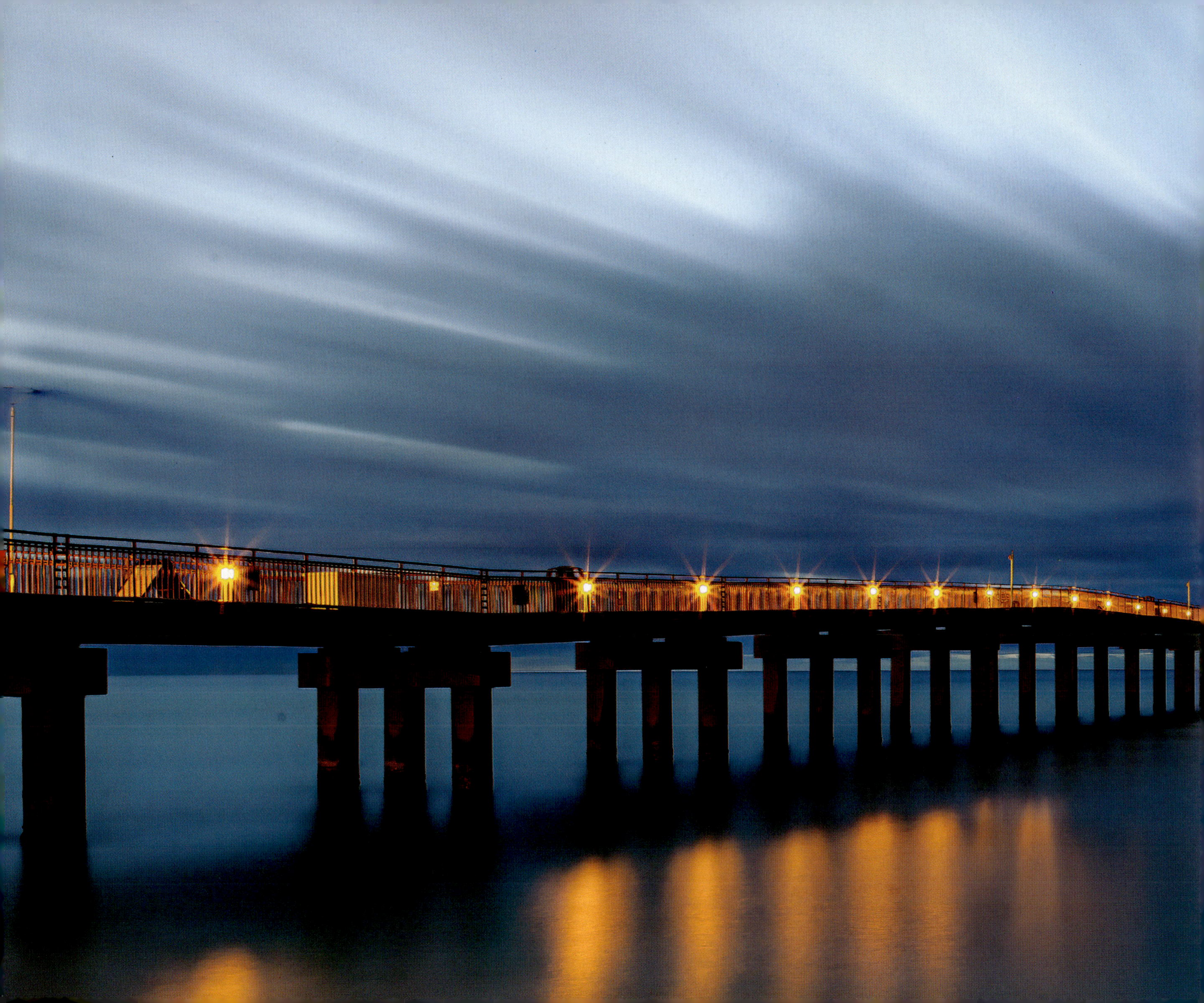

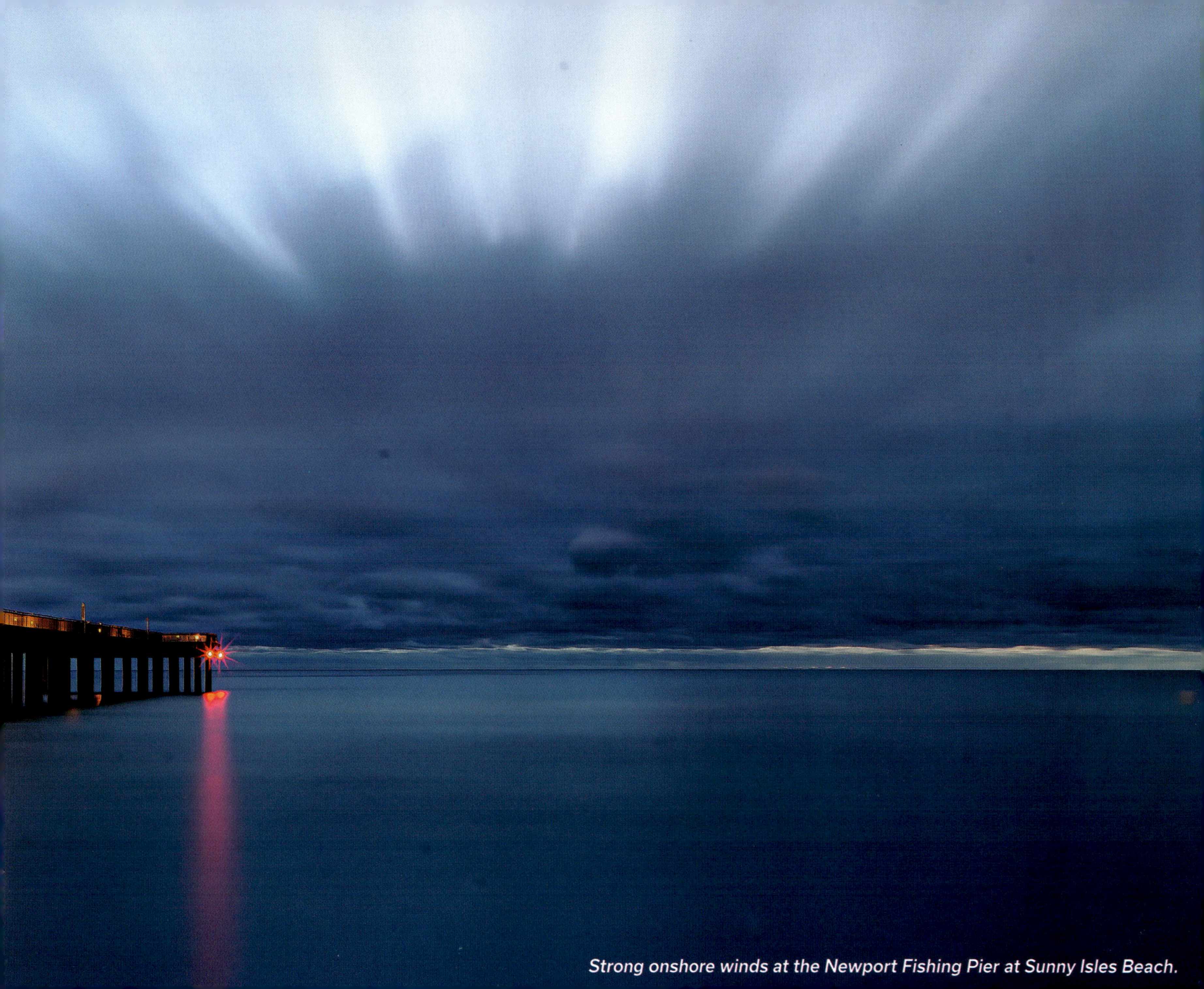

Strong onshore winds at the Newport Fishing Pier at Sunny Isles Beach.

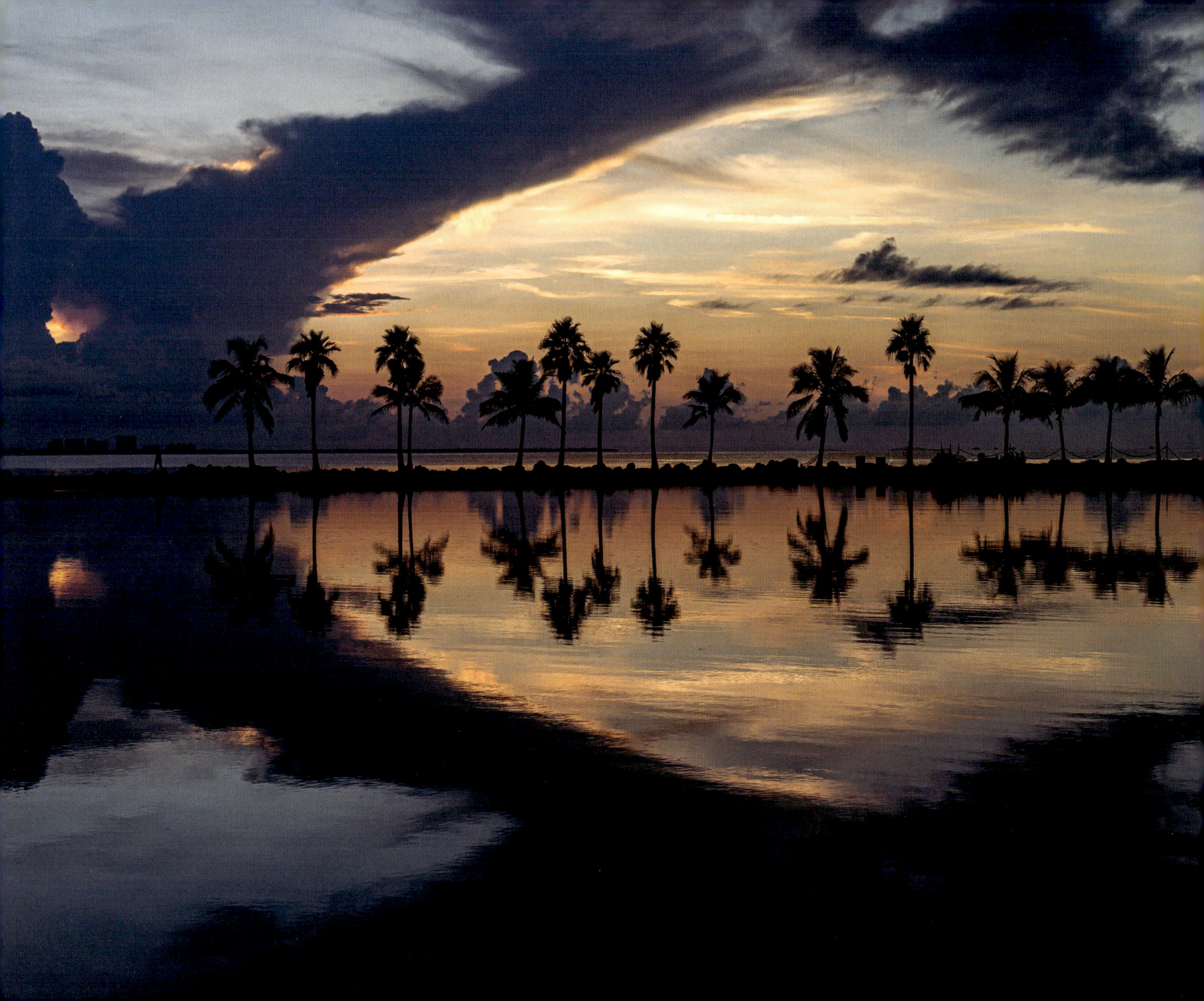

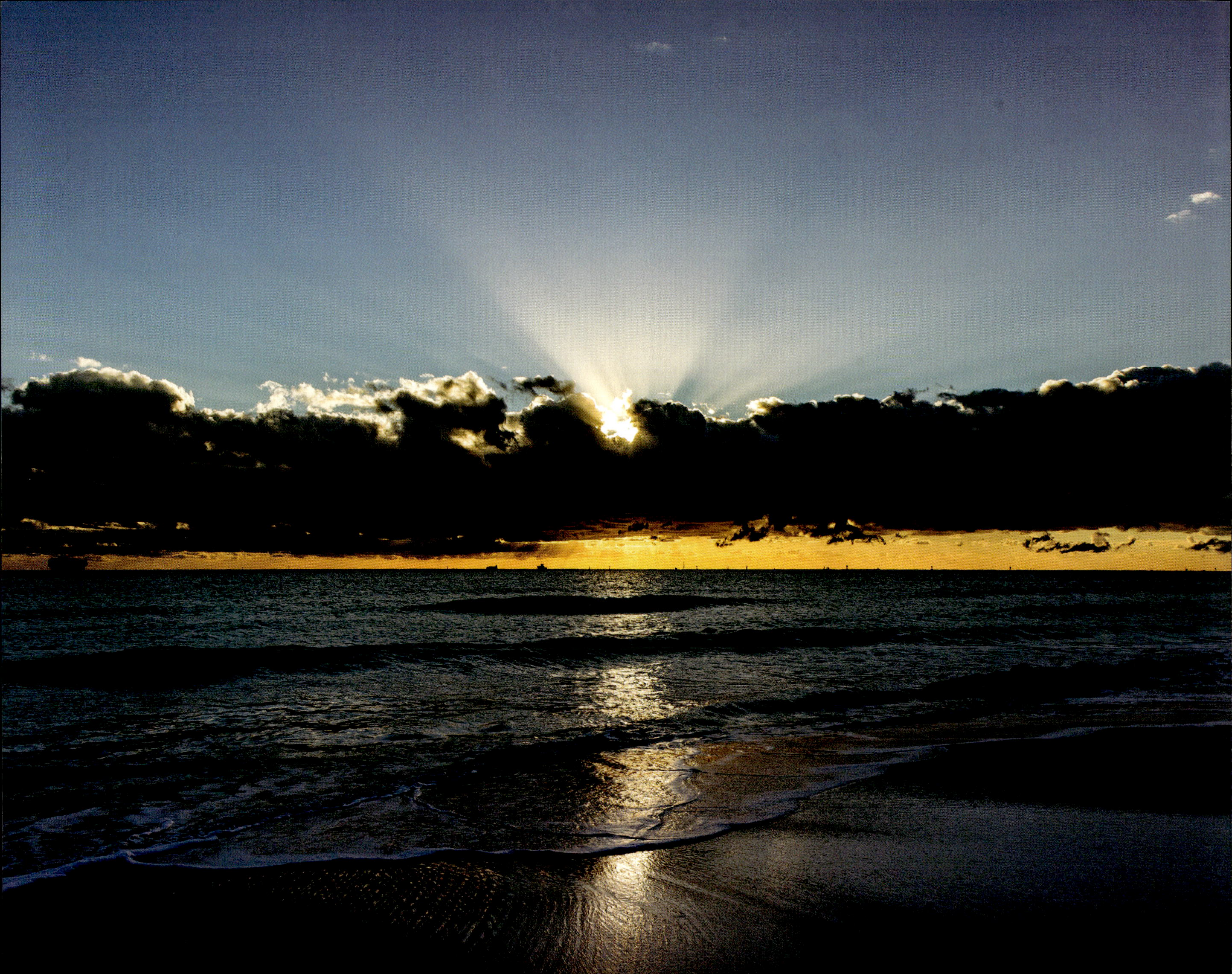

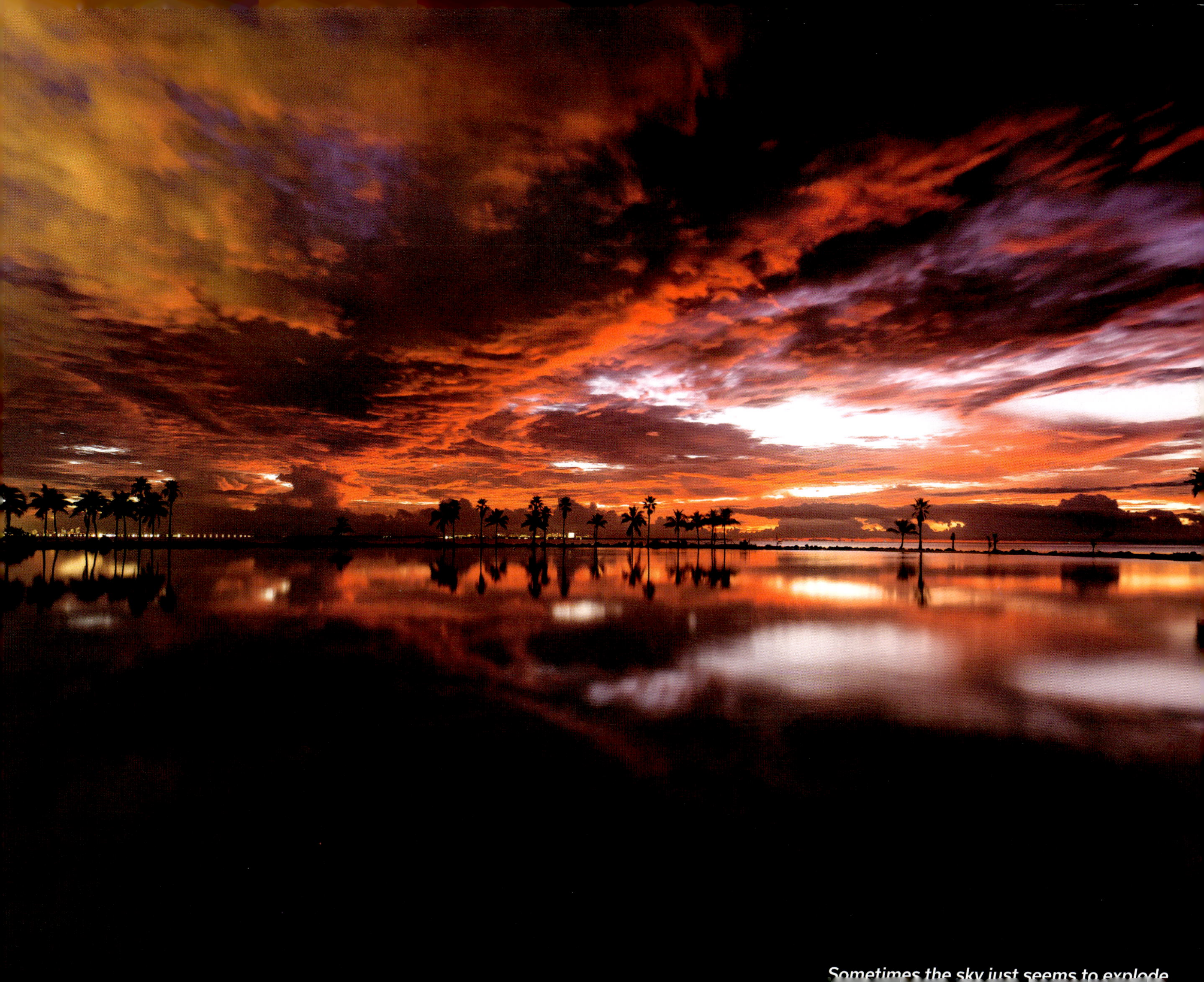

Sometimes the sky just seems to explode

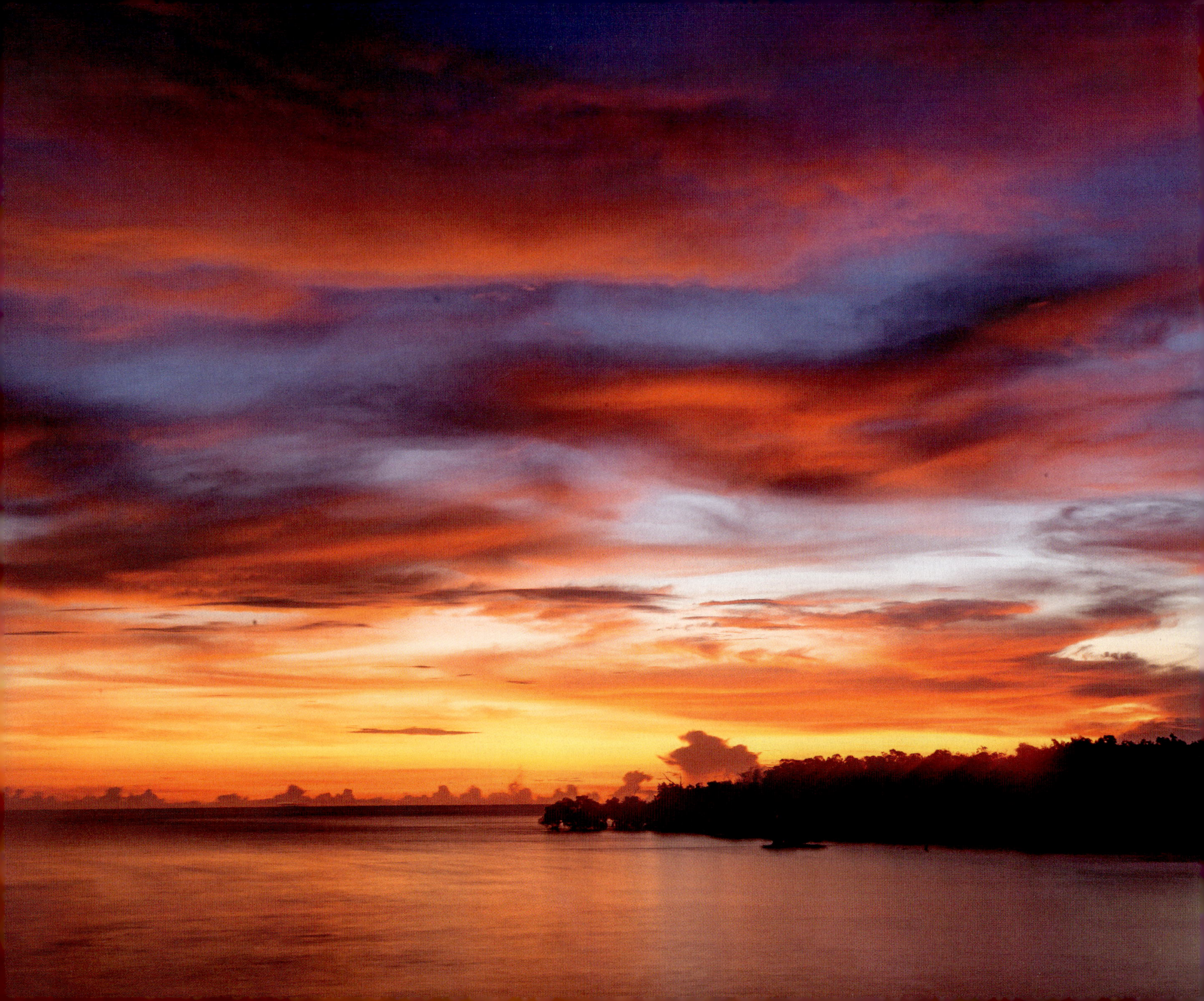

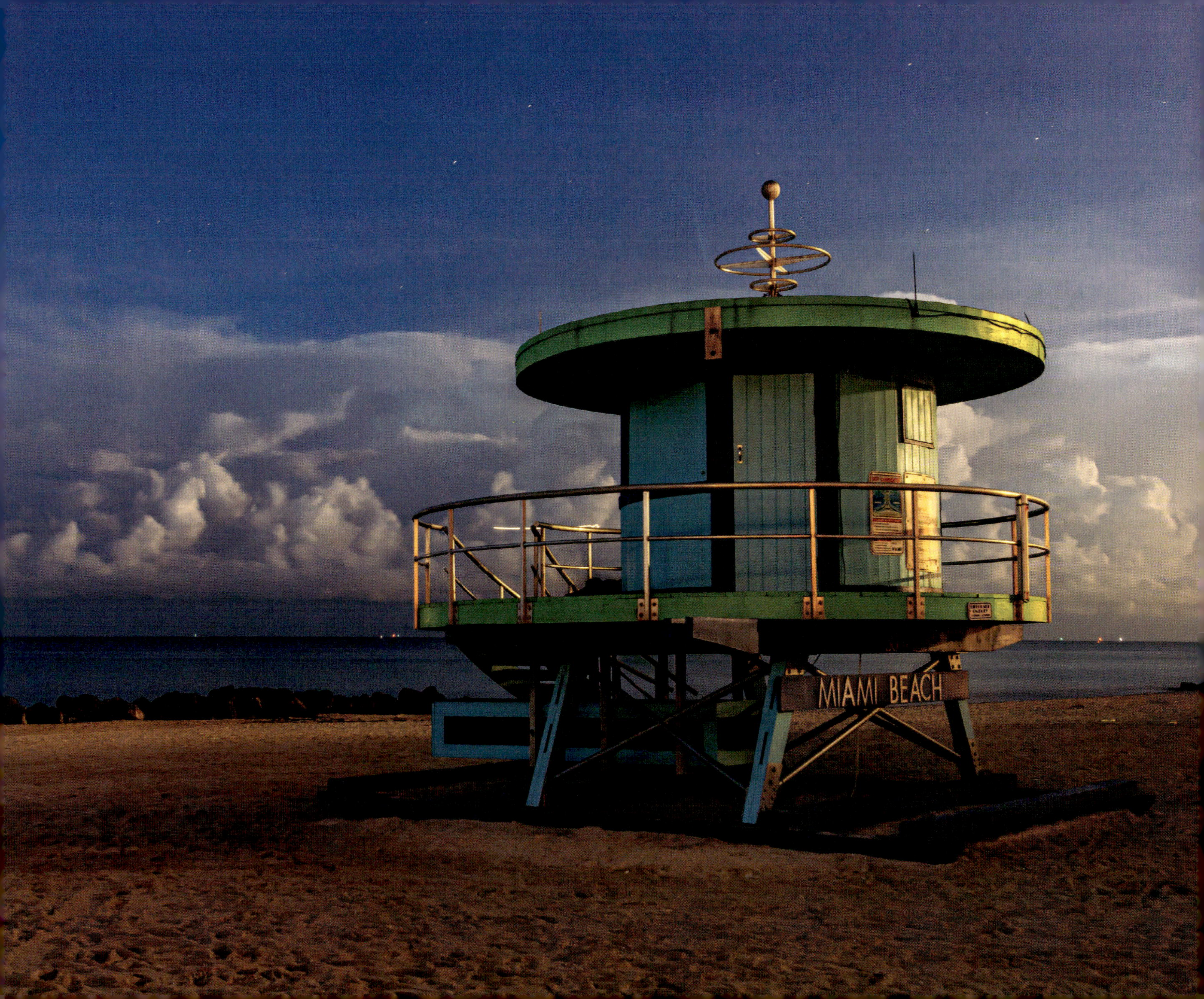
MIAMI BEACH

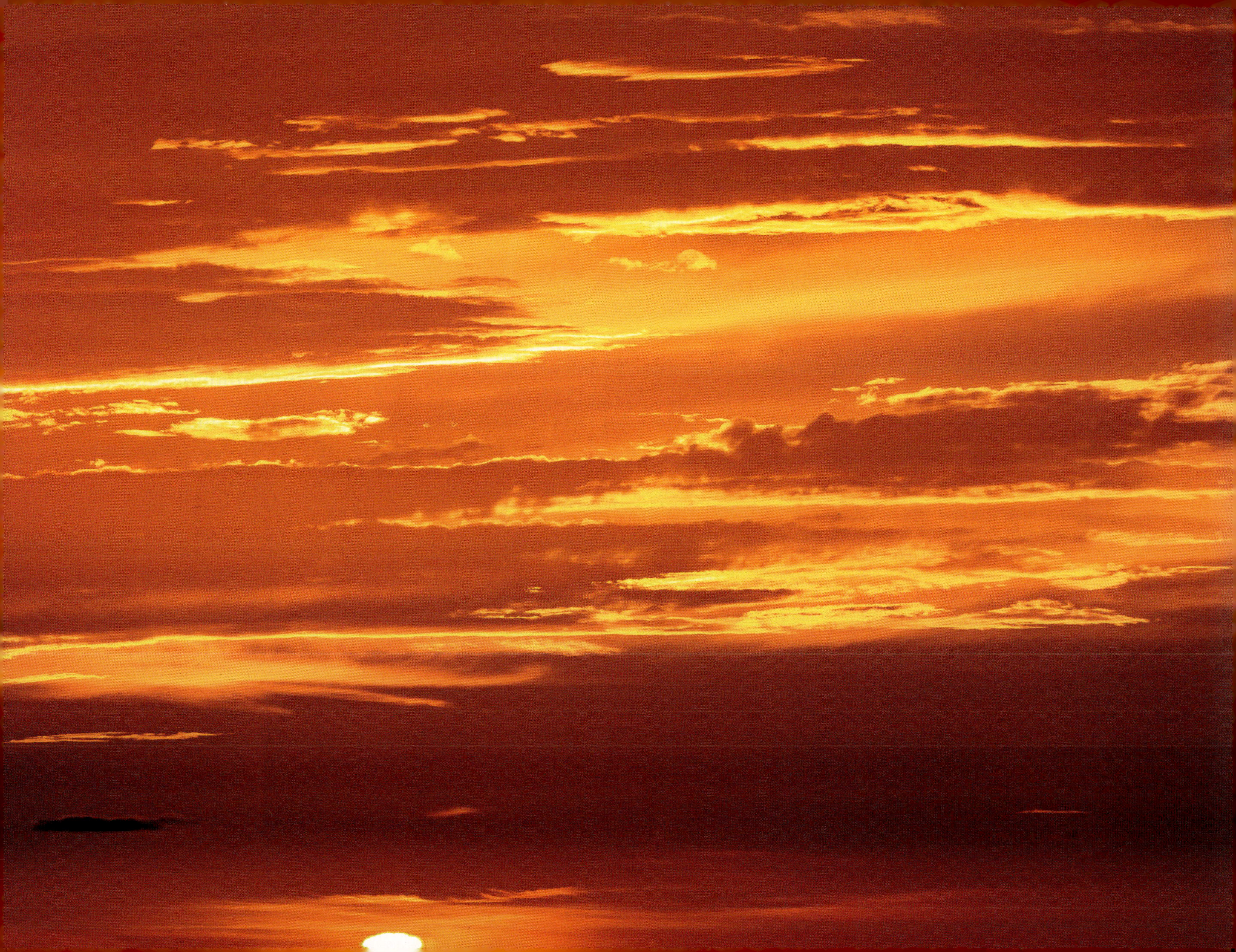

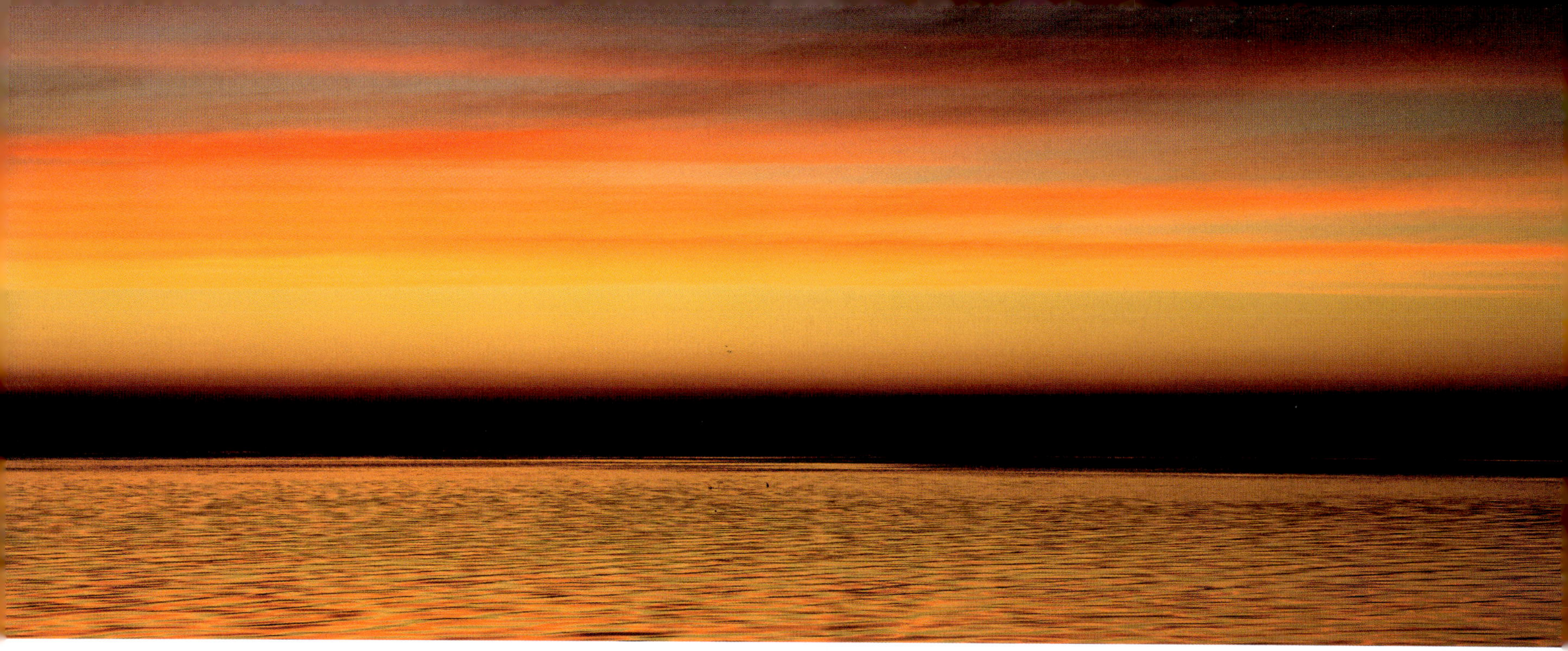

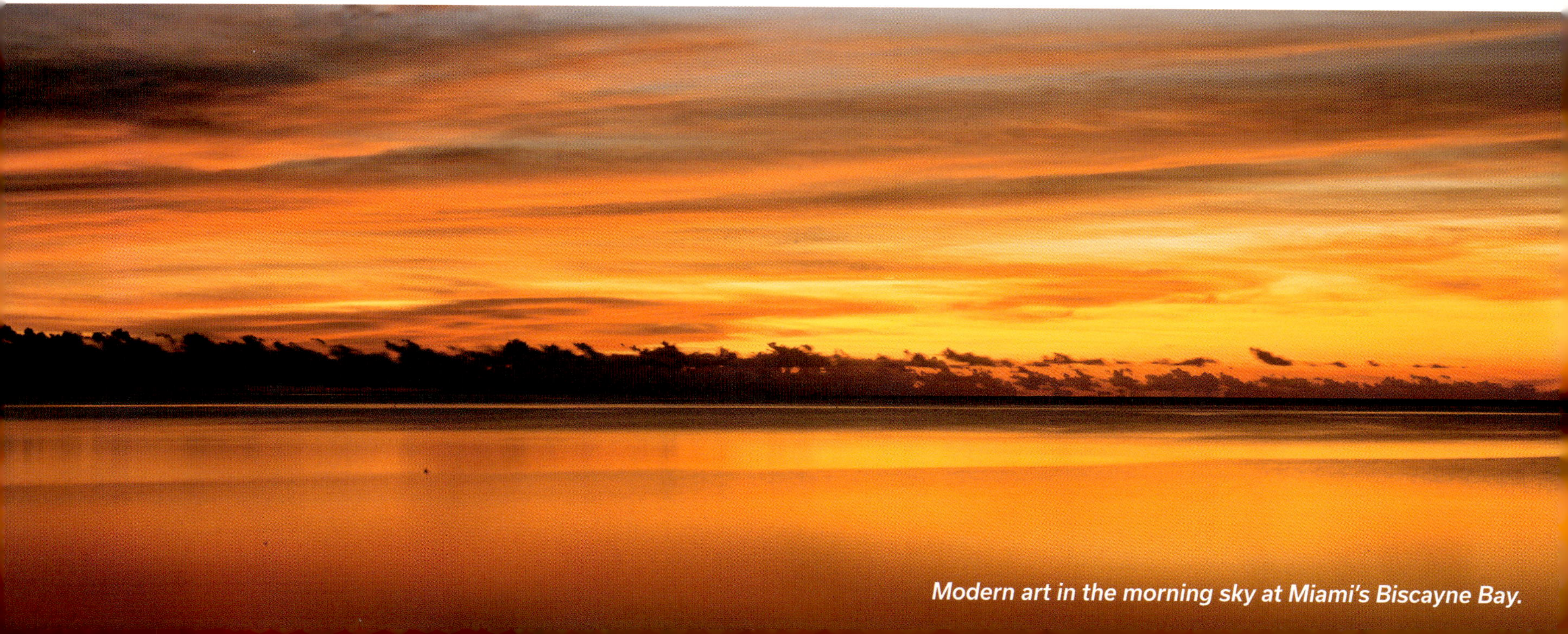

Modern art in the morning sky at Miami's Biscayne Bay.

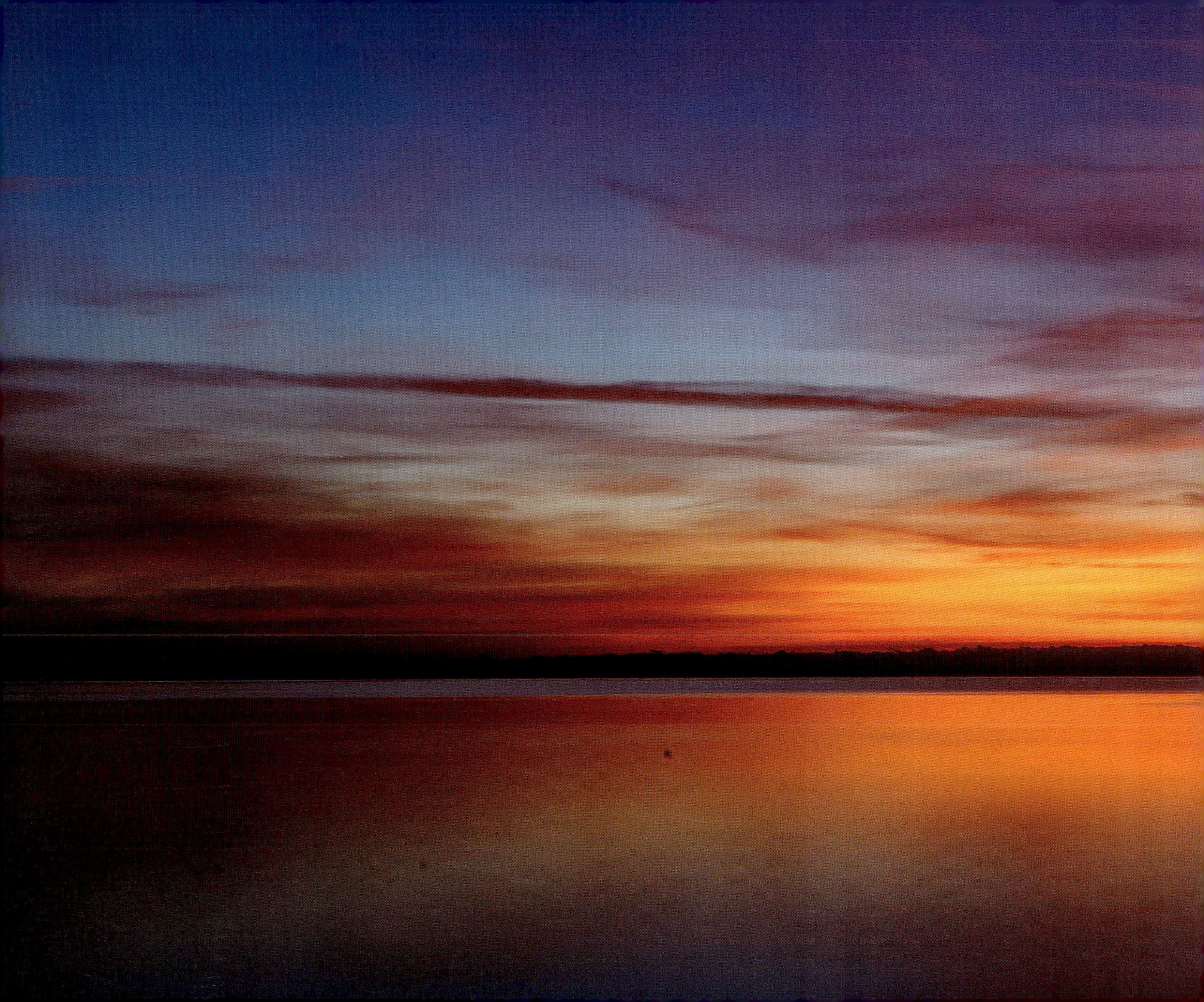

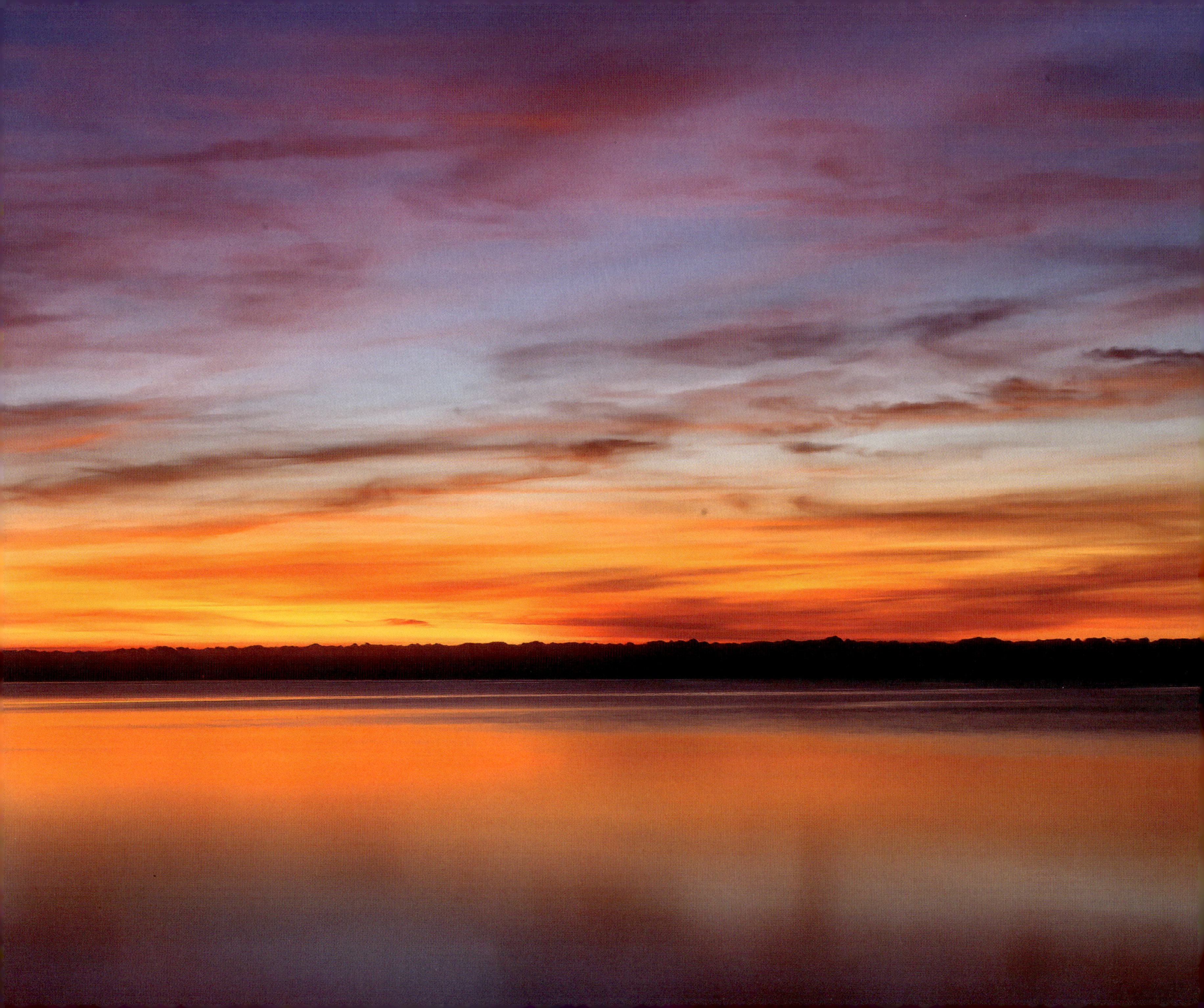

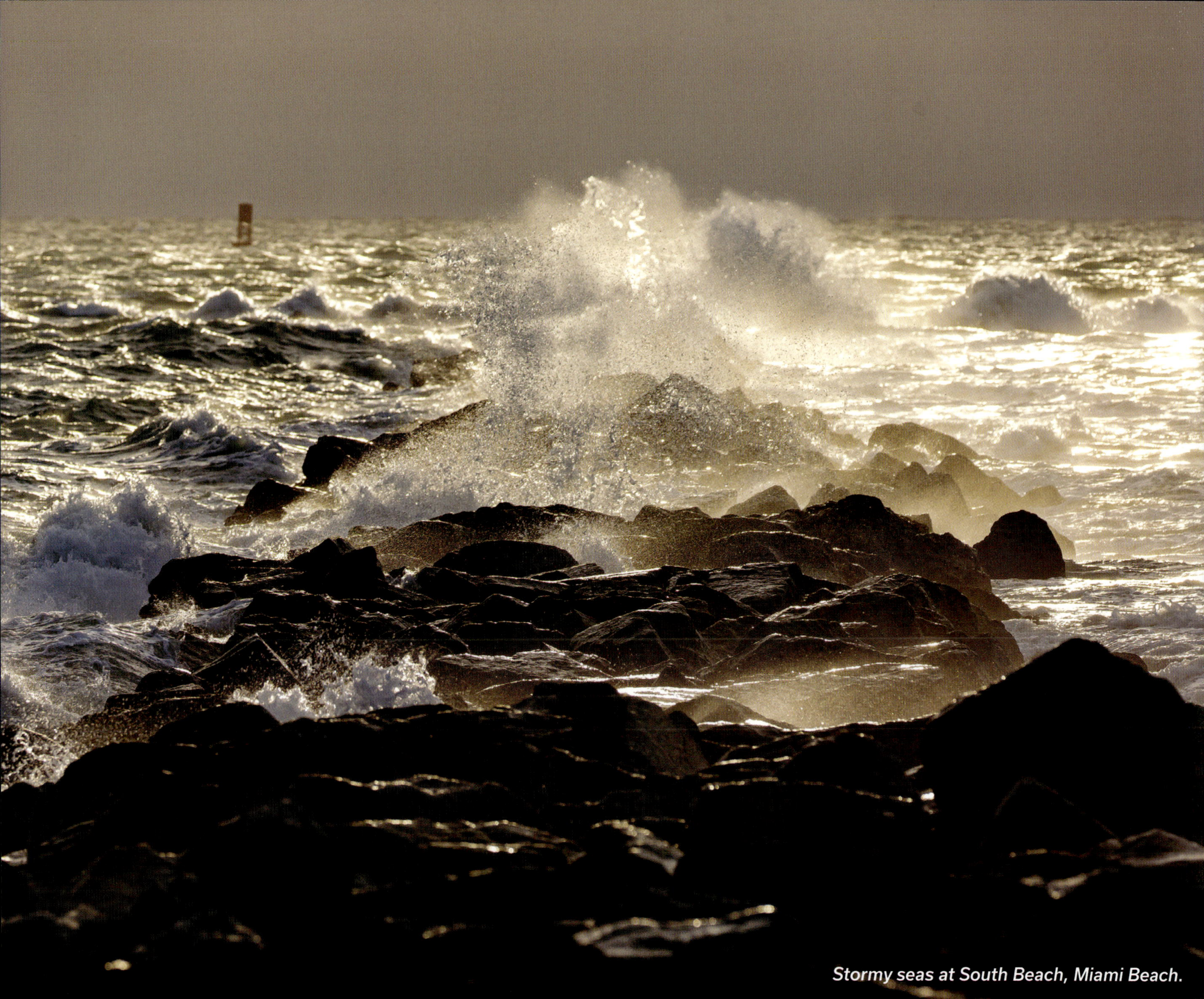

Stormy seas at South Beach, Miami Beach.

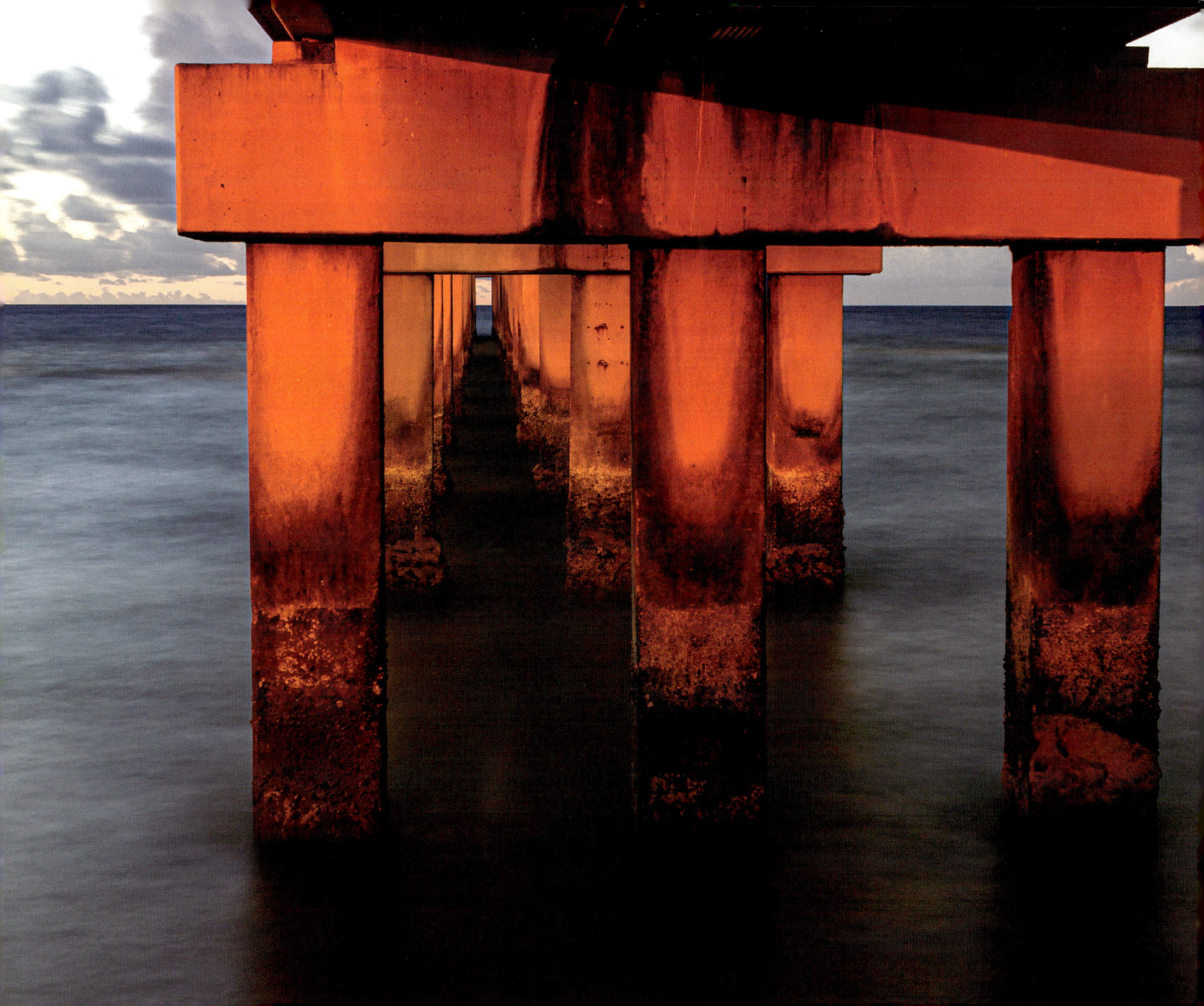

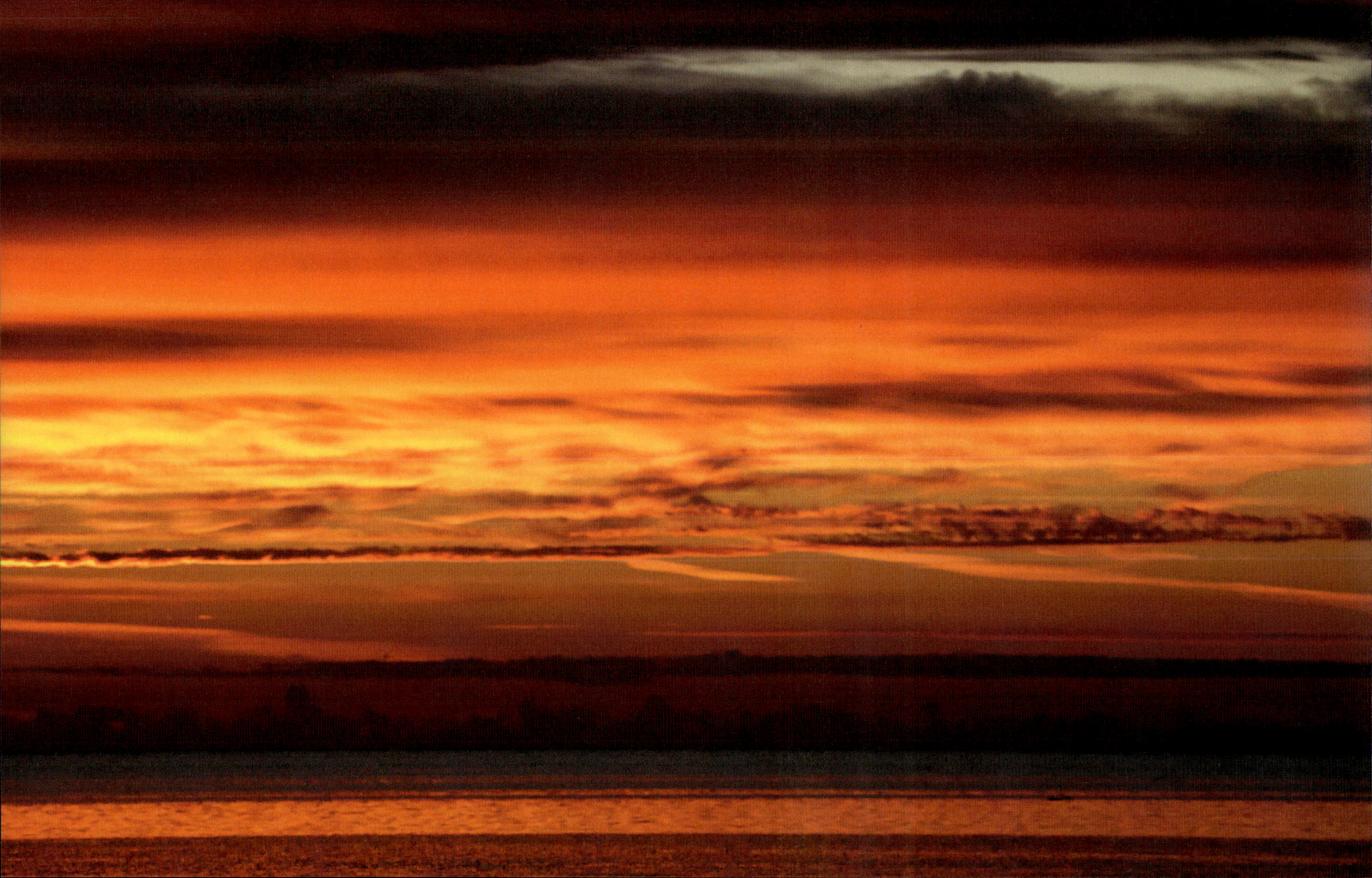

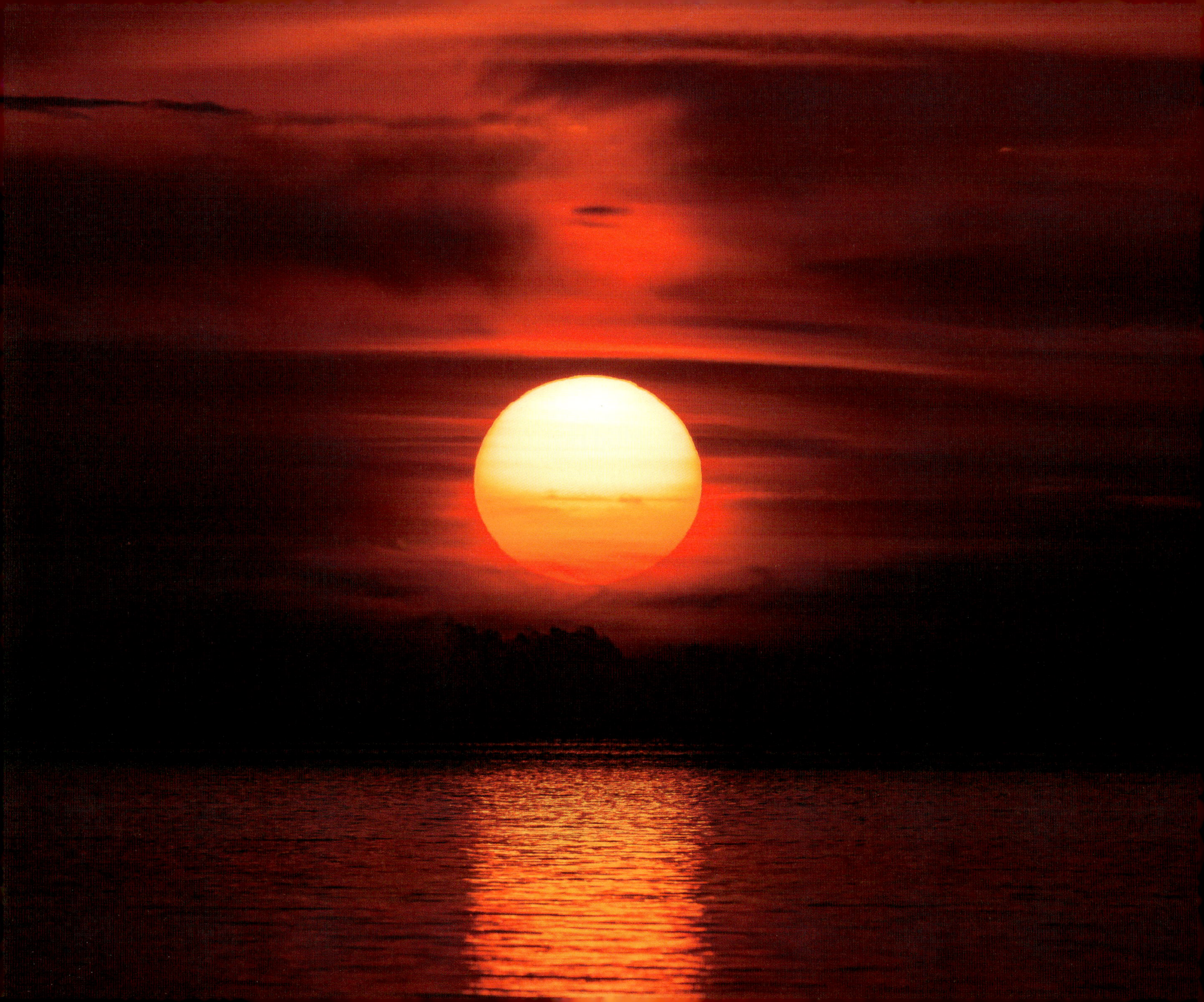

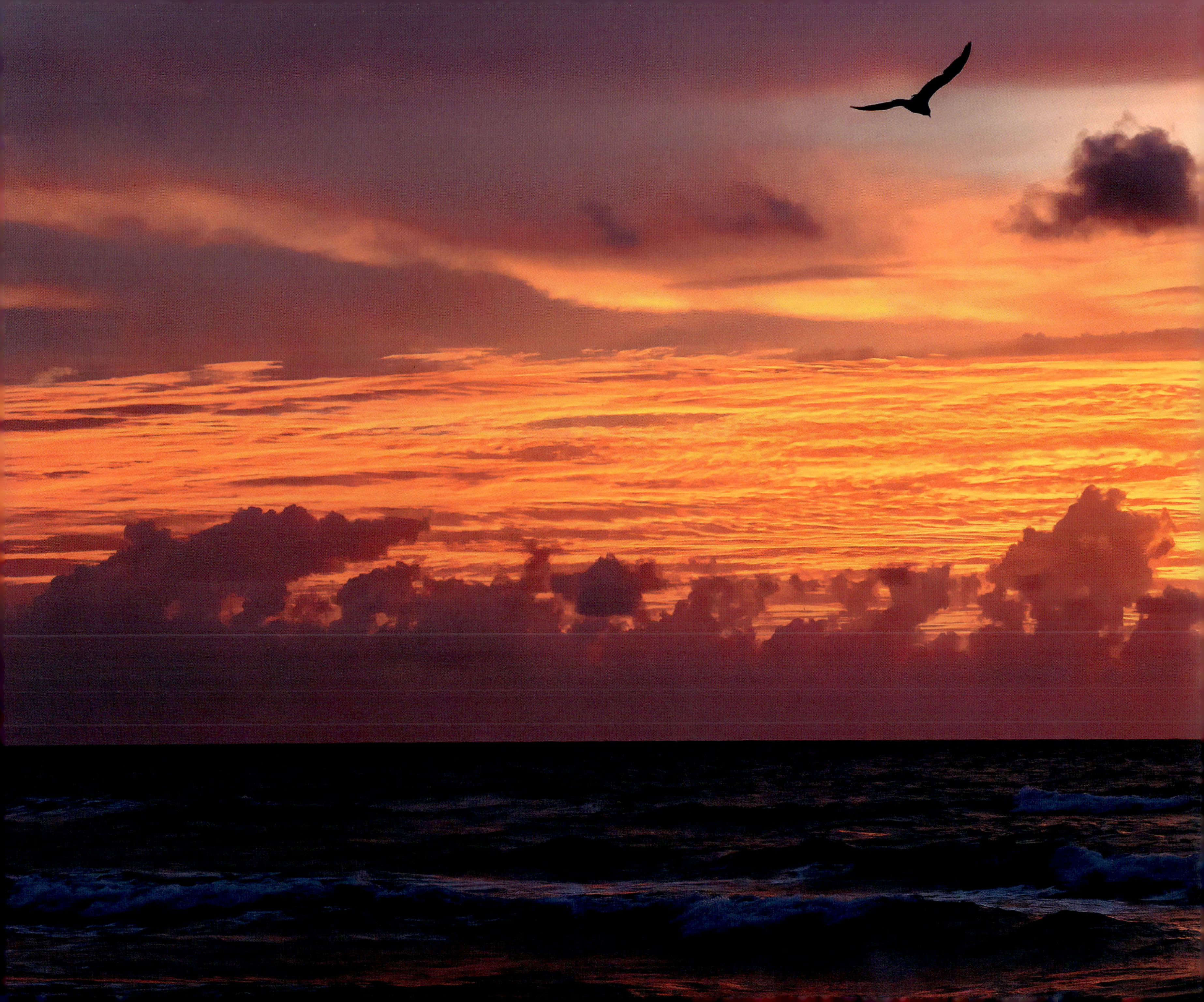

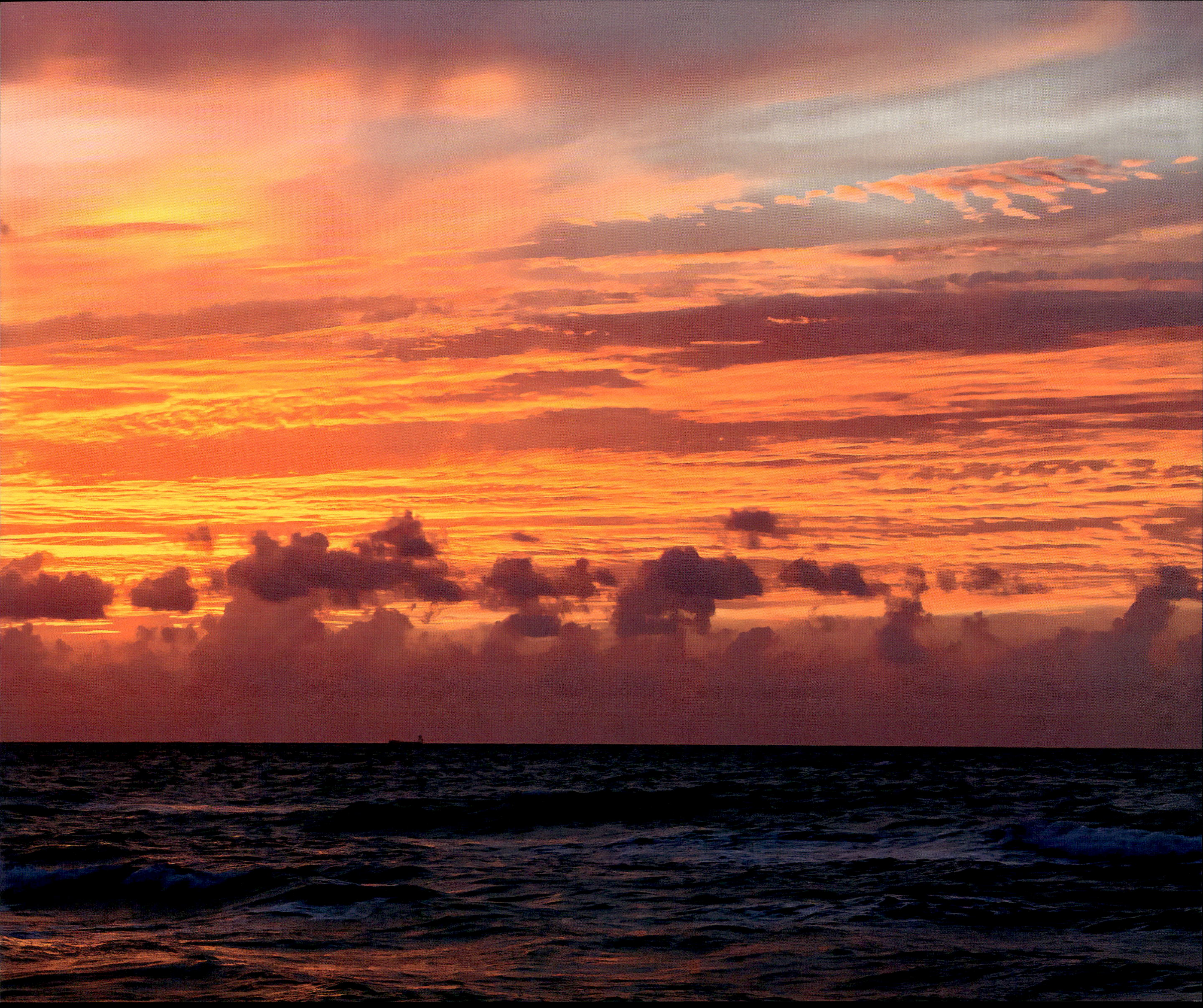

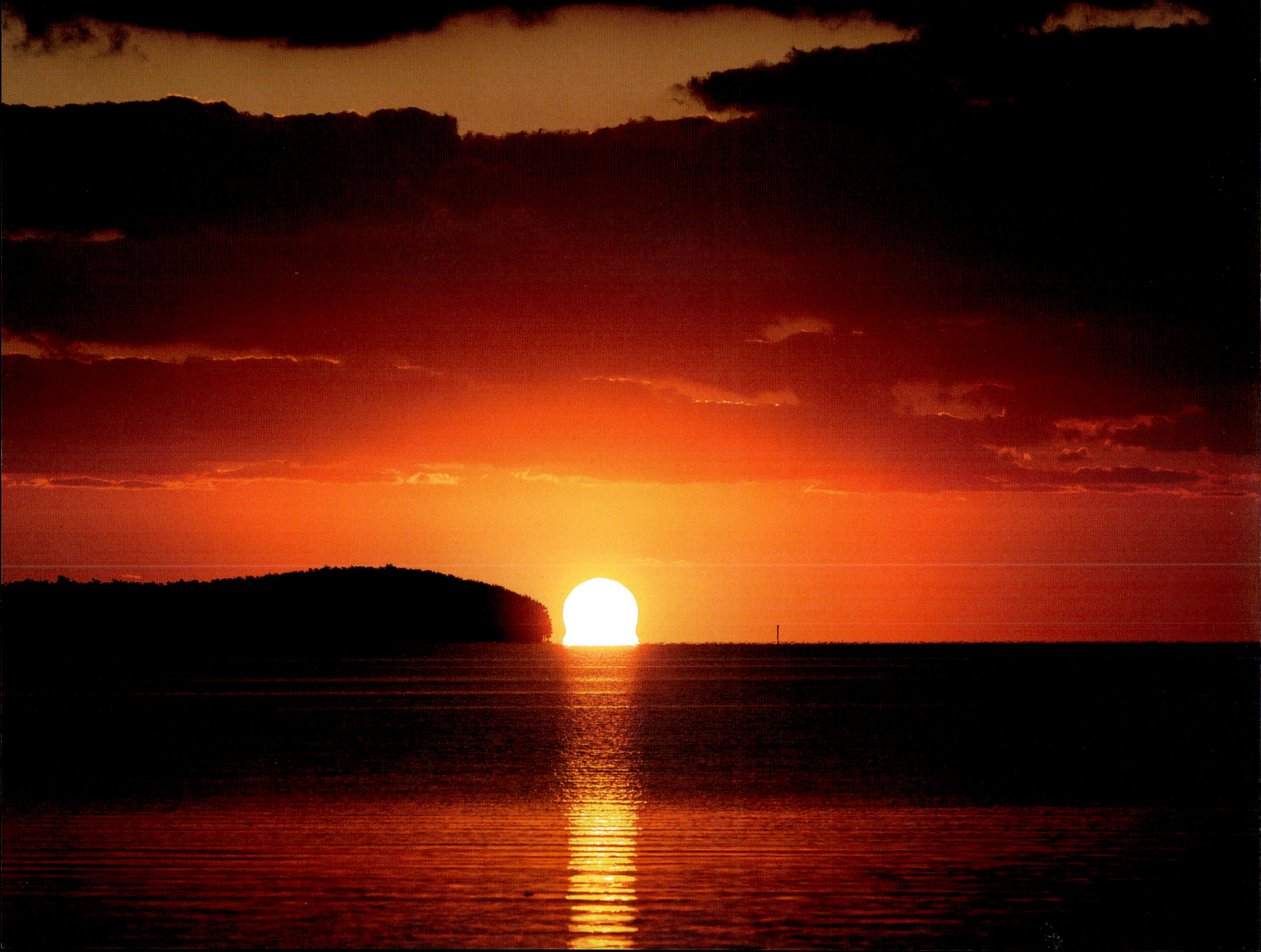

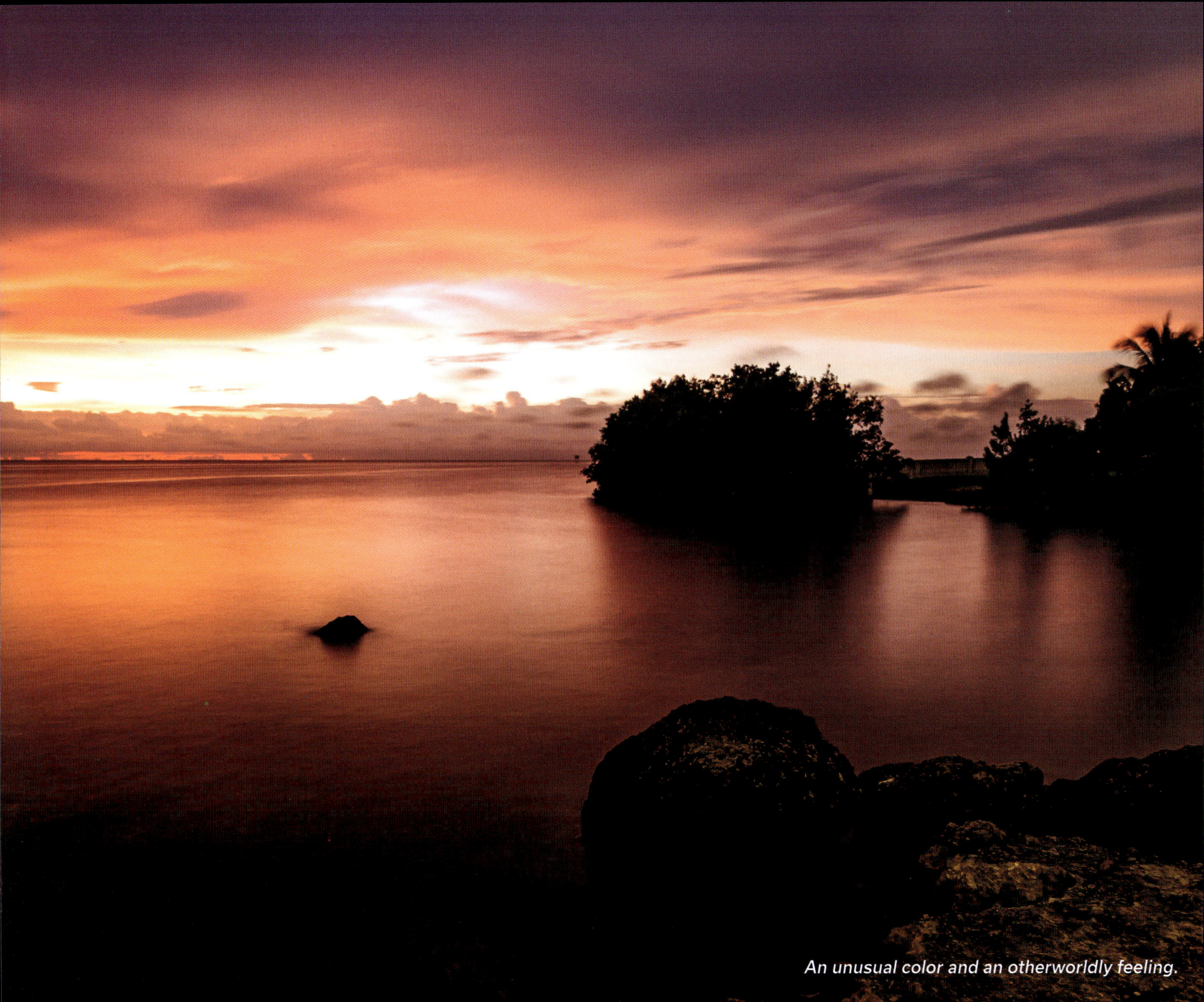

An unusual color and an otherworldly feeling.

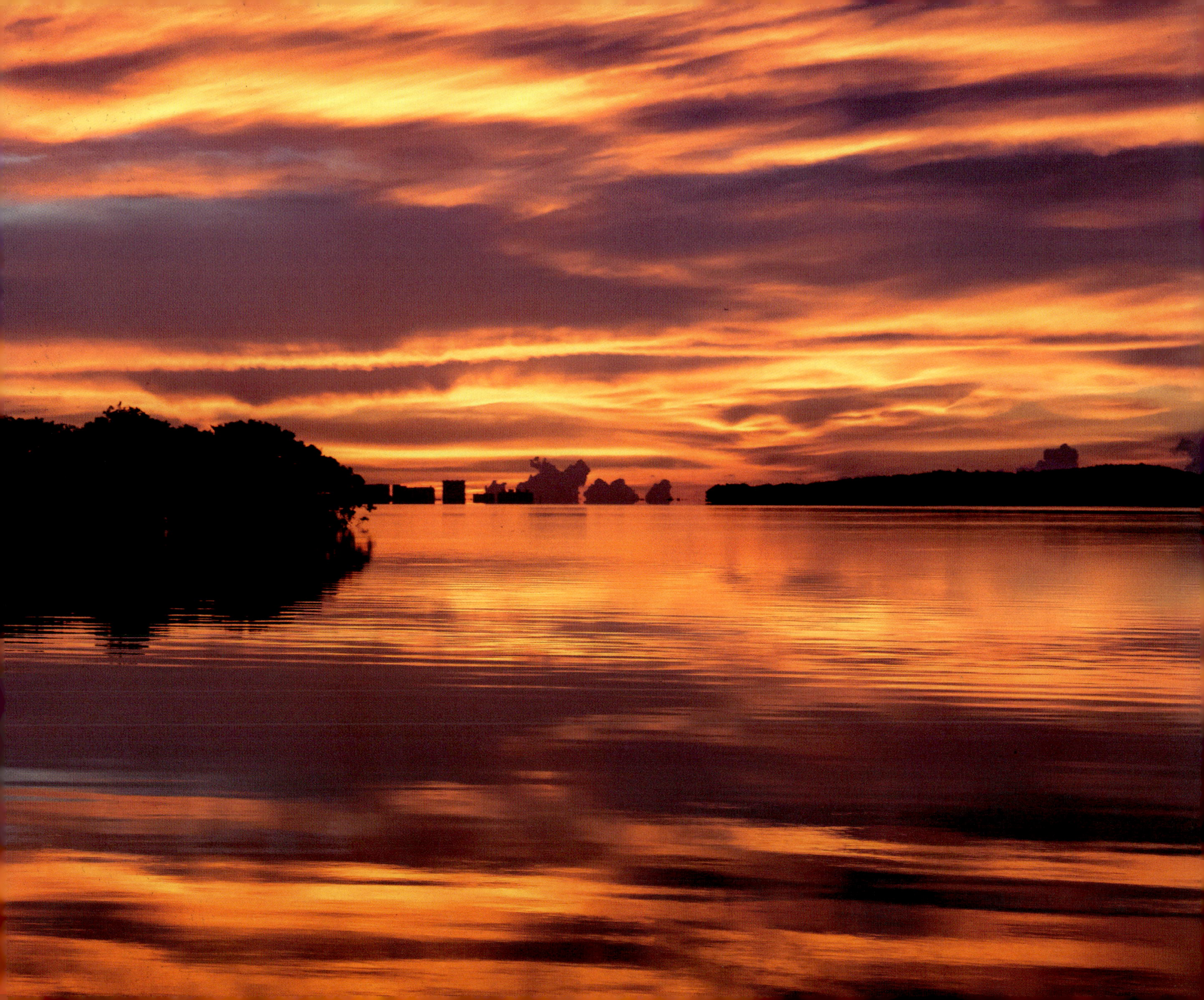

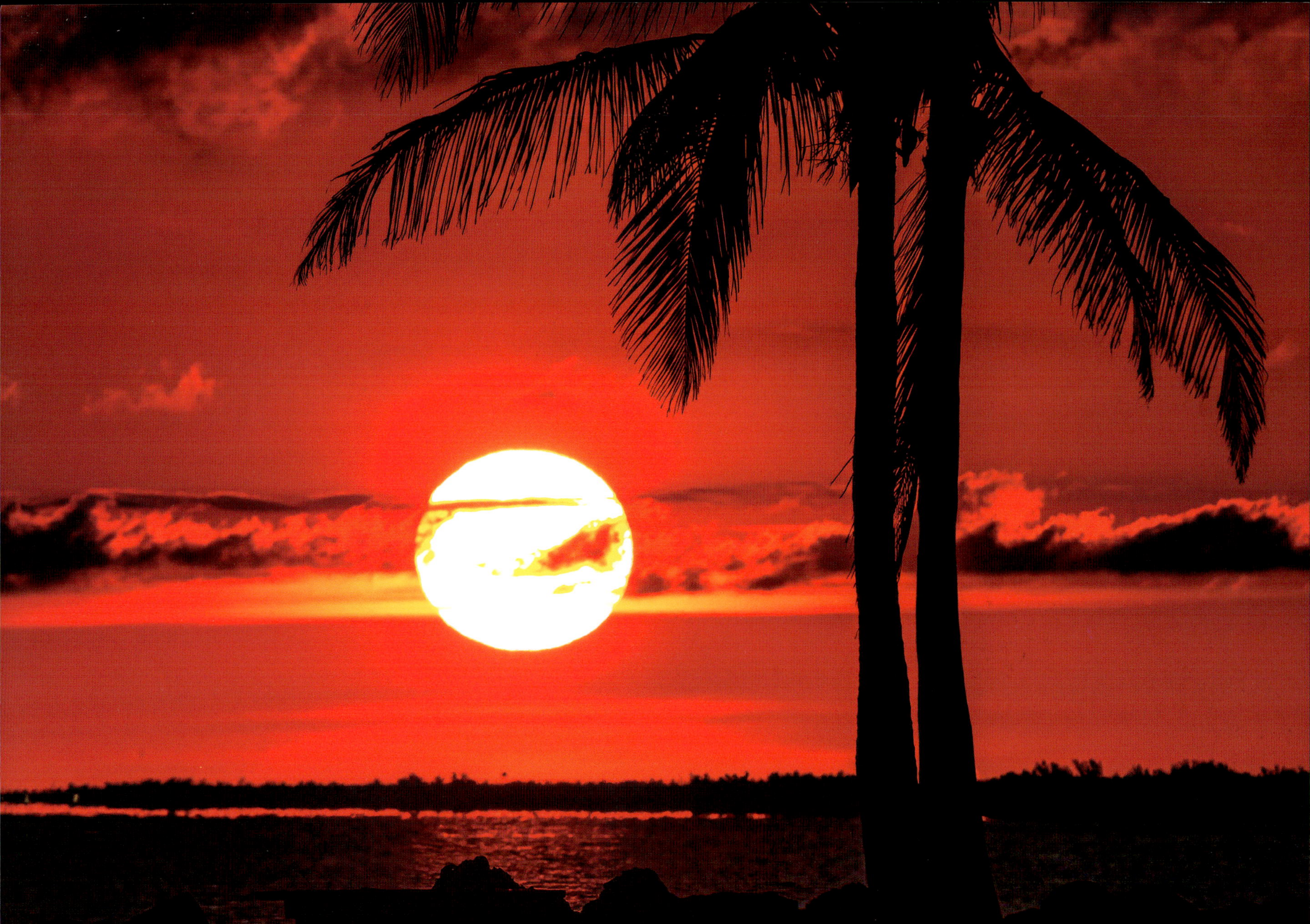

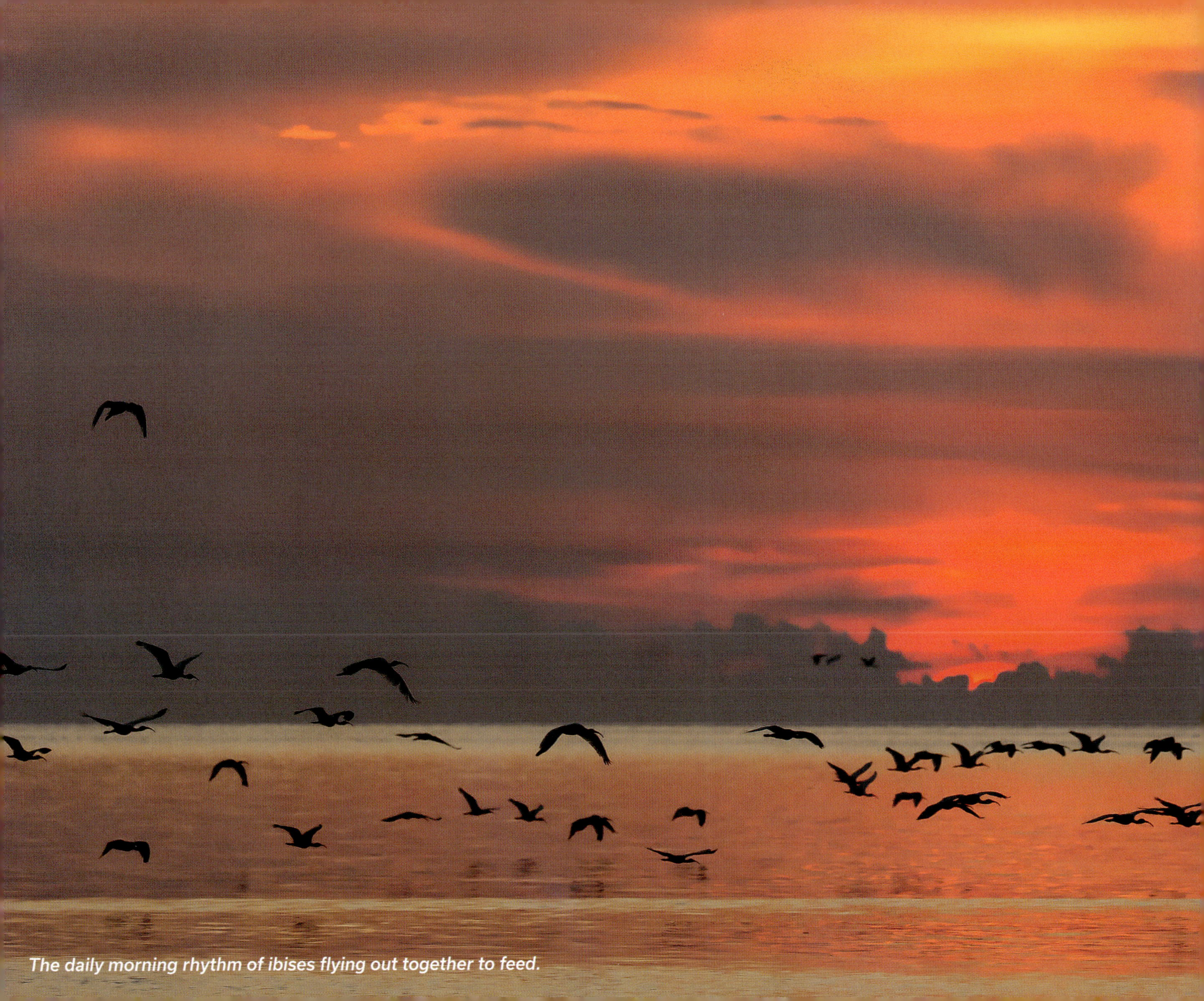

The daily morning rhythm of ibises flying out together to feed.

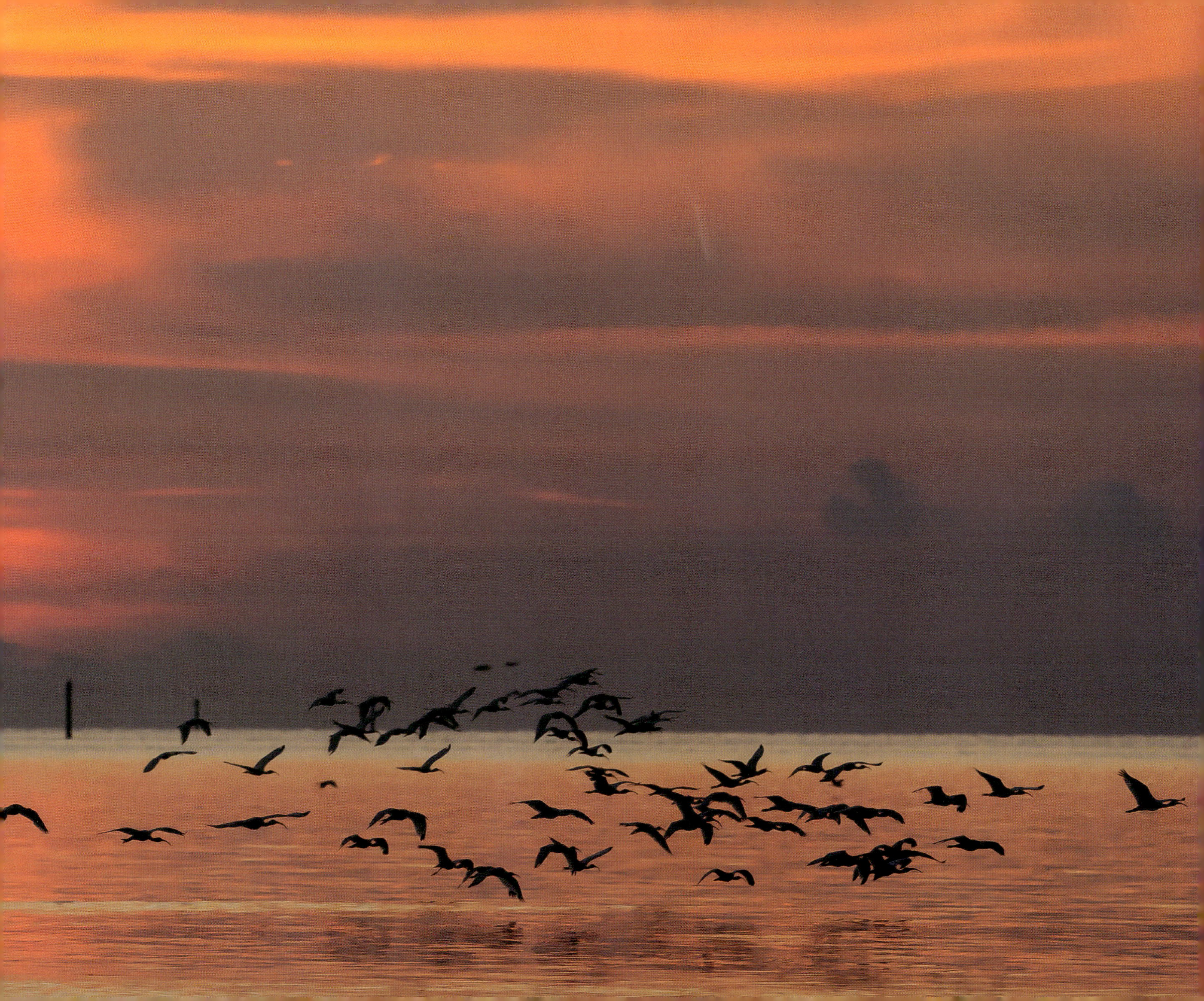

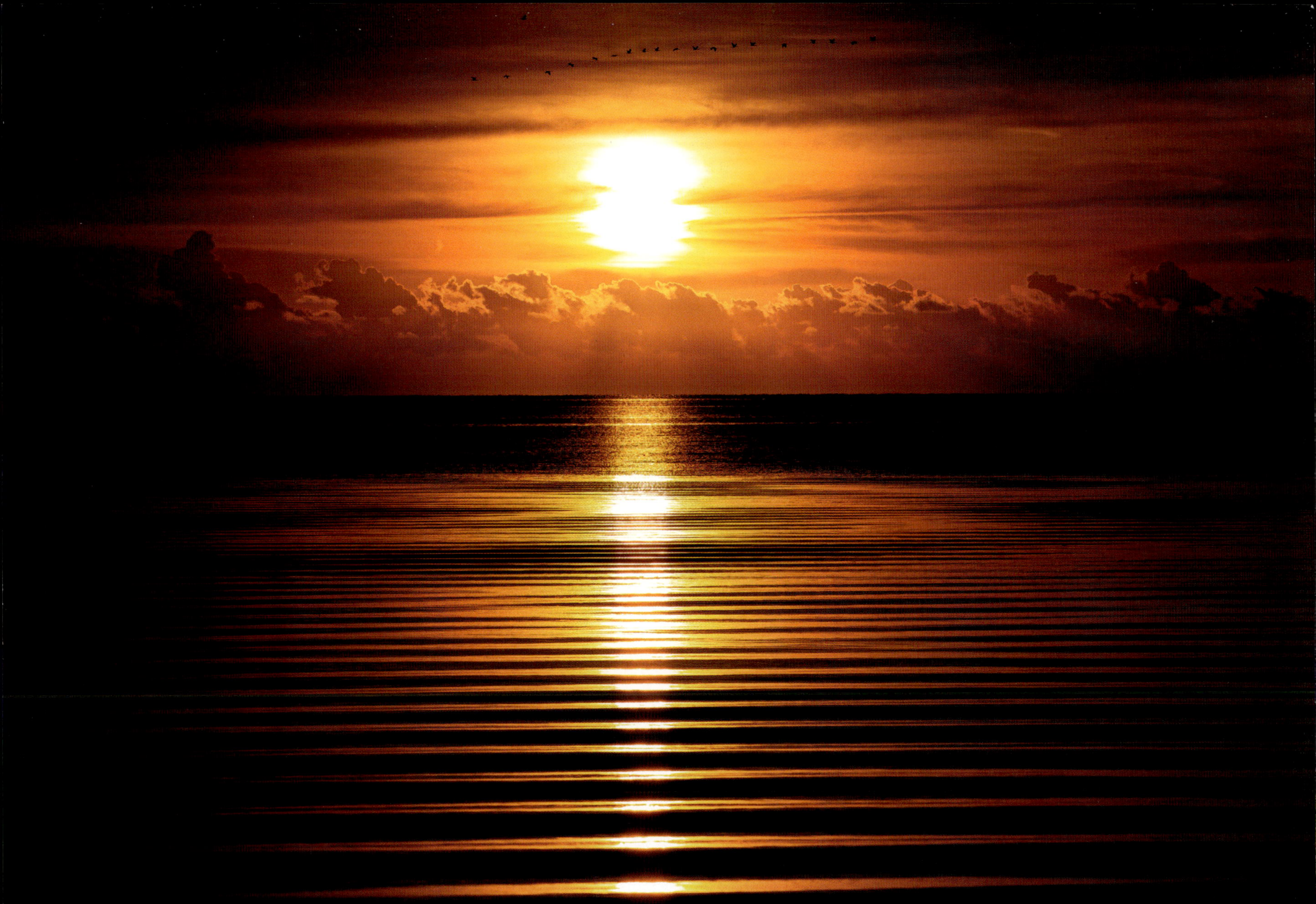

A lifelong friend calls this photograph, above, "New Beginning." A perfect description.

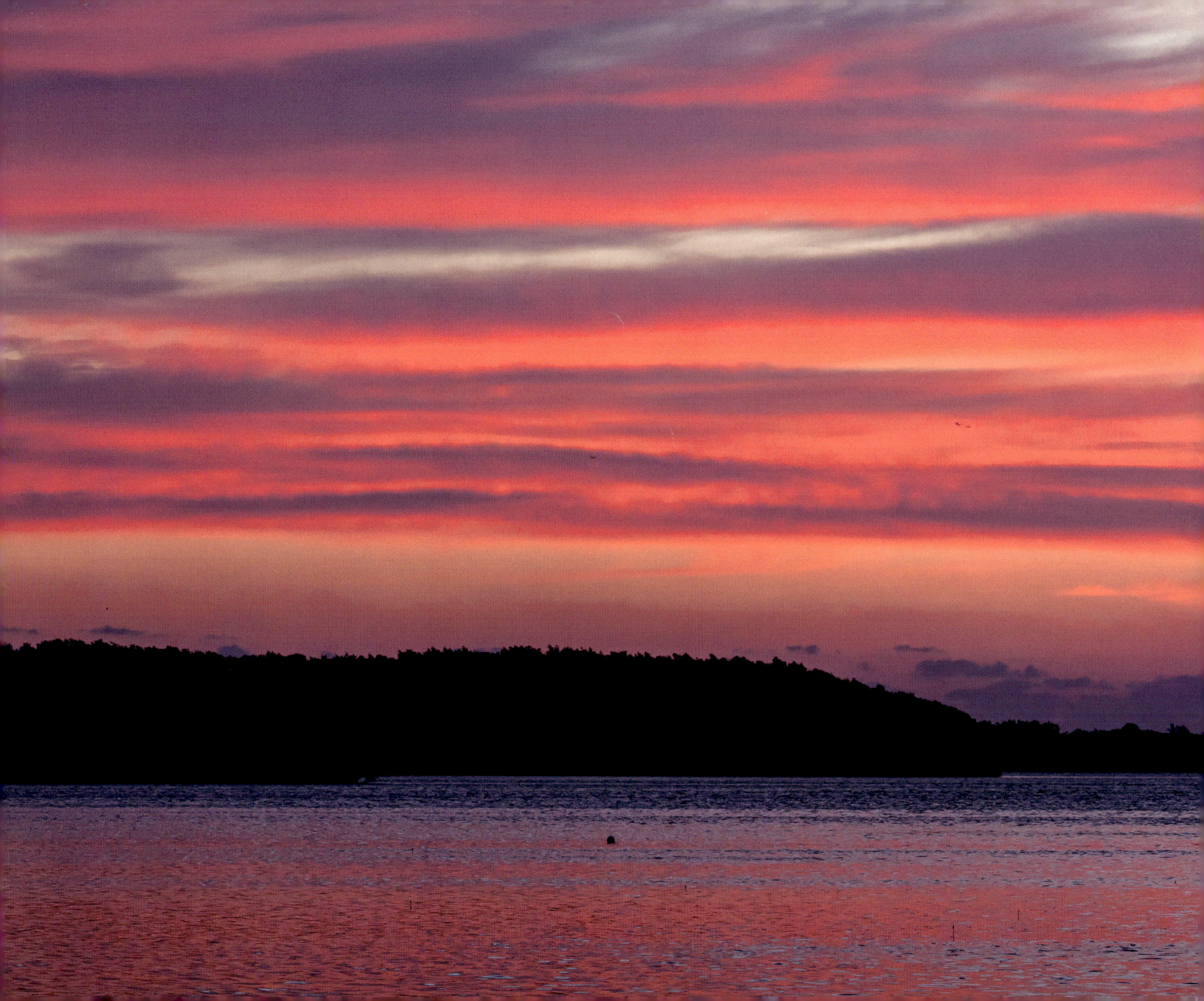

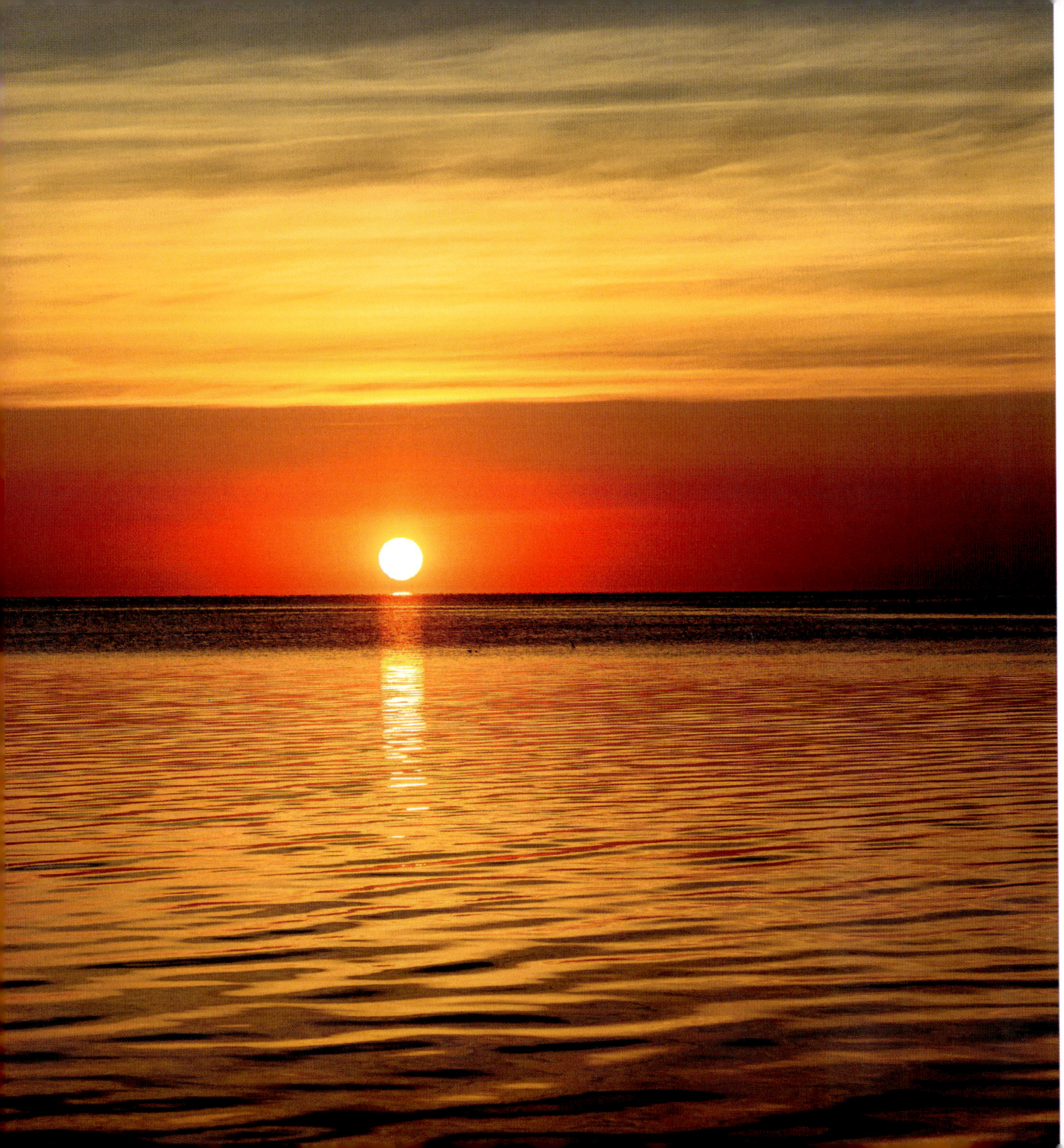

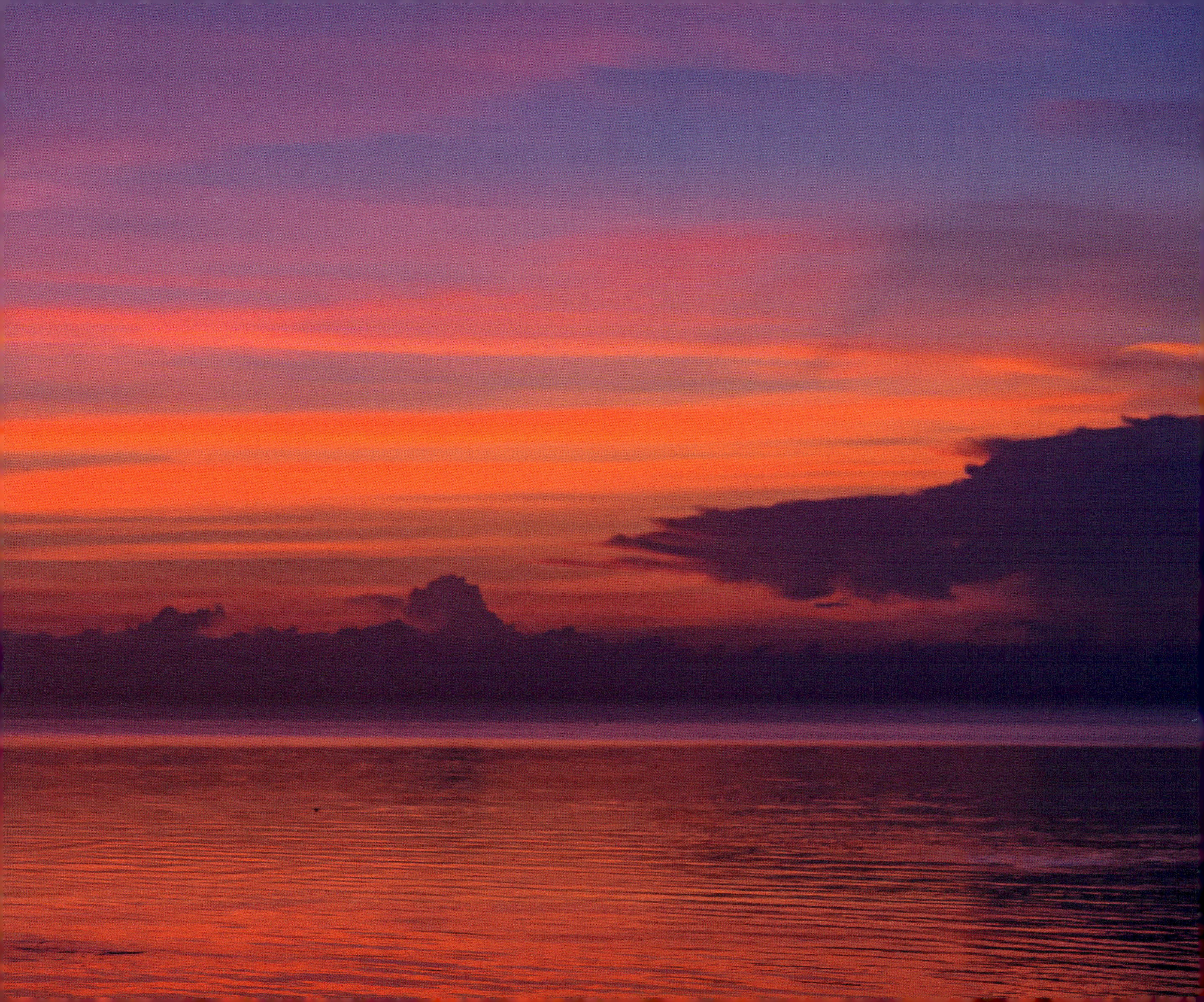

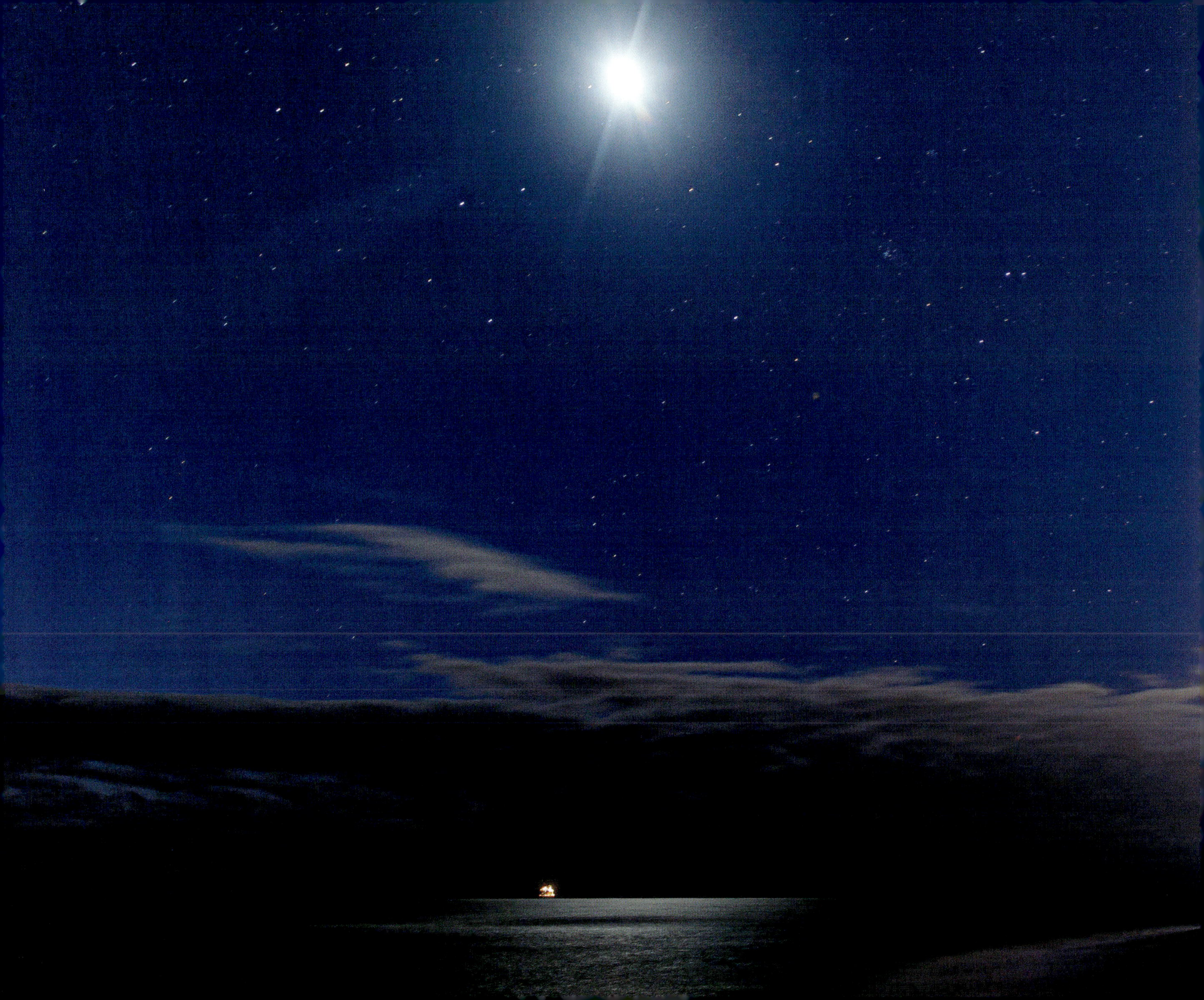

Dark of Night and Twilight Awakening

This is where the chronological march toward sunrise begins. The first thing you notice in the early-morning darkness on Florida beaches, in the Everglades, at marinas, or along a city skyline is just how quiet everything is. Looking up, you can see the blackened sky filled with stars and planets. When the moon is high, the low-lying clouds appear luminescent as they glide with the wind through the humid air. As the light slowly brightens, the sky at the horizon turns gray or even light blue. We are now heading for sunrise, and a brand-new day is upon us.

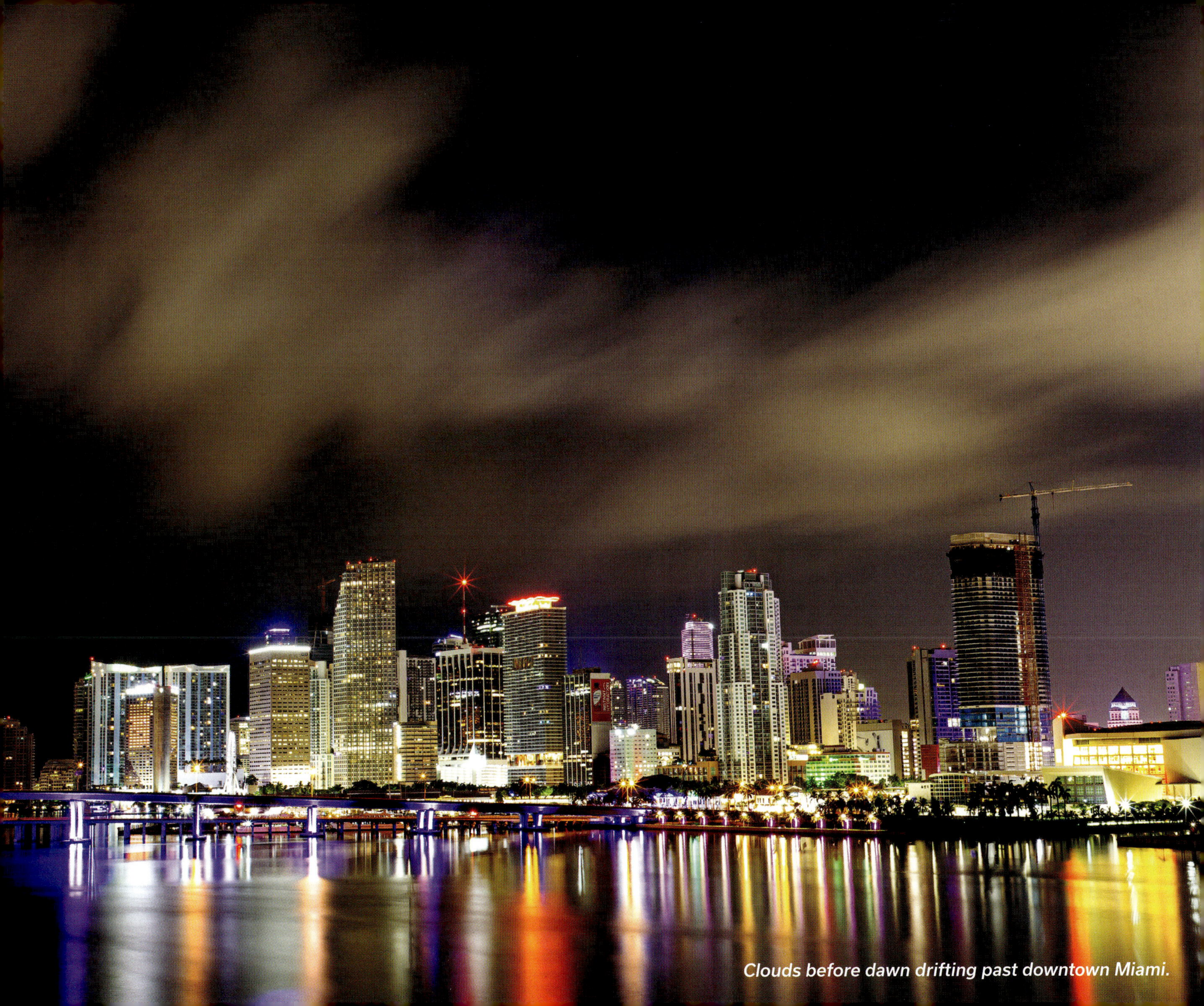

Clouds before dawn drifting past downtown Miami.

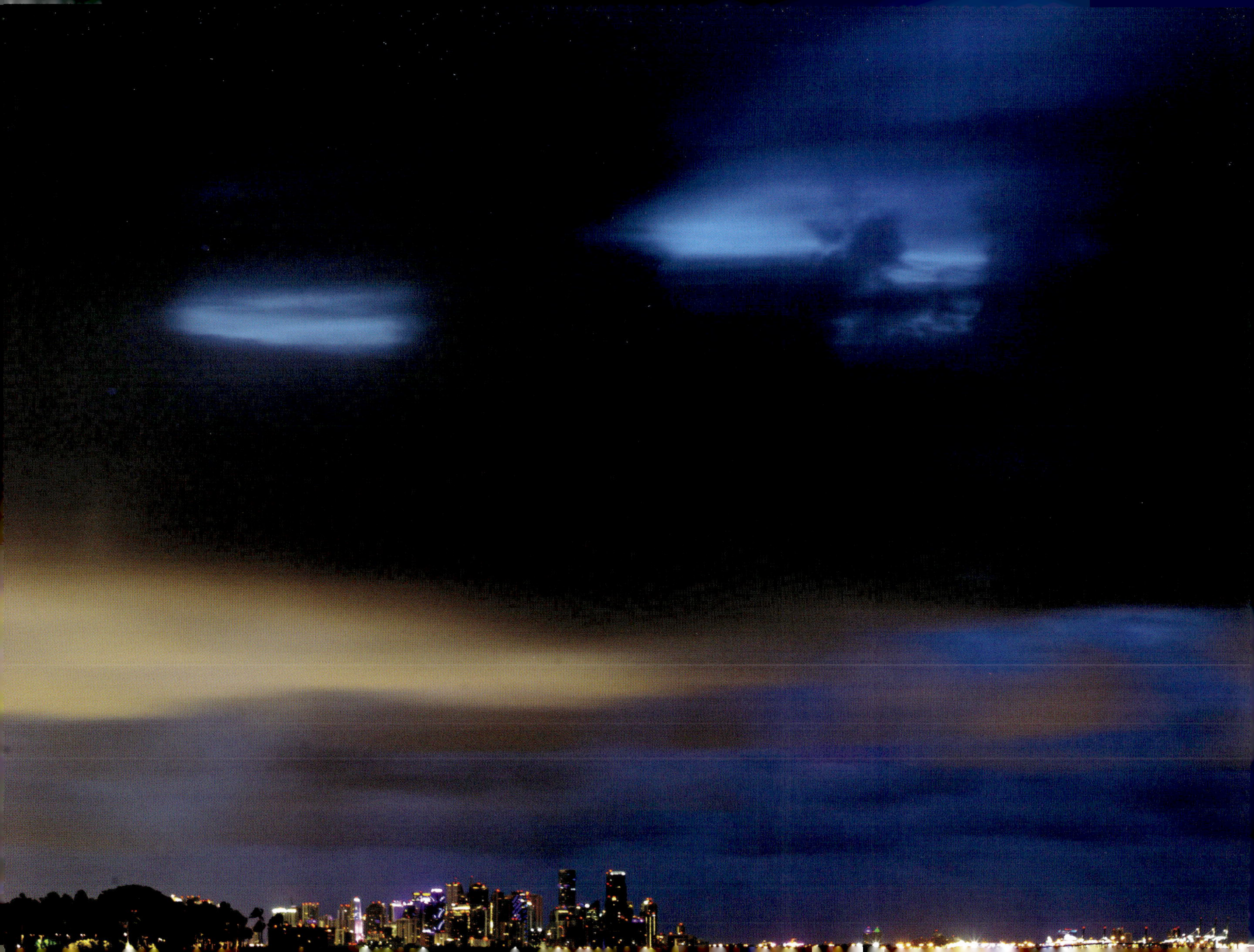

"The fog comes on little cat feet. It sits looking over harbor and city on silent haunches and then moves on" —Carl Sandburg, 1916

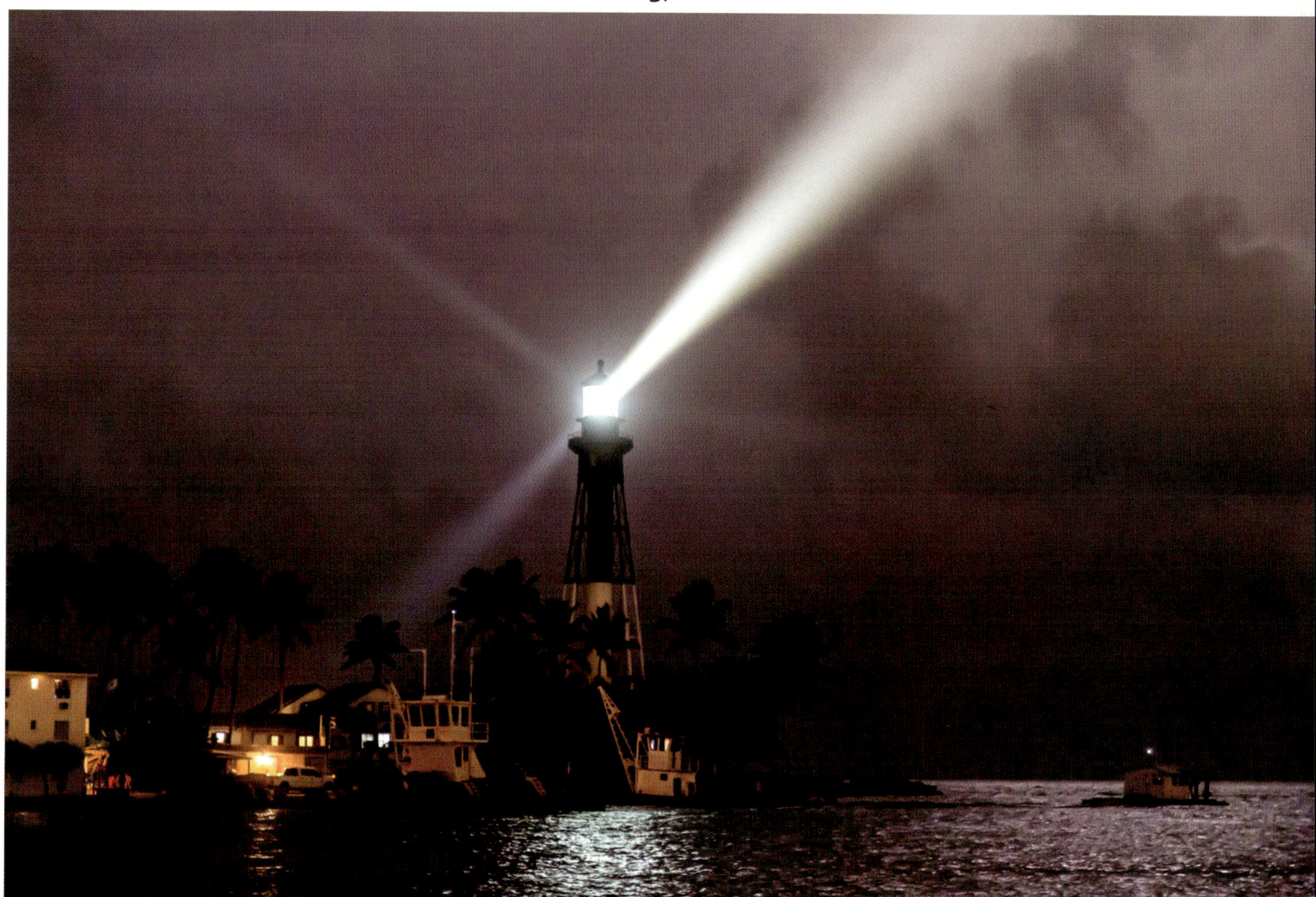

A twilight glow at Sunny Isles.

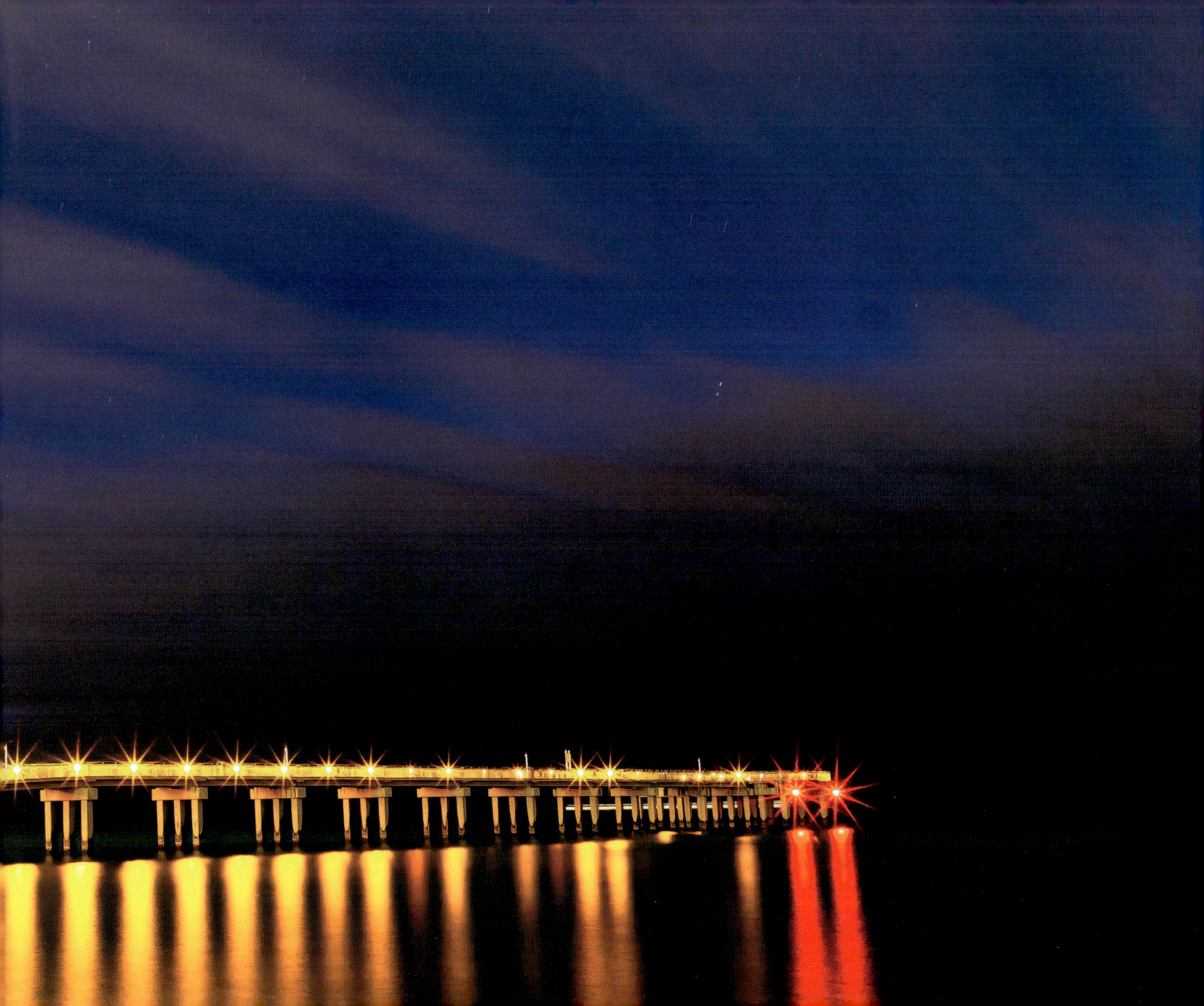

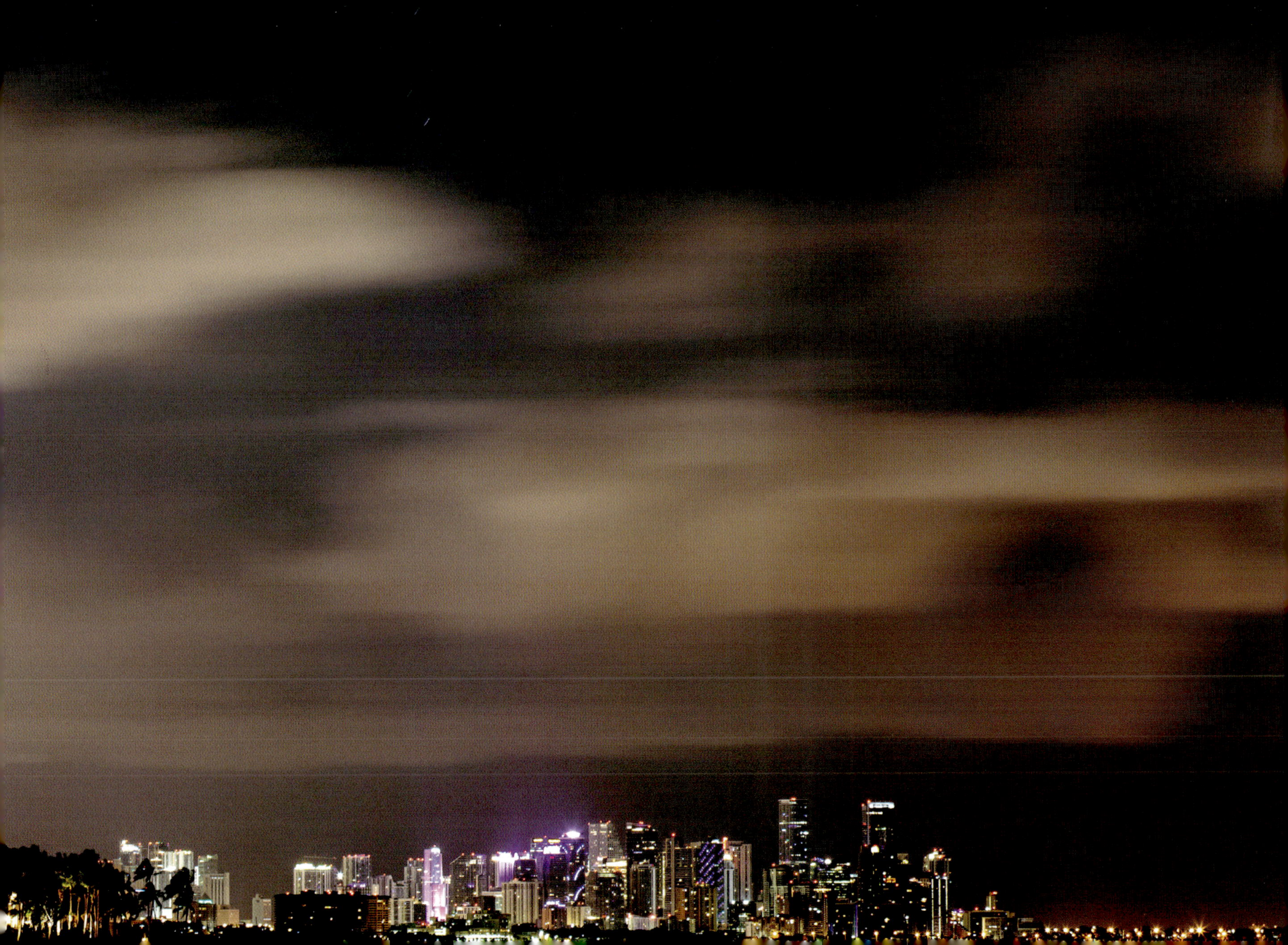

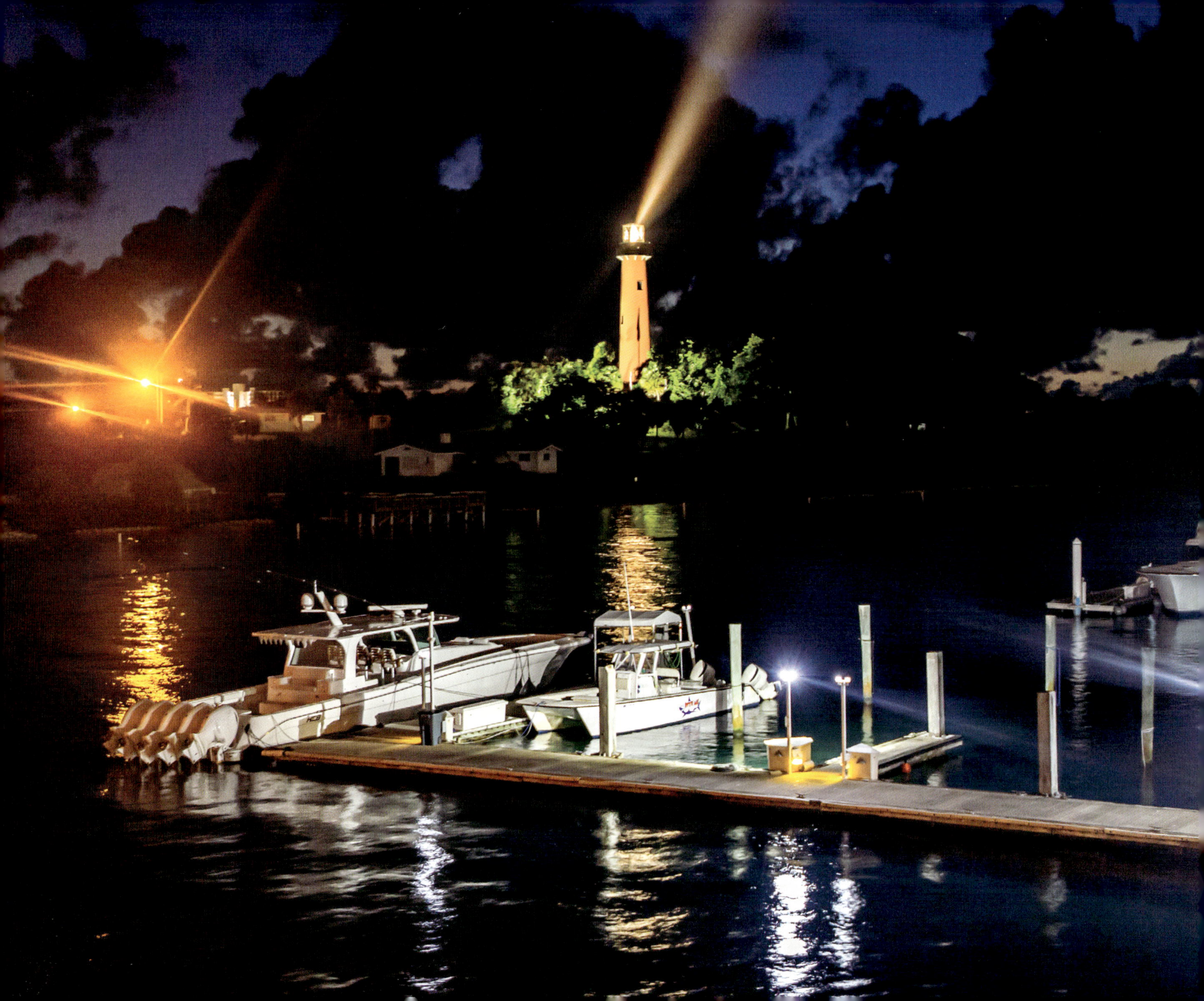

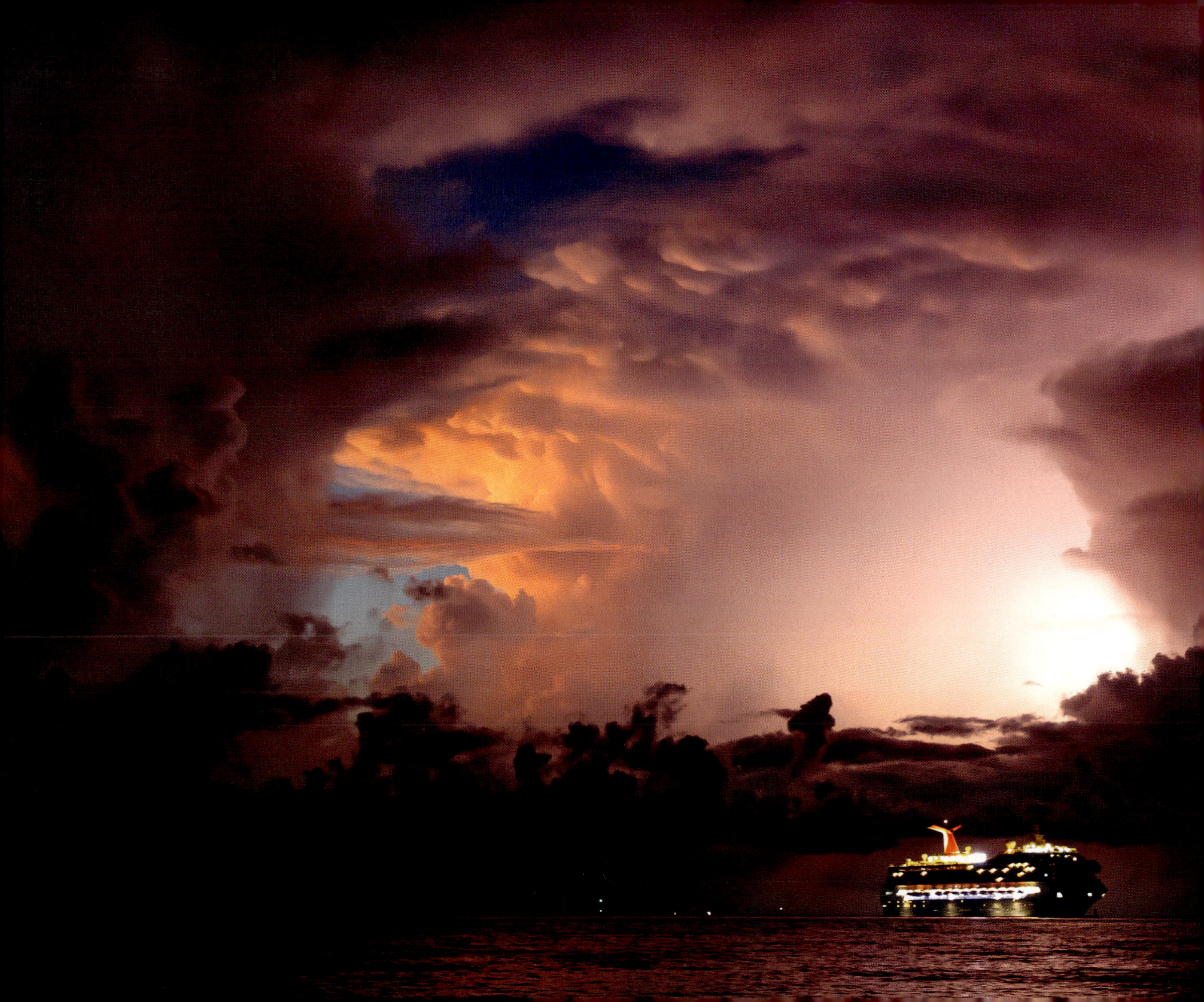

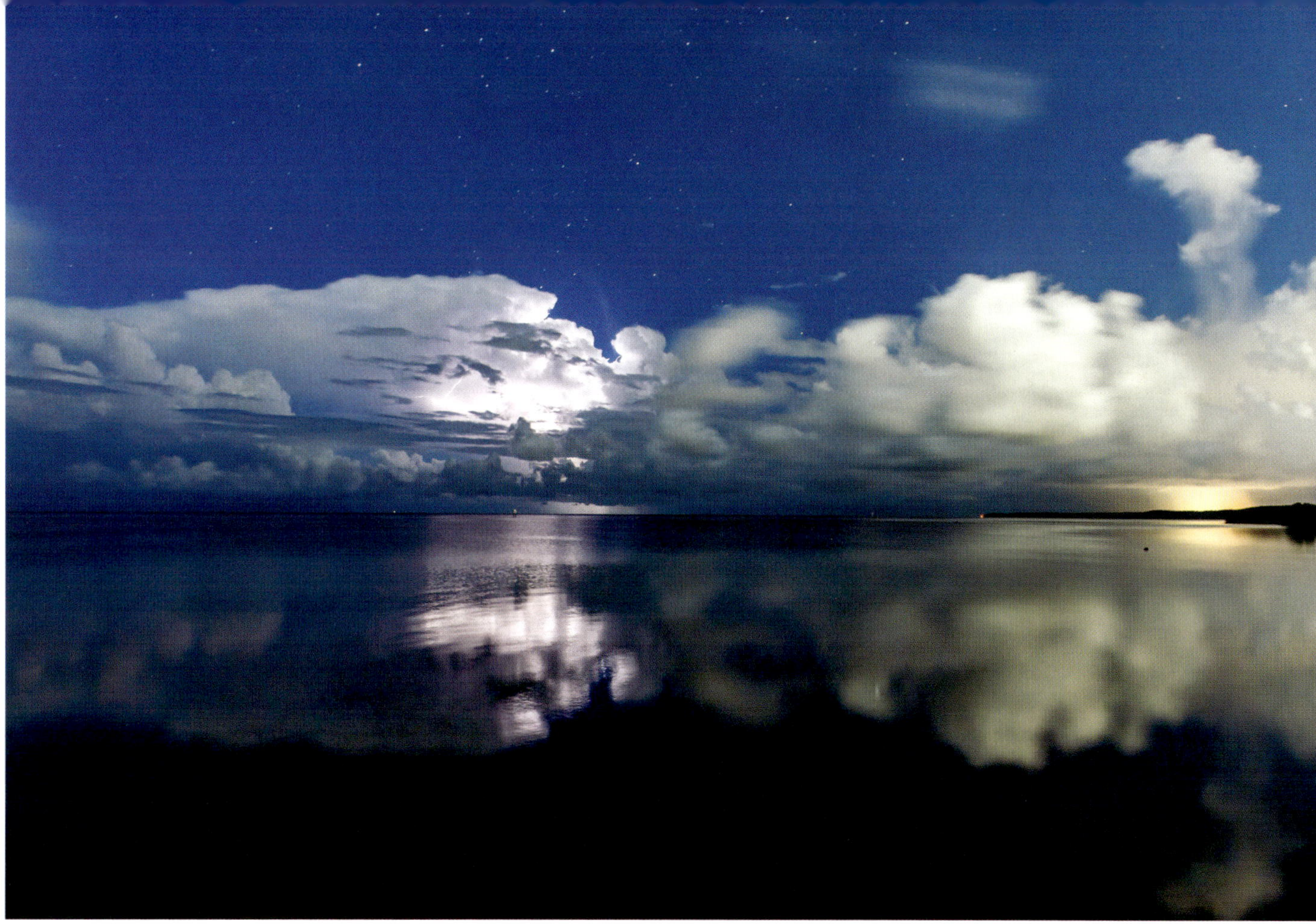

Lightning storms offshore illuminating the sky before dawn. Witnessing the awesome power of nature.

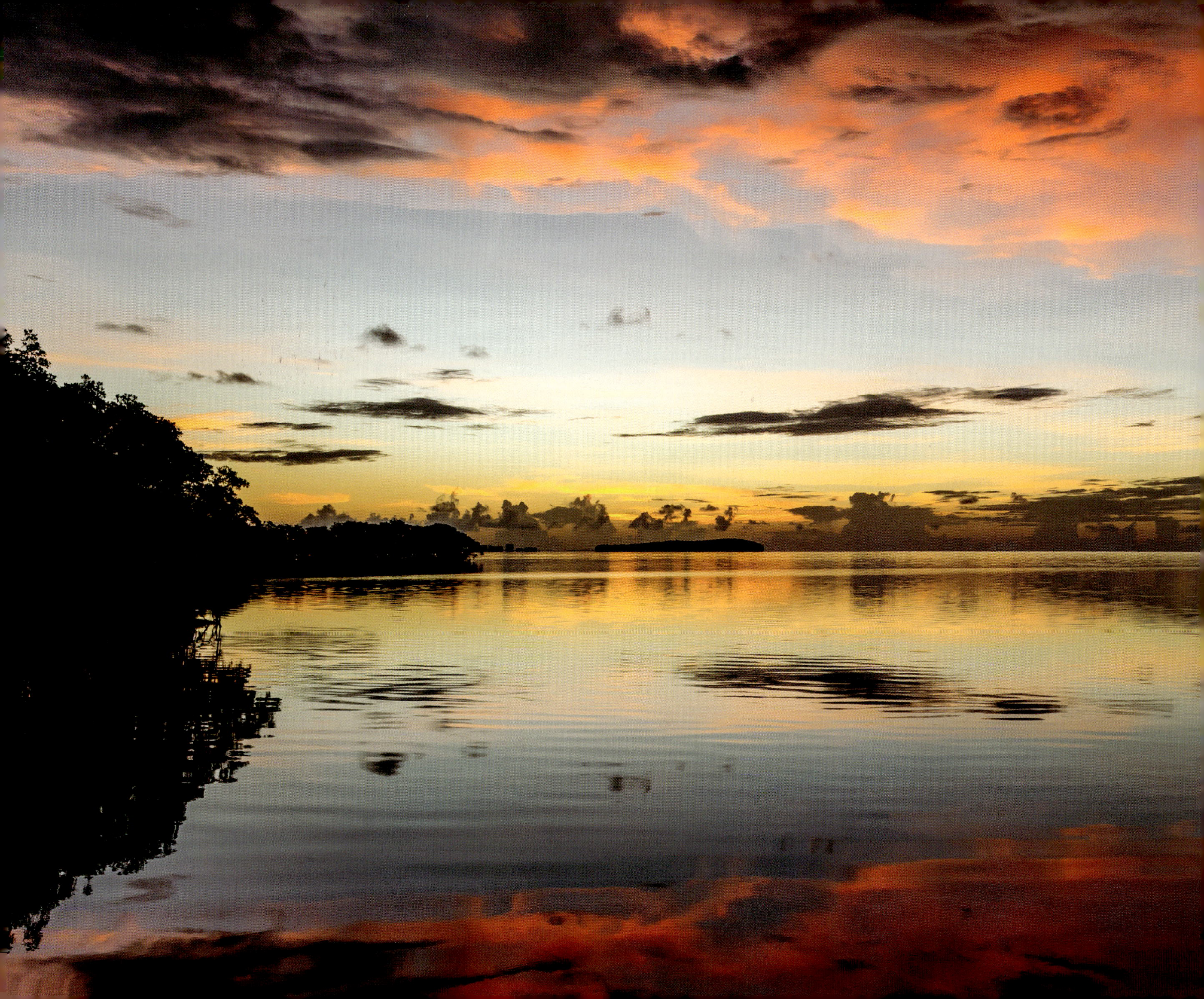

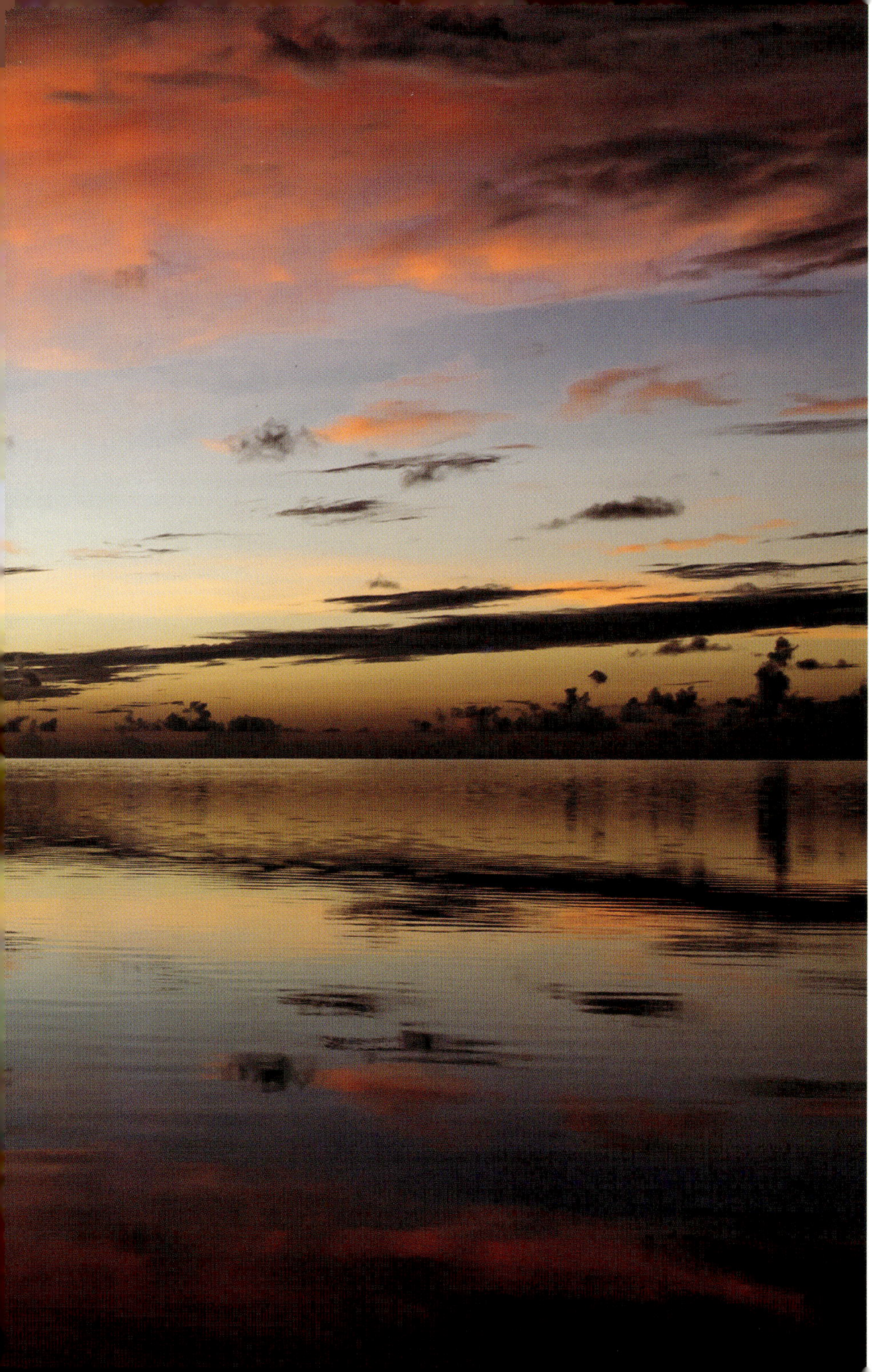

Dawn's Early Light

The dawn half-hour before sunrise is when the magic show above us is usually most exciting. More times than not, it begins with bright orange or yellow rays of light shooting upward from the horizon. When atmospheric conditions are right, the clouds will turn amazingly vibrant colors—red, magenta, orange, yellow and purple—which deepen minute by minute until the sky before you seems to be on fire. This stunning sensation is amplified even more dramatically when the vivid colors are also reflected on waters of the ocean, bays, lagoons, lakes and the Everglades.

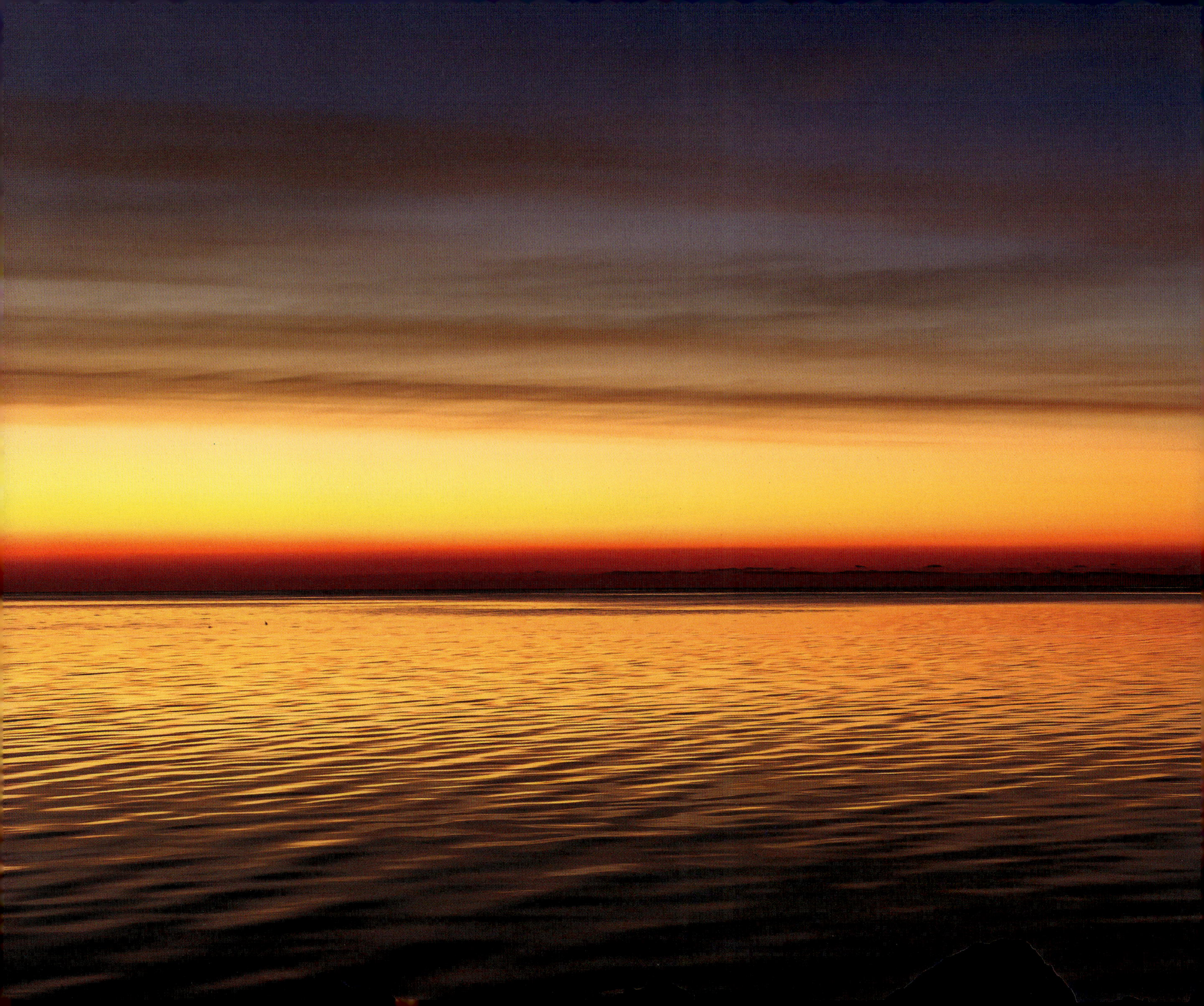

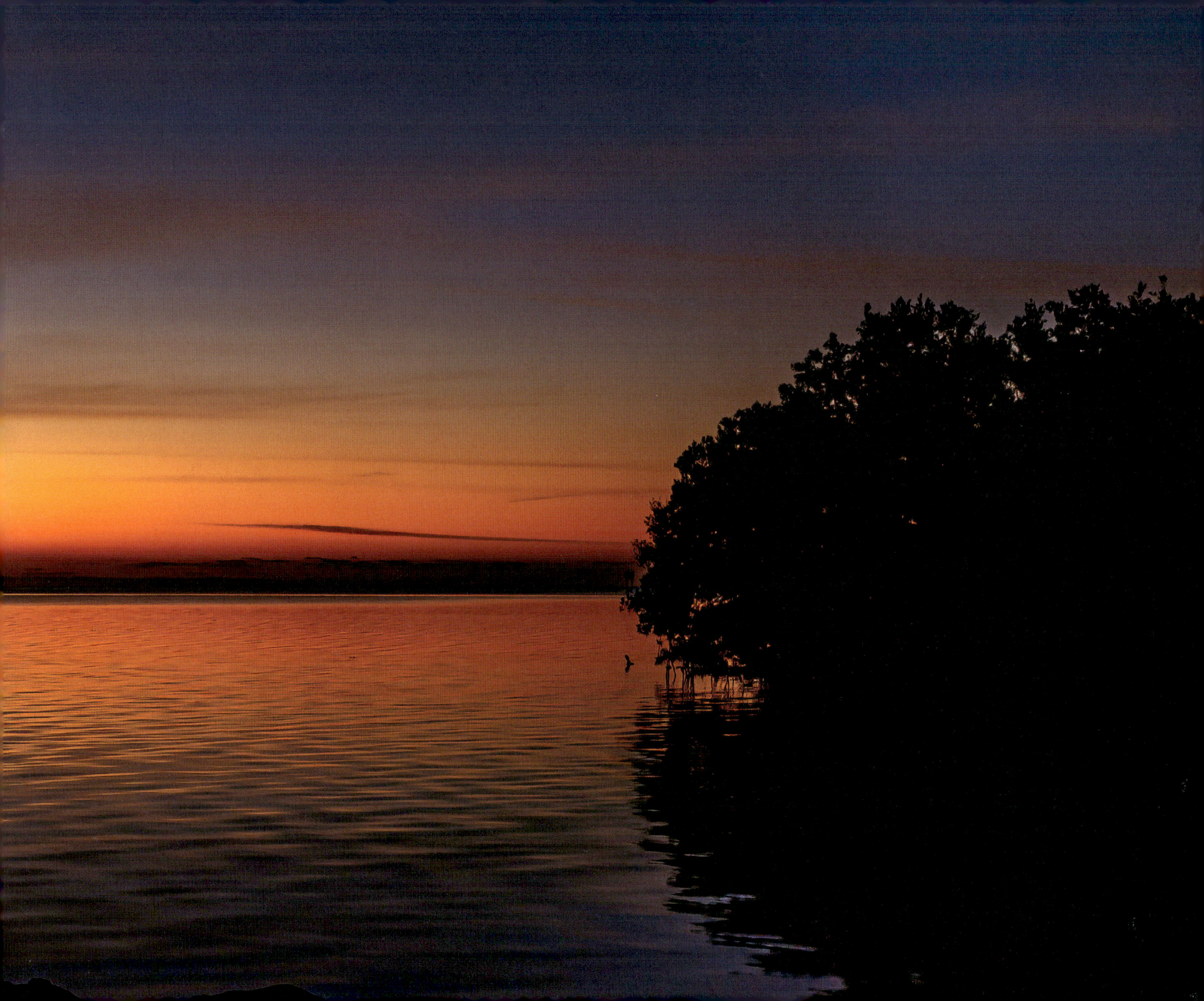

Early-morning fishermen on the Miami Beach rock jetty.

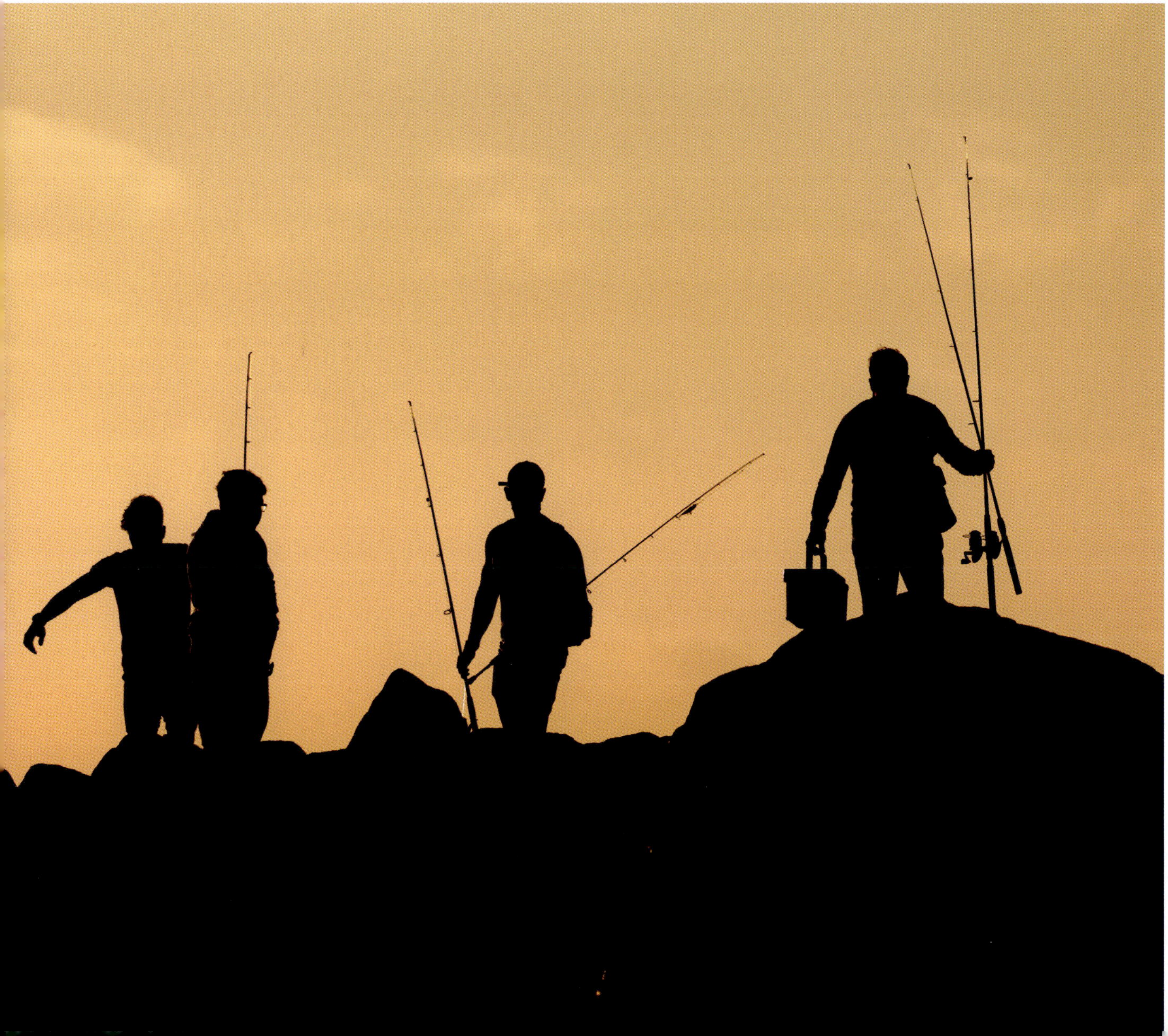

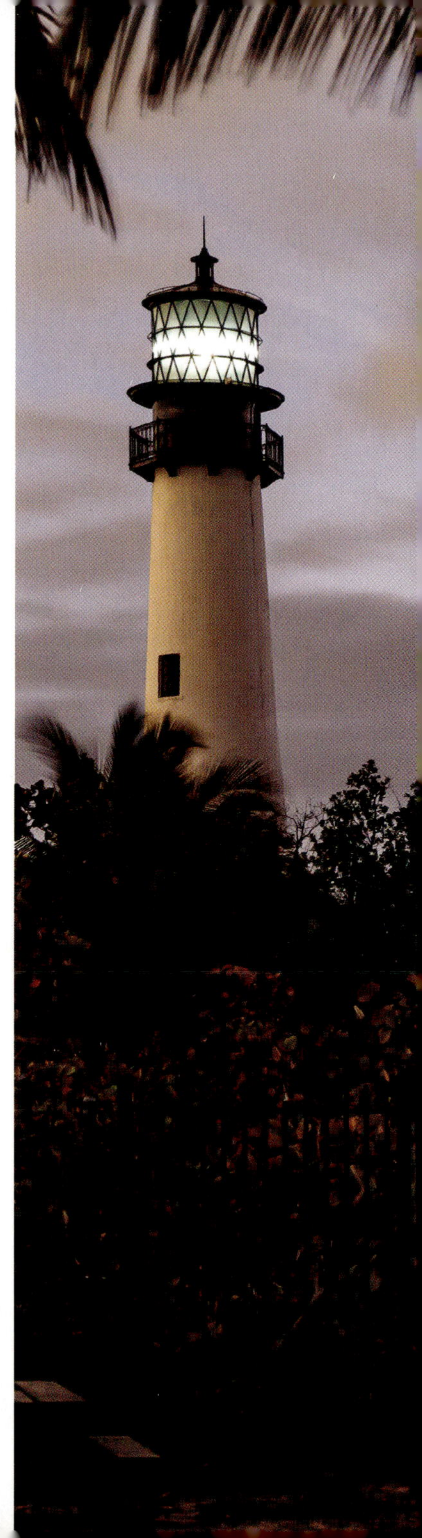

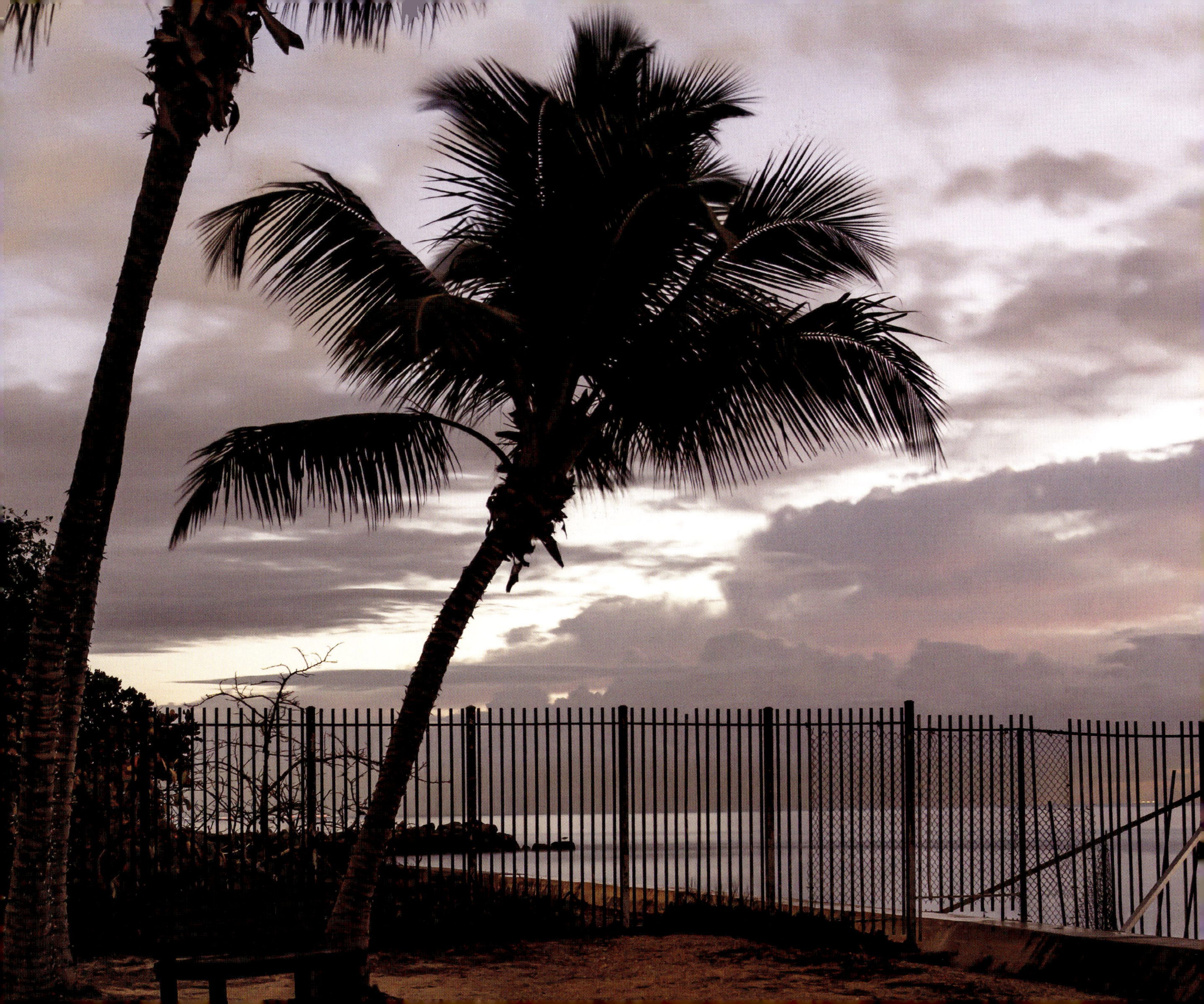

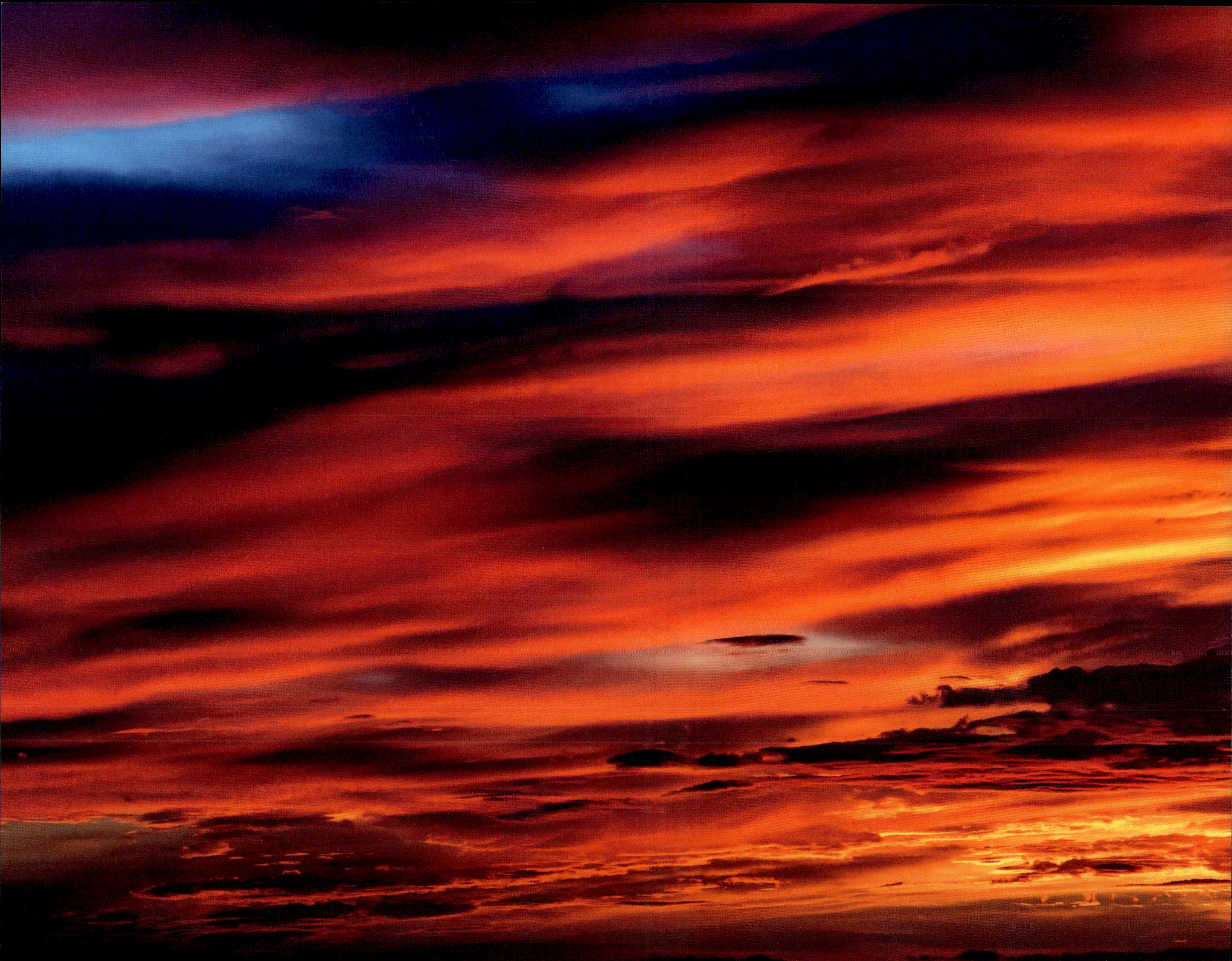

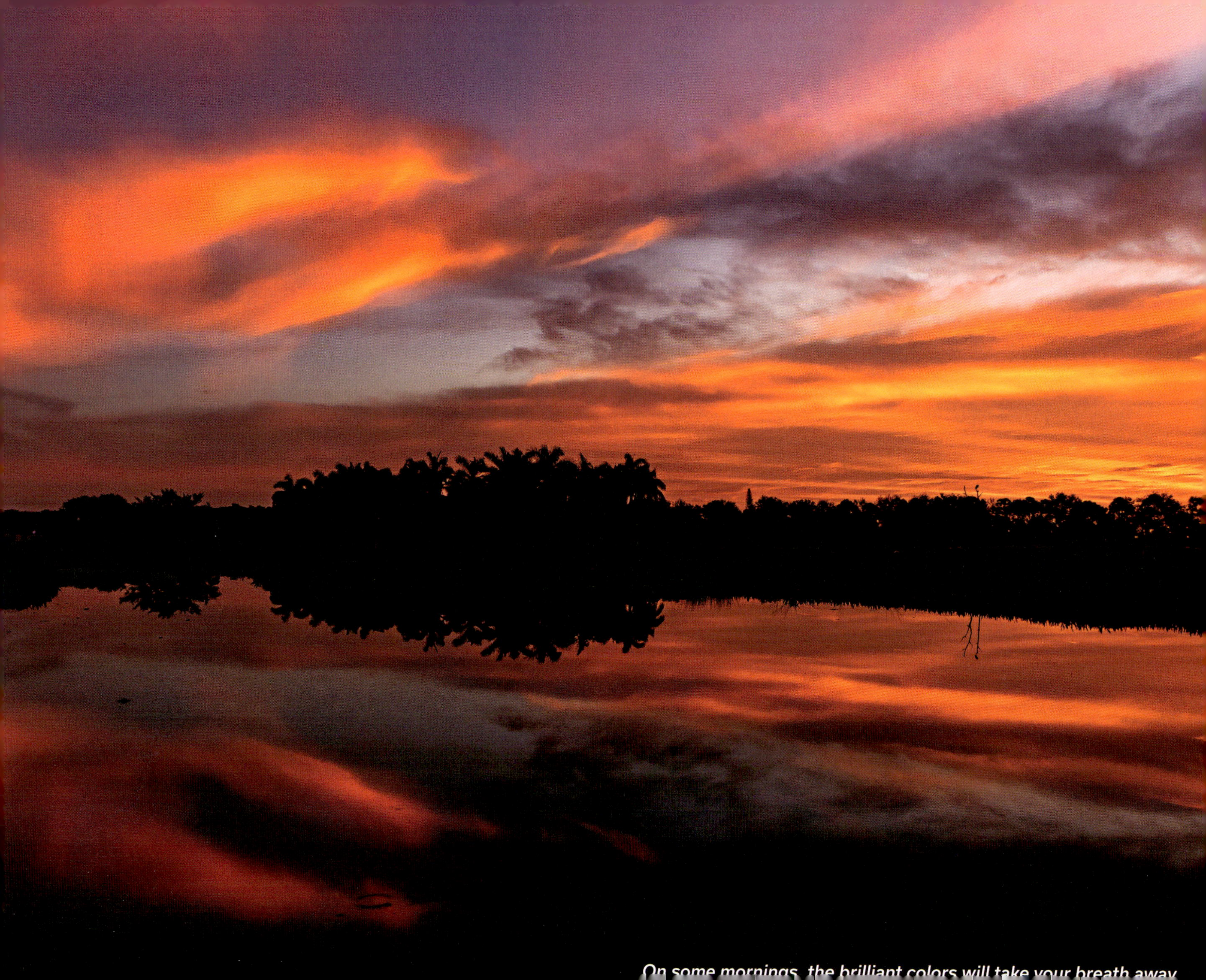

On some mornings, the brilliant colors will take your breath away.

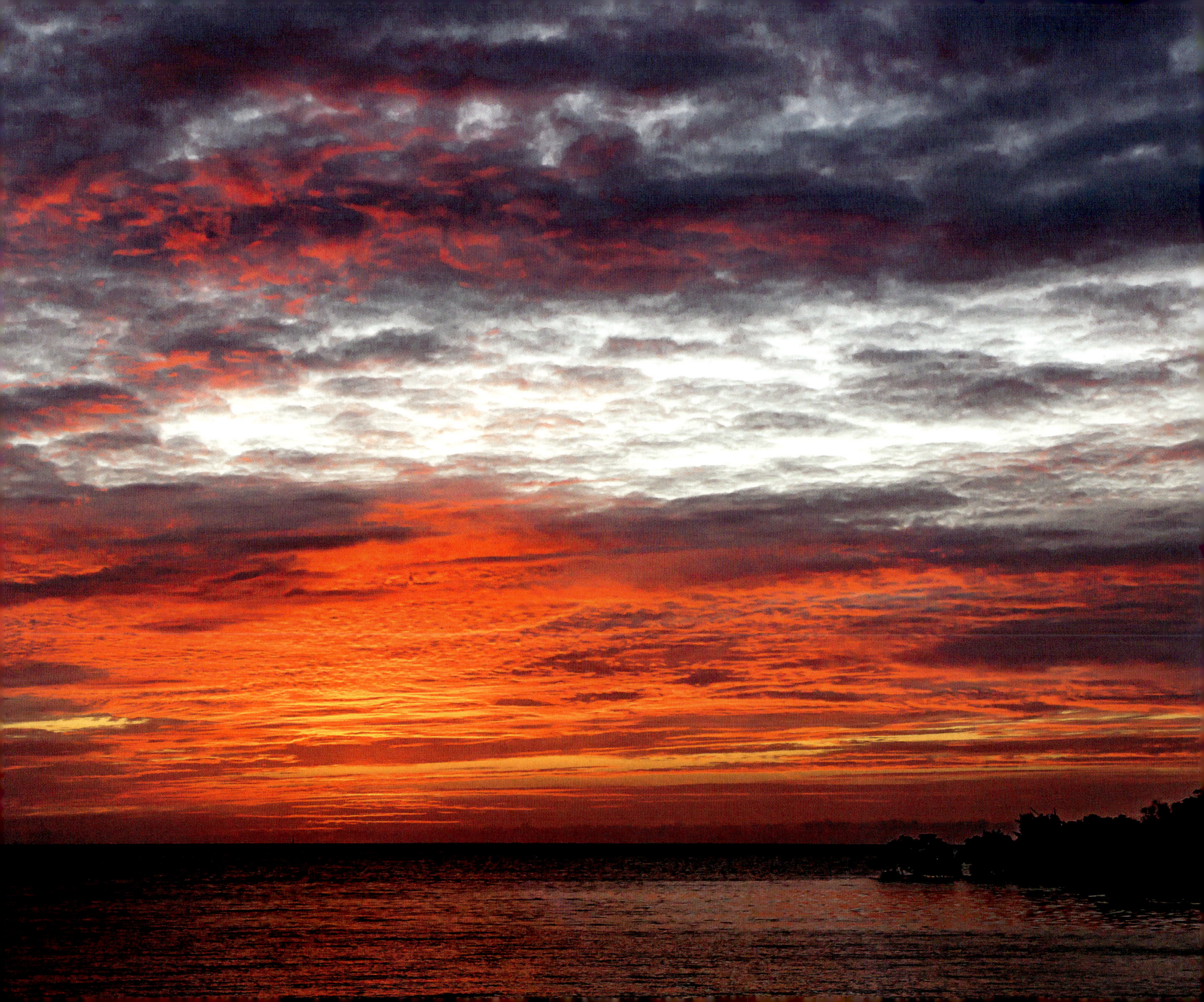

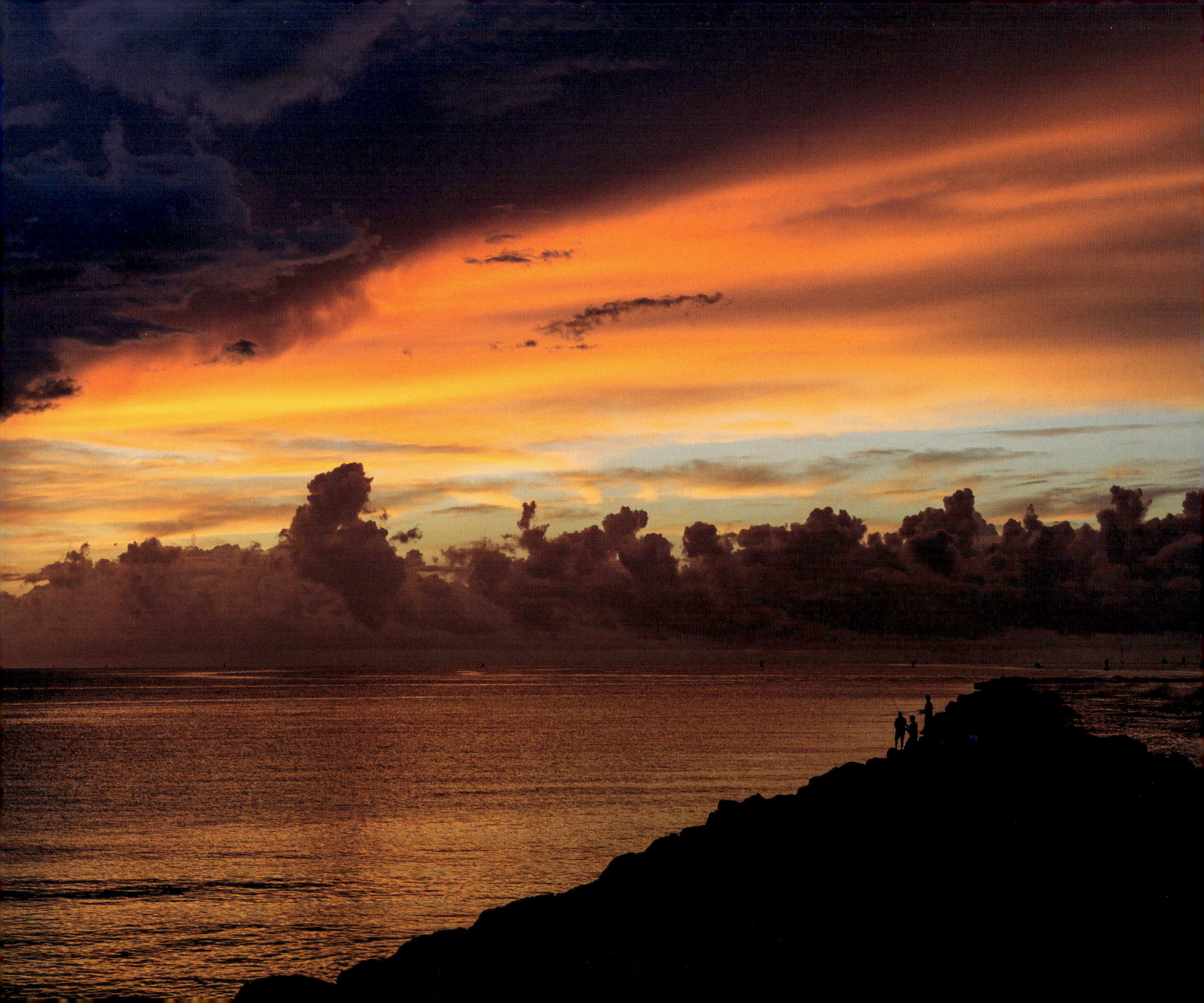

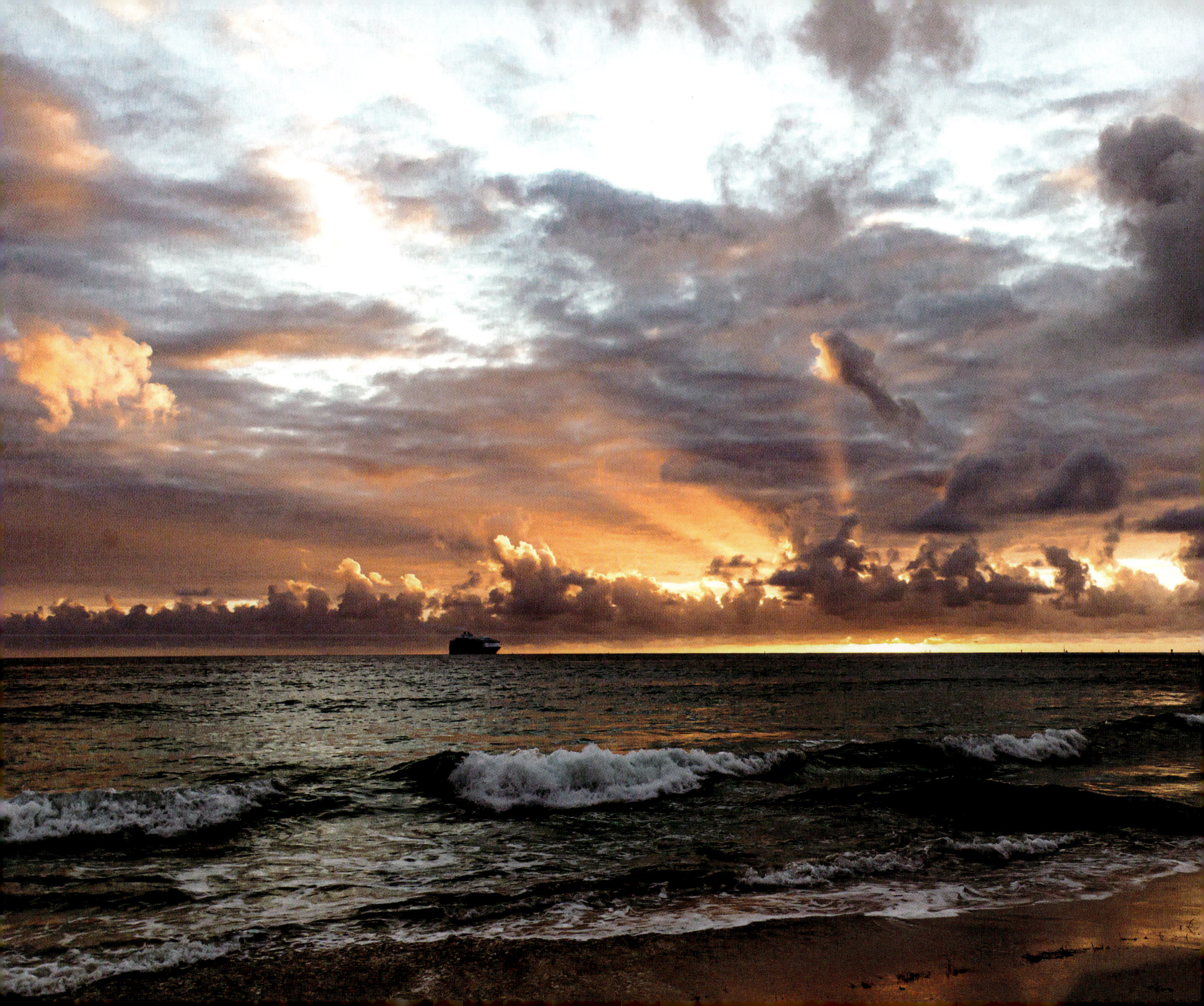

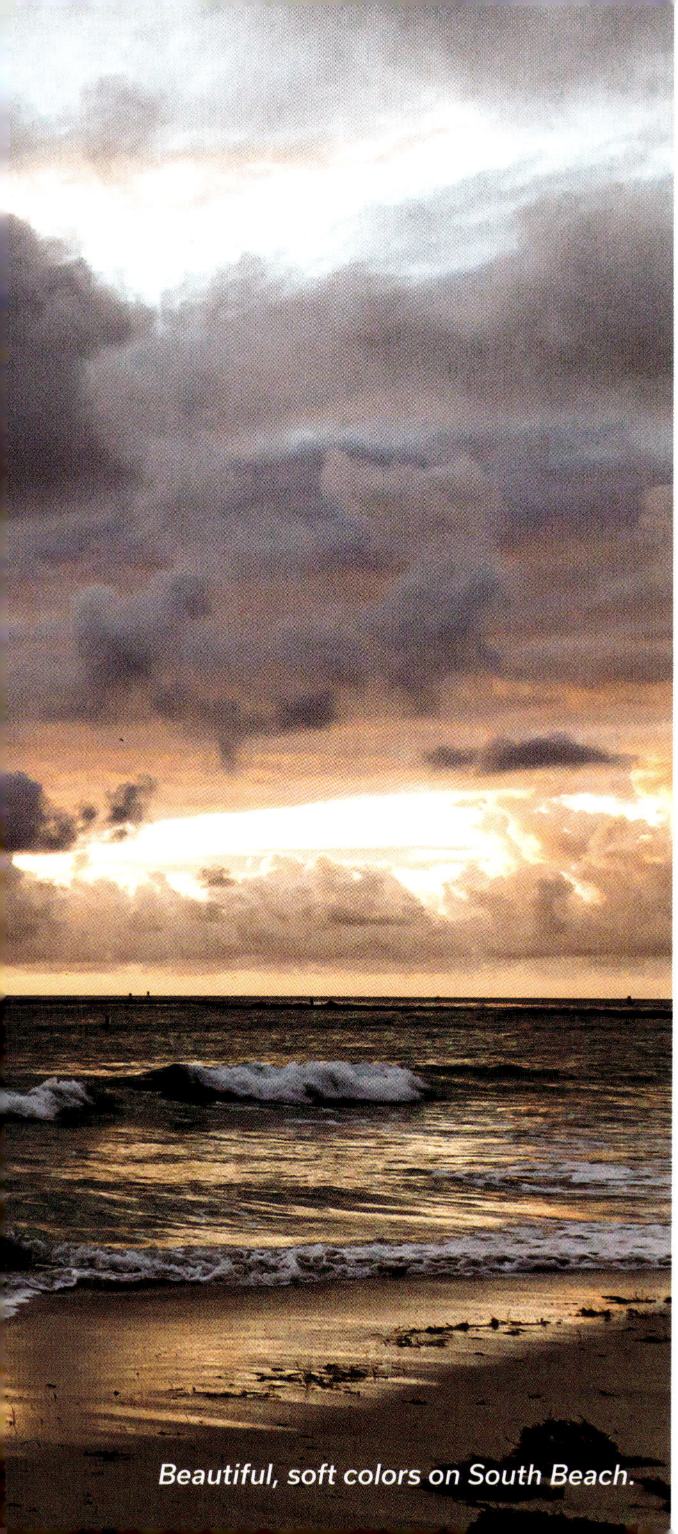

Beautiful, soft colors on South Beach.

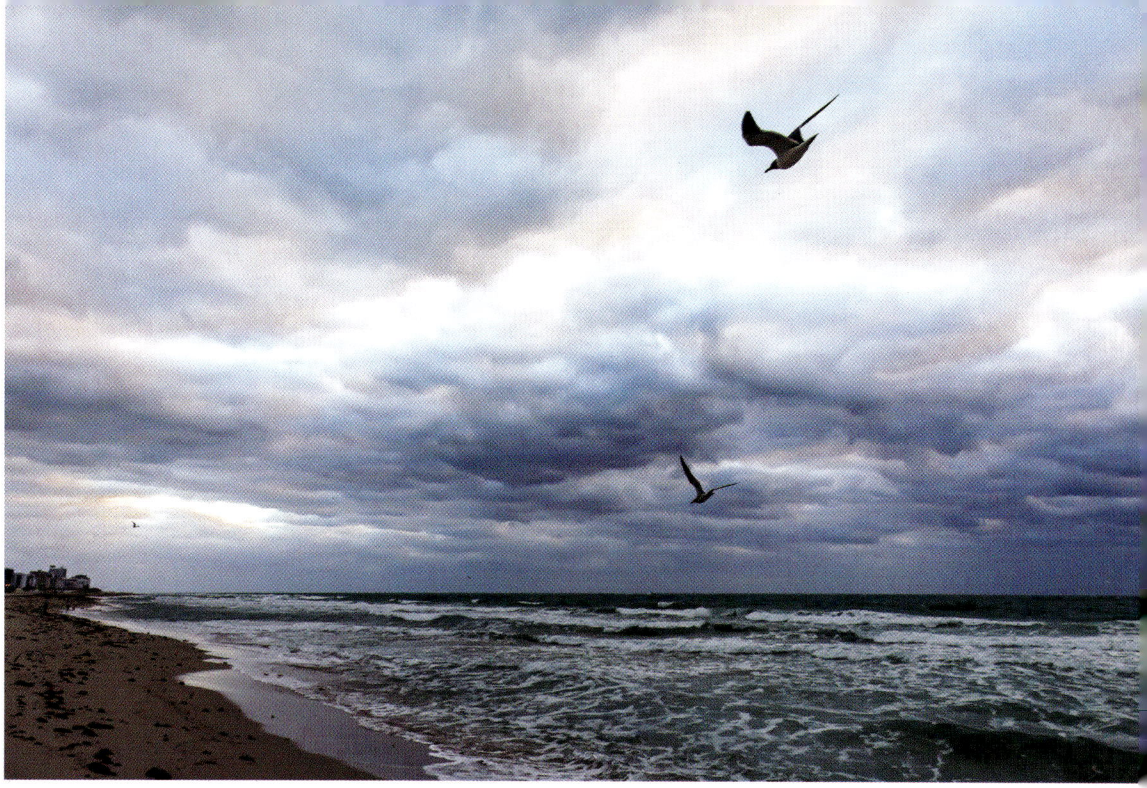

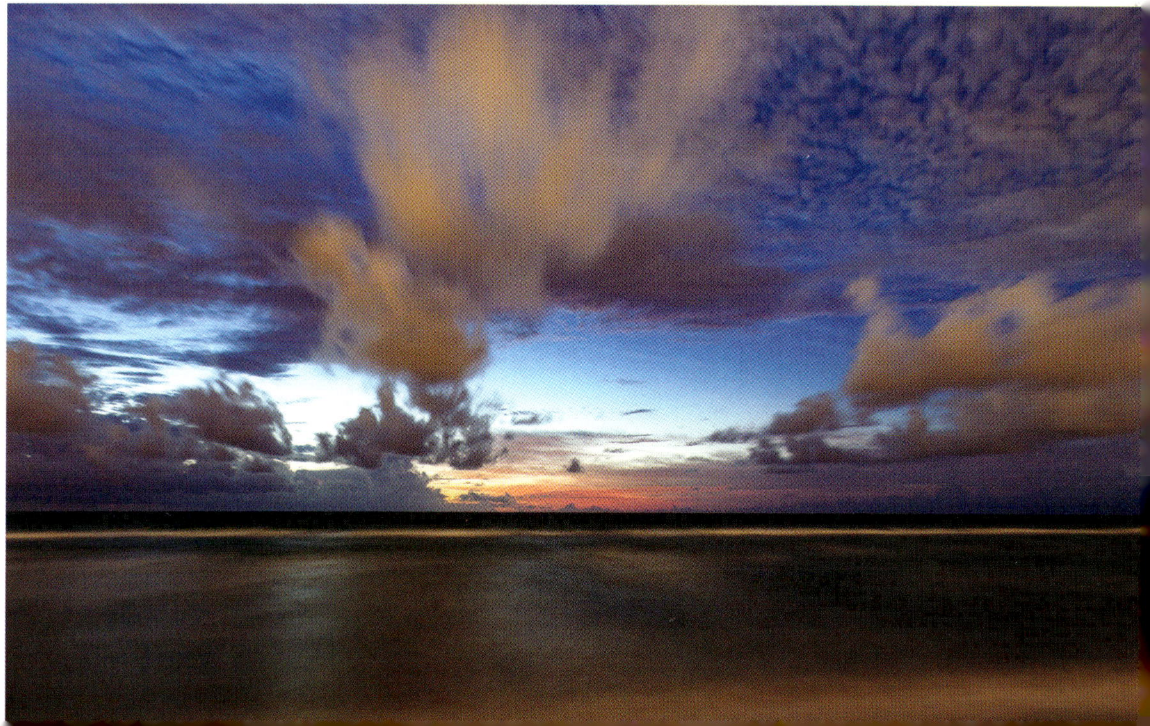

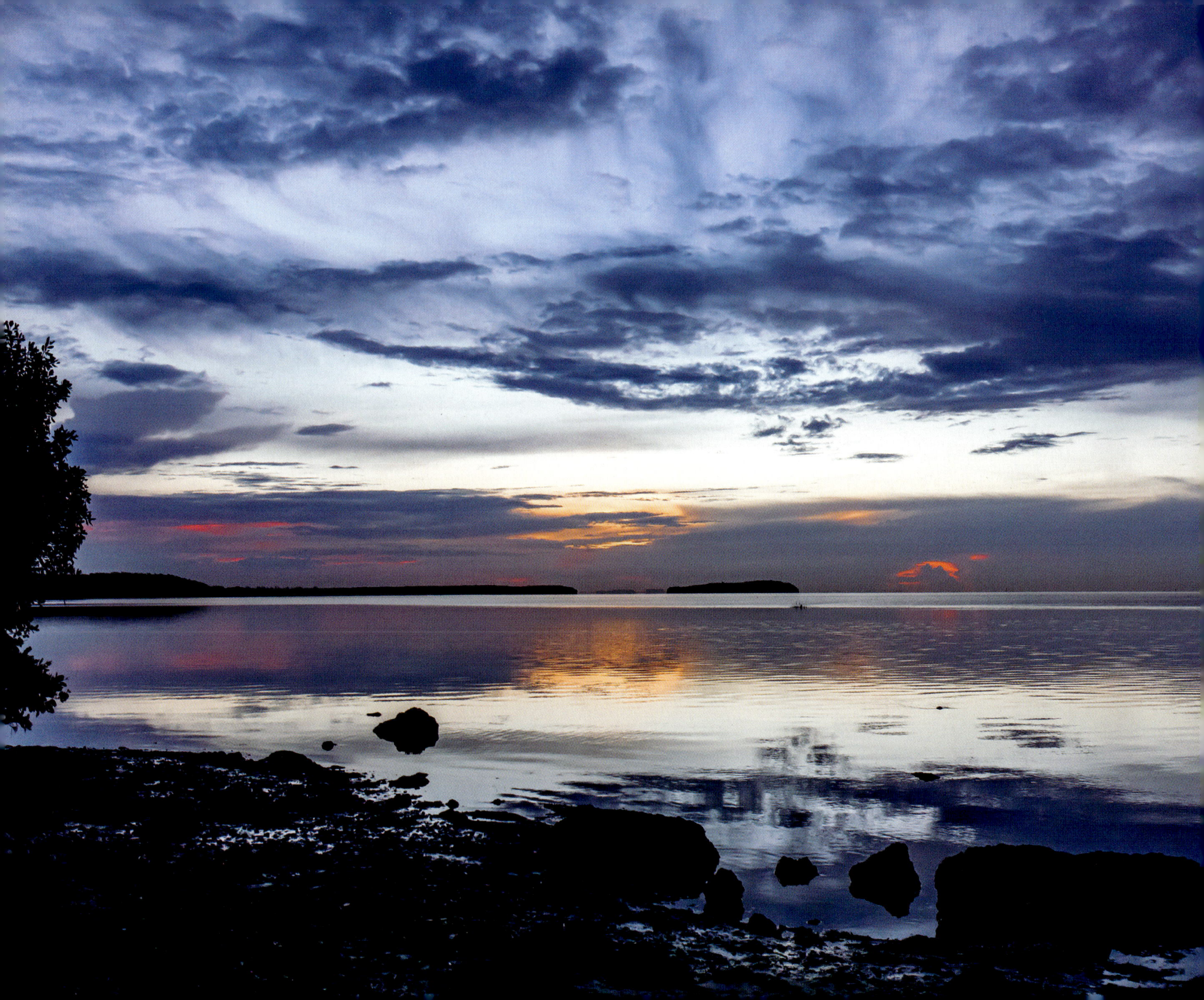

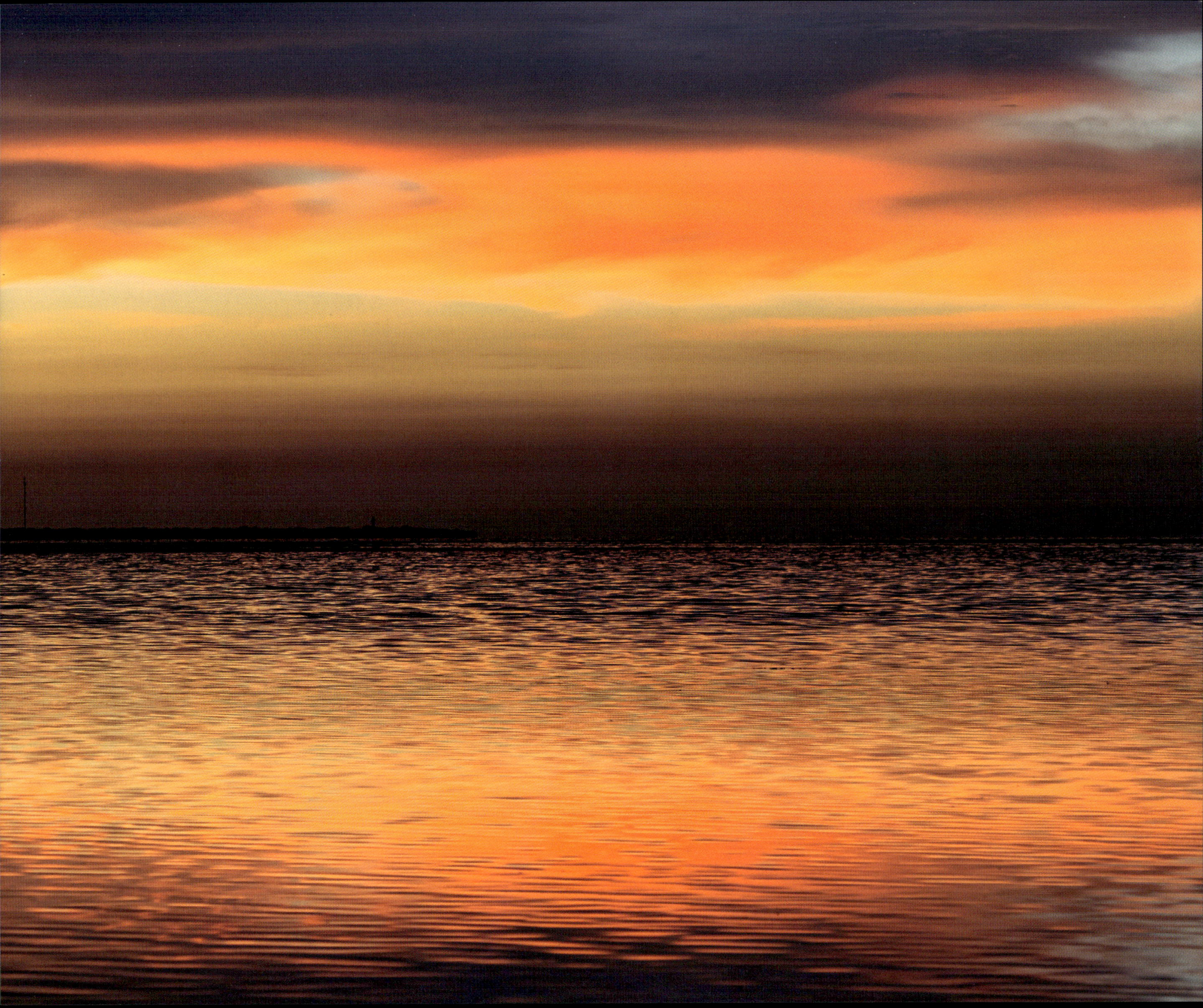

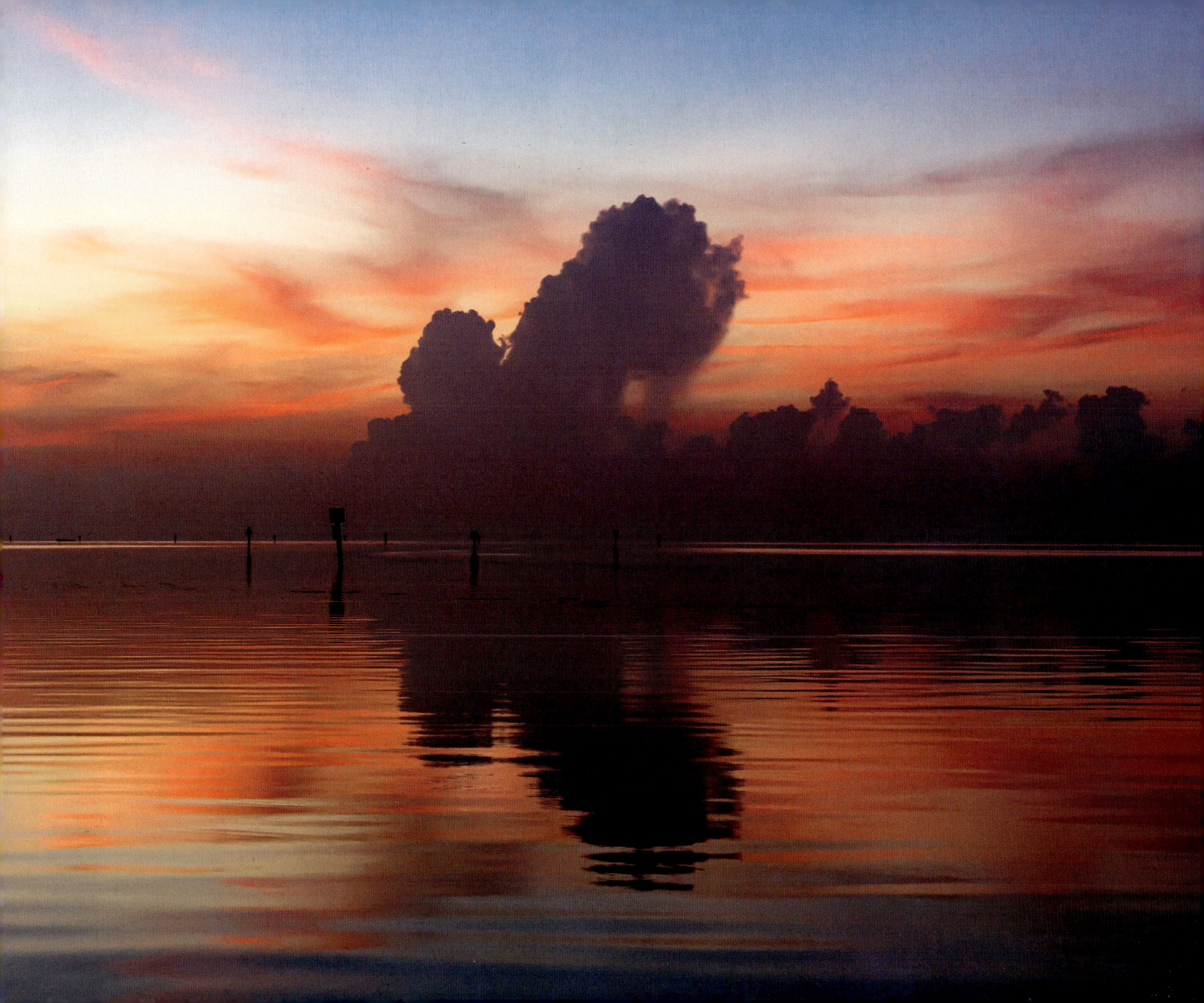

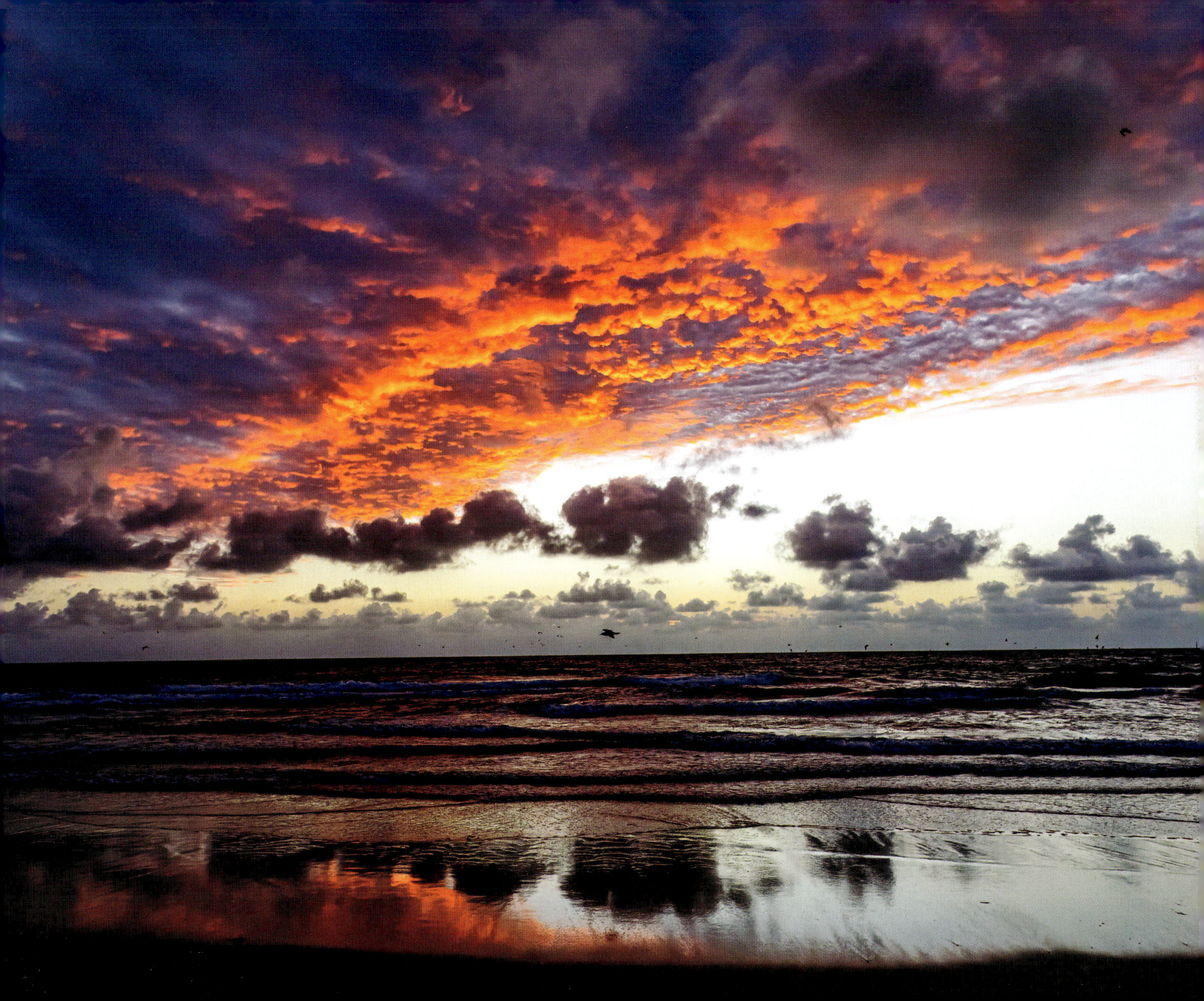

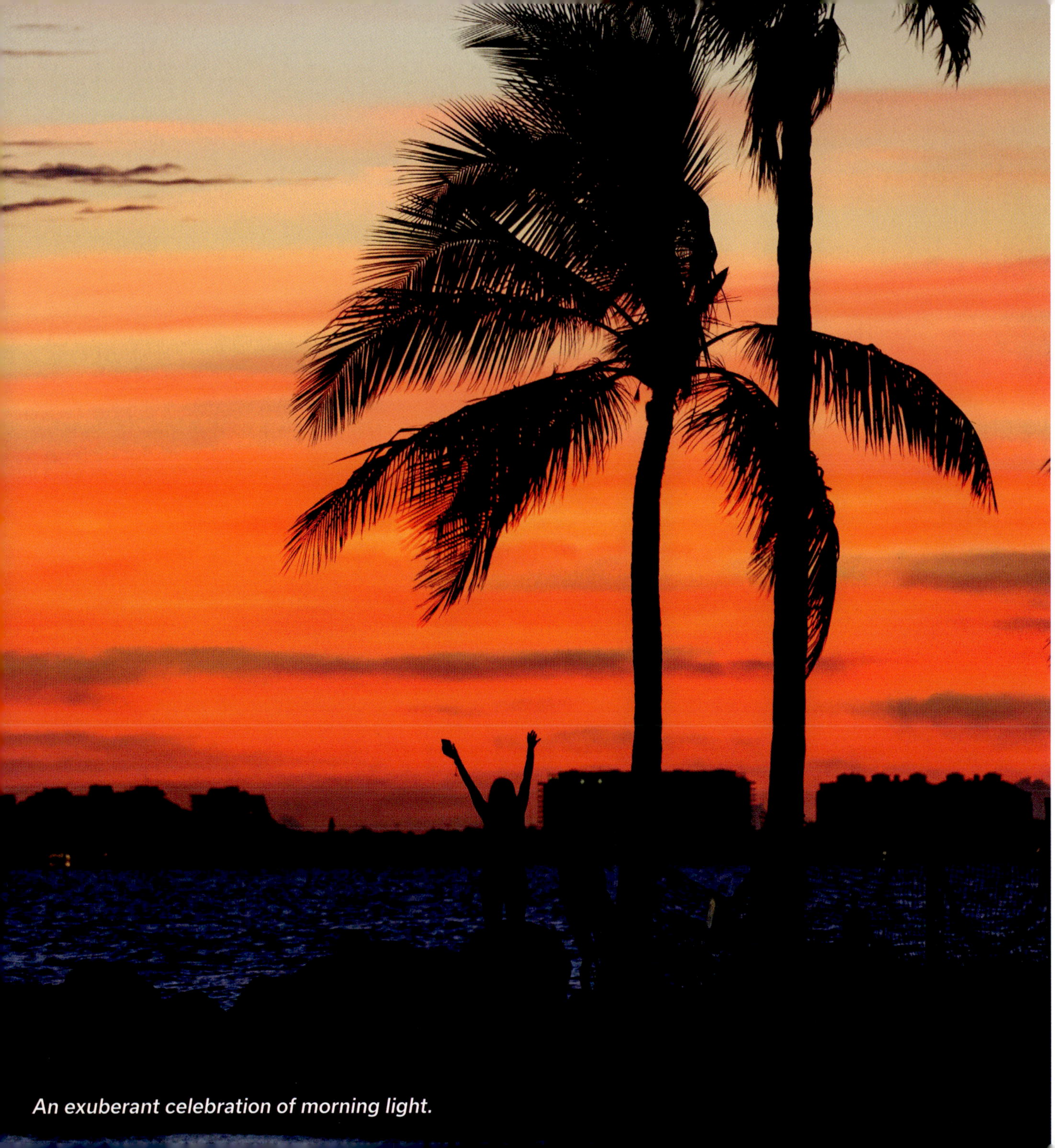

An exuberant celebration of morning light.

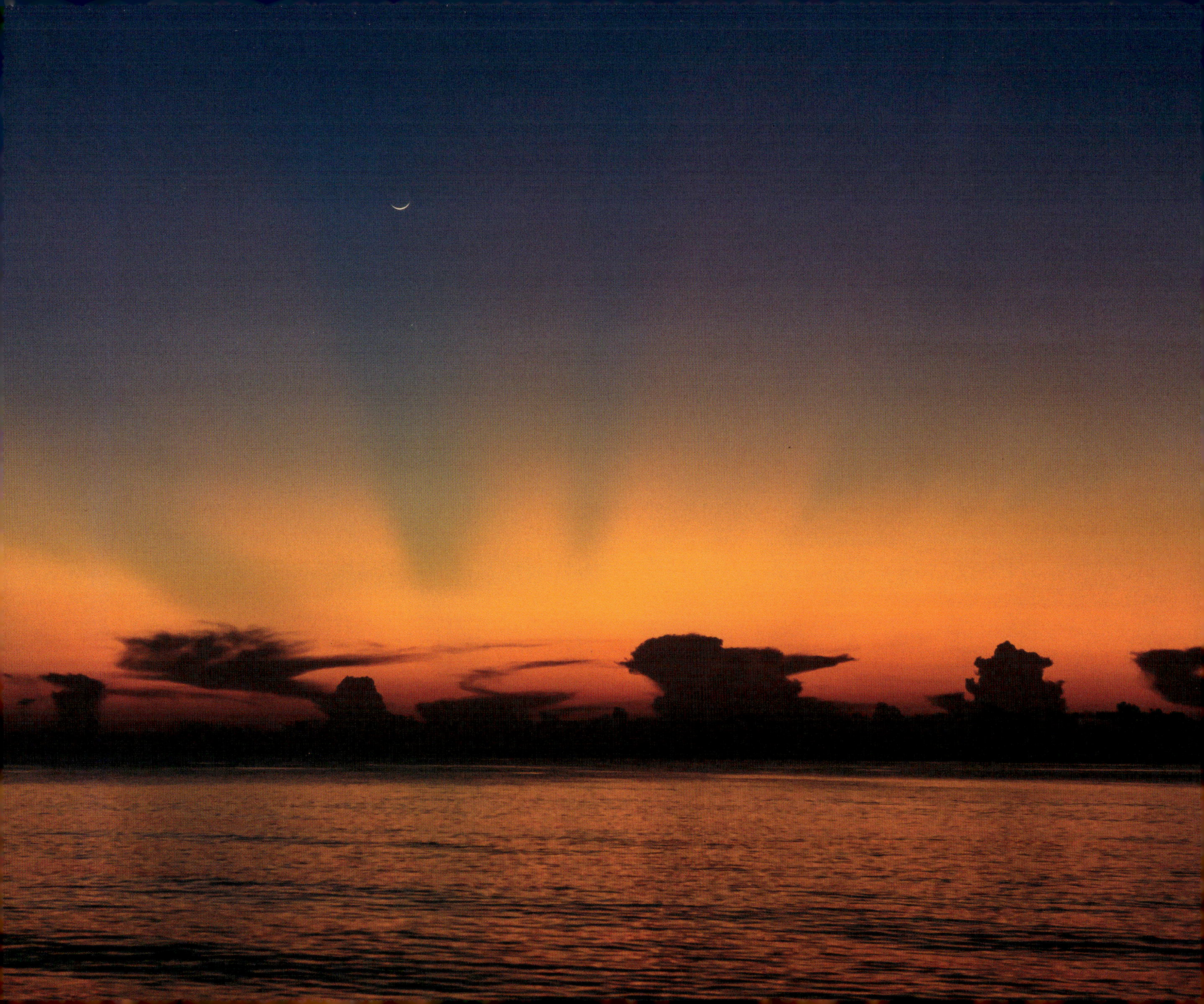

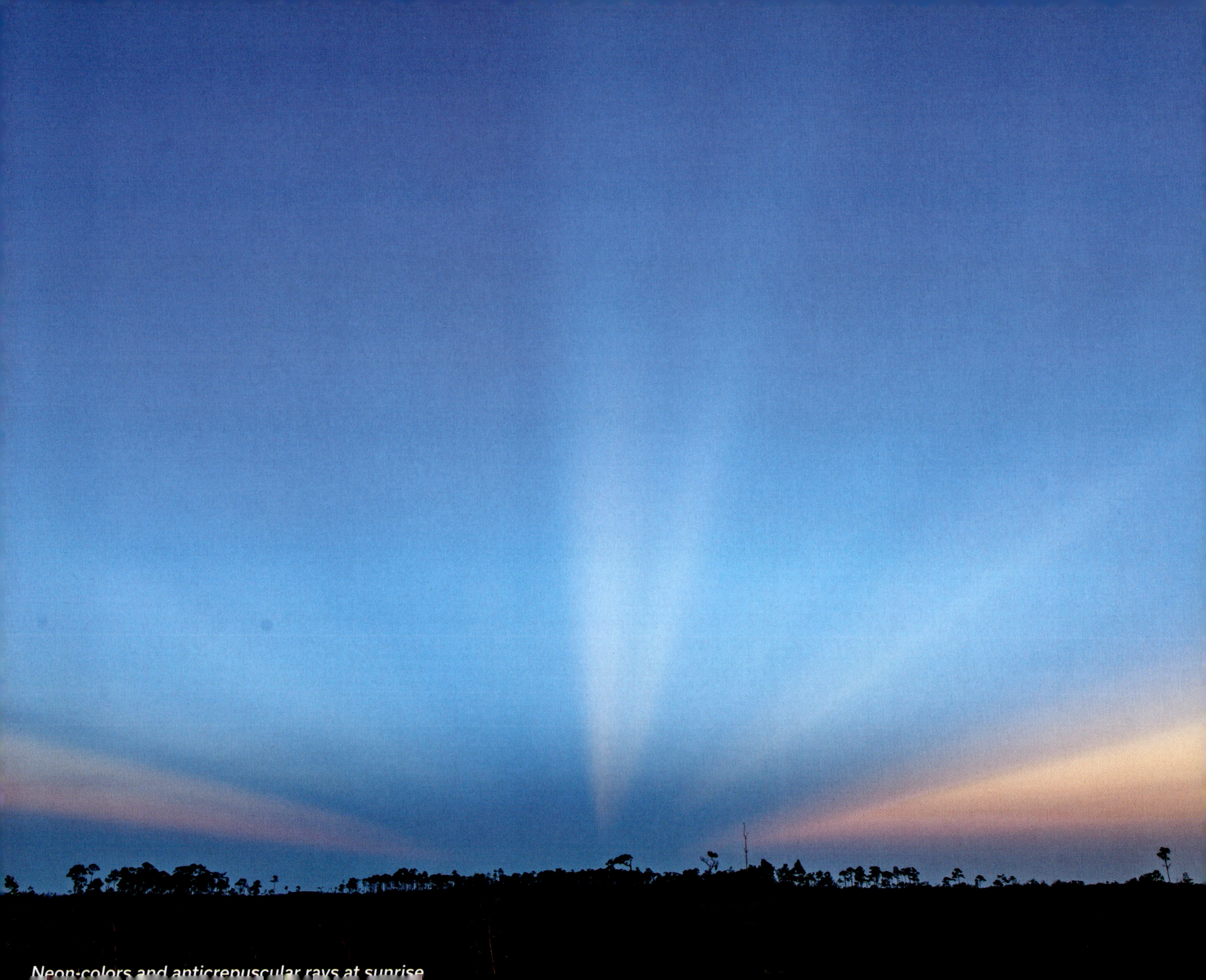

Neon-colors and anticrepuscular rays at sunrise

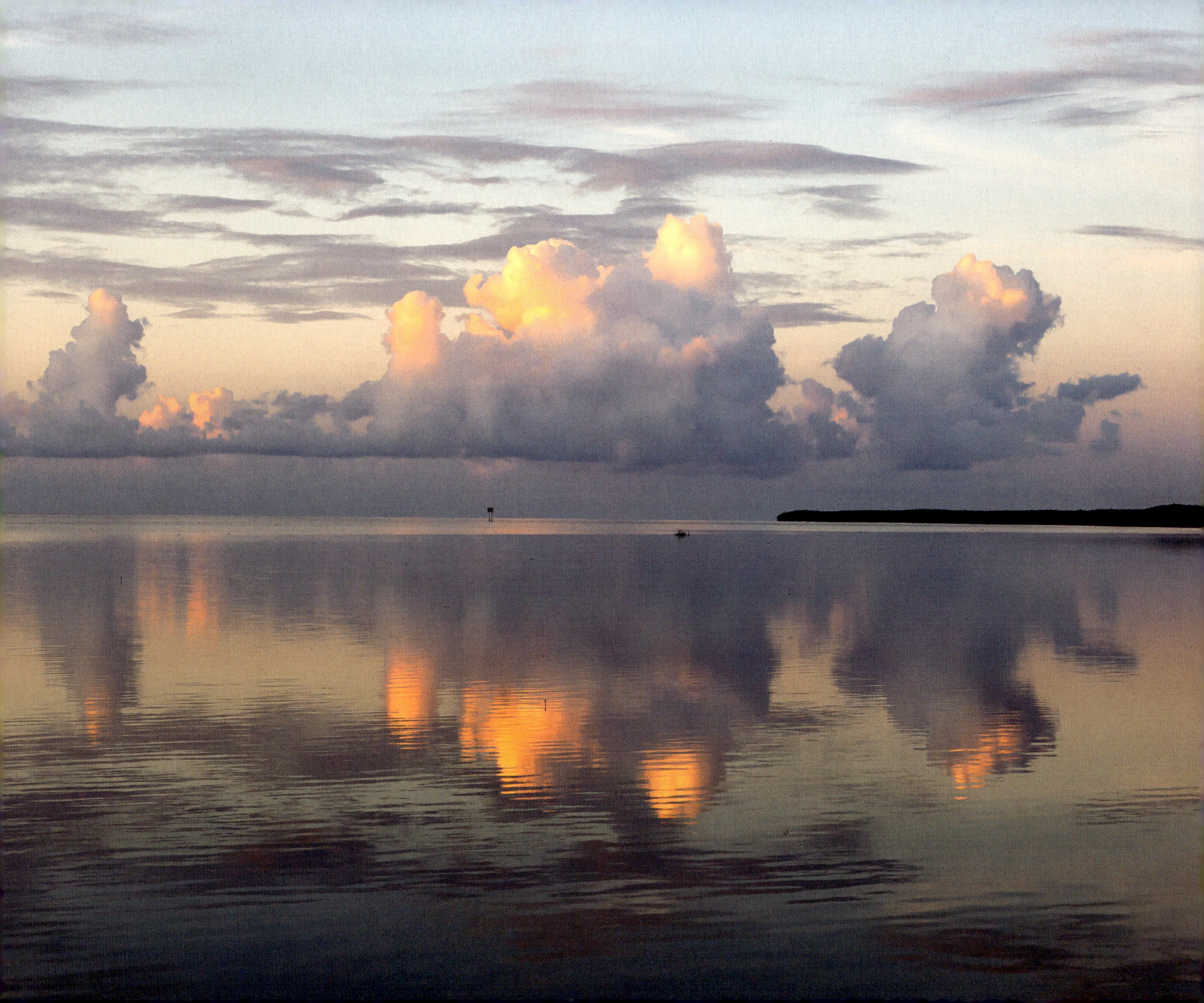

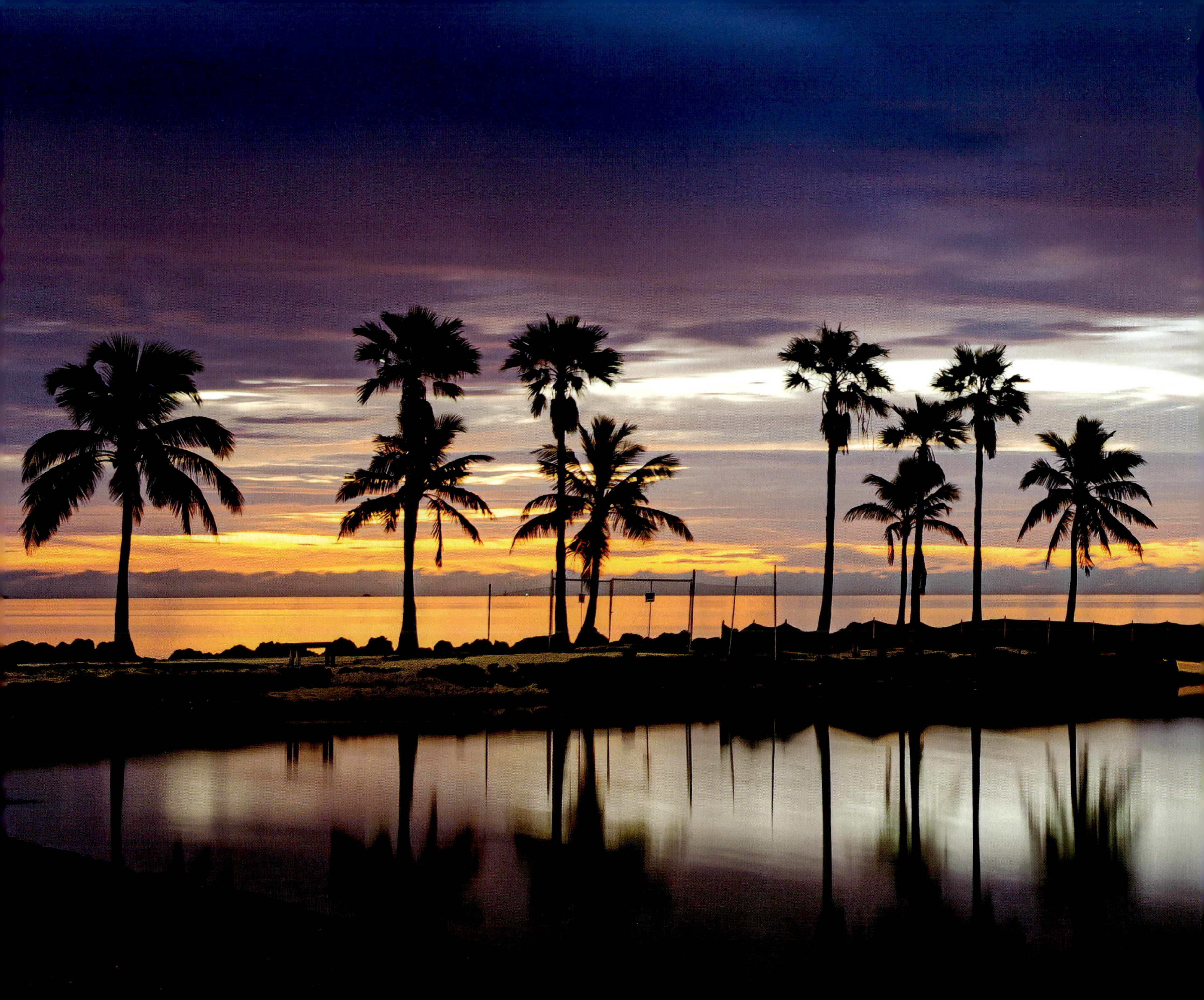

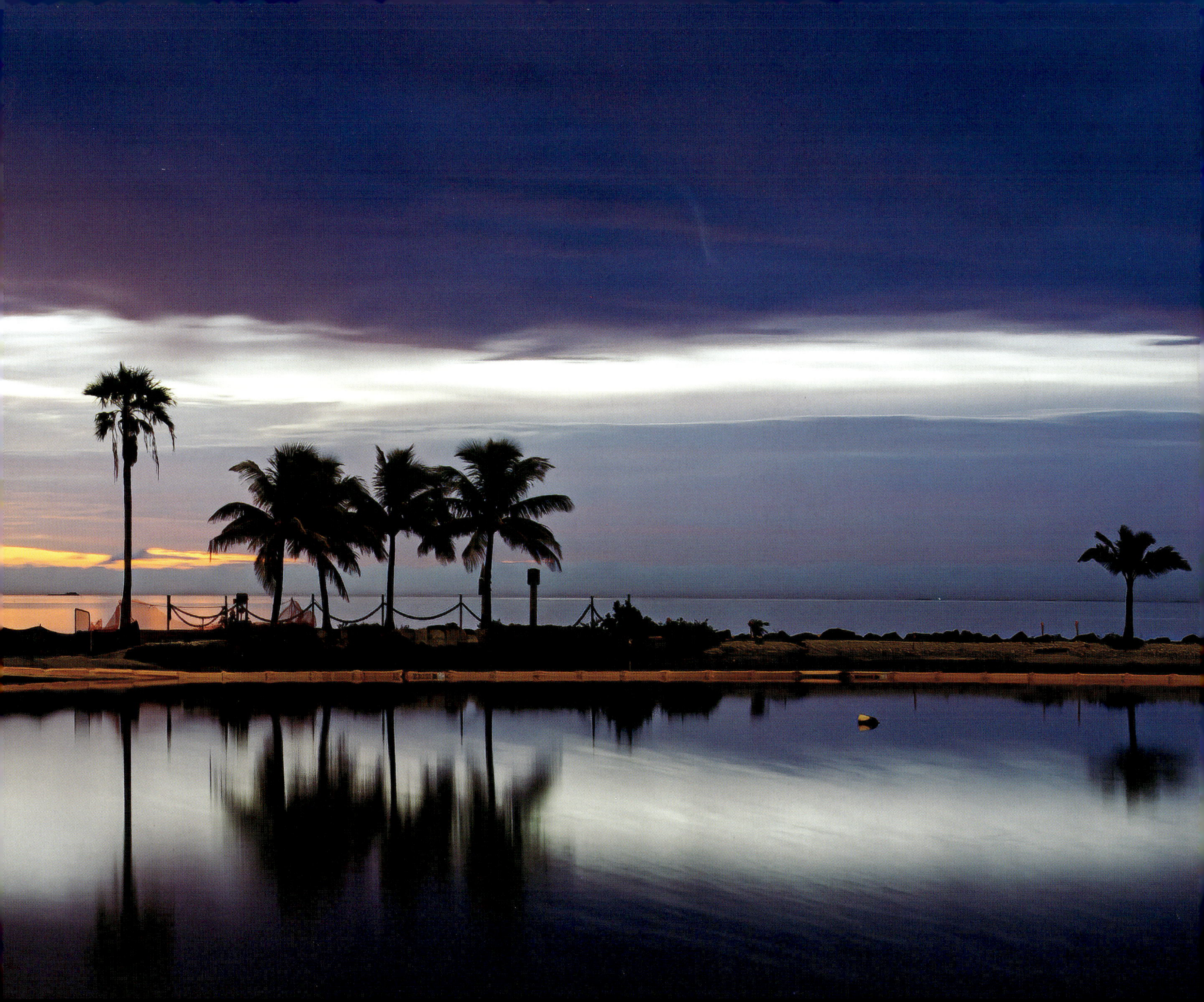

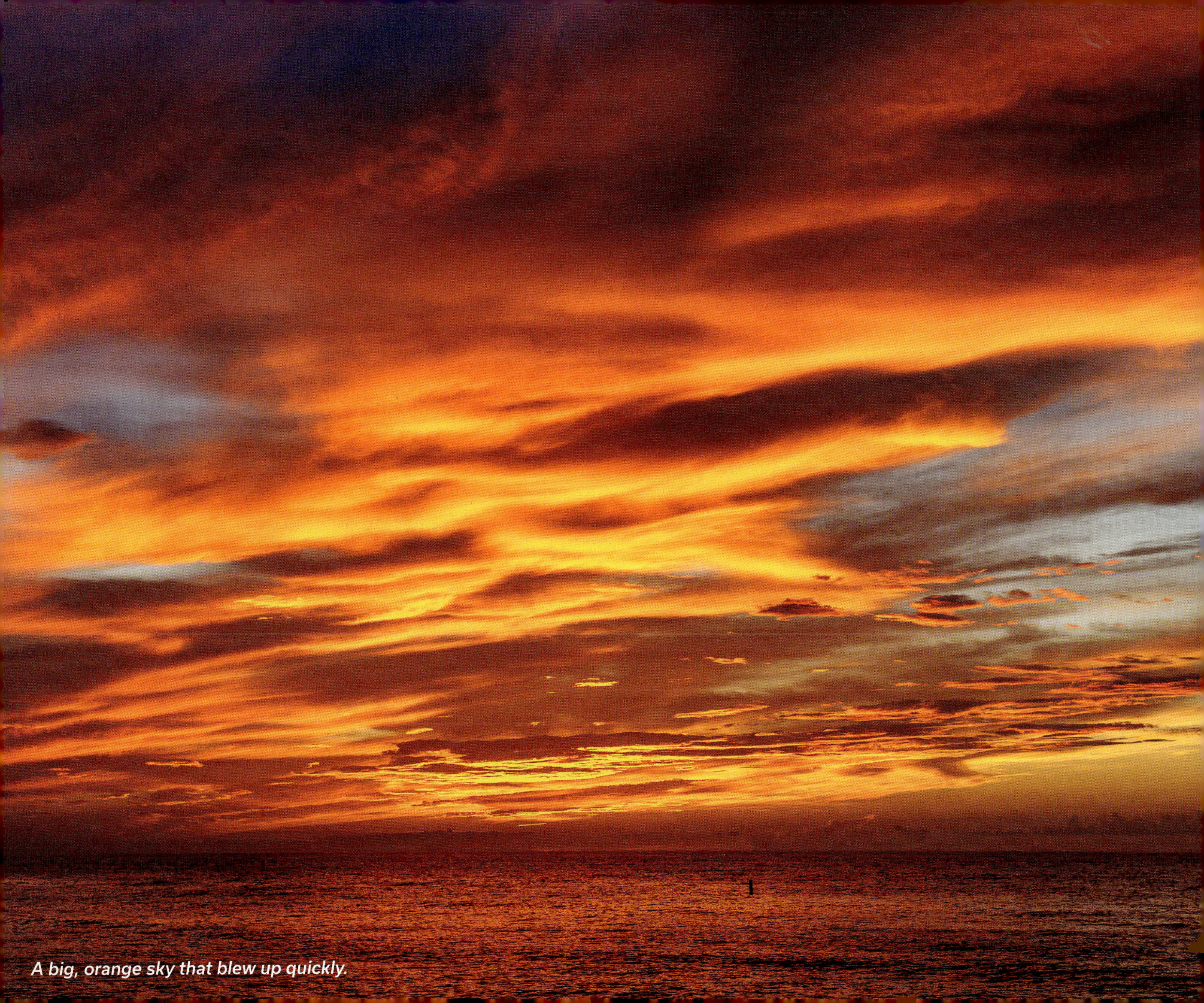
A big, orange sky that blew up quickly.

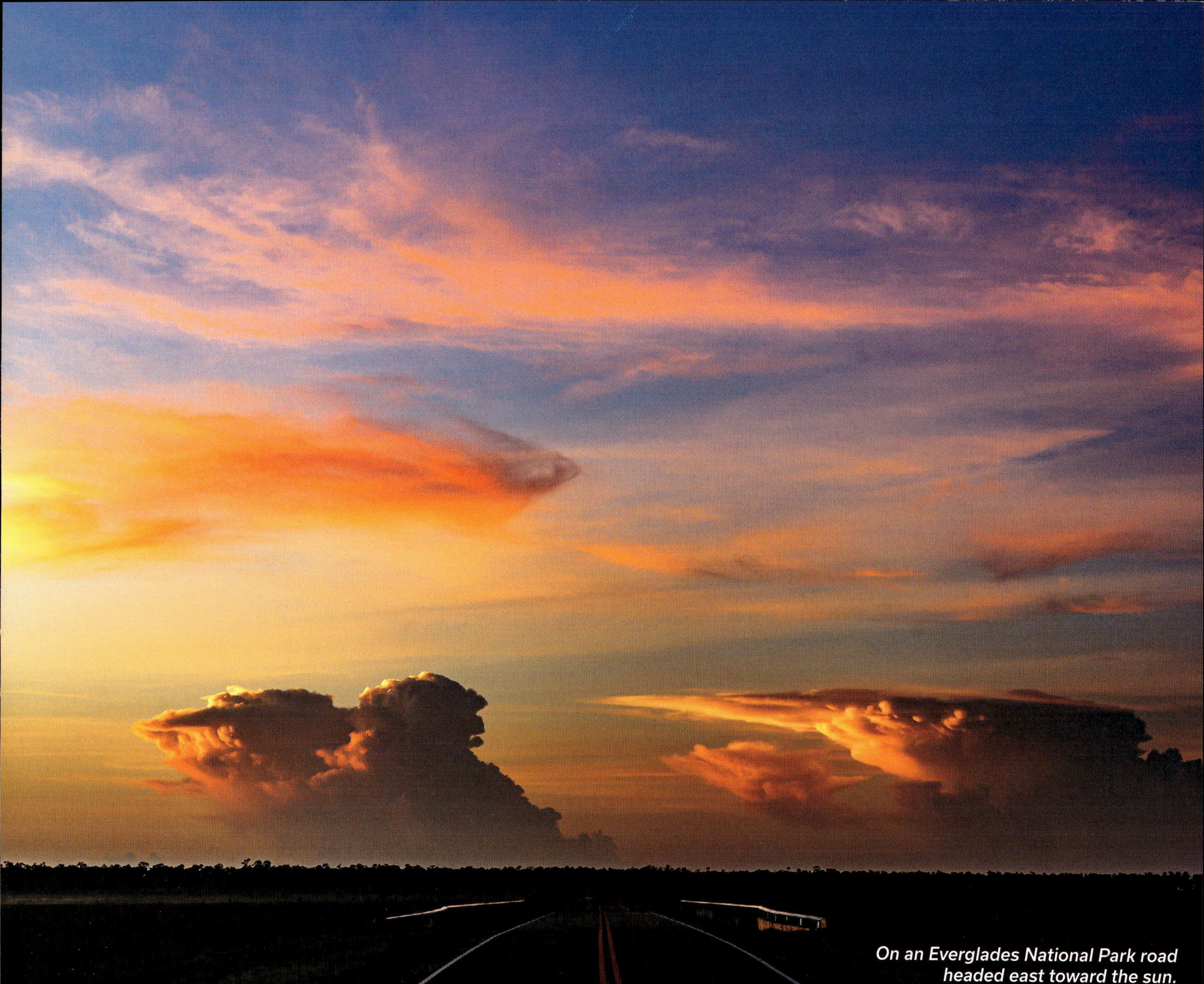

On an Everglades National Park road
headed east toward the sun.

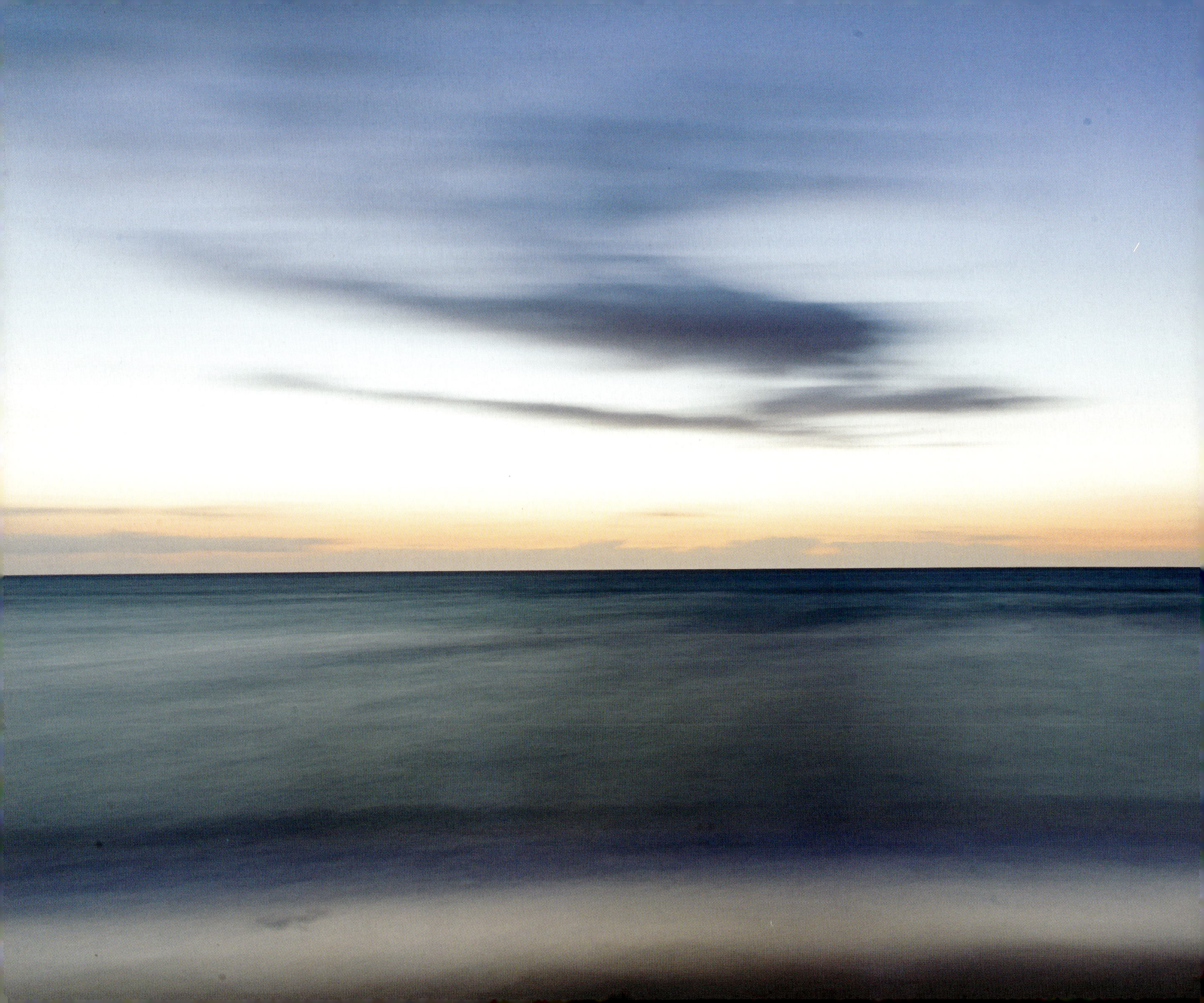

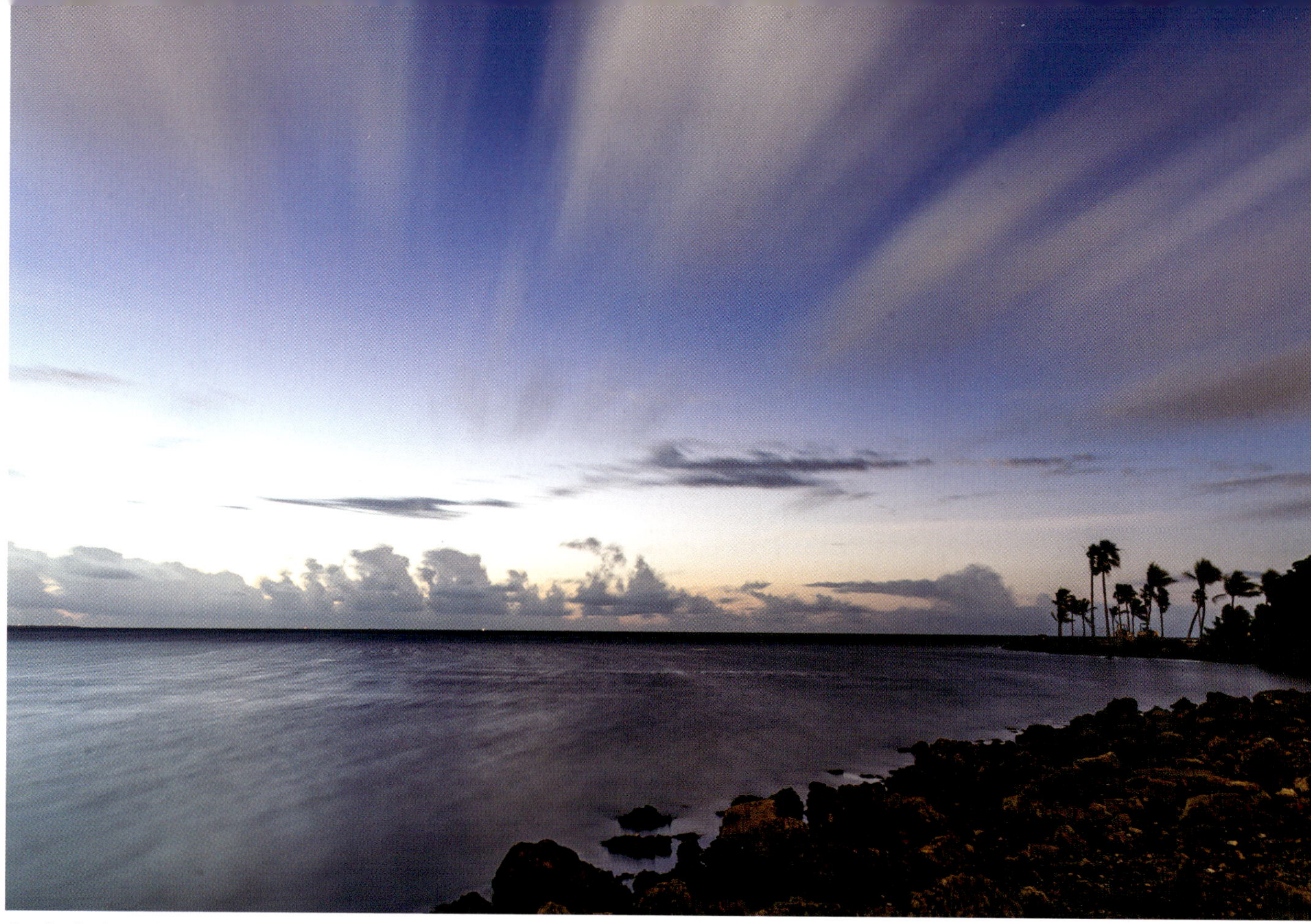

Artistic brush strokes of light and color along the waters edge on windy days.

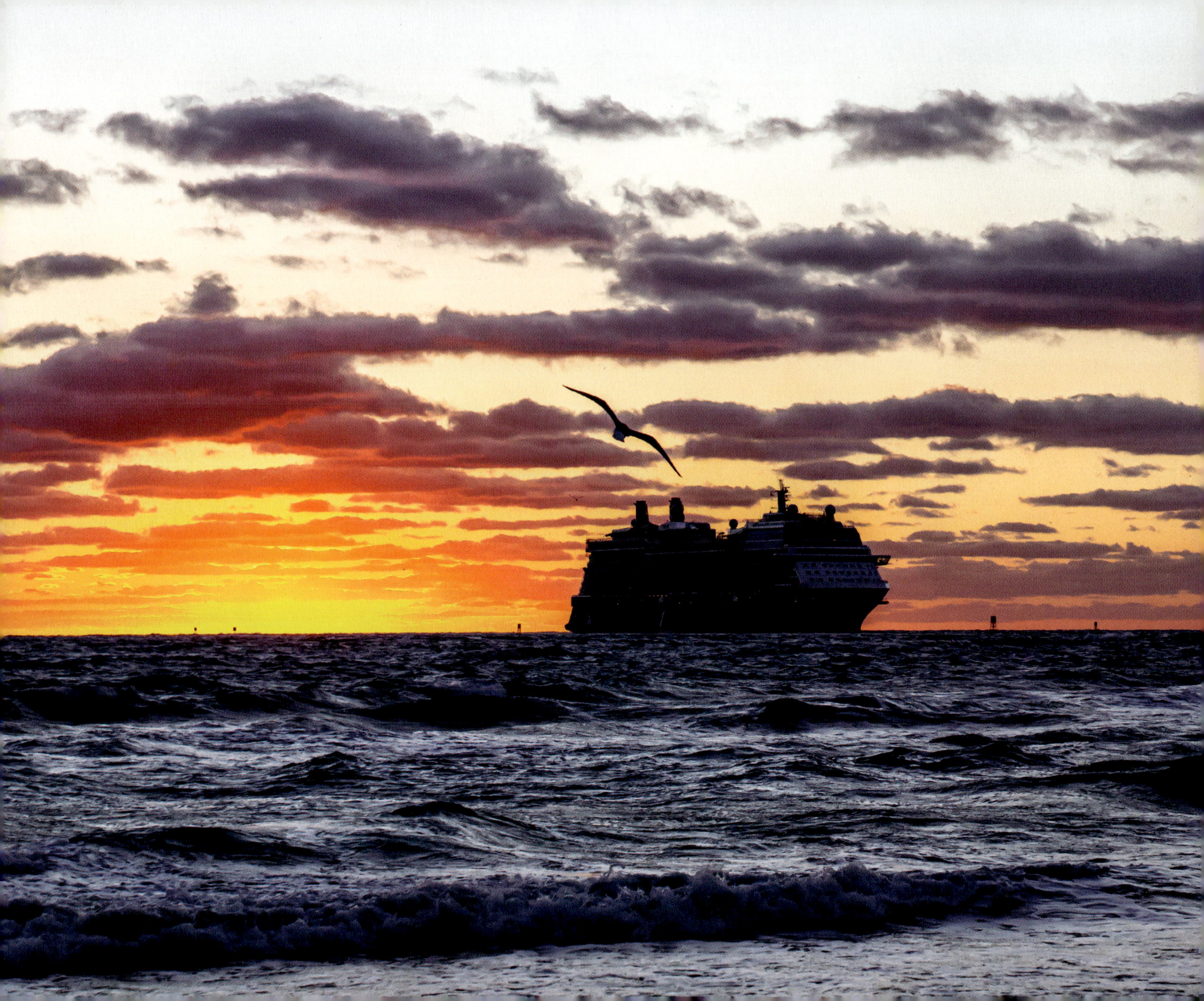

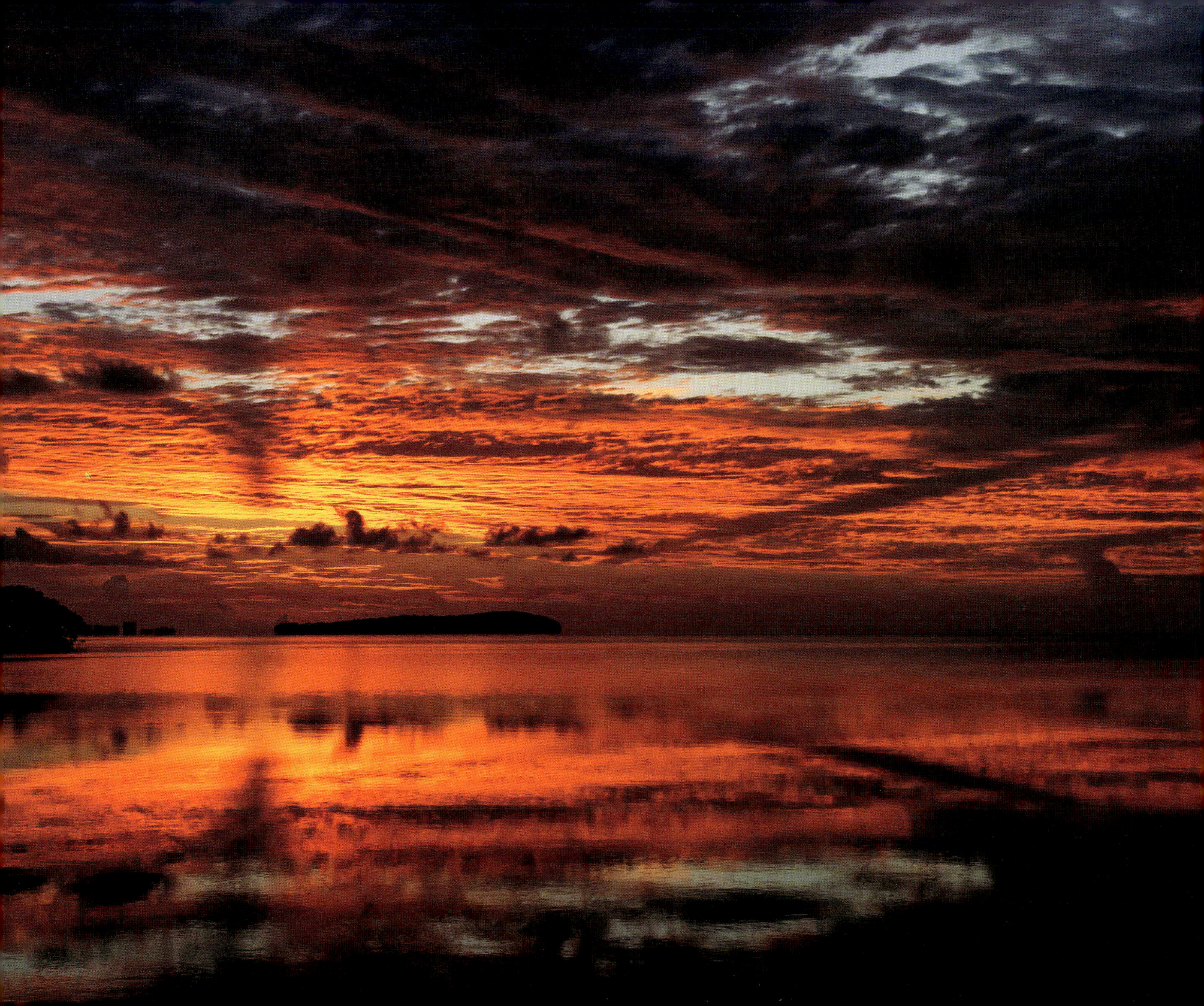

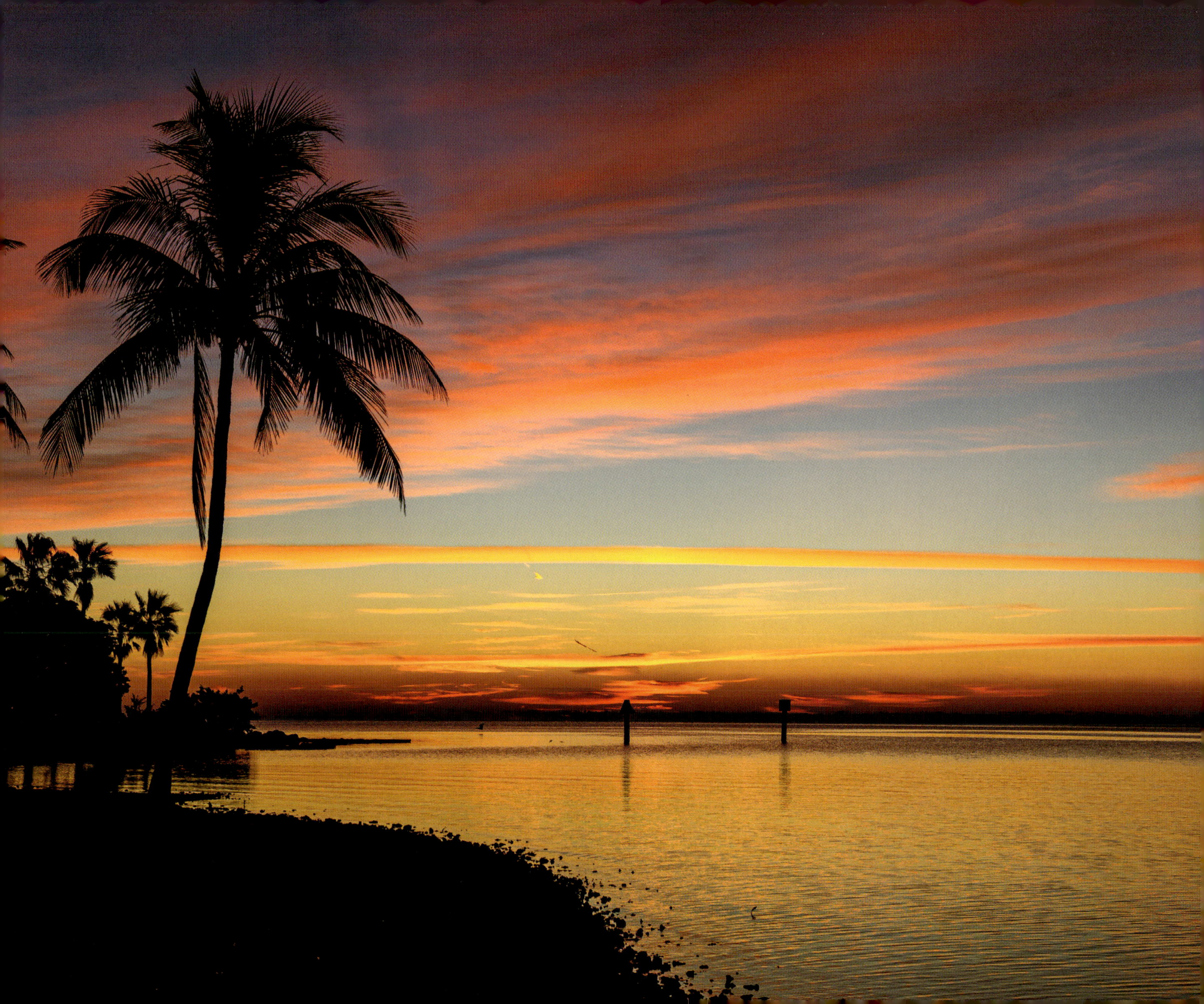

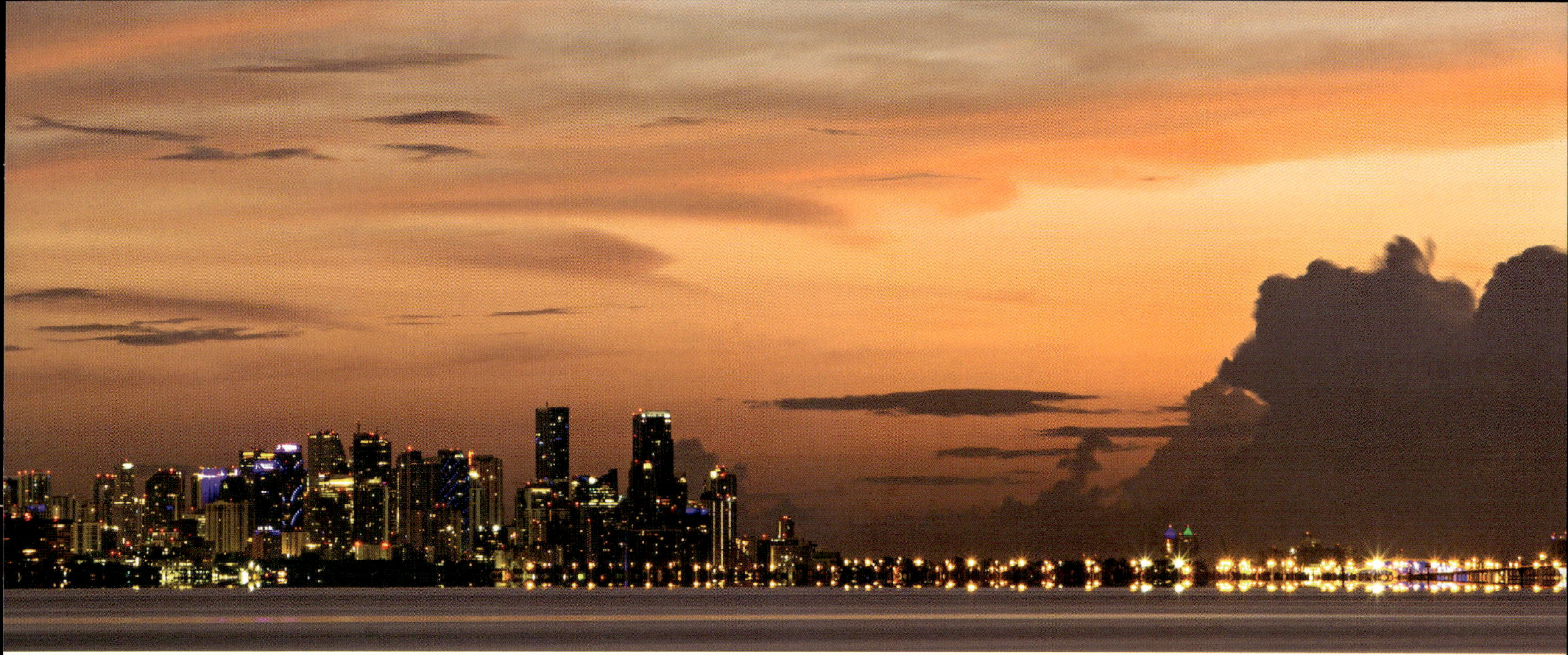

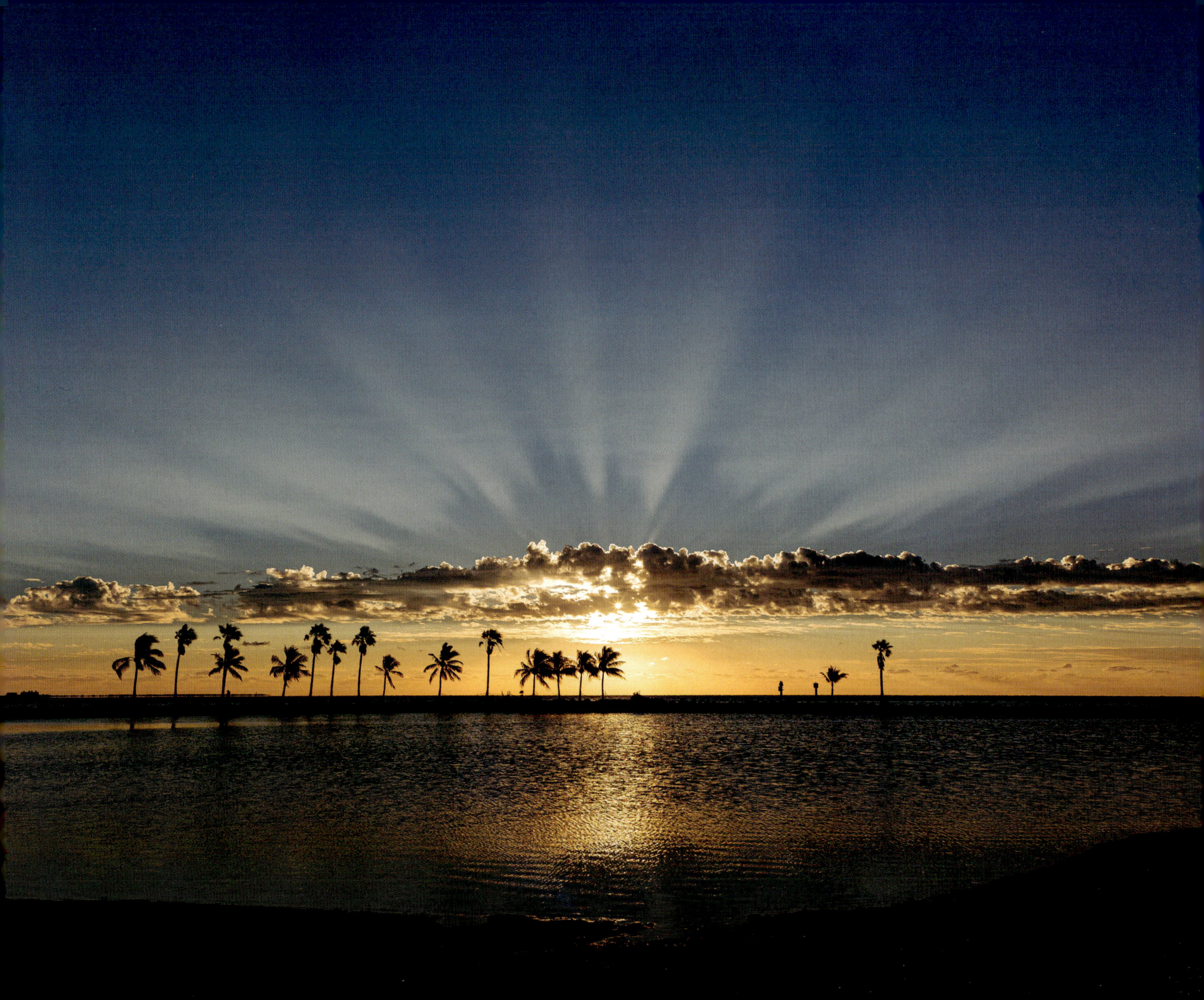

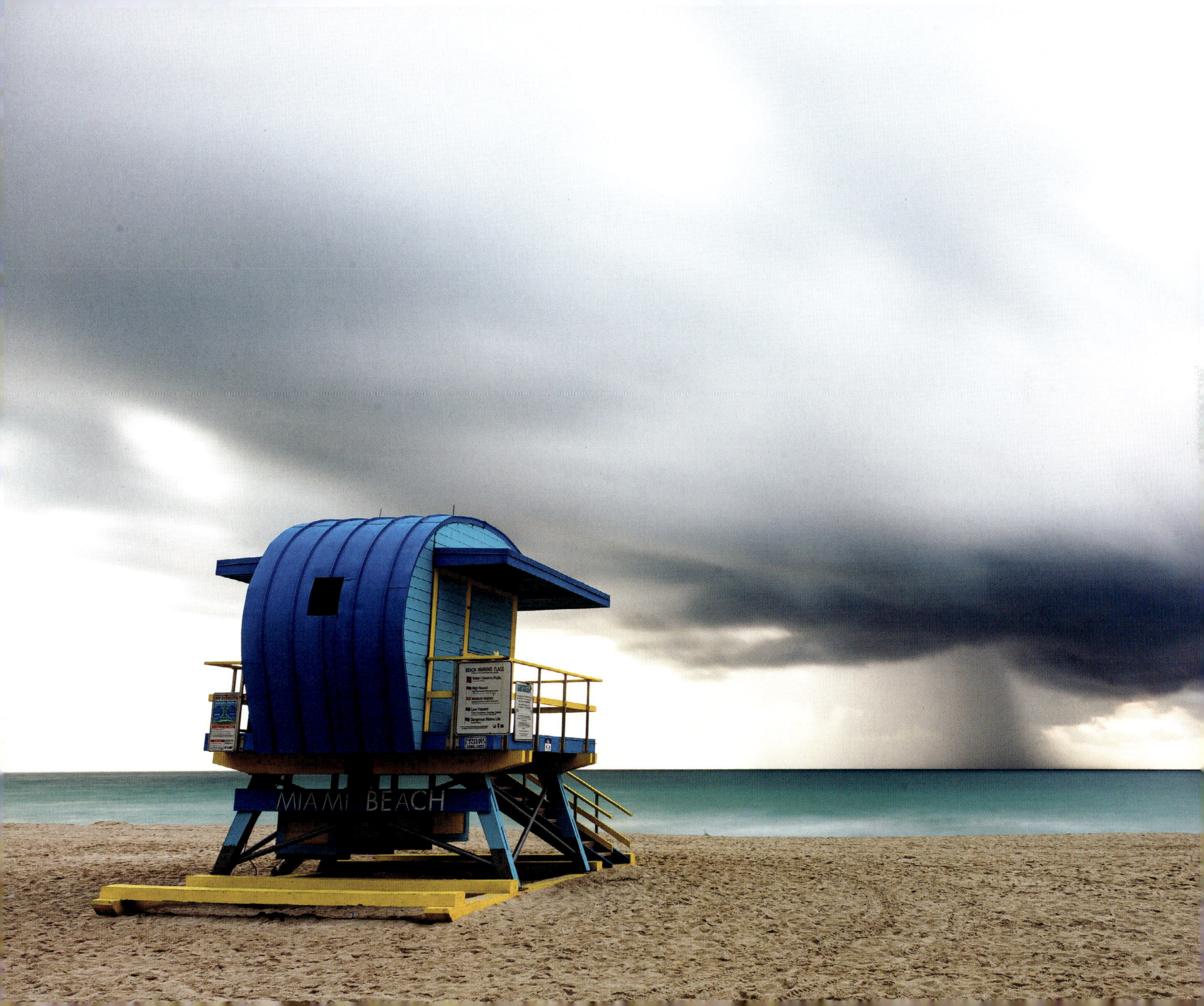
MIAMI BEACH

When I arrived on these beaches in the dark, I had no idea the sky would turn out like this. It's often a pleasant surprise.

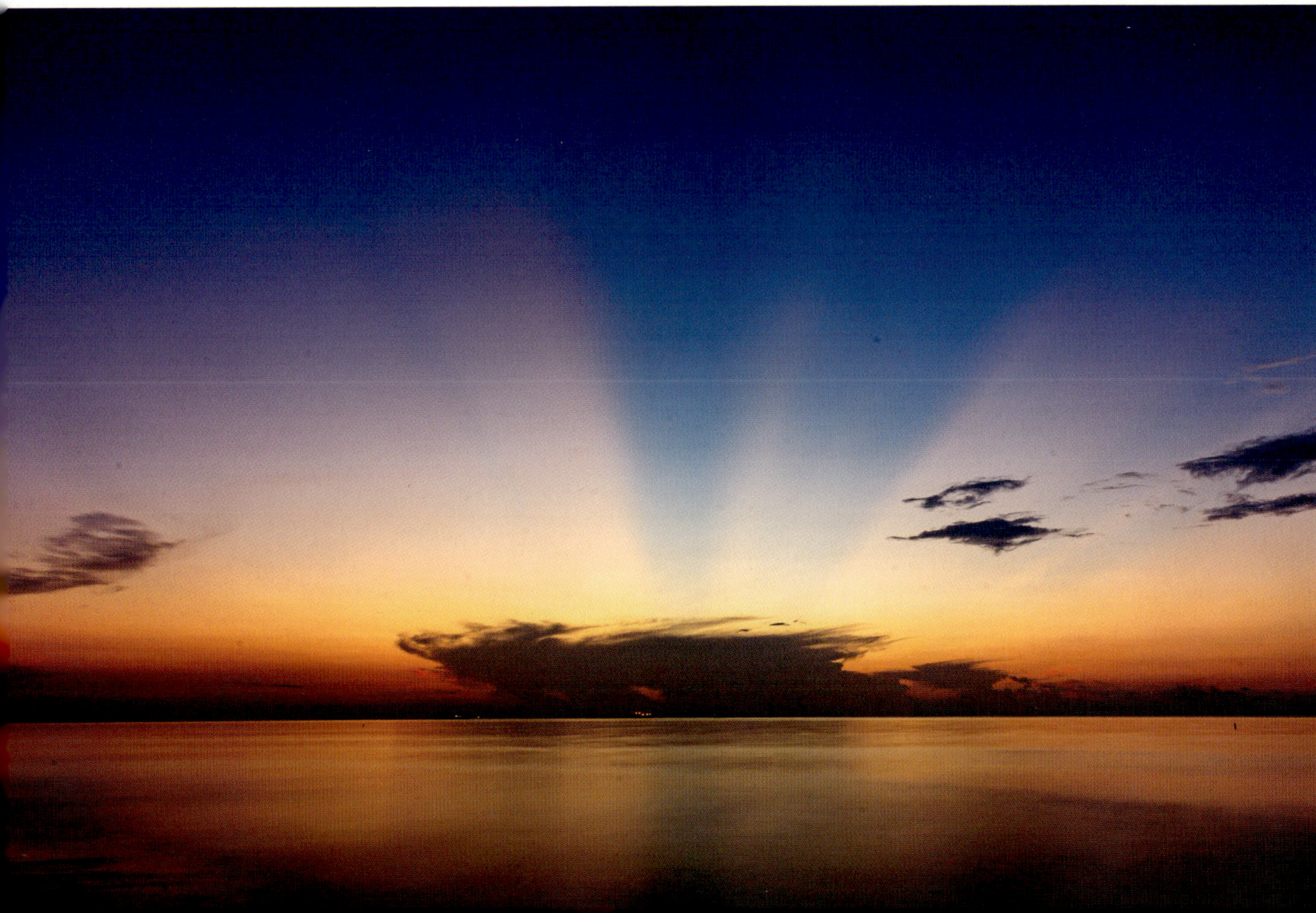

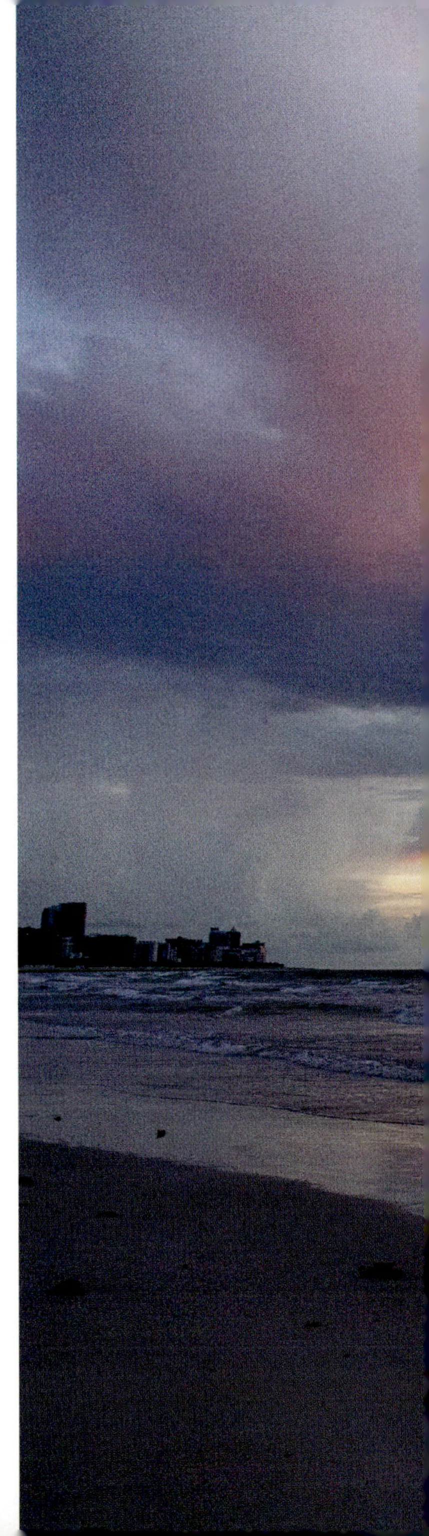

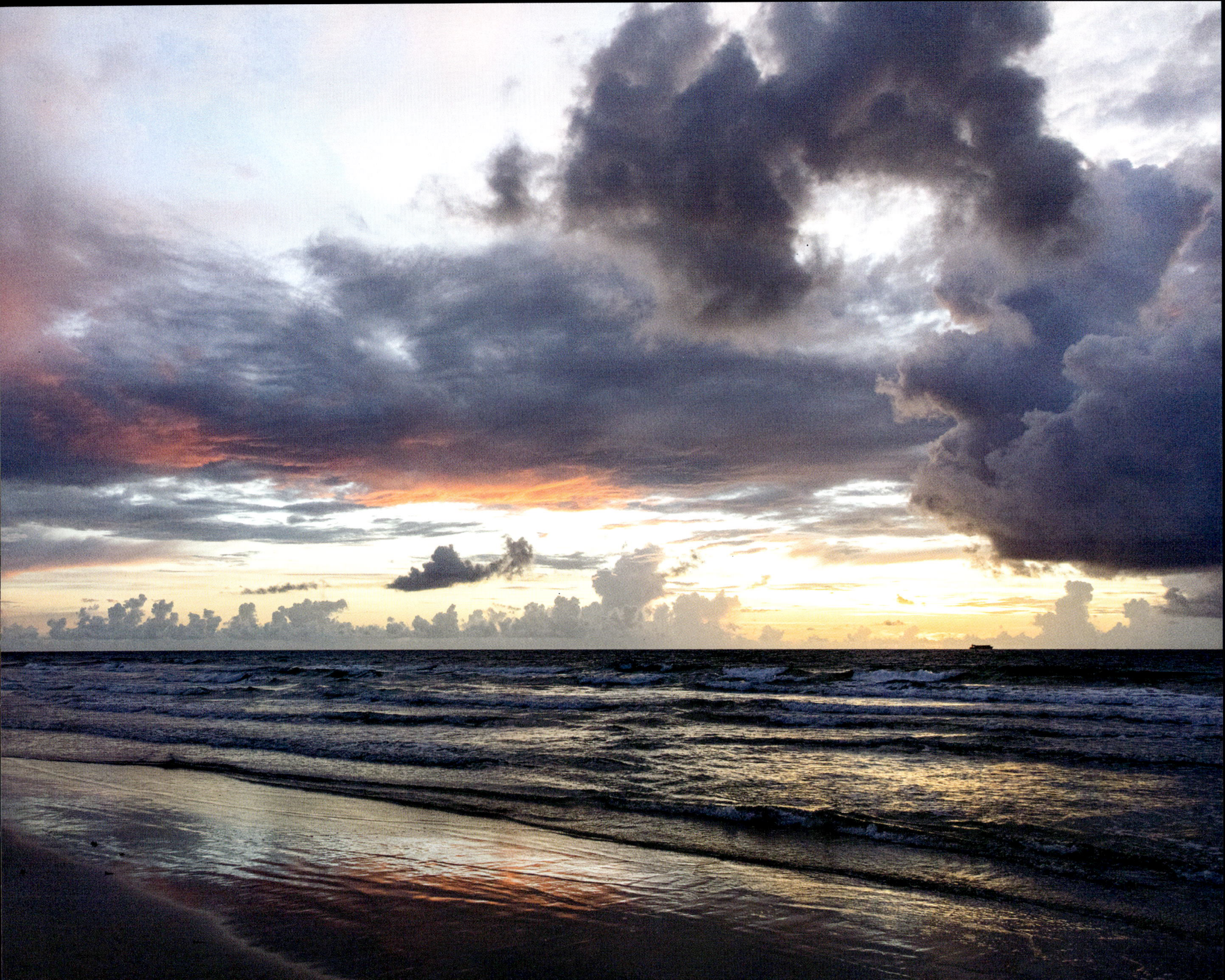

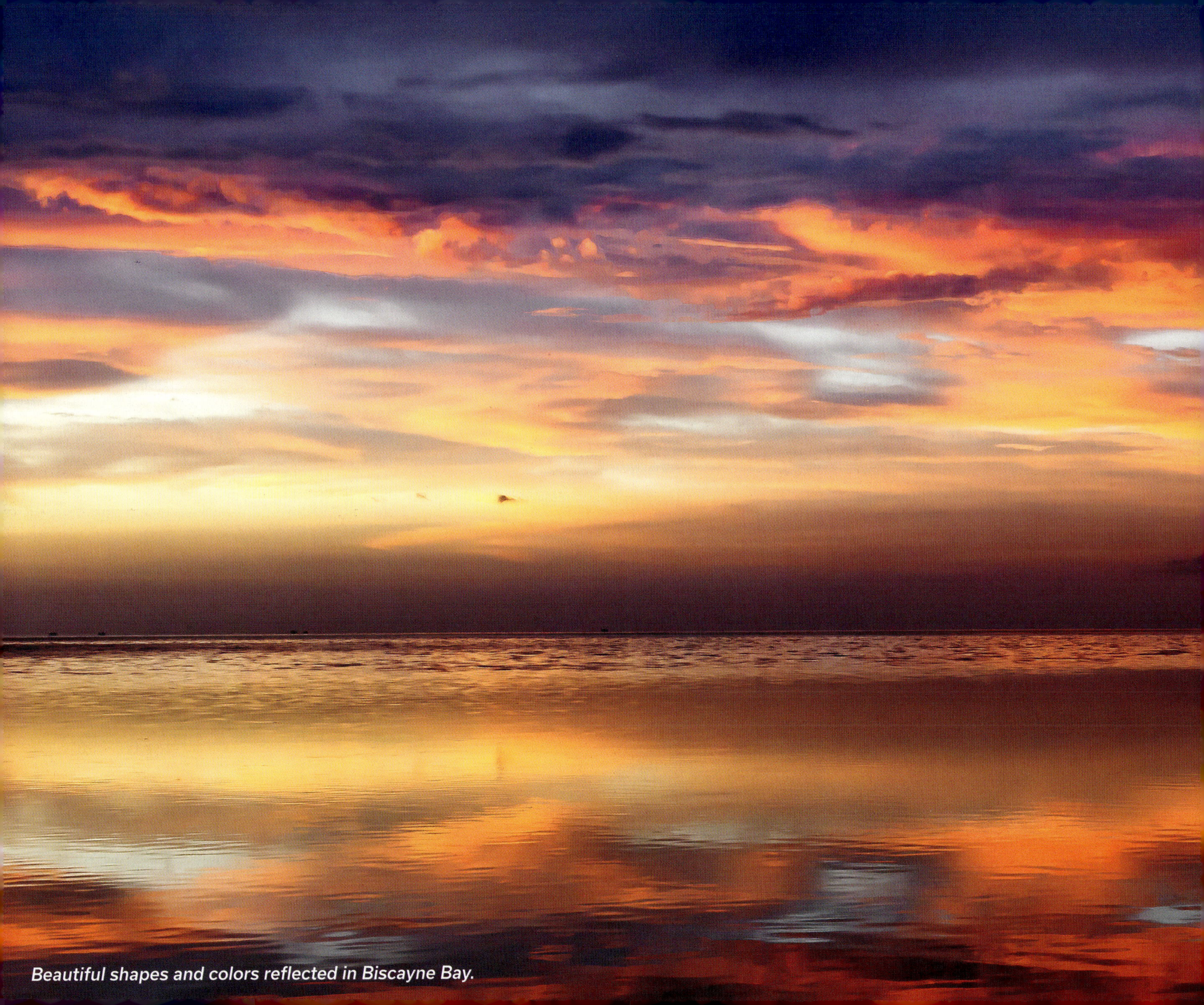

Beautiful shapes and colors reflected in Biscayne Bay.

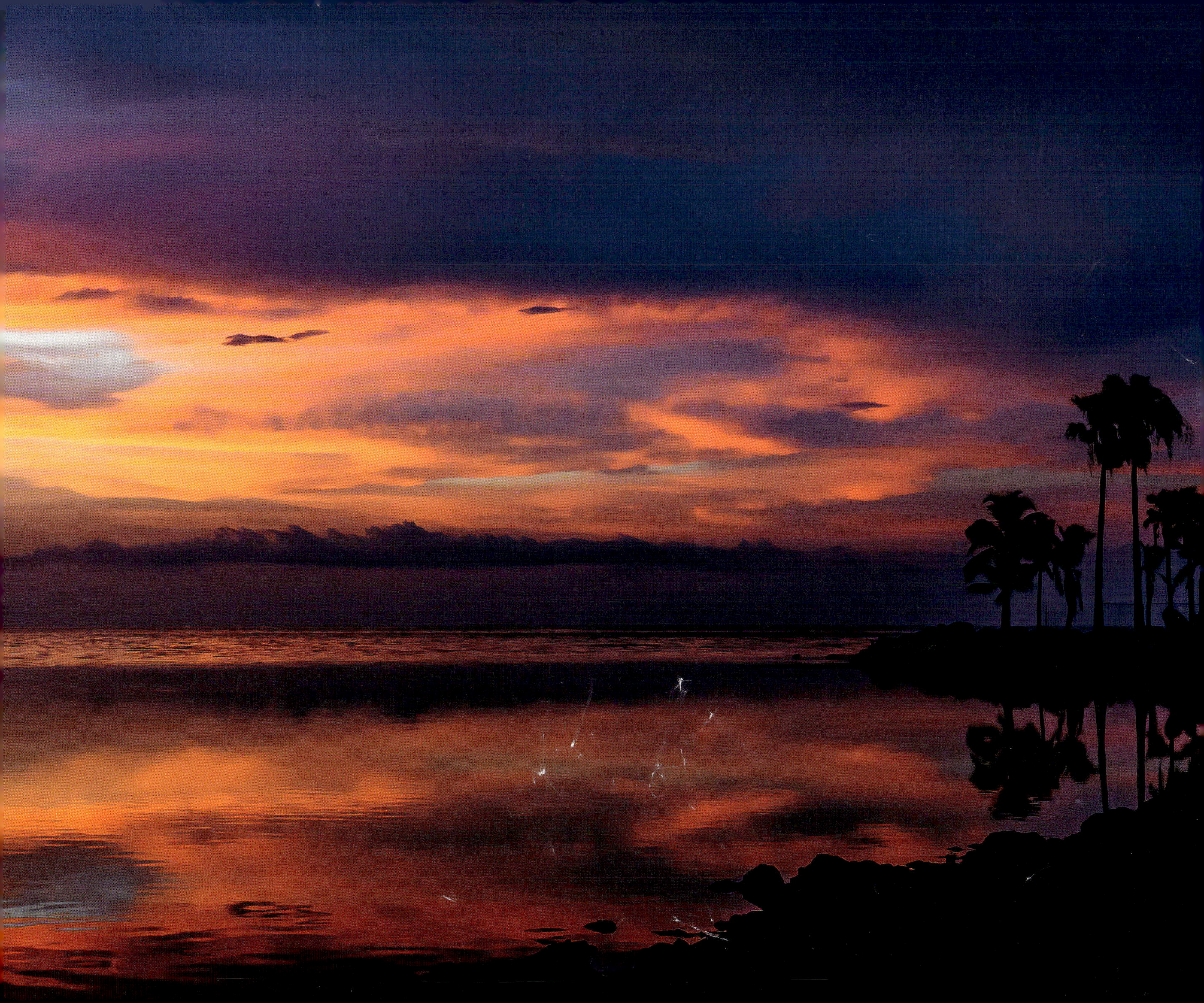

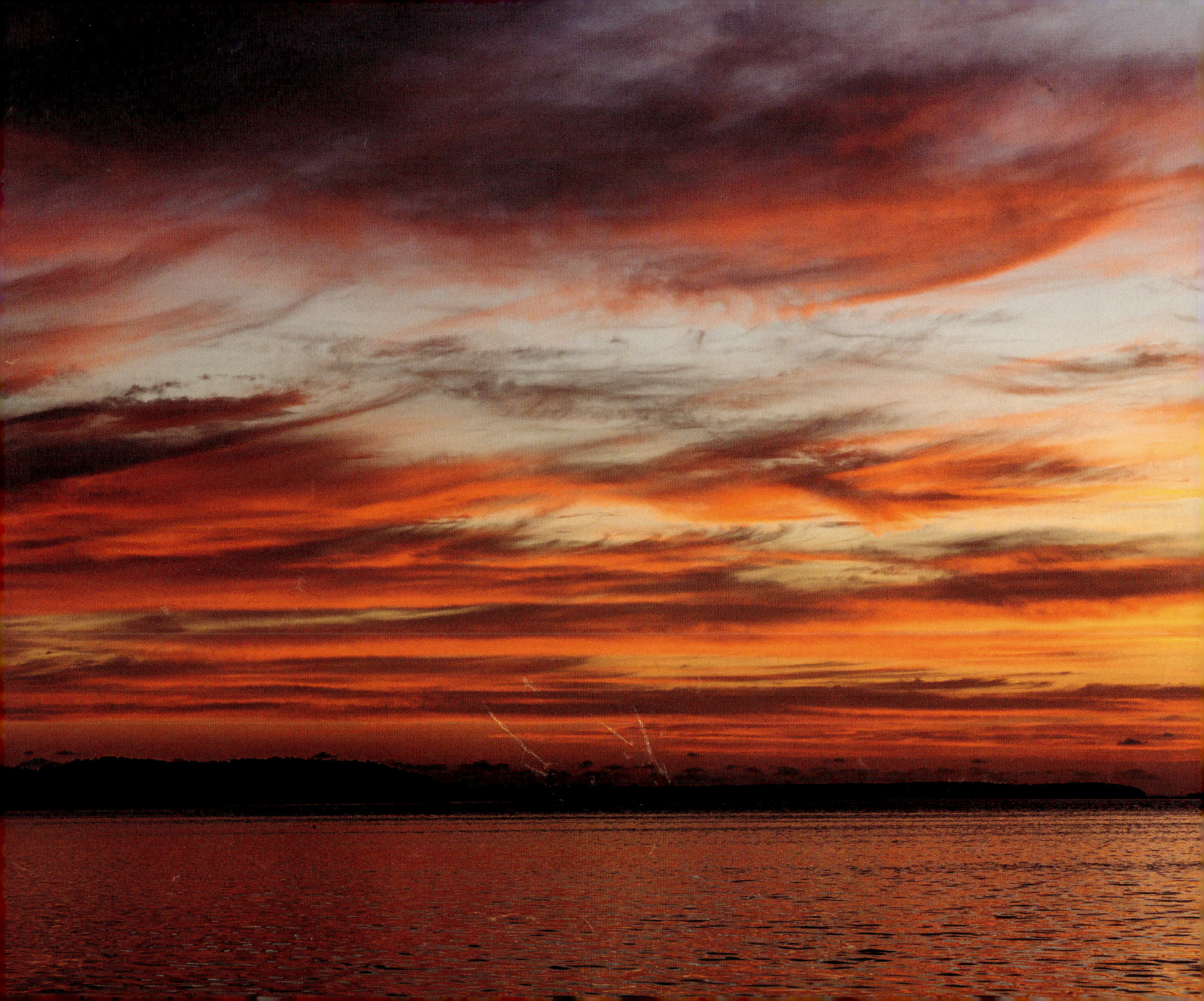

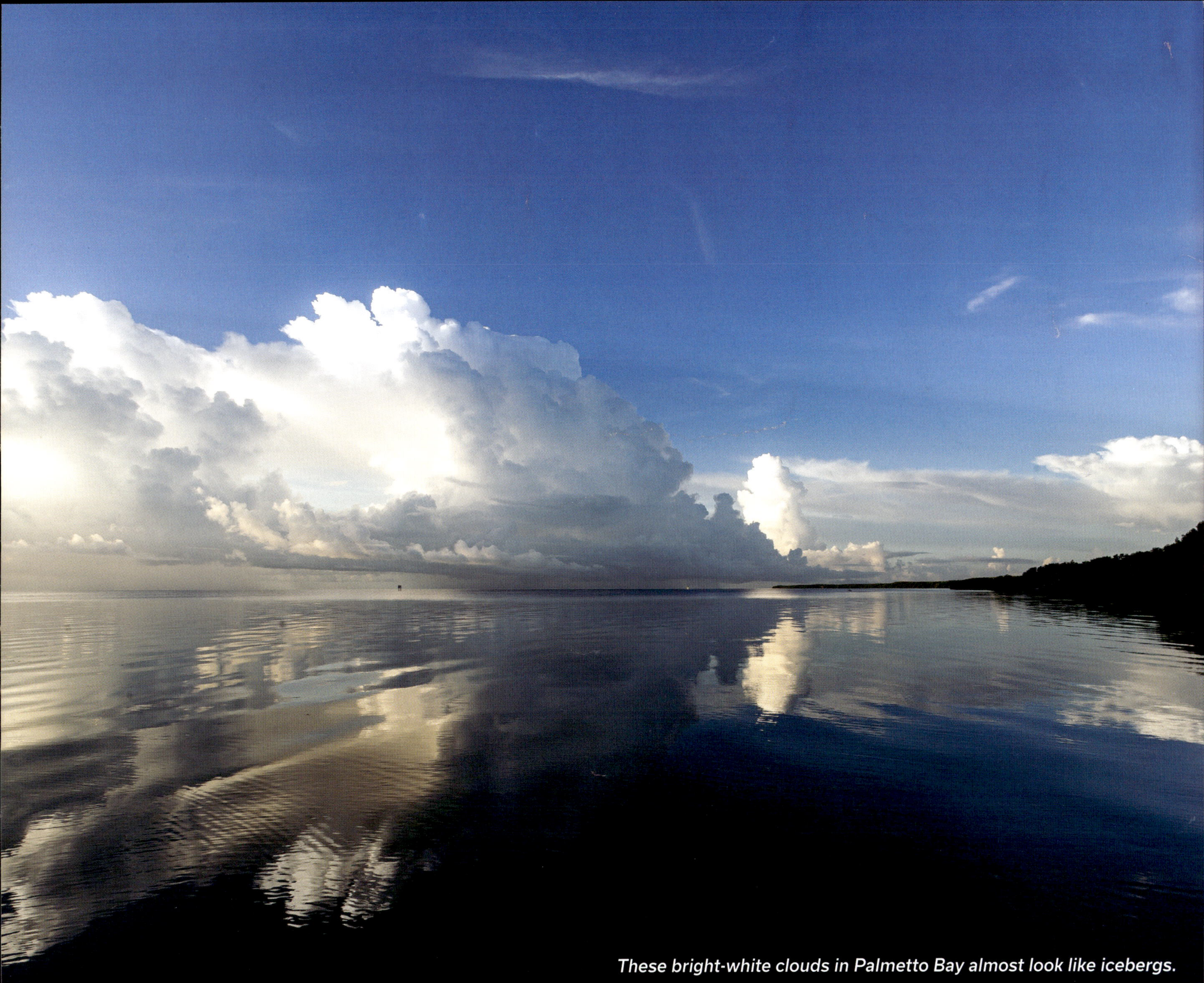

These bright-white clouds in Palmetto Bay almost look like icebergs.

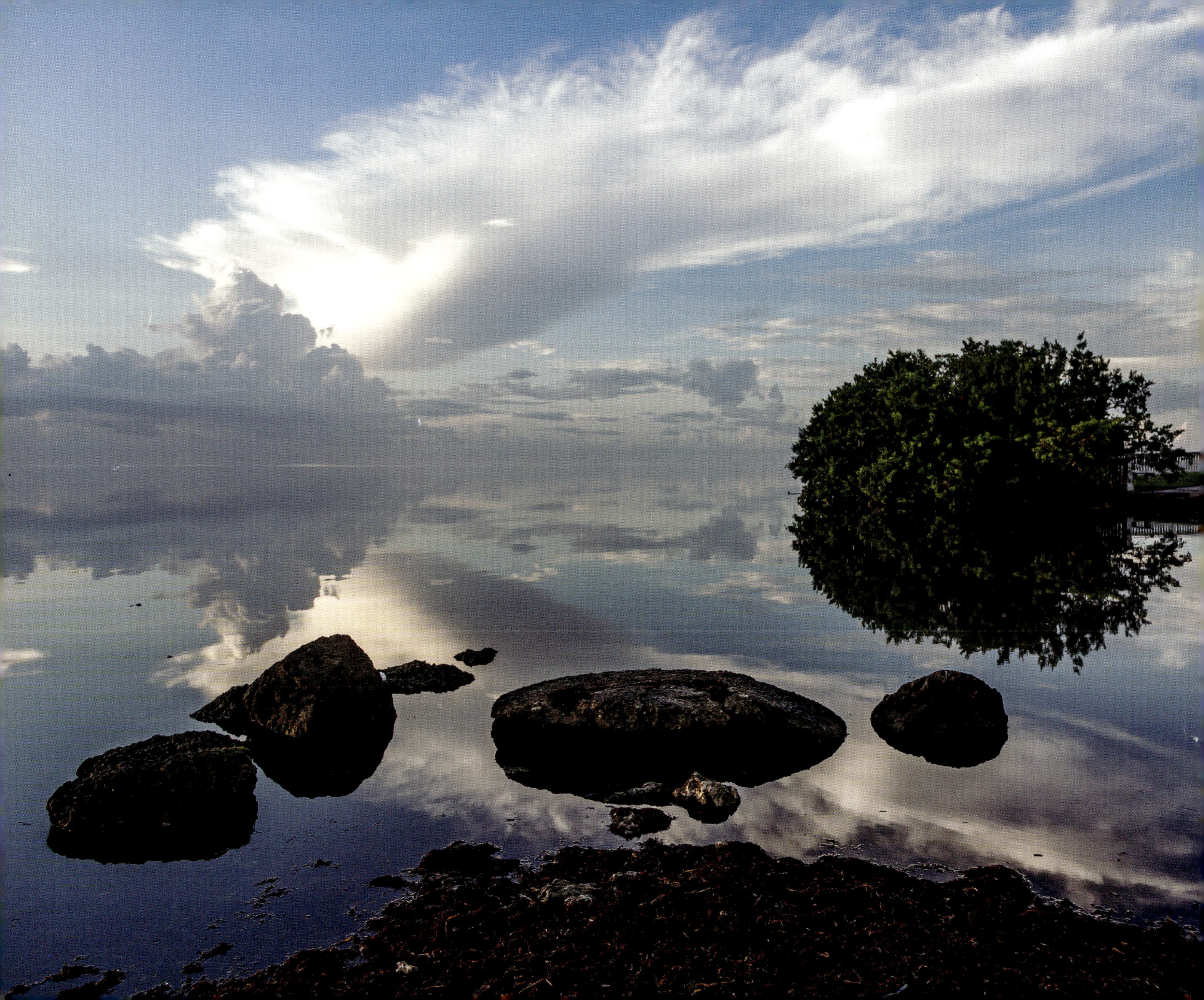

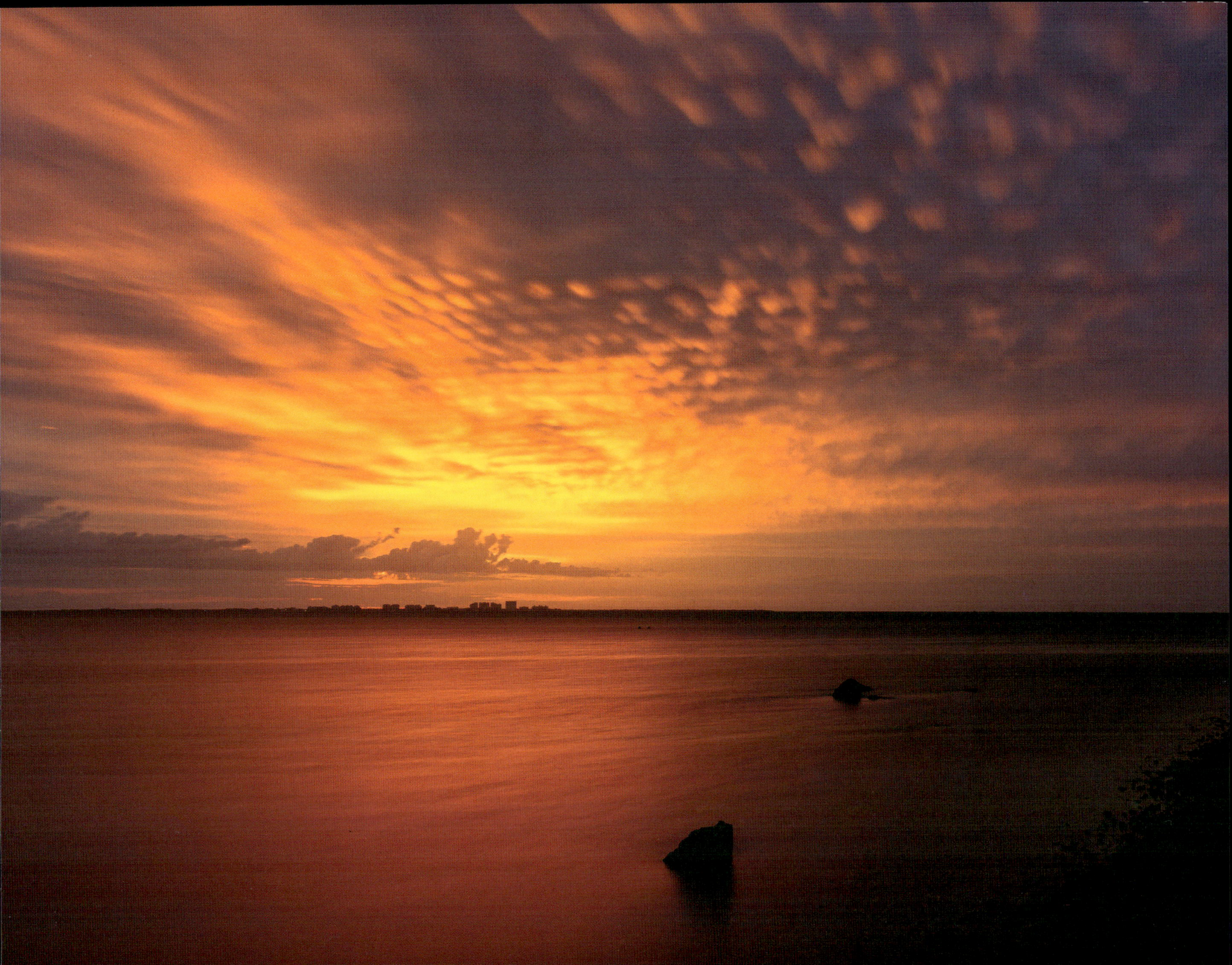

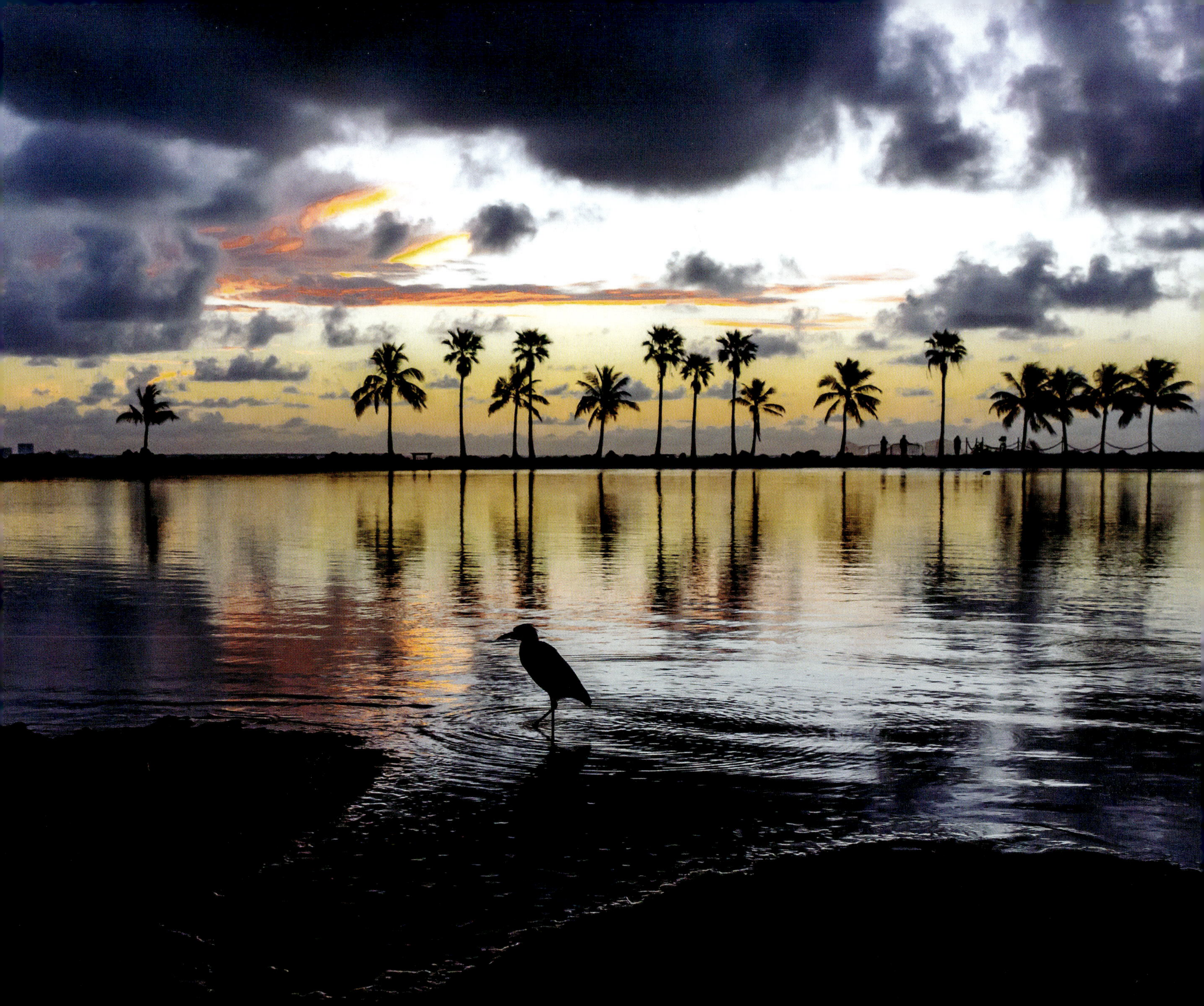

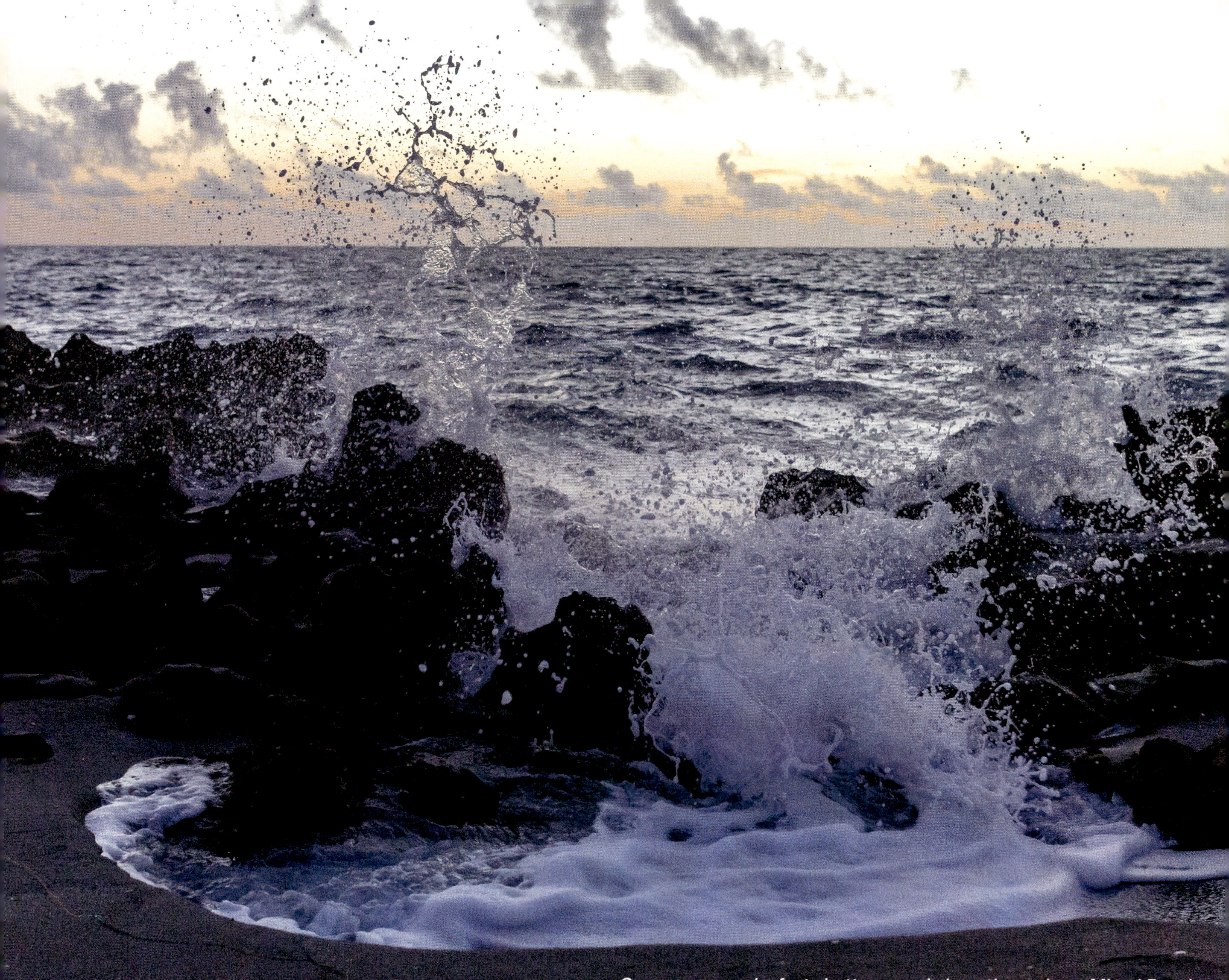

Ocean spray and a fast shutter speed along the rocks at Miami Beach

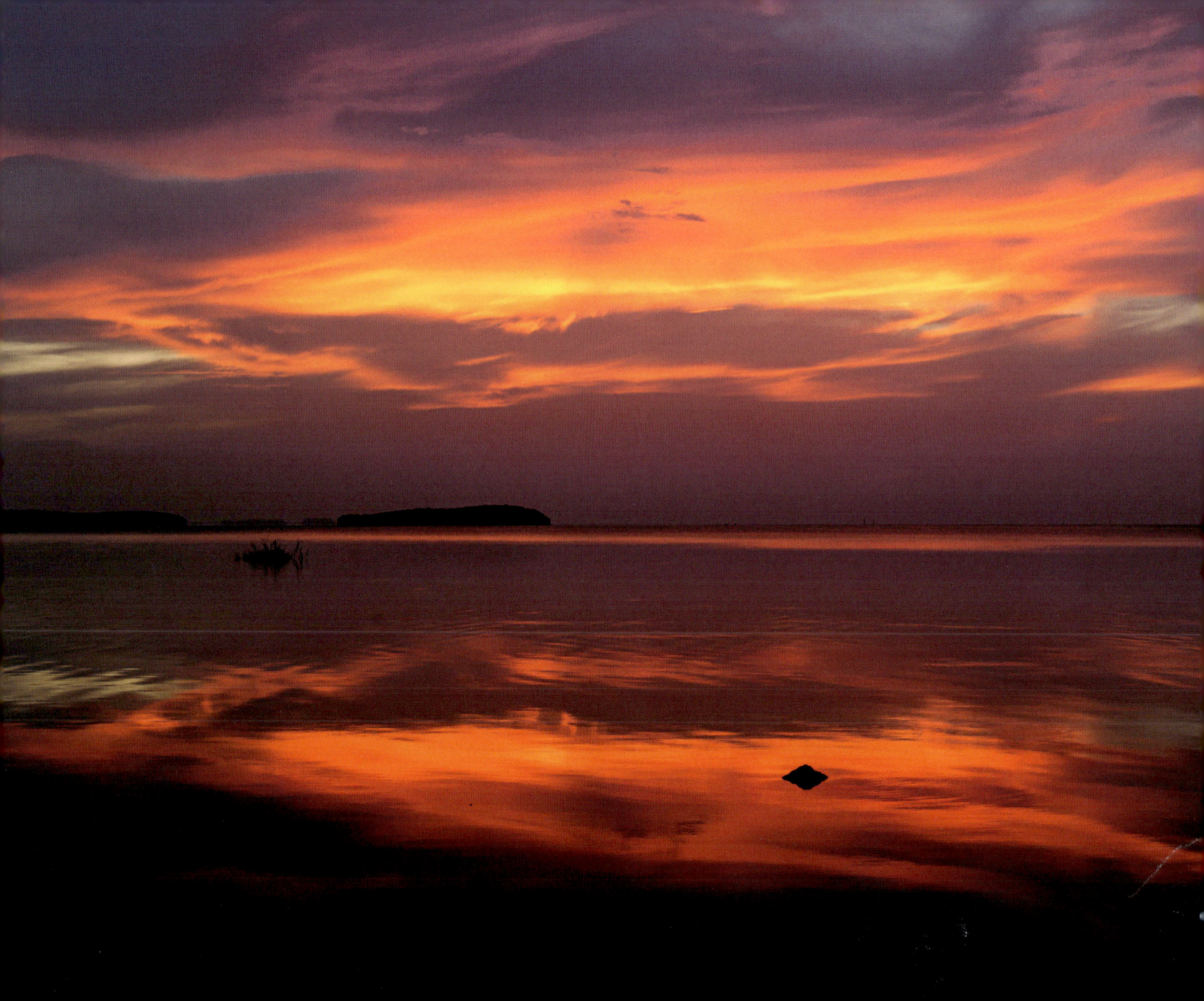

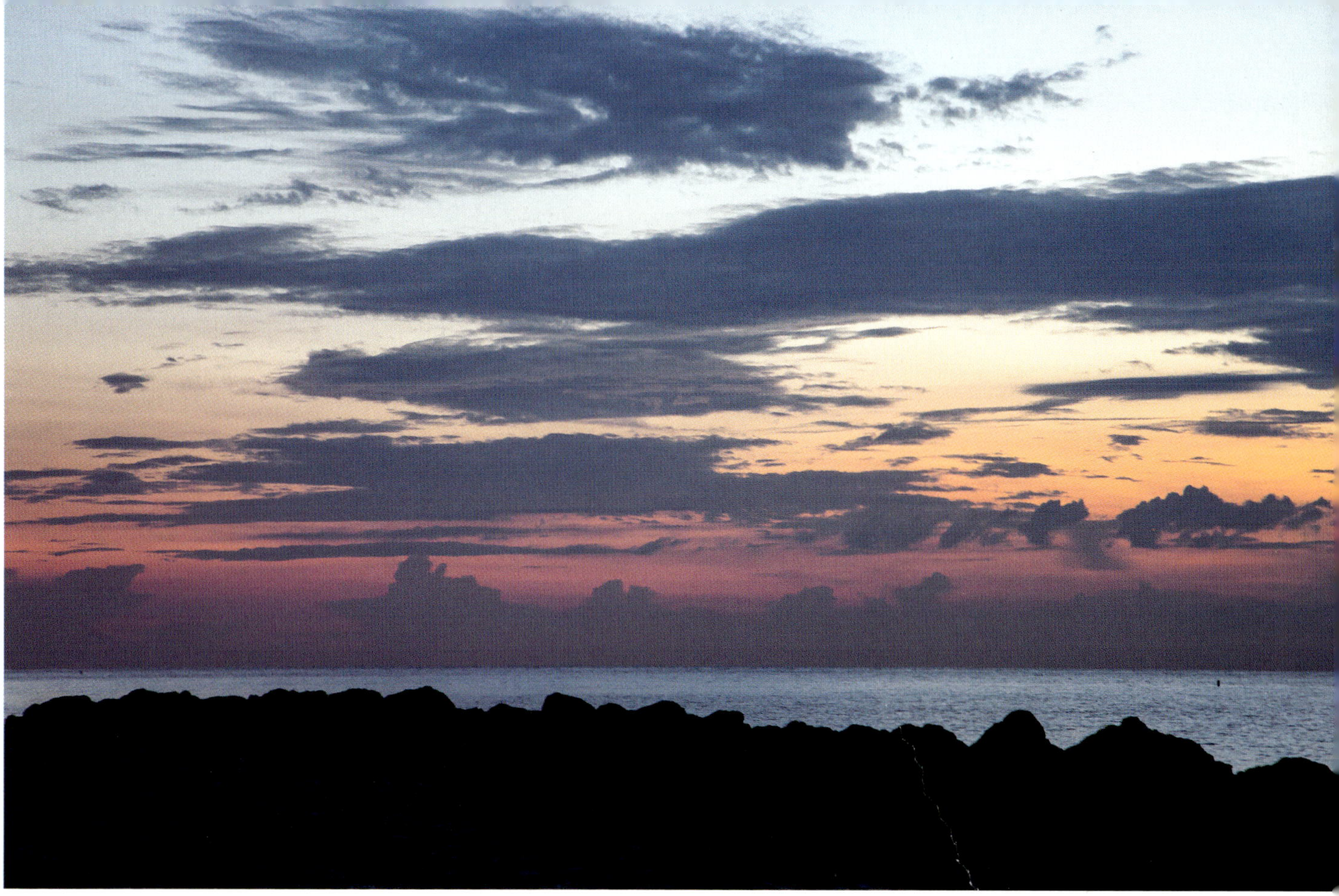

It's always a calming morning when the sky painter decides to work with soft colors and pastels.

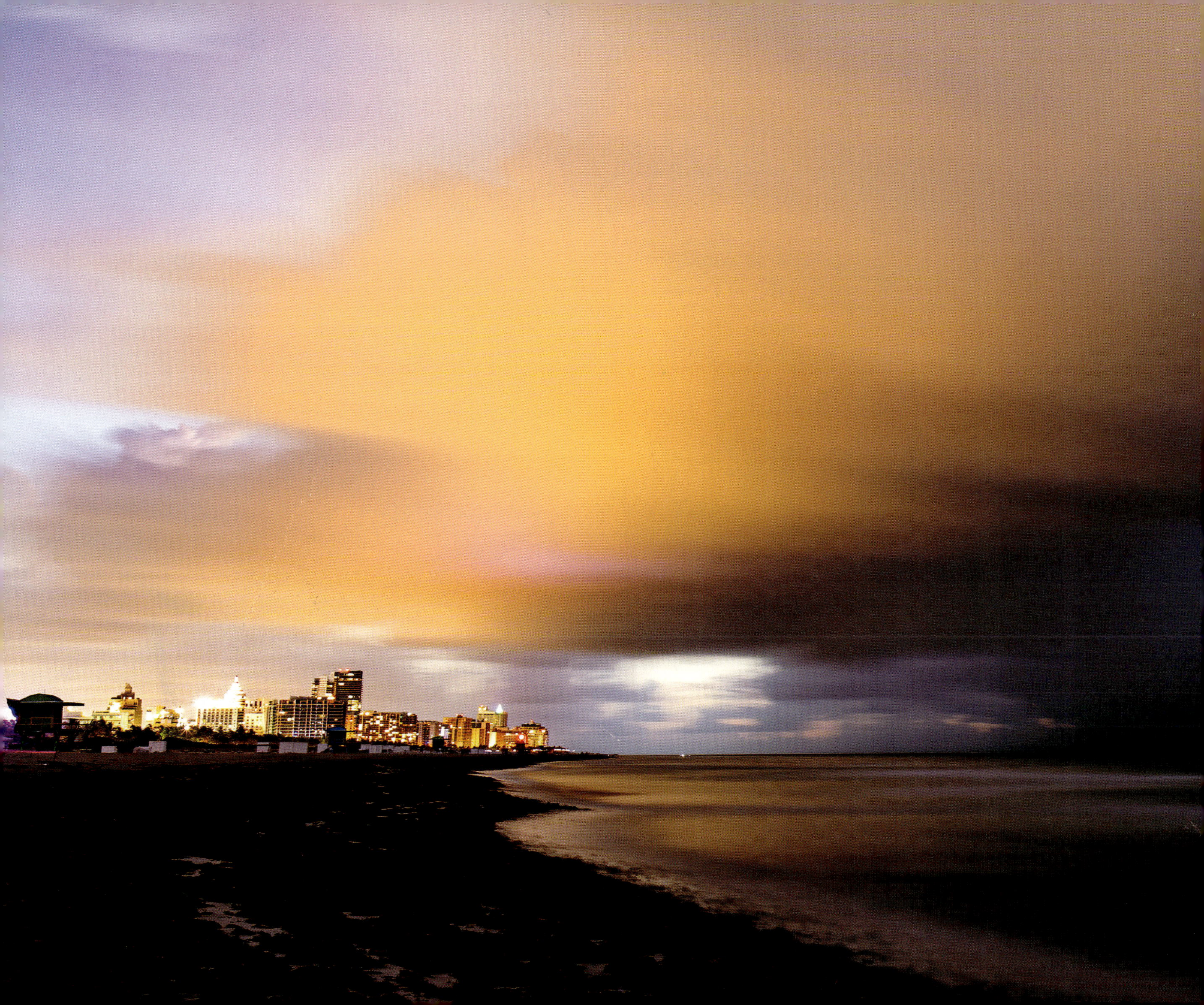

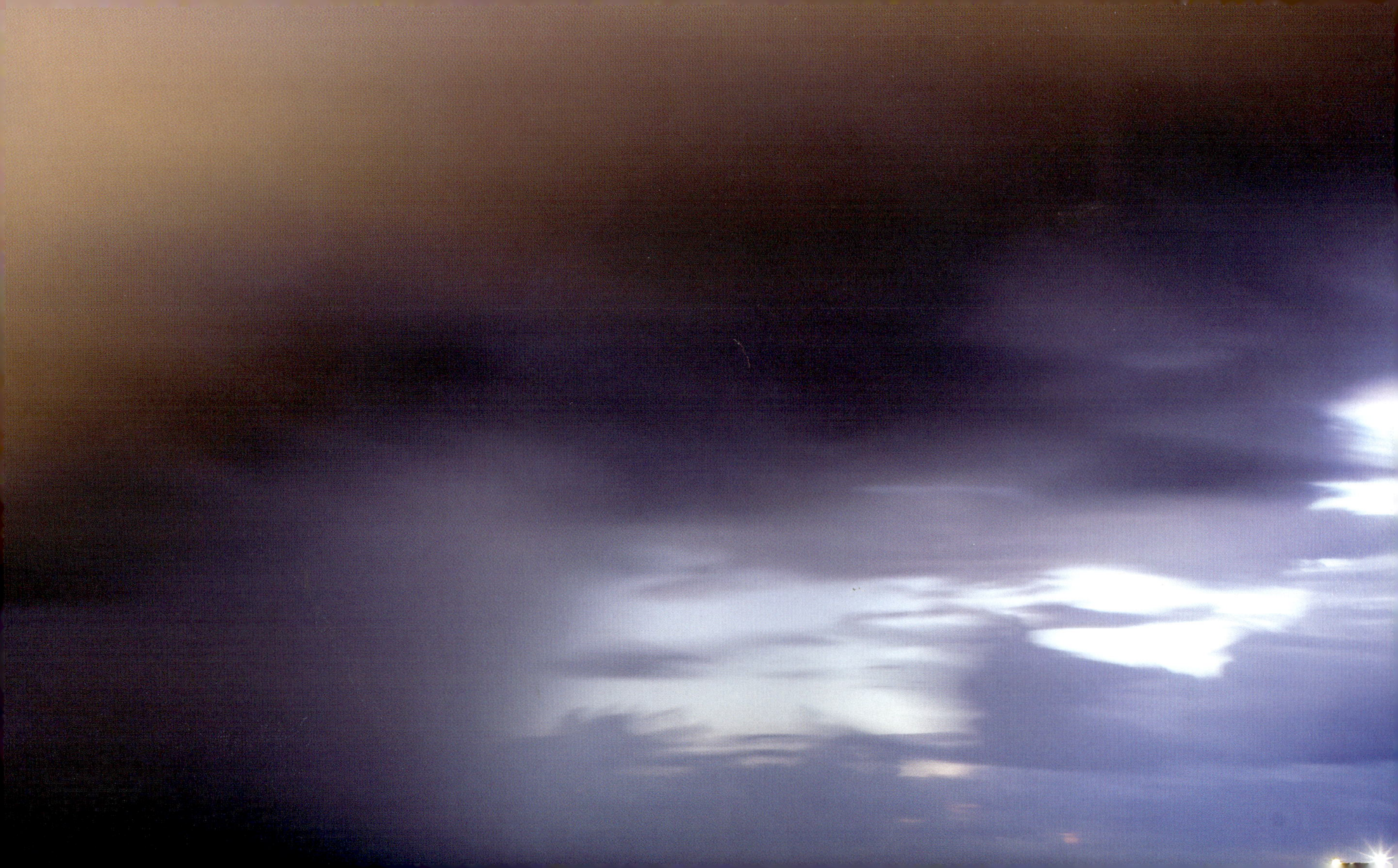

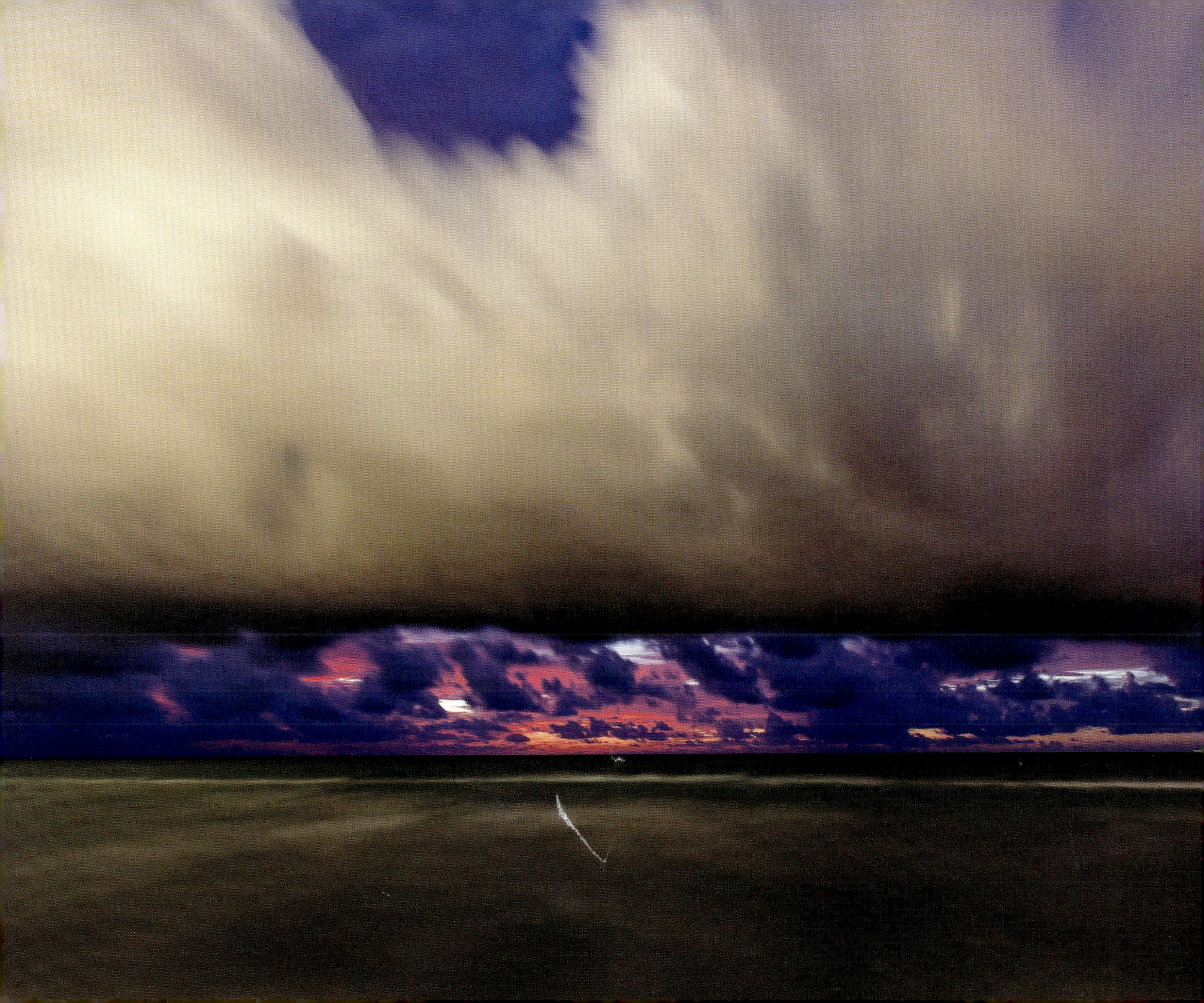

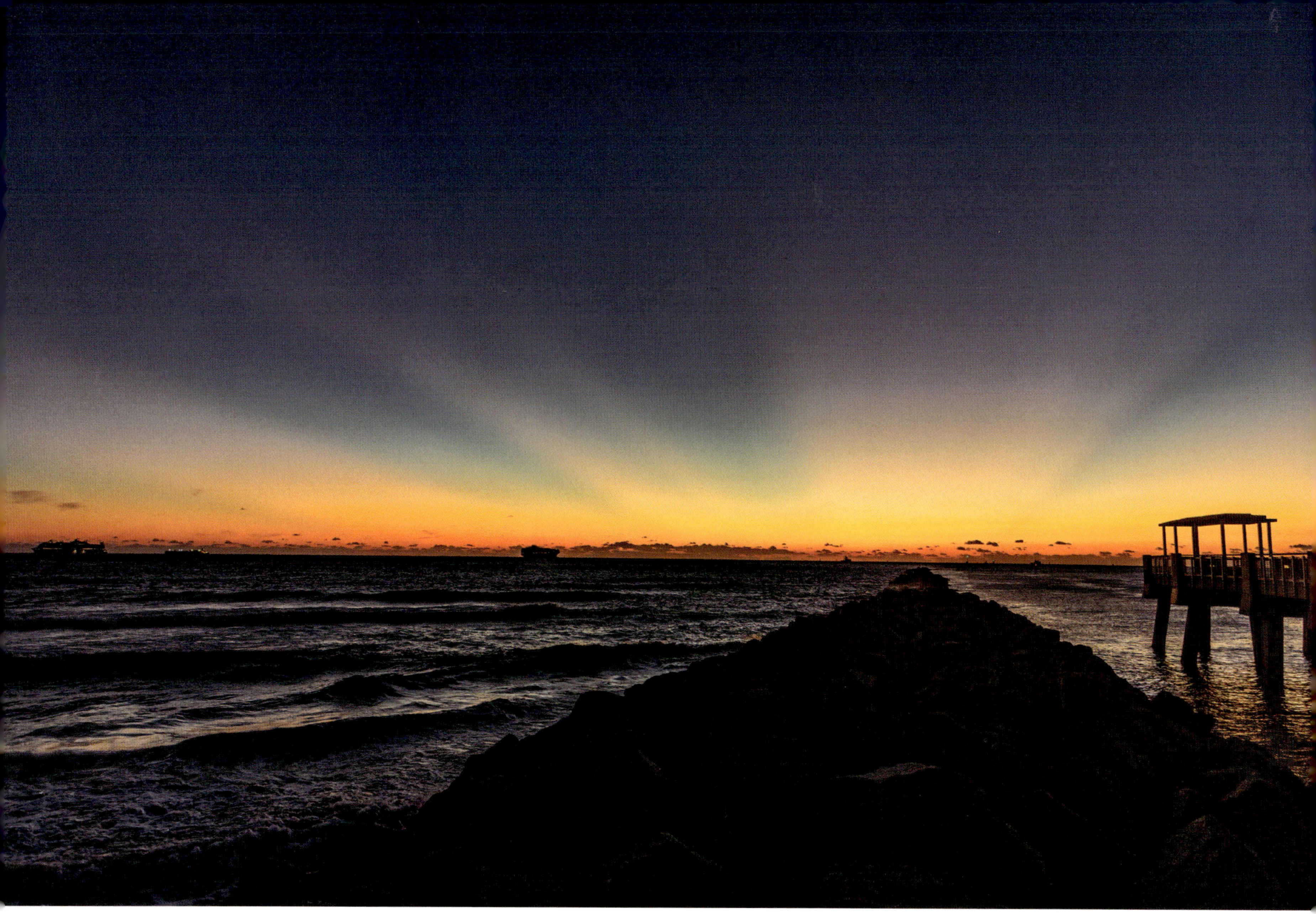

Wind-blown clouds and sun rays piercing the horizon. Celestial theater at its best.

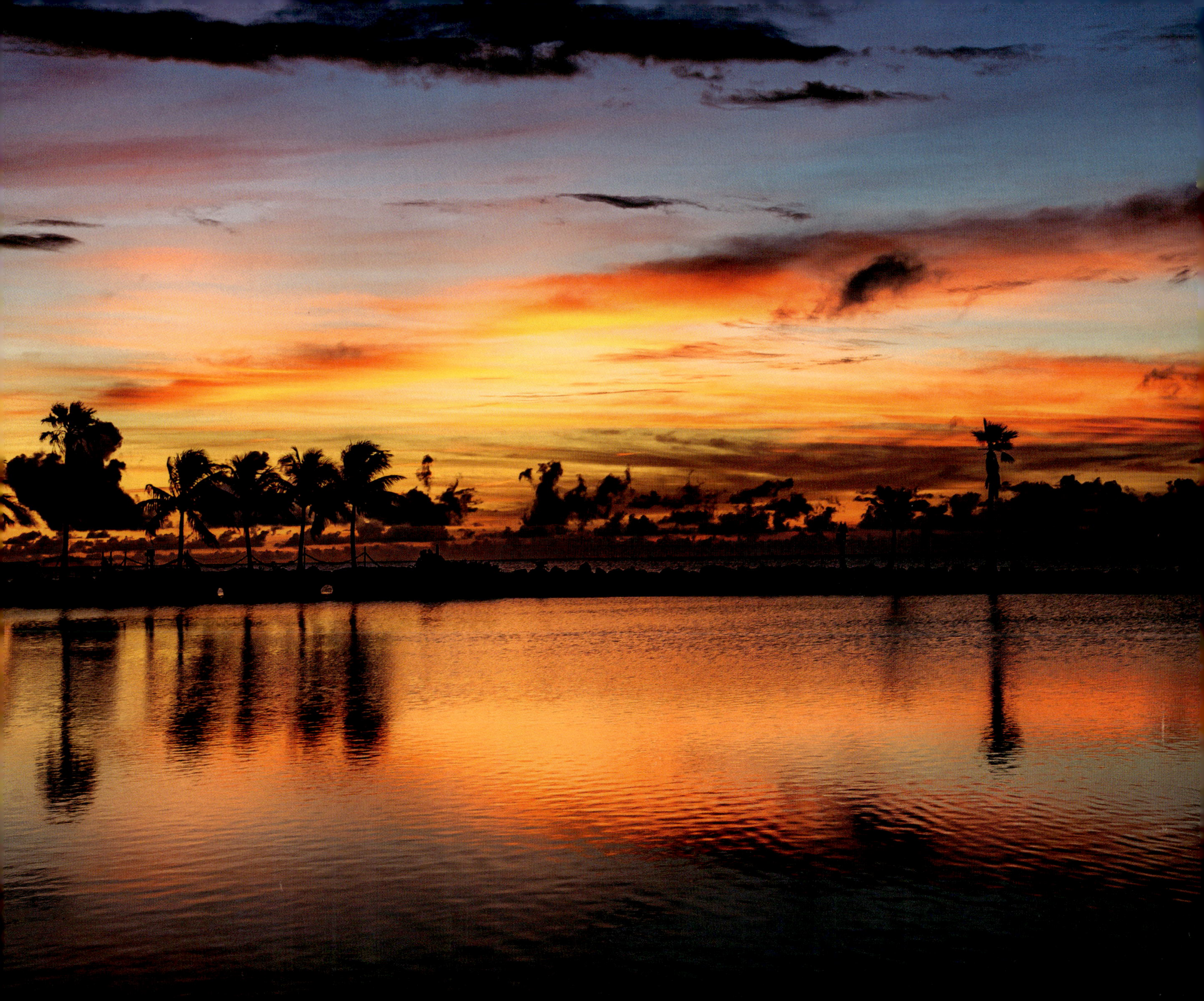

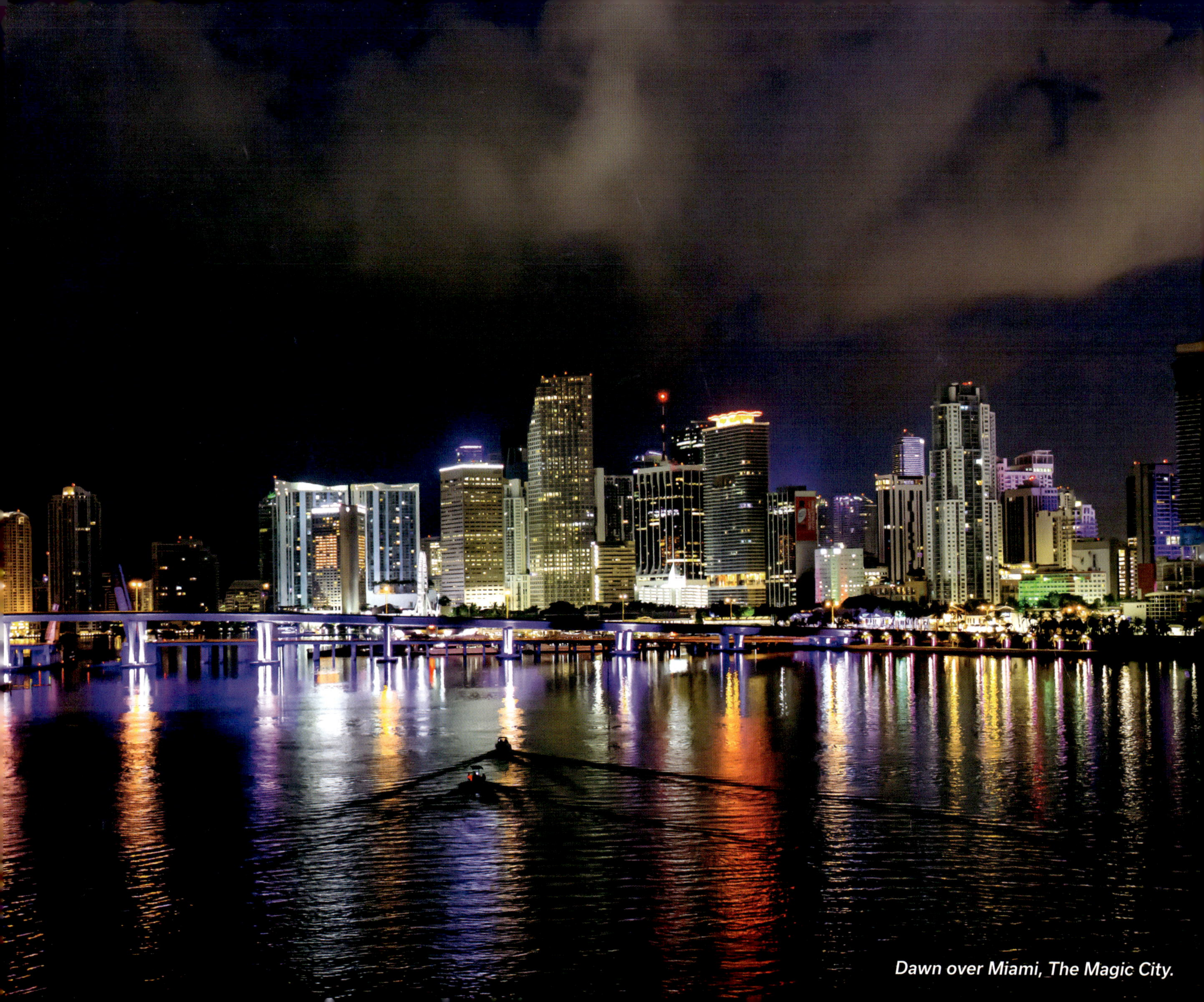

Dawn over Miami, The Magic City.

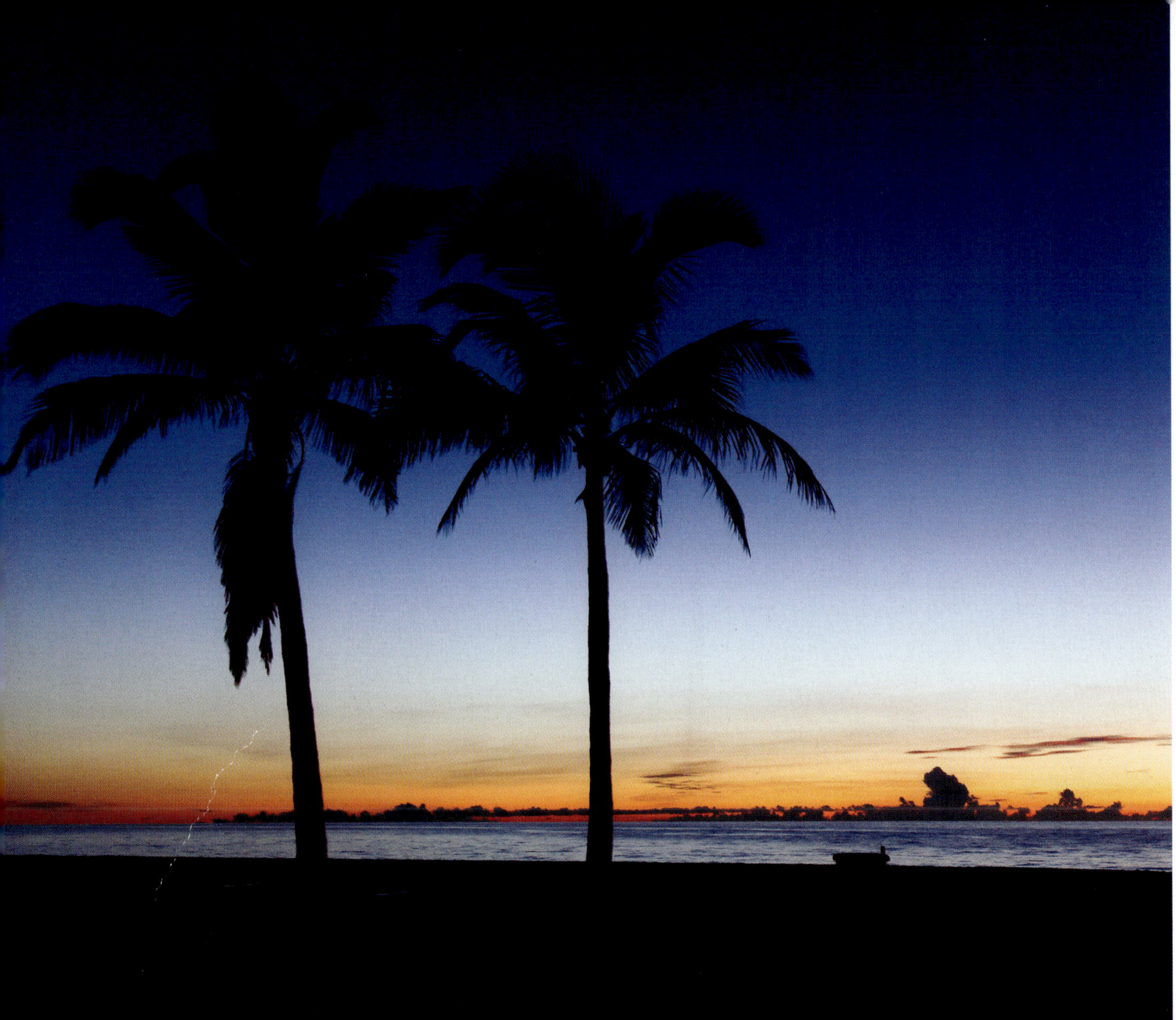

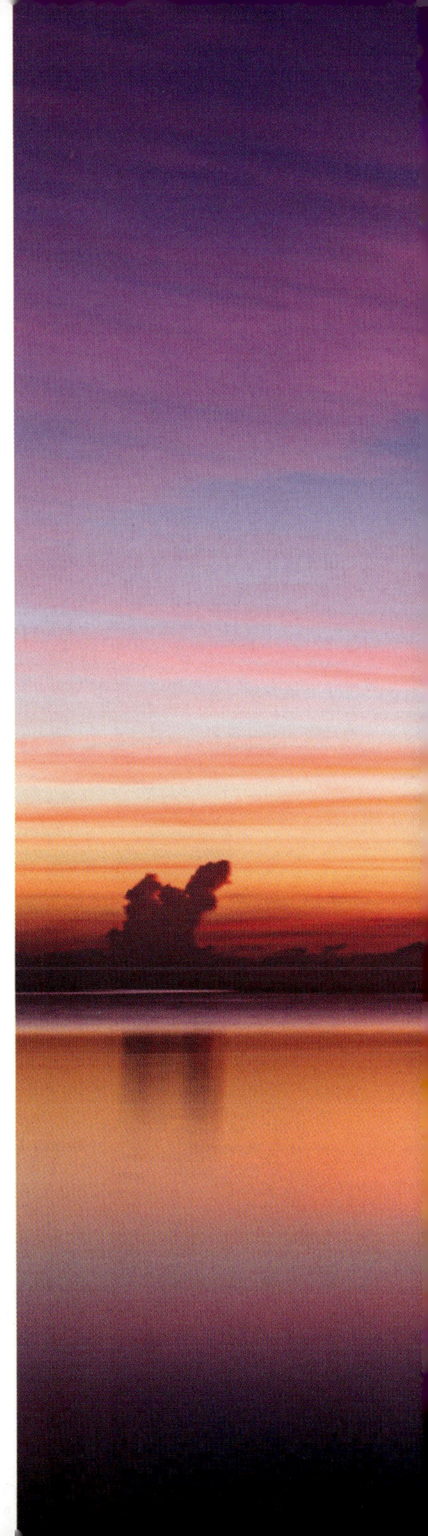

The most varied and stylish colors are almost always before the sunrise. A good reason to wake up even earlier.

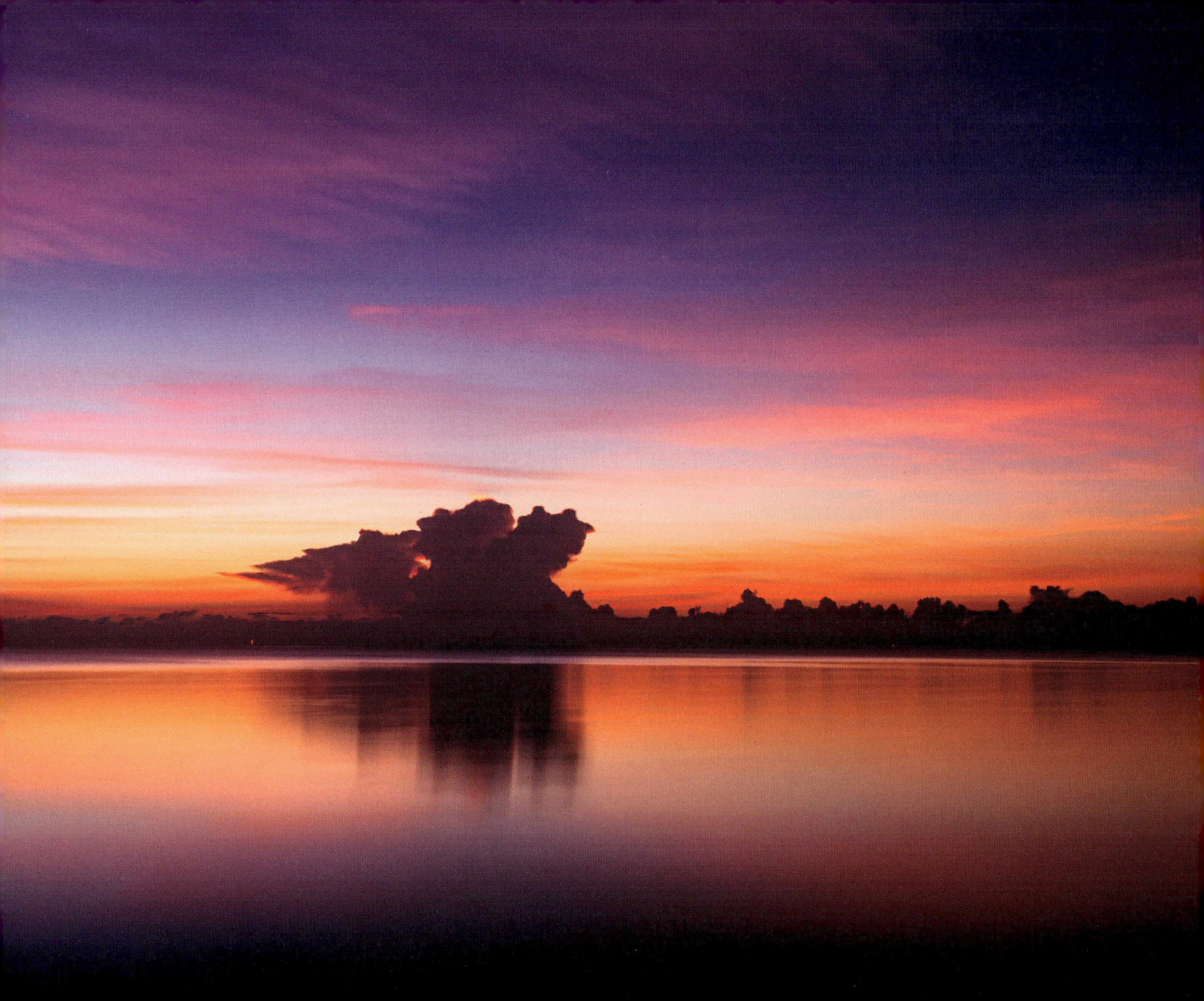

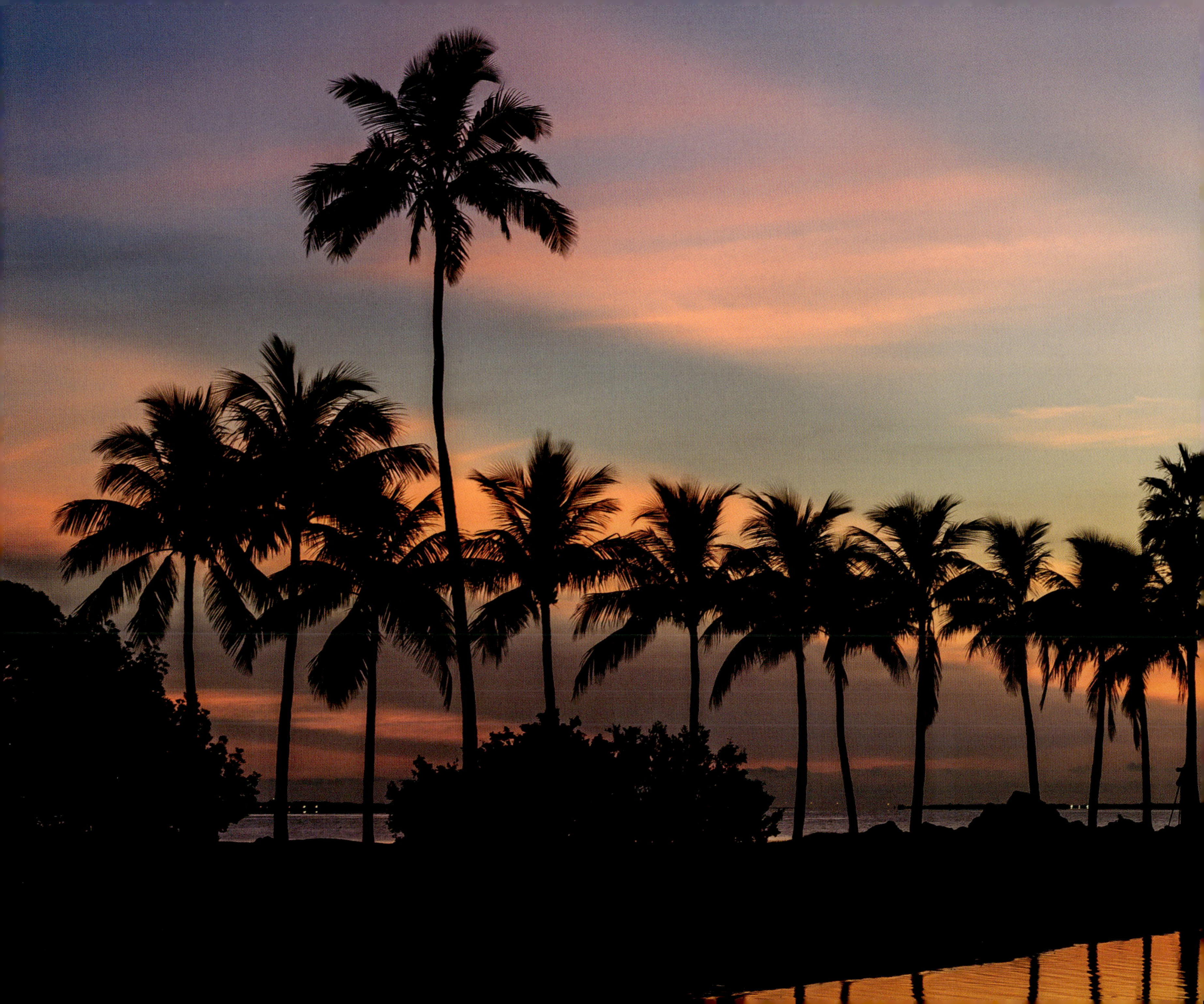

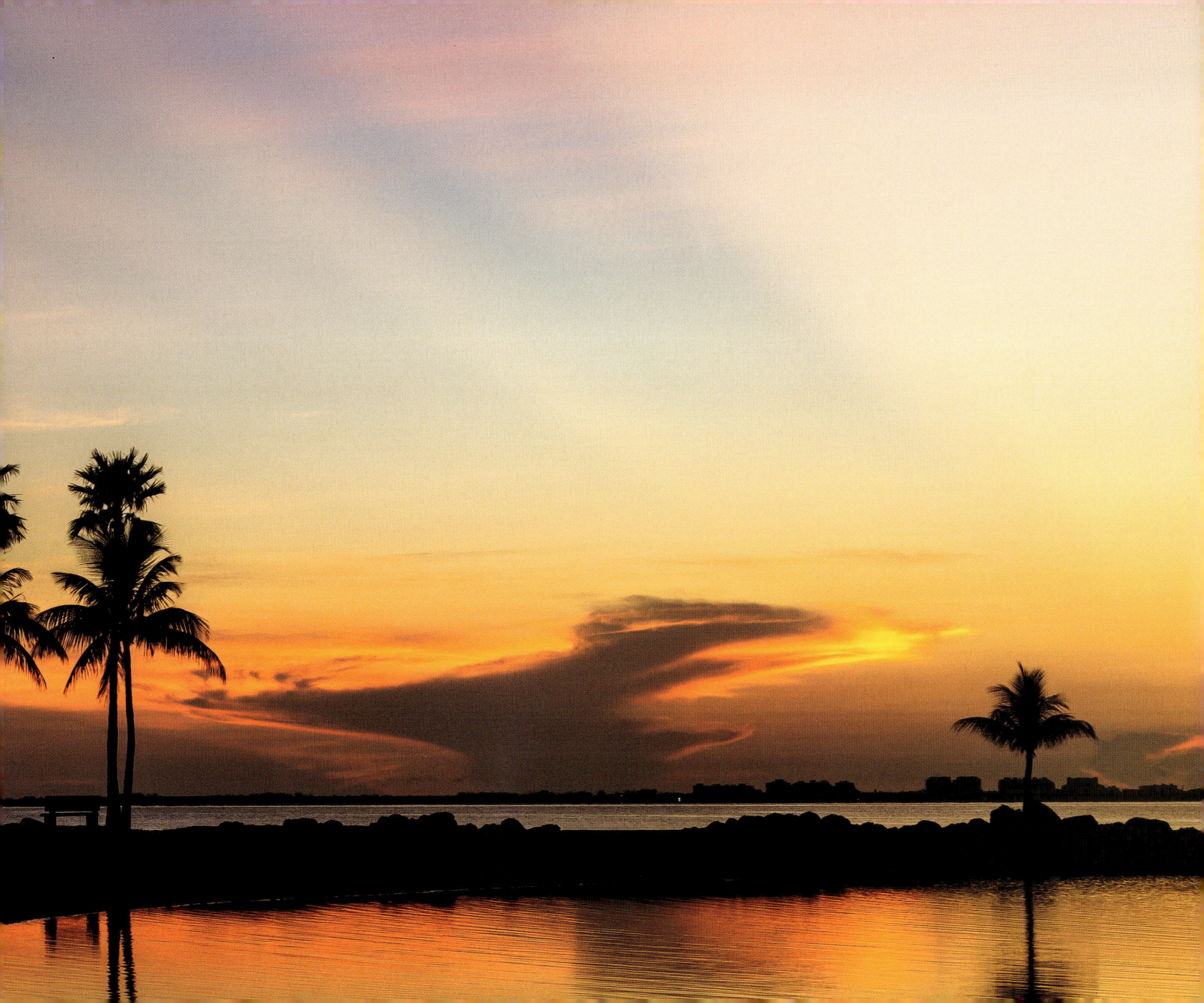

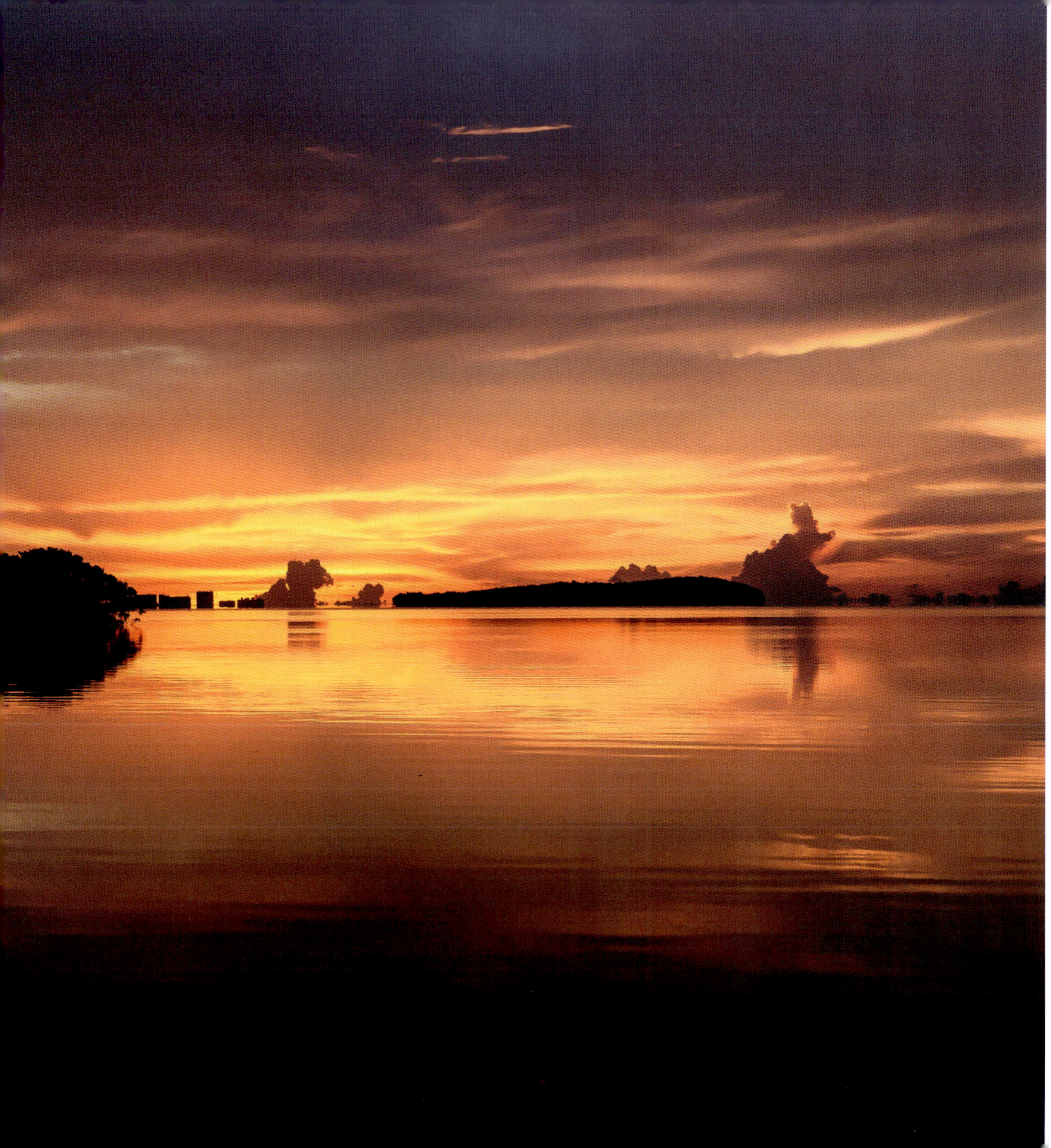
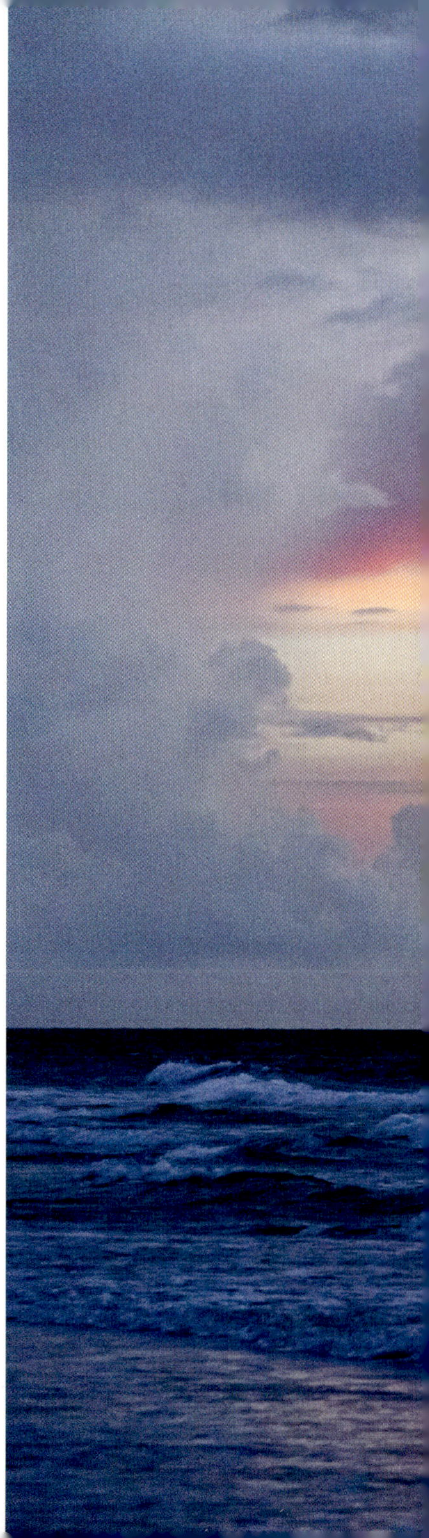

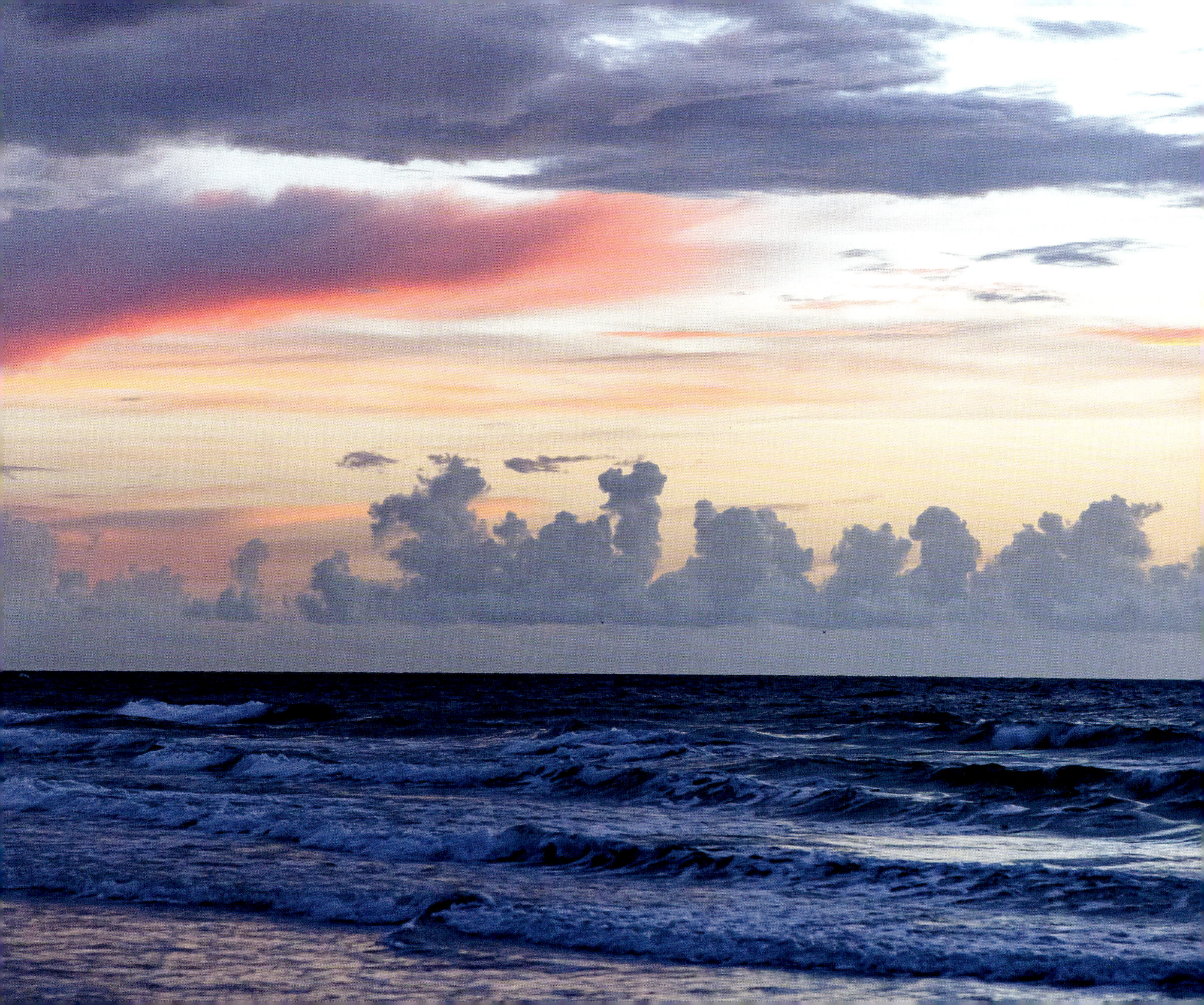

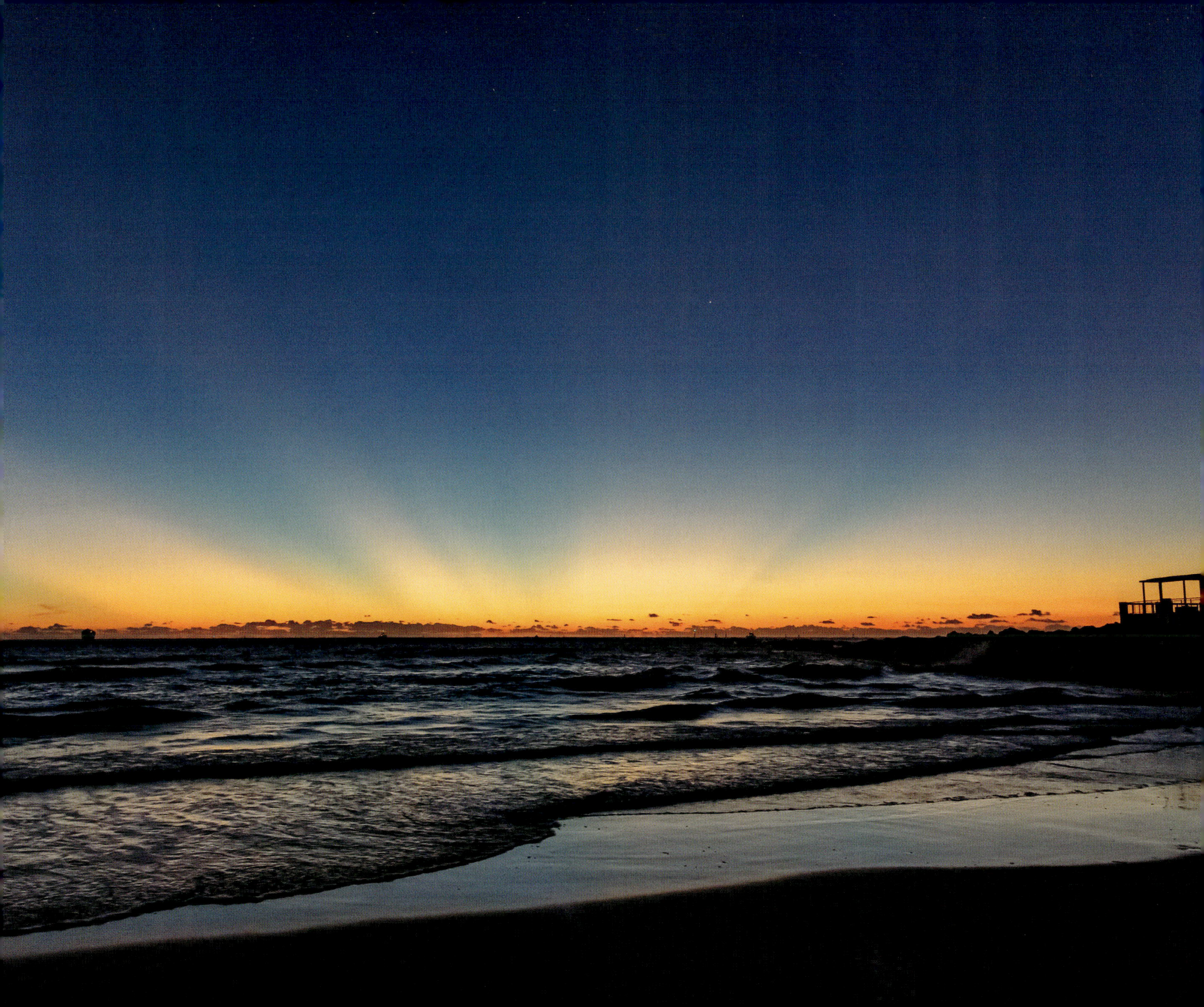

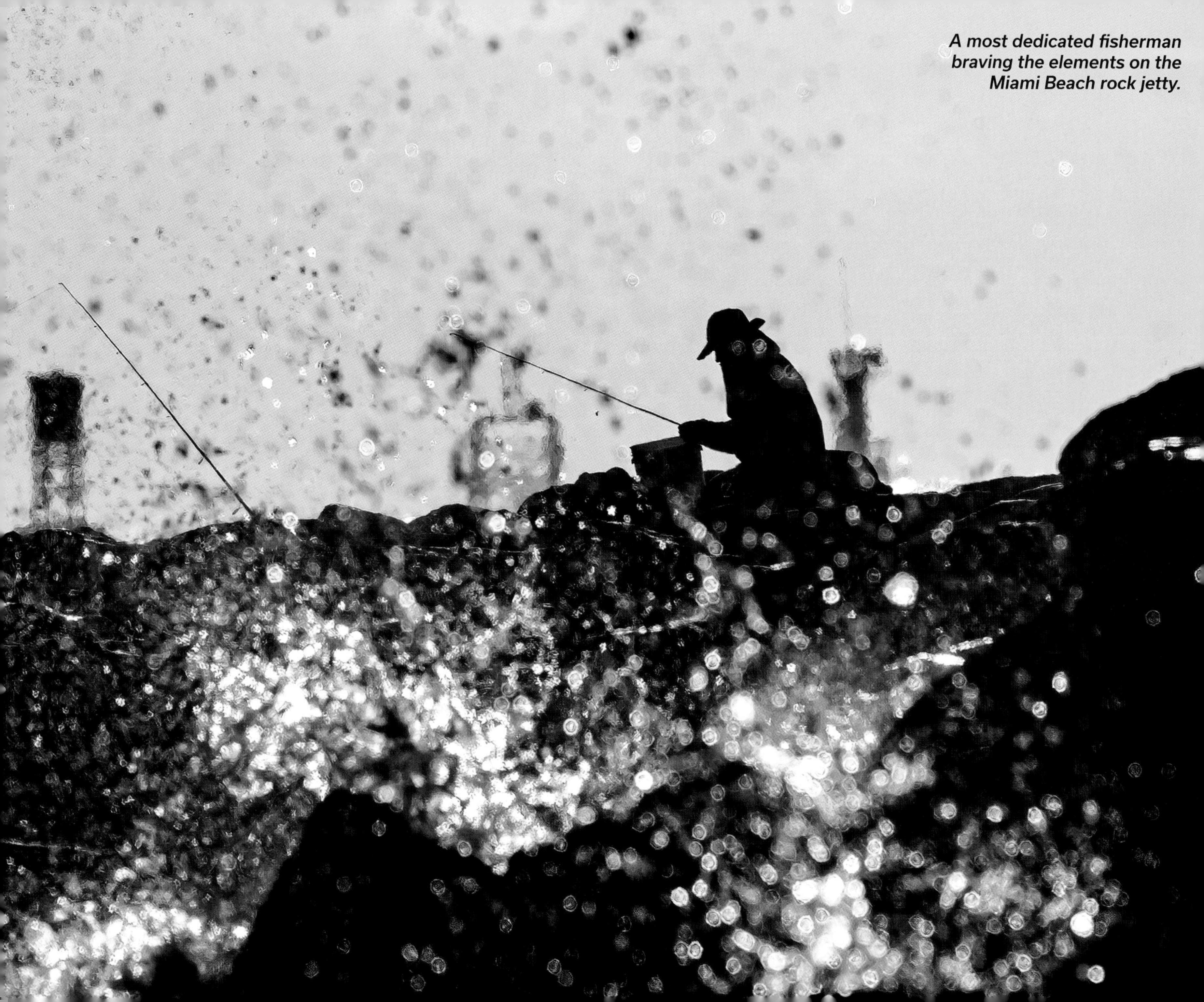

A most dedicated fisherman braving the elements on the Miami Beach rock jetty.

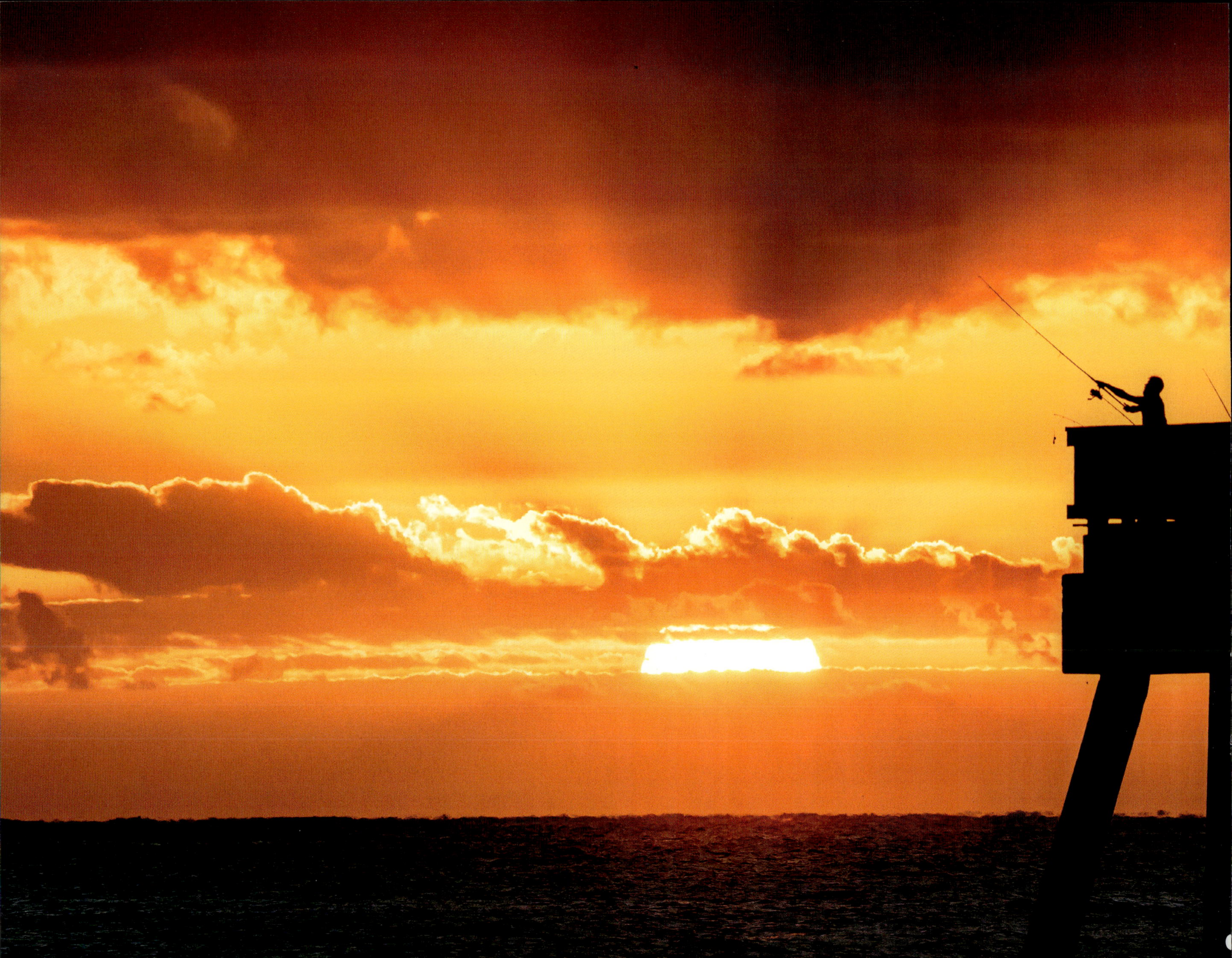

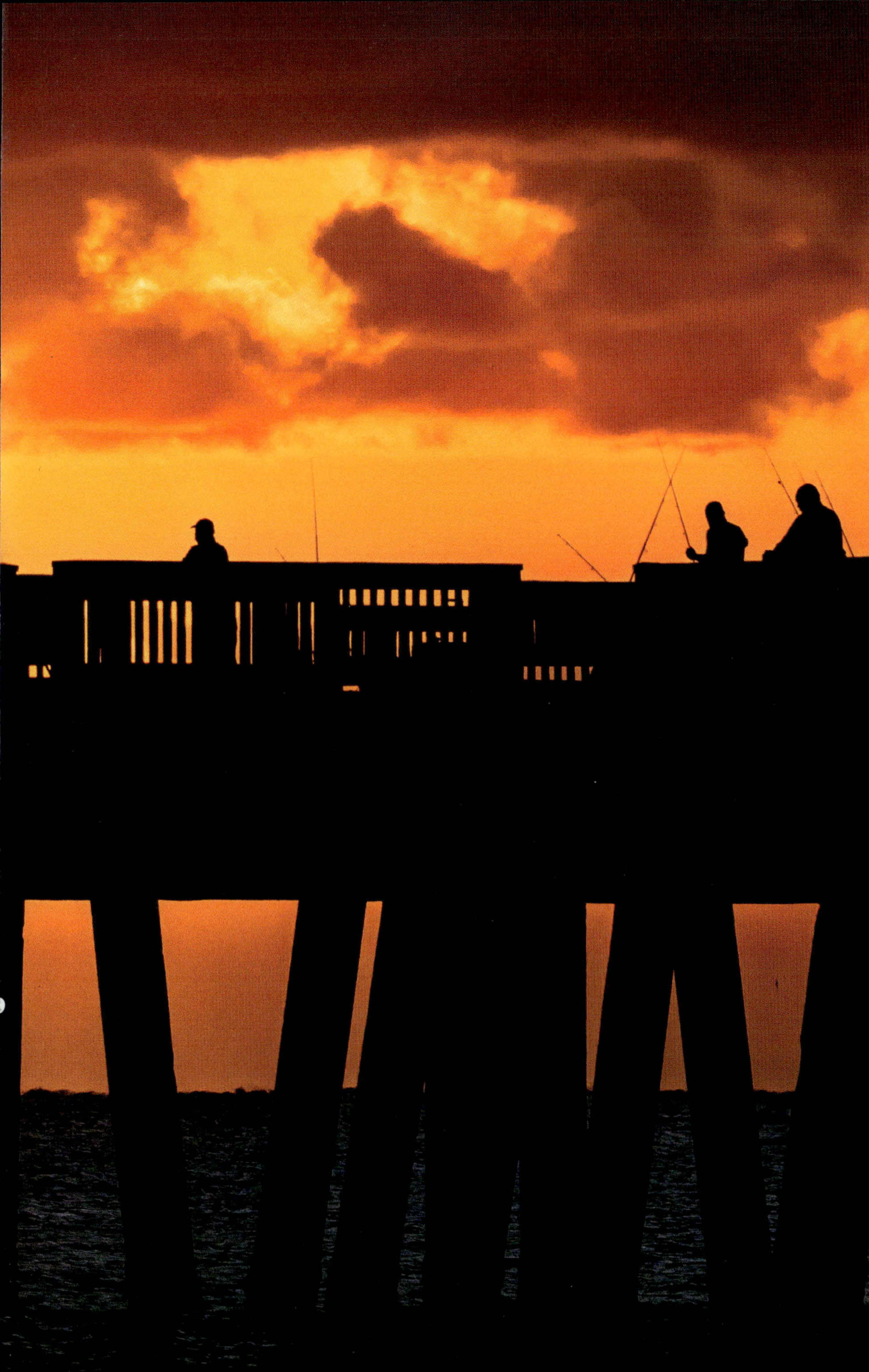

Sunrise and the Morning Celebration

The beauty of patiently waiting to experience the sunrise on a shoreline is that when the earth finally turns just far enough, you are rewarded with a brilliant celestial glow that has been worshiped for all the ages. You, too, now join the ancestral chain. That hot, glowing ember on the horizon is welcoming and exciting to see, and it means we are heading for a new beginning. The sunrise symbolizes healing, restoration, strength, hope, warmth, redemption and a second chance. It also comforts us with the knowledge that no matter what we think and do, there is always something big and bright out there upon which we can always rely.

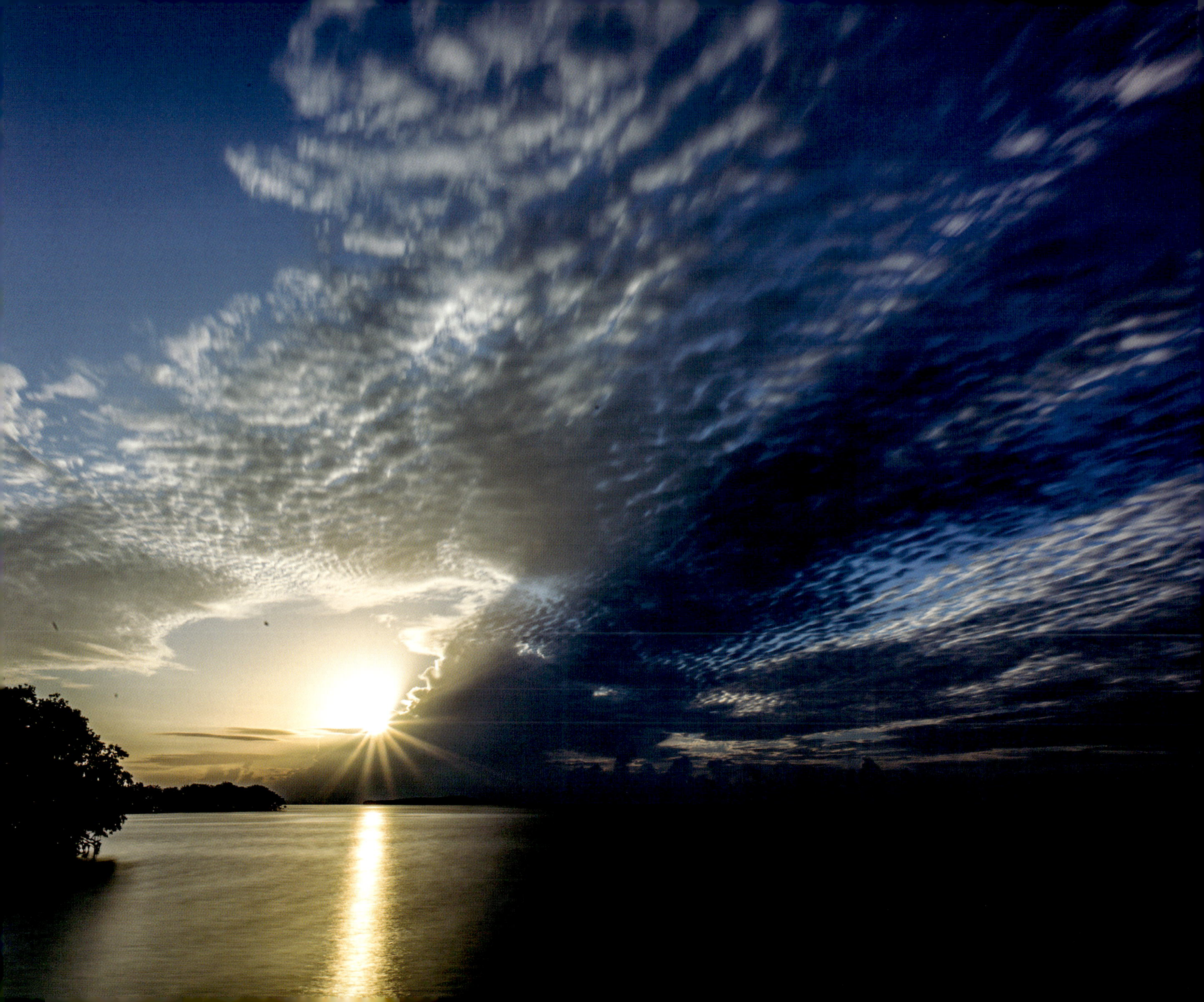

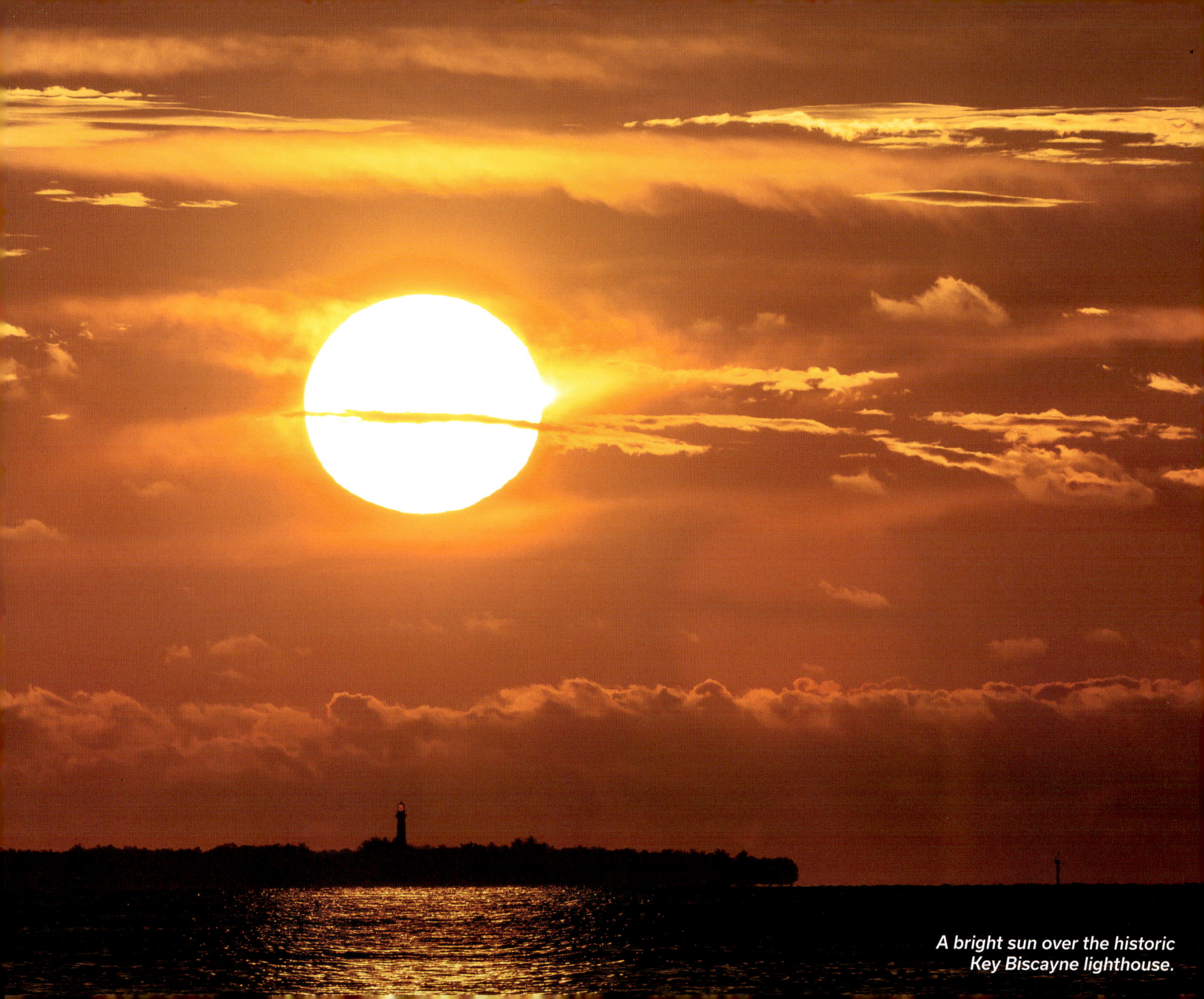

A bright sun over the historic Key Biscayne lighthouse.

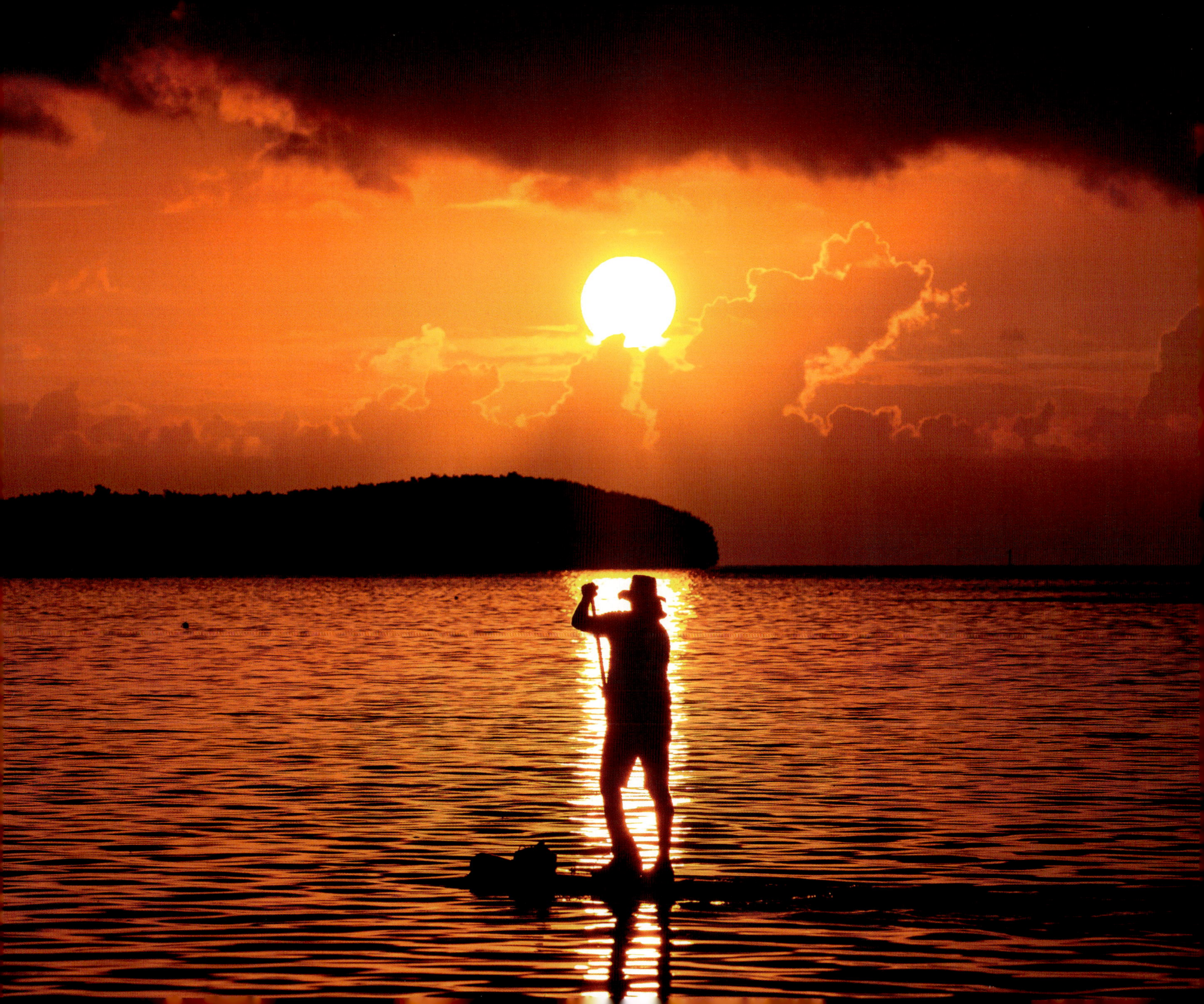

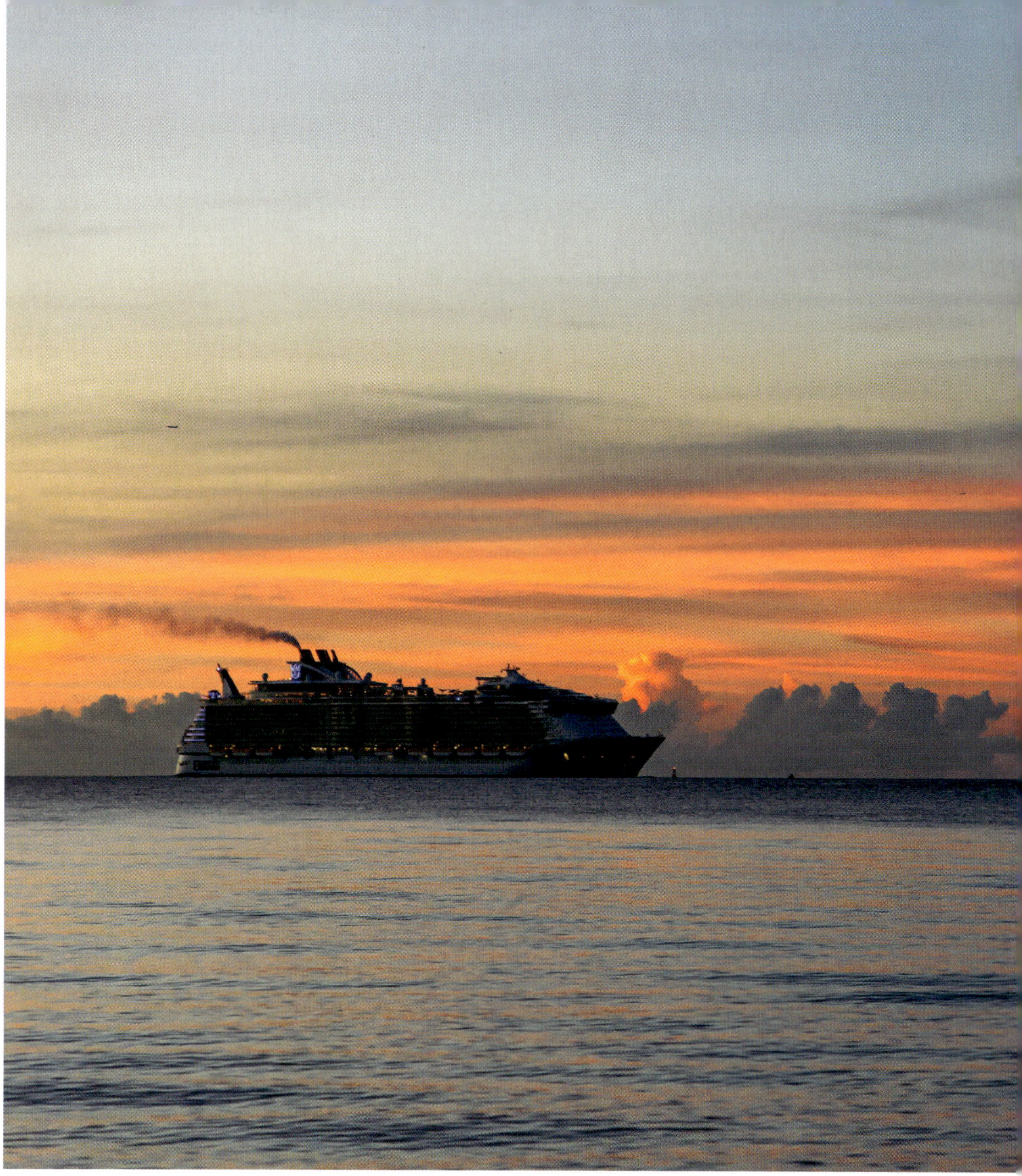

Bathed in light and paddling toward the sun in Miami's Biscayne Bay.

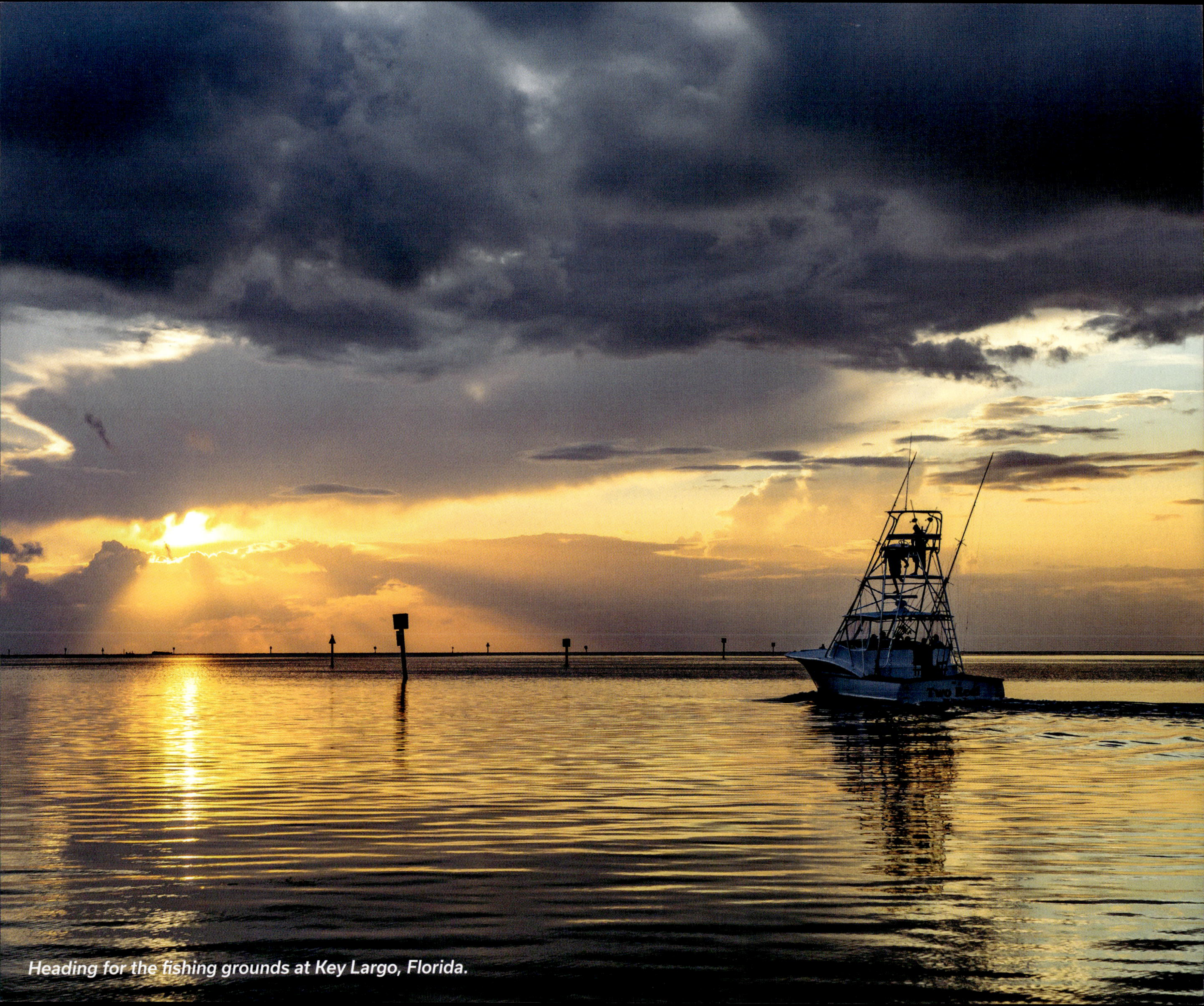

Heading for the fishing grounds at Key Largo, Florida.

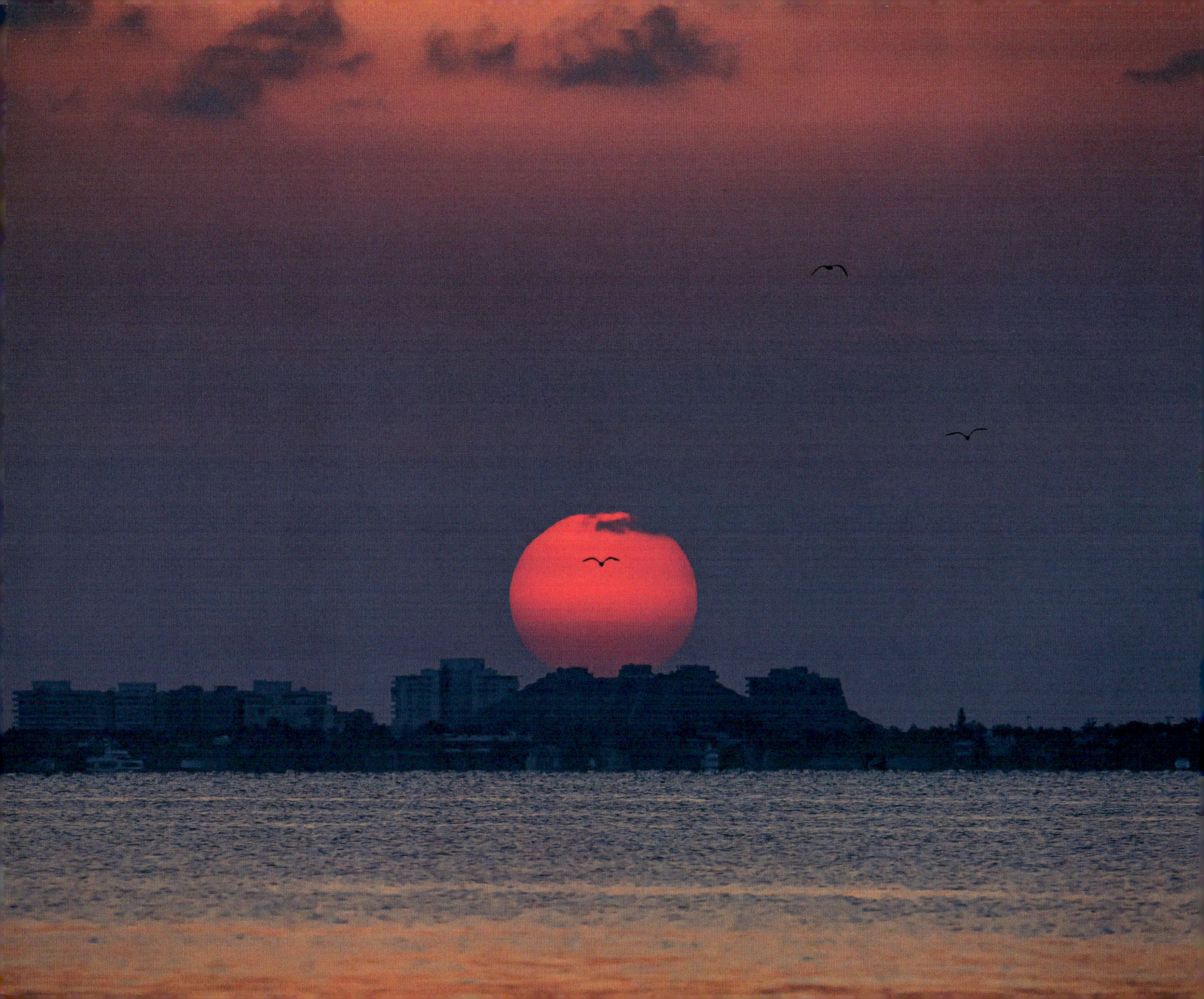

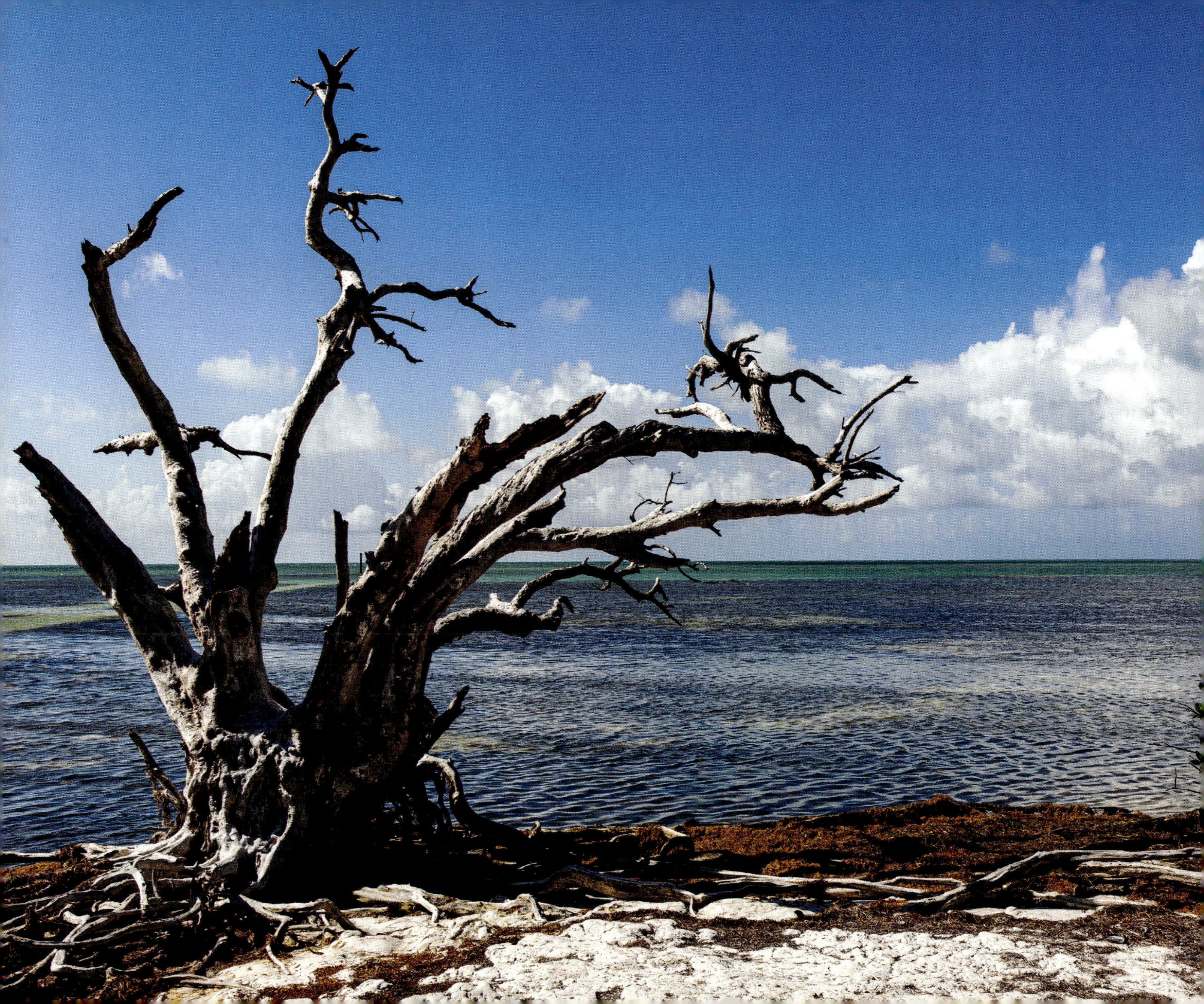

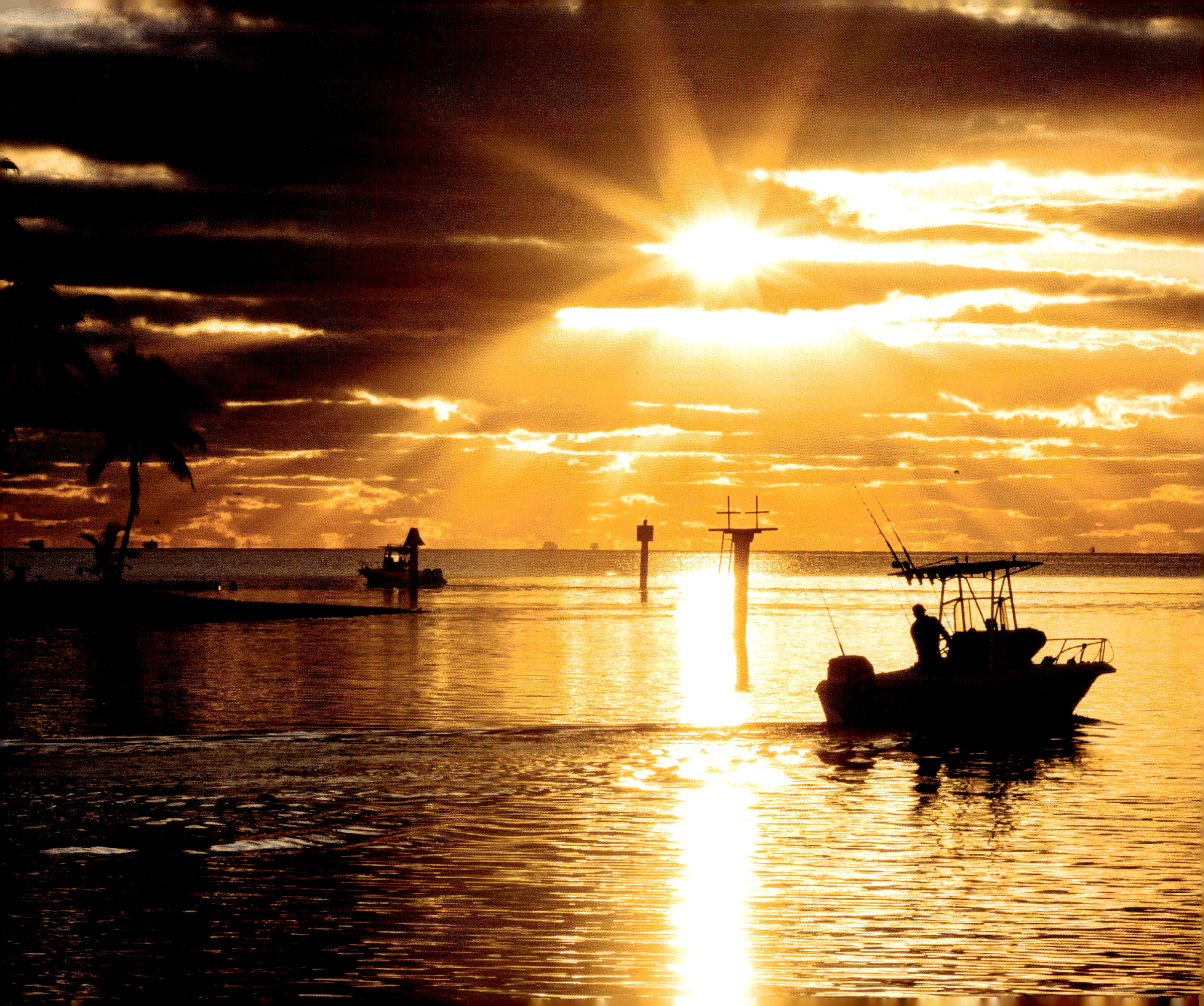

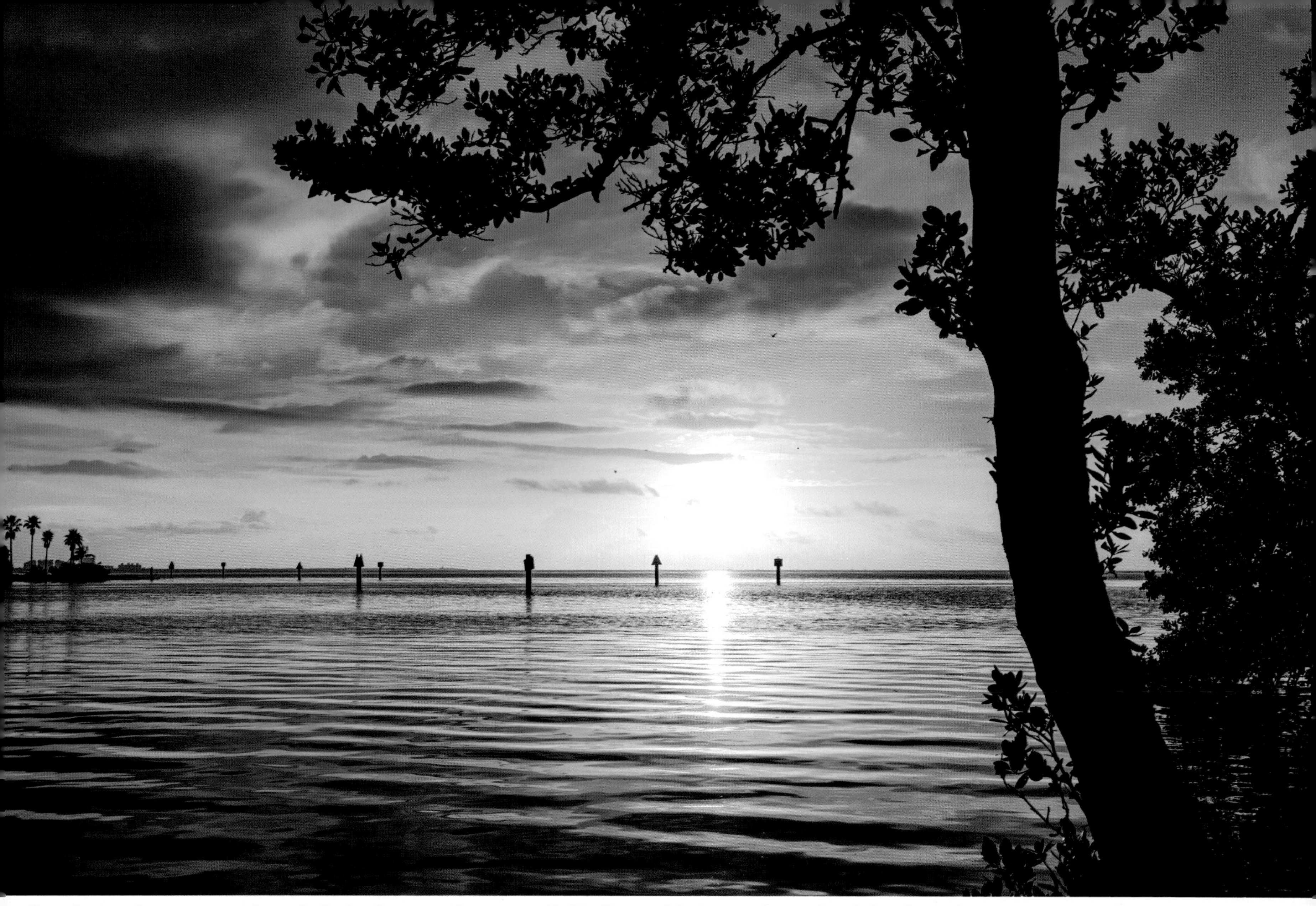

On a hot and sunny morning, dark shadows on the waves (left). On a cold-air morning, mist rising from the warmer water (right).

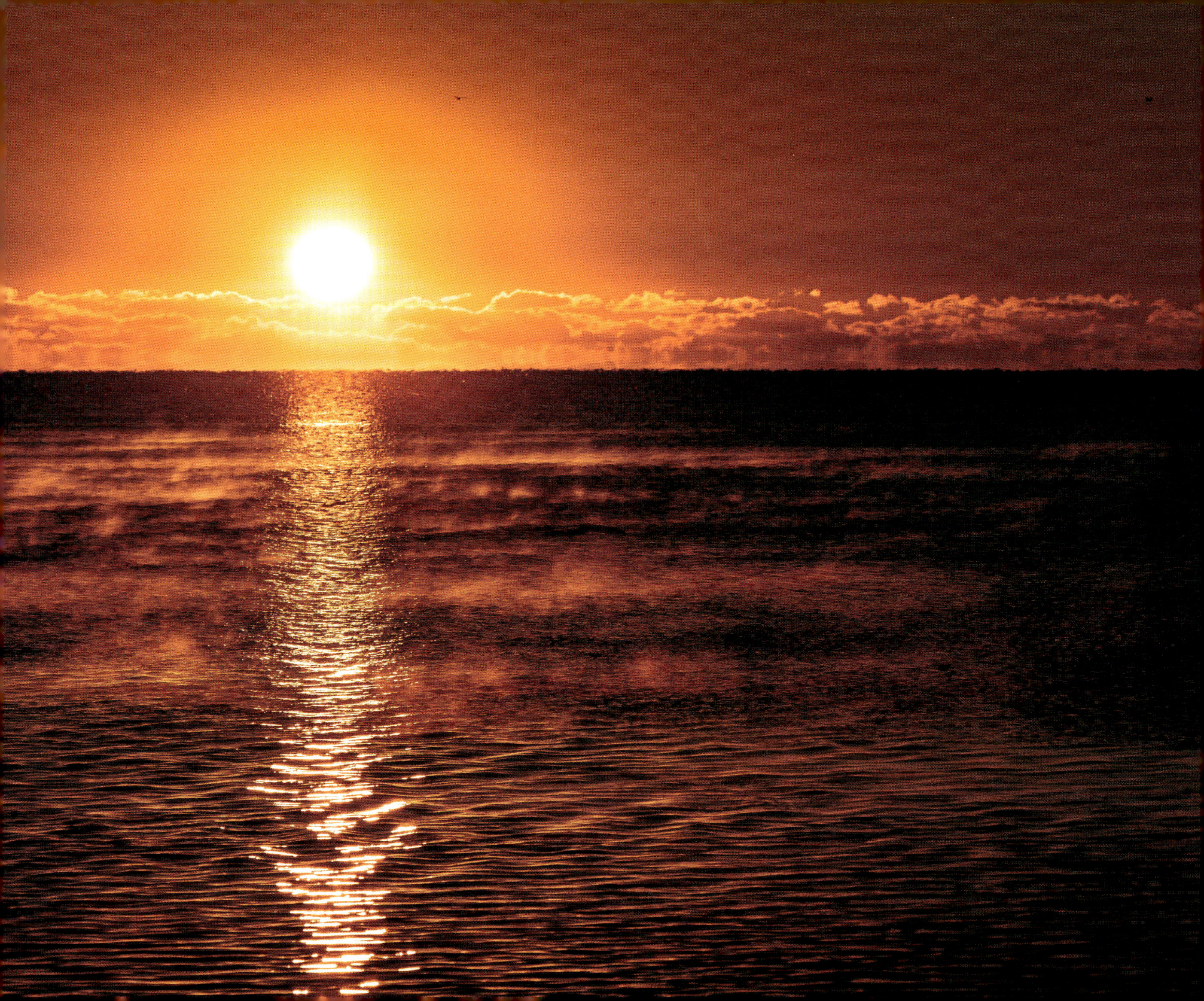

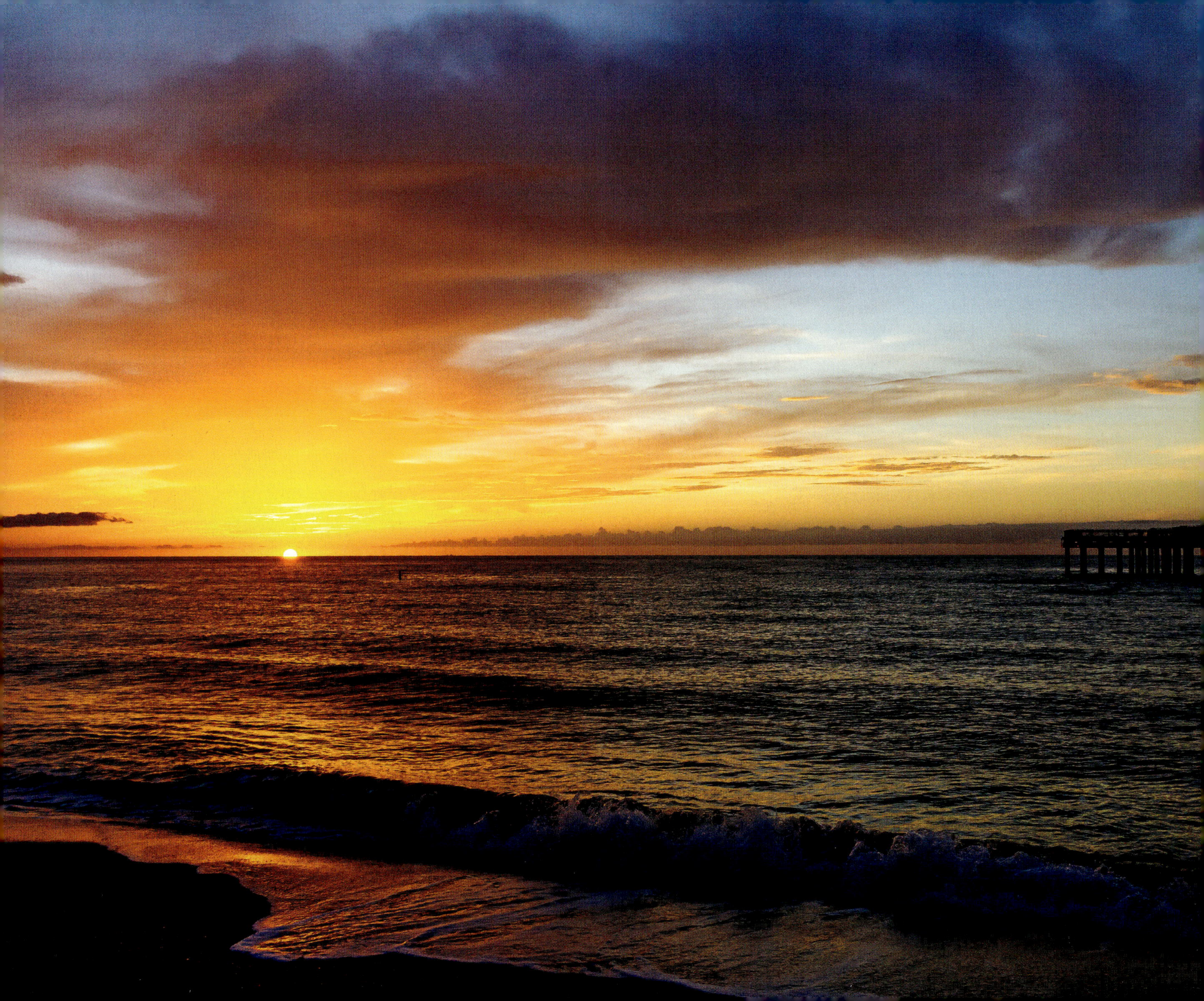

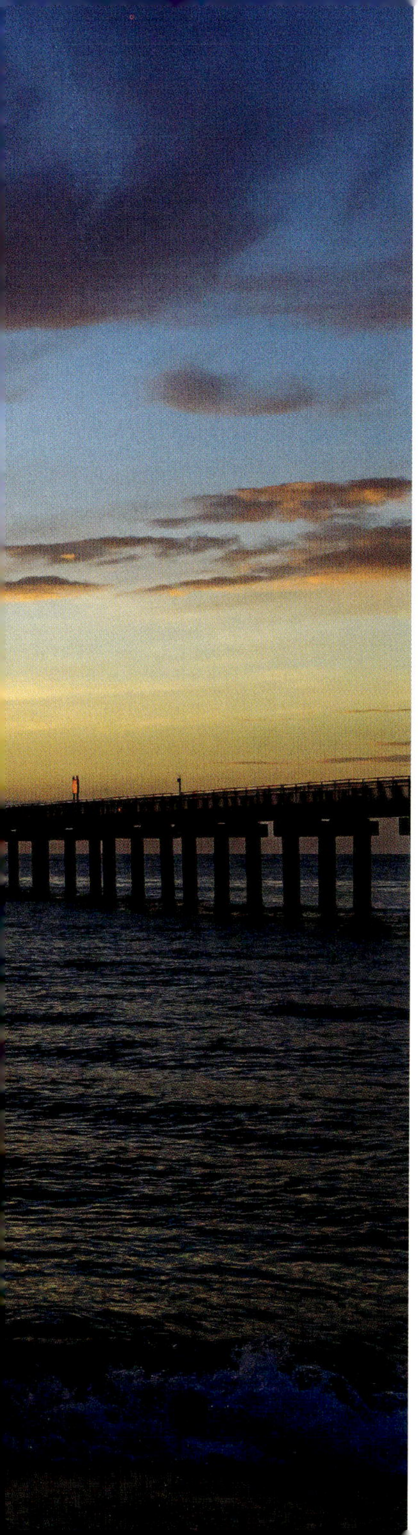

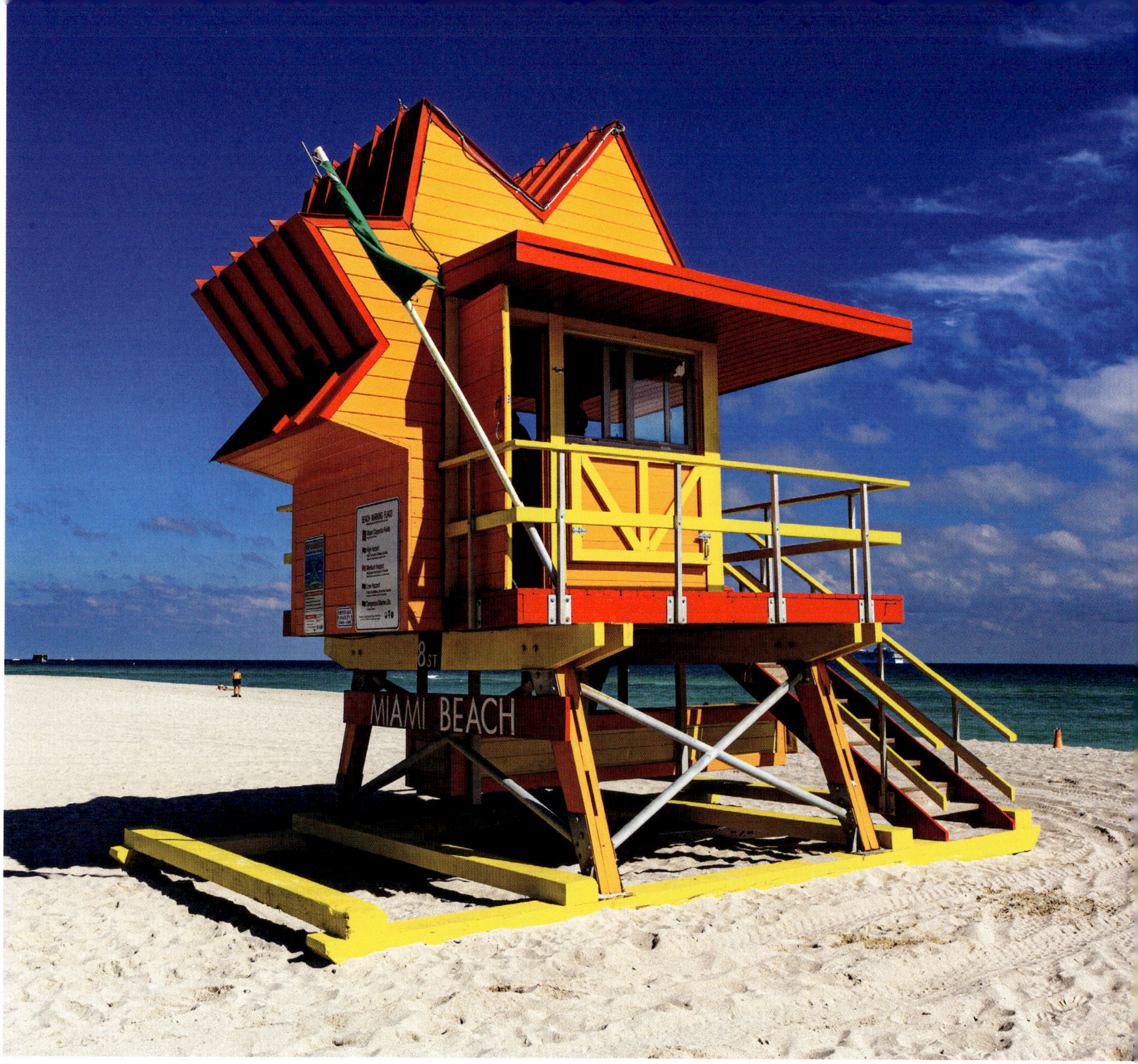

One of the many whimsical and colorful Art Deco lifeguard towers on Miami Beach.

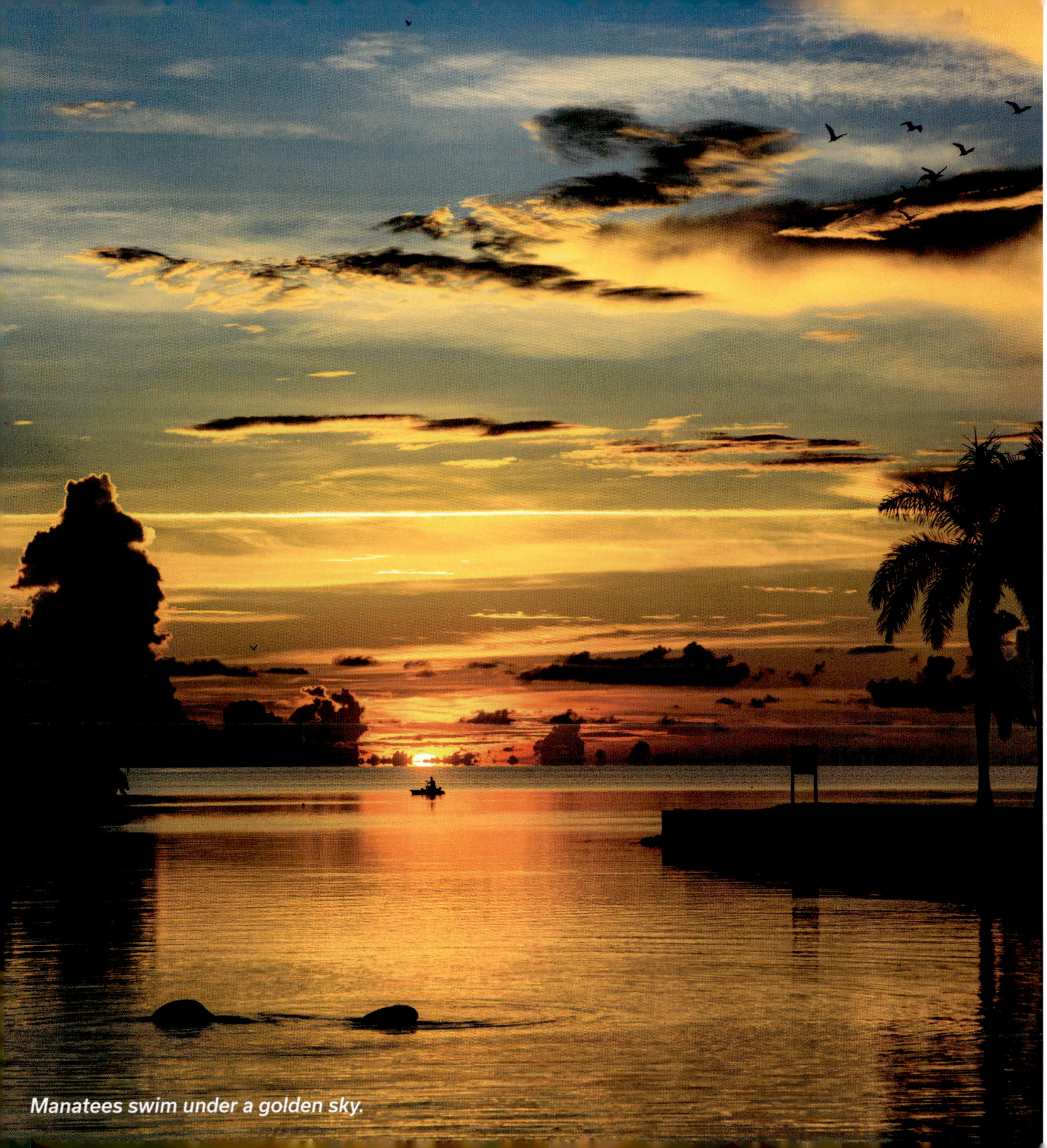

Manatees swim under a golden sky.

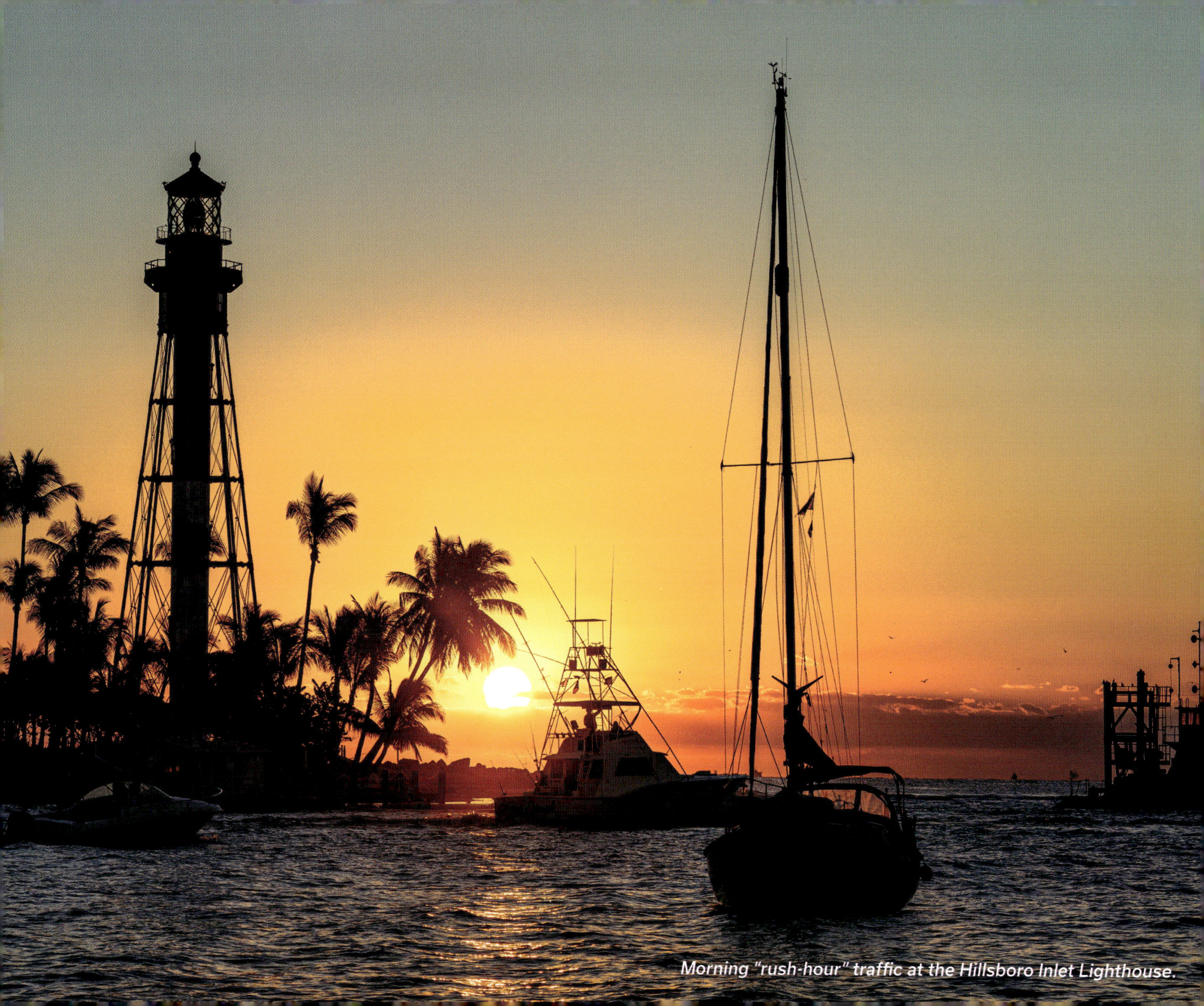

Morning "rush-hour" traffic at the Hillsboro Inlet Lighthouse.

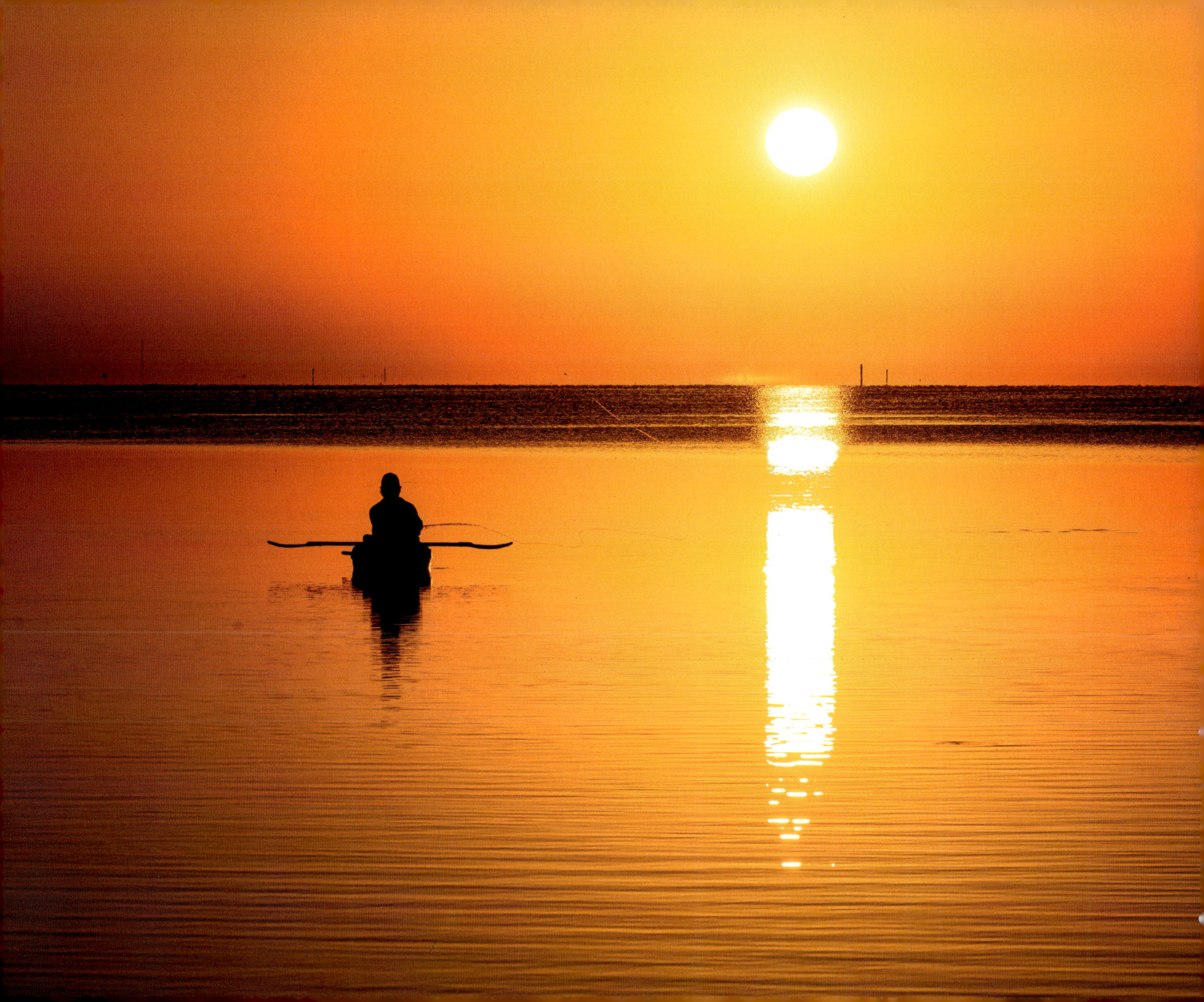

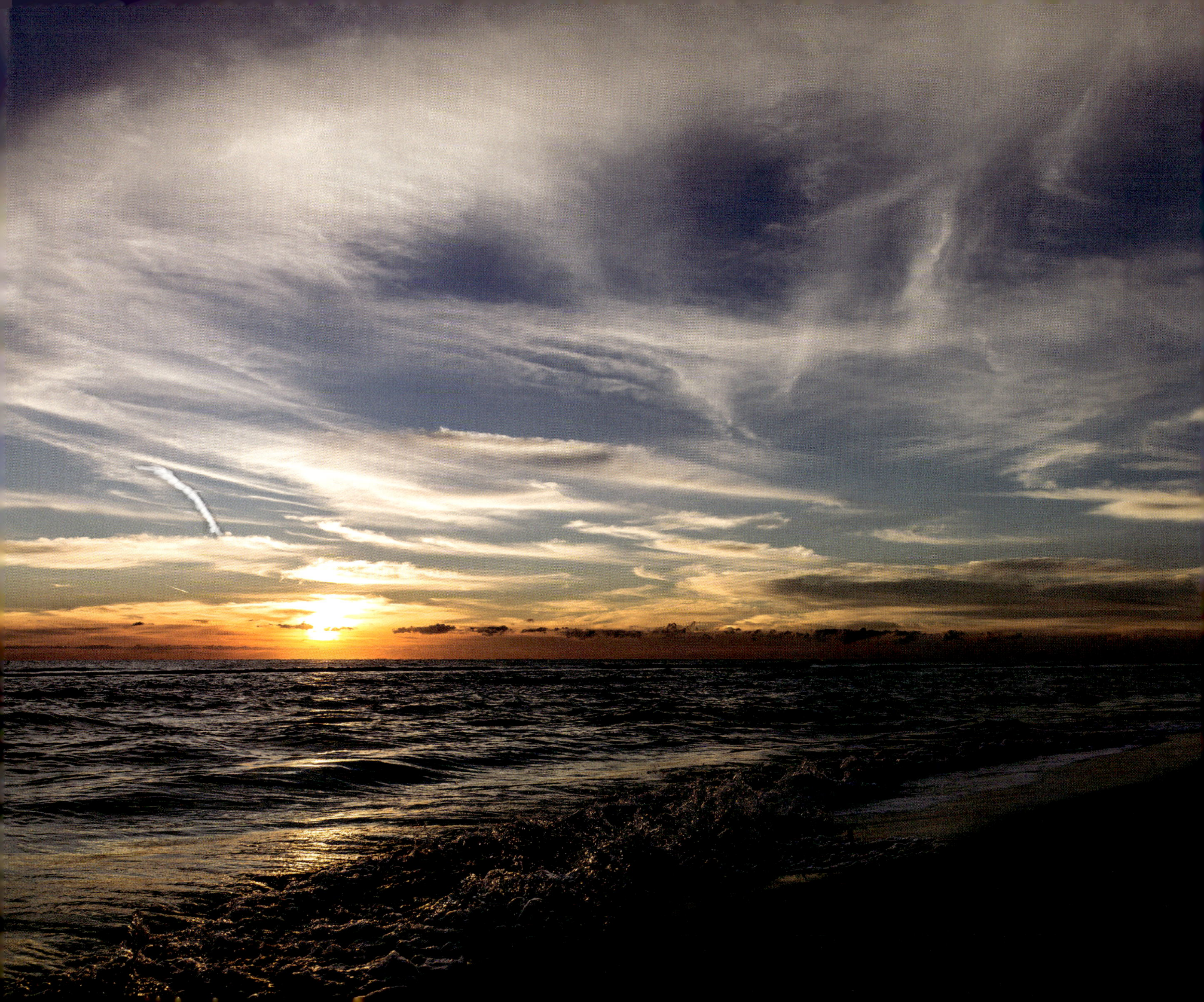

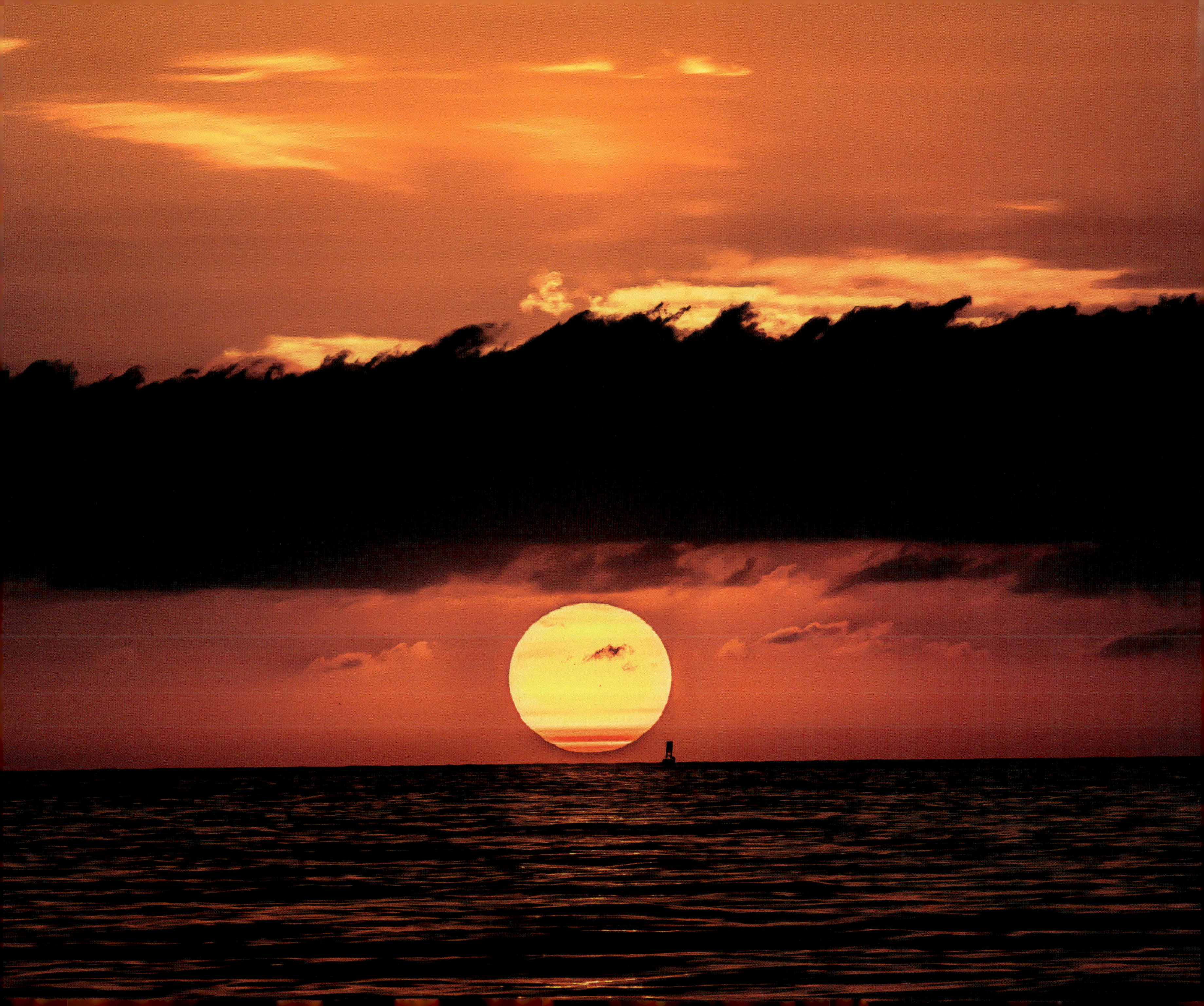

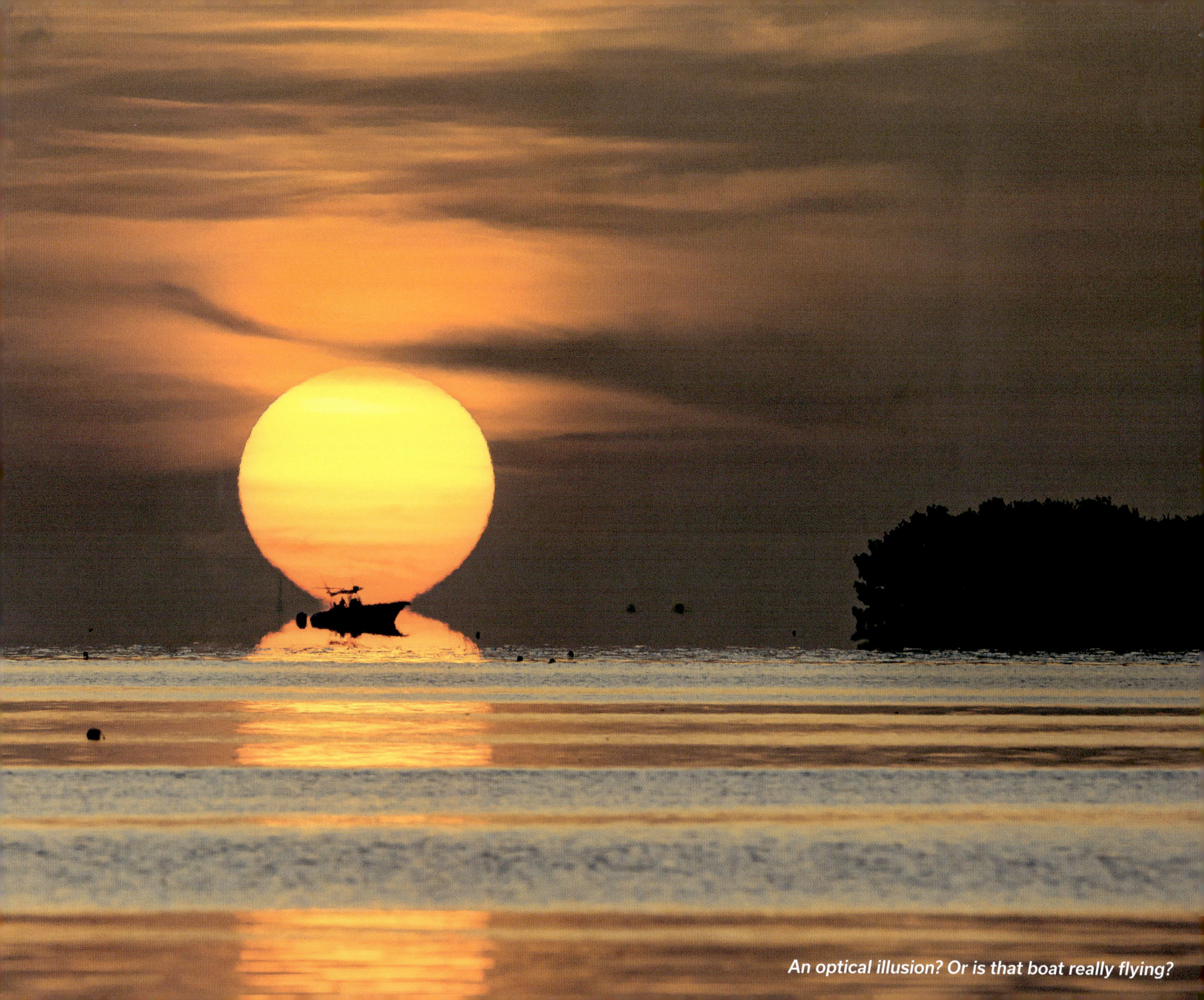

An optical illusion? Or is that boat really flying?

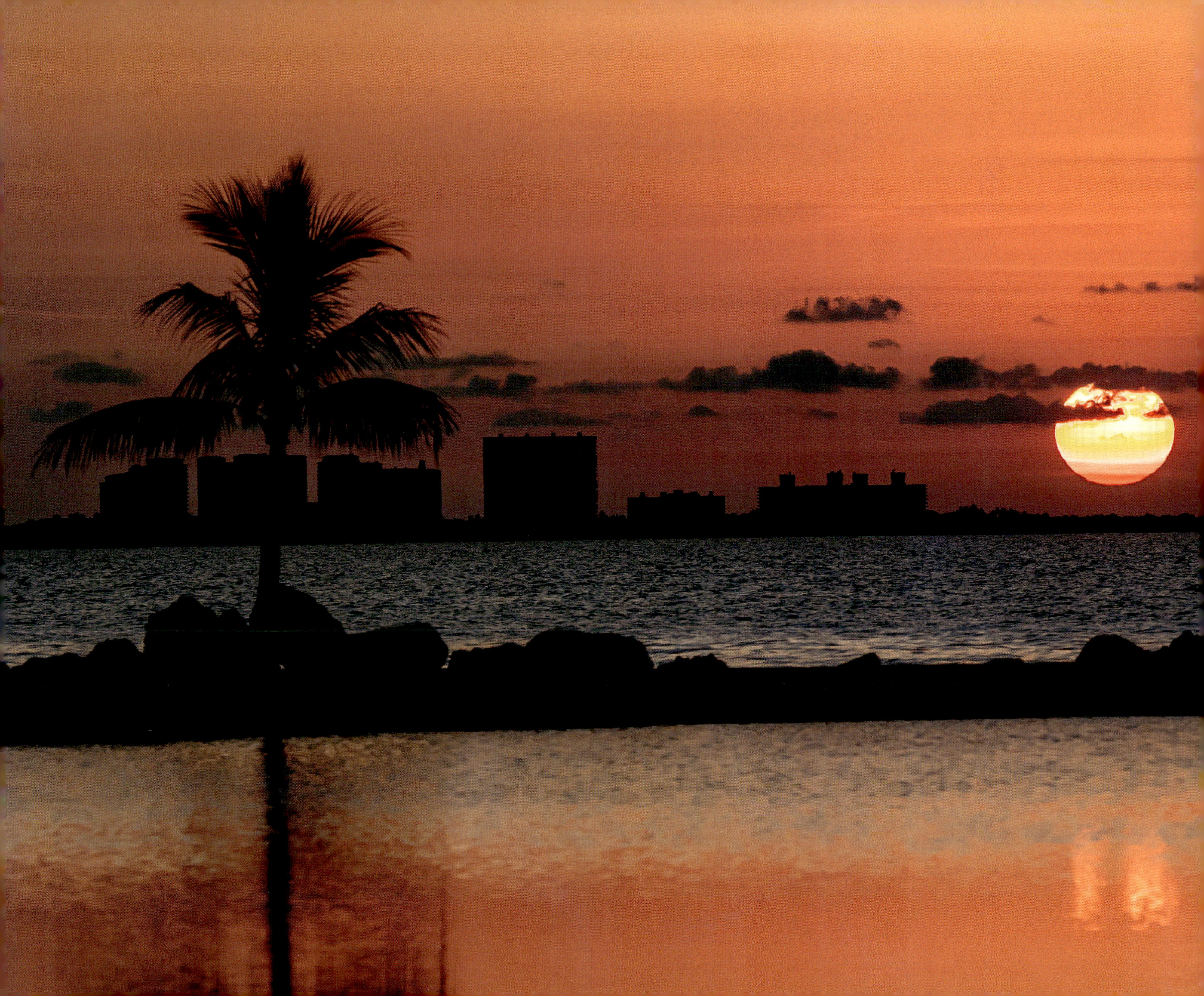

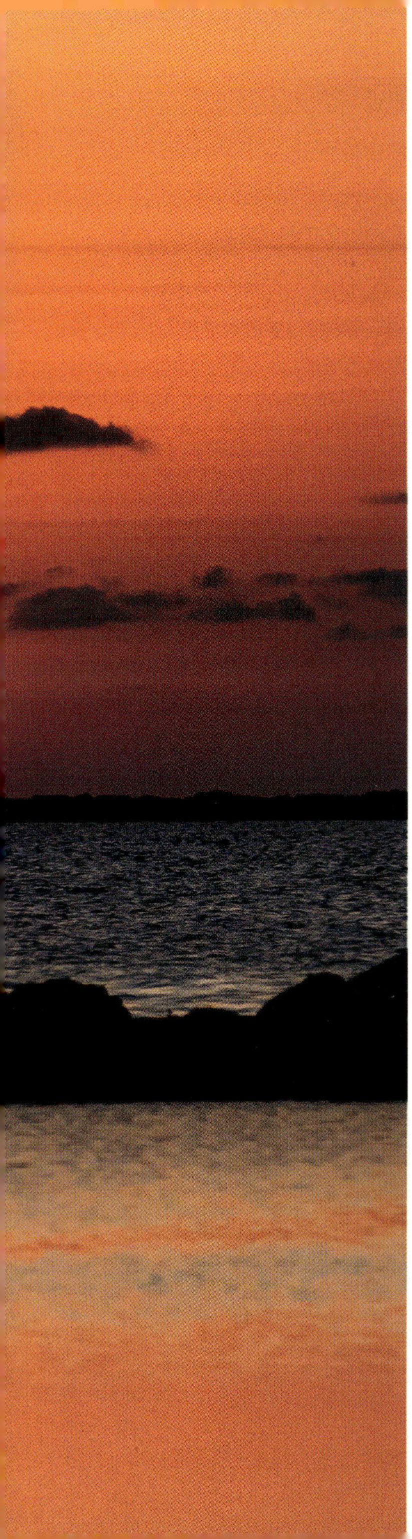

I wonder why the ibis on the right is looking down and so far backward while flying forward? The things you see out here.

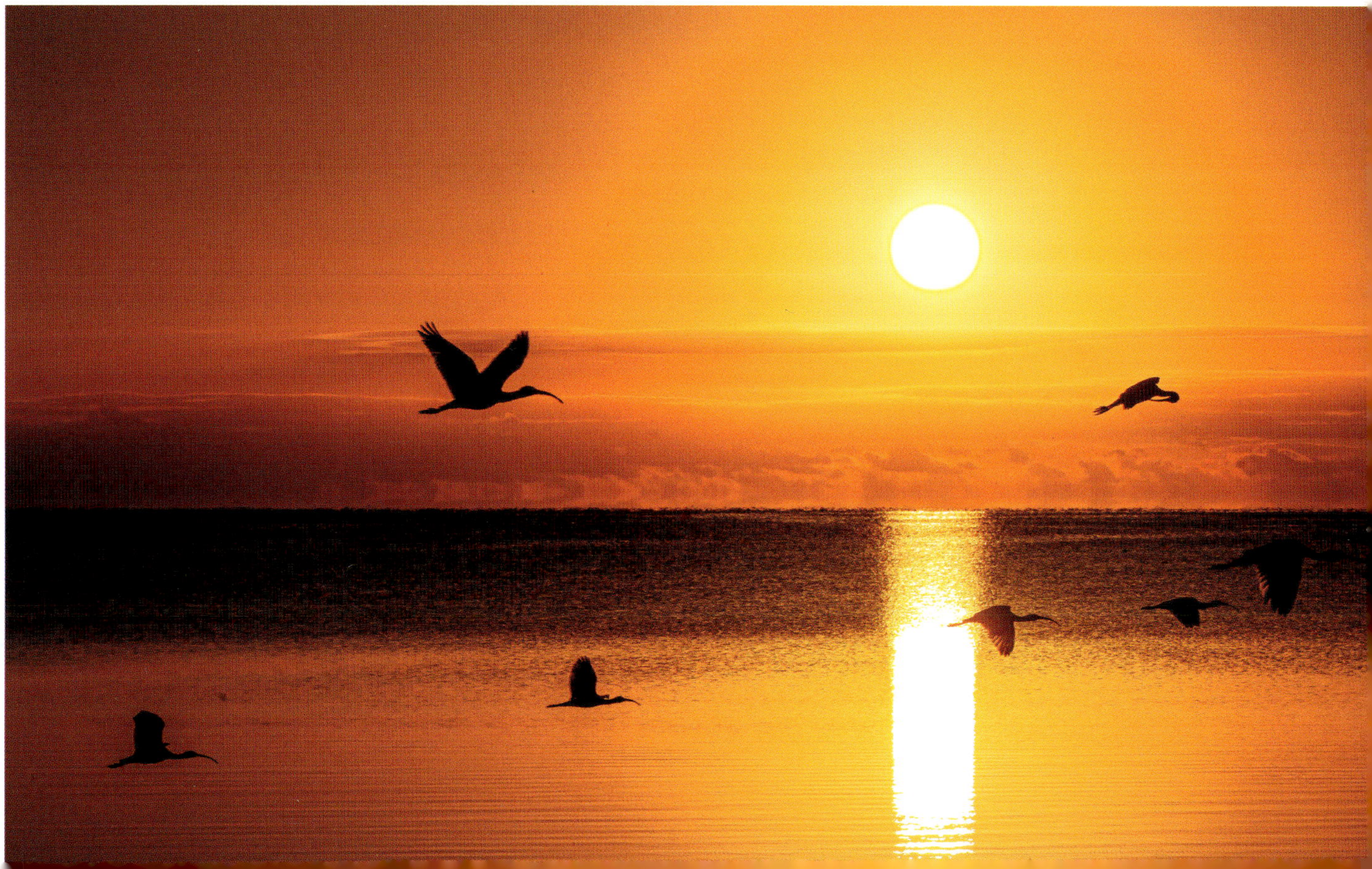

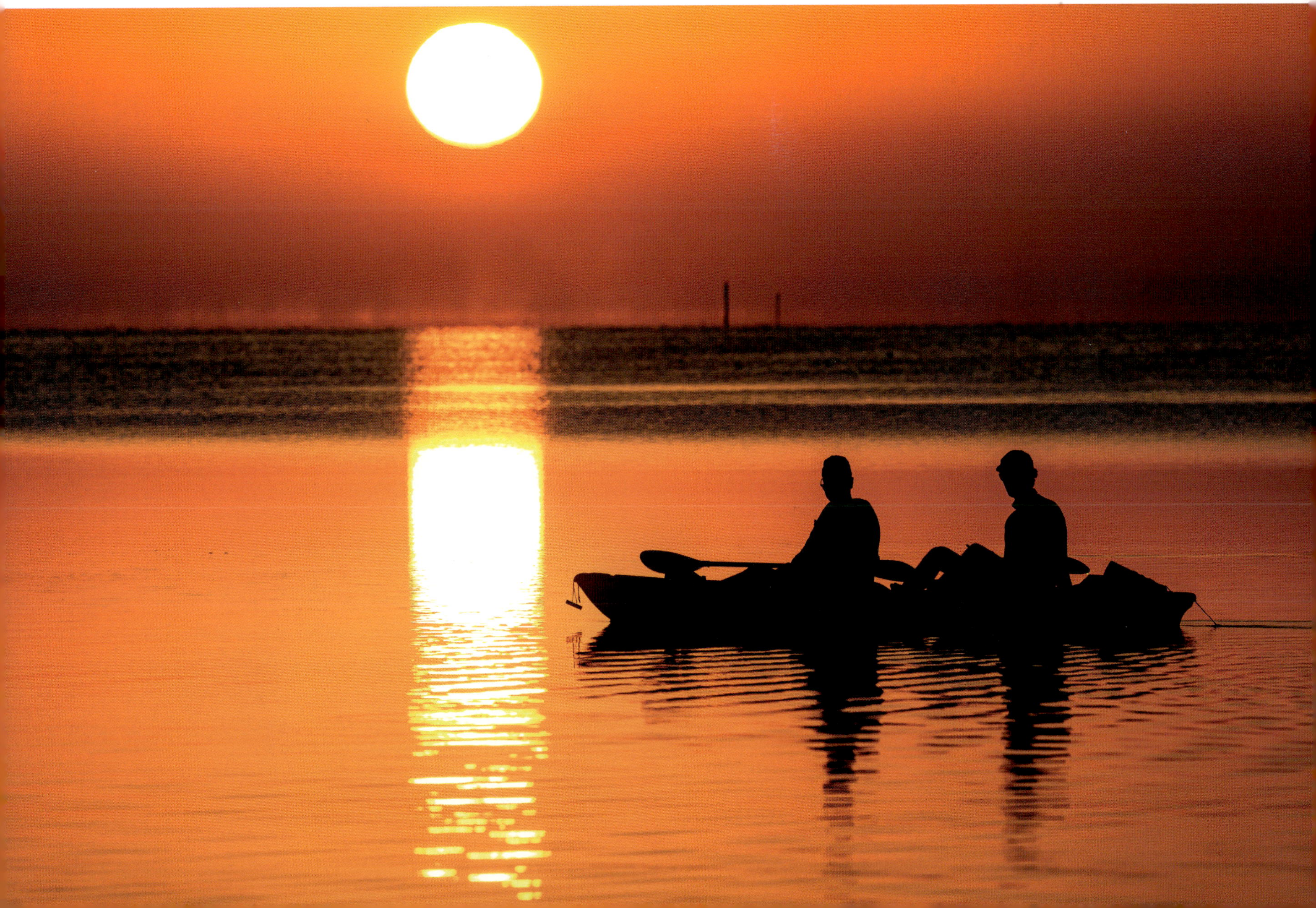

Taking a break to enjoy the view from the best seat in the house.

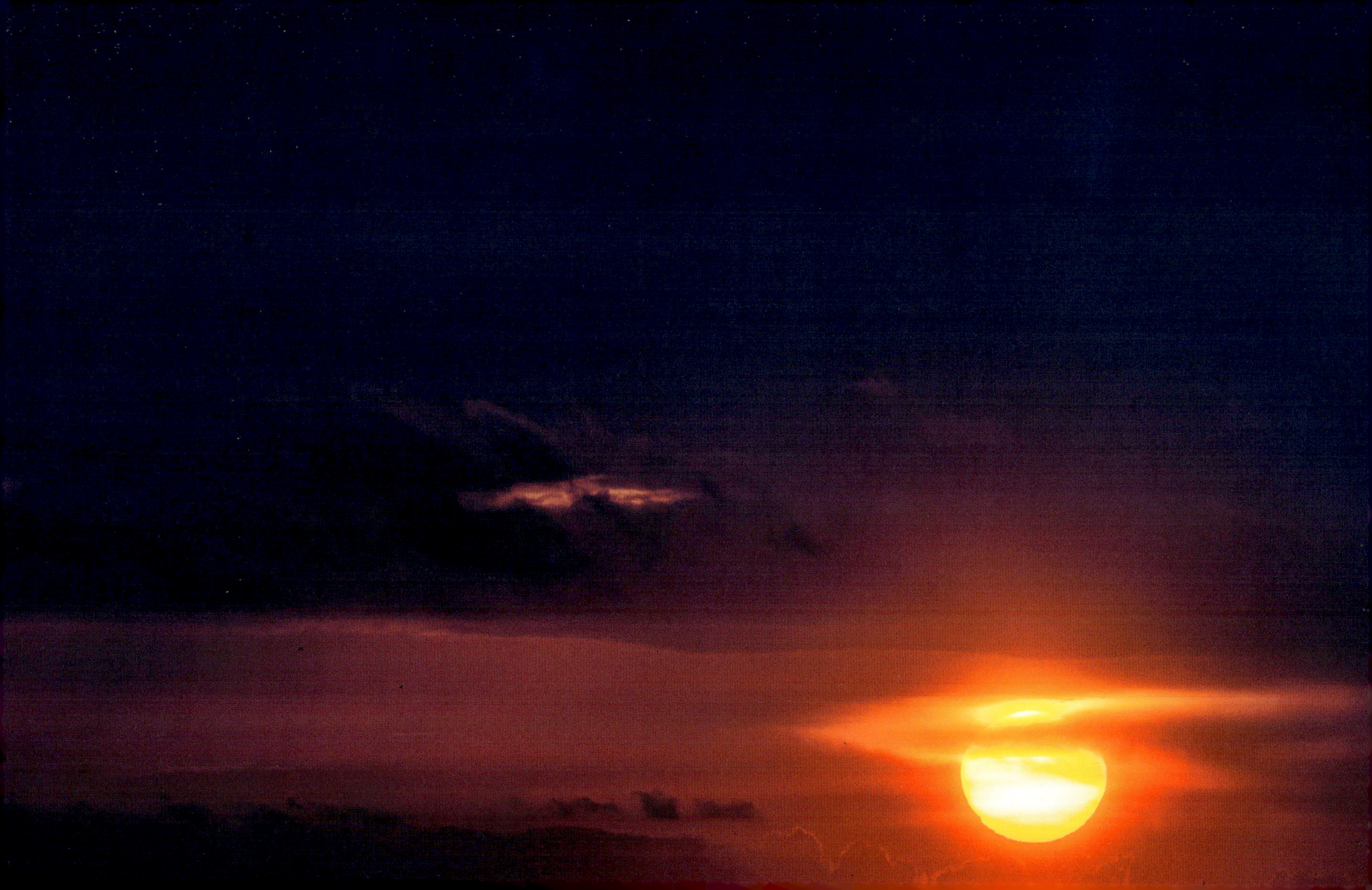

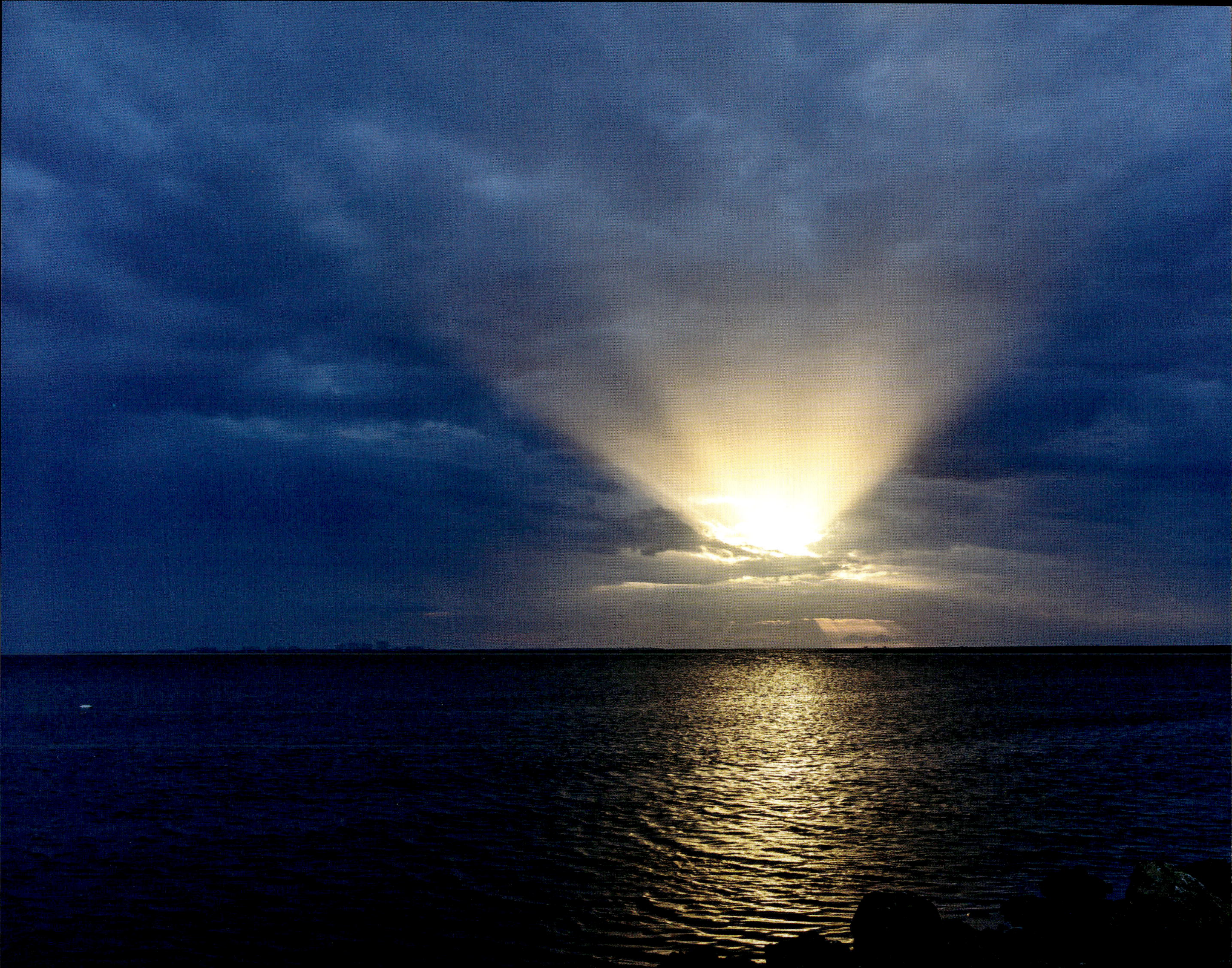

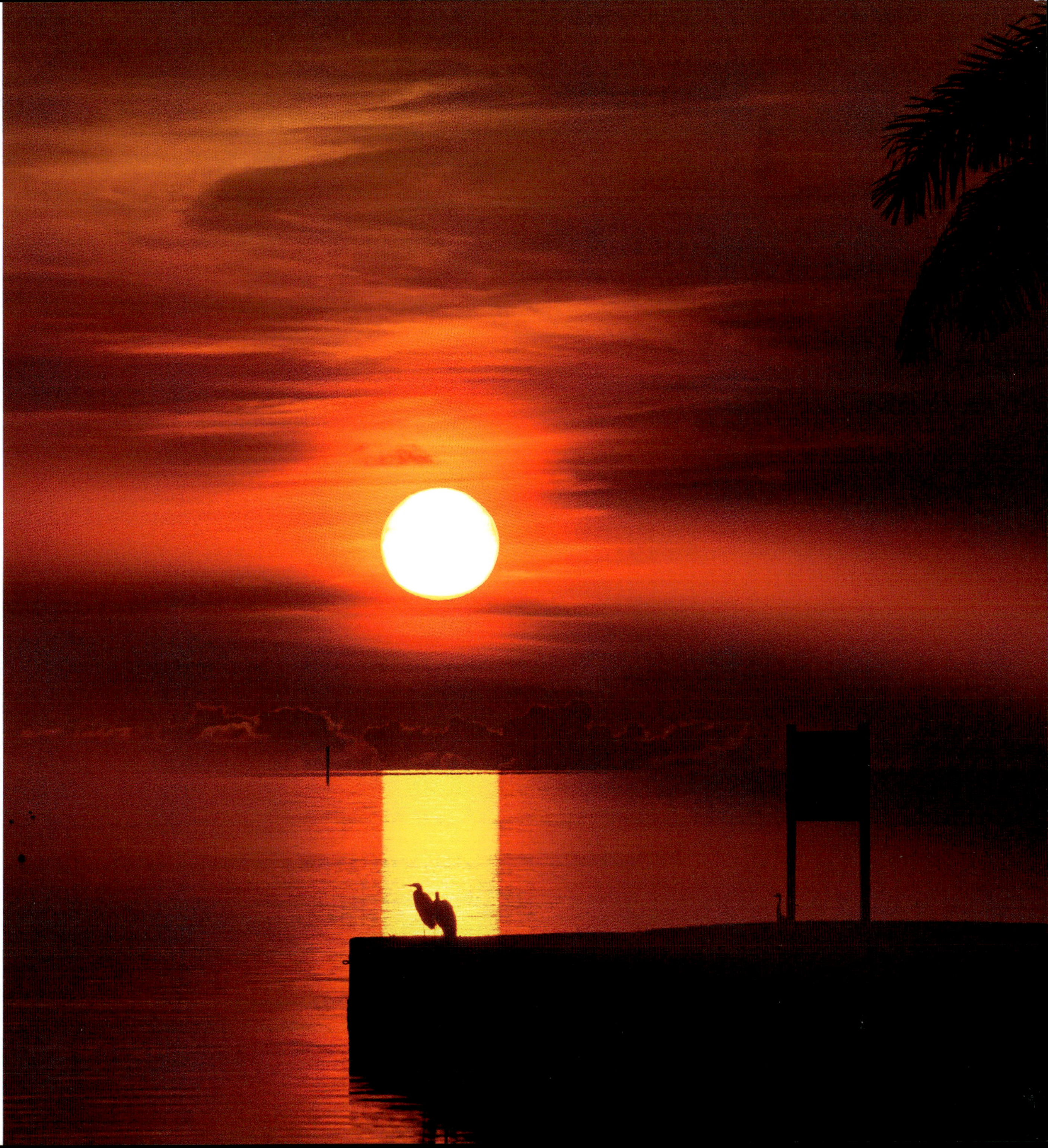

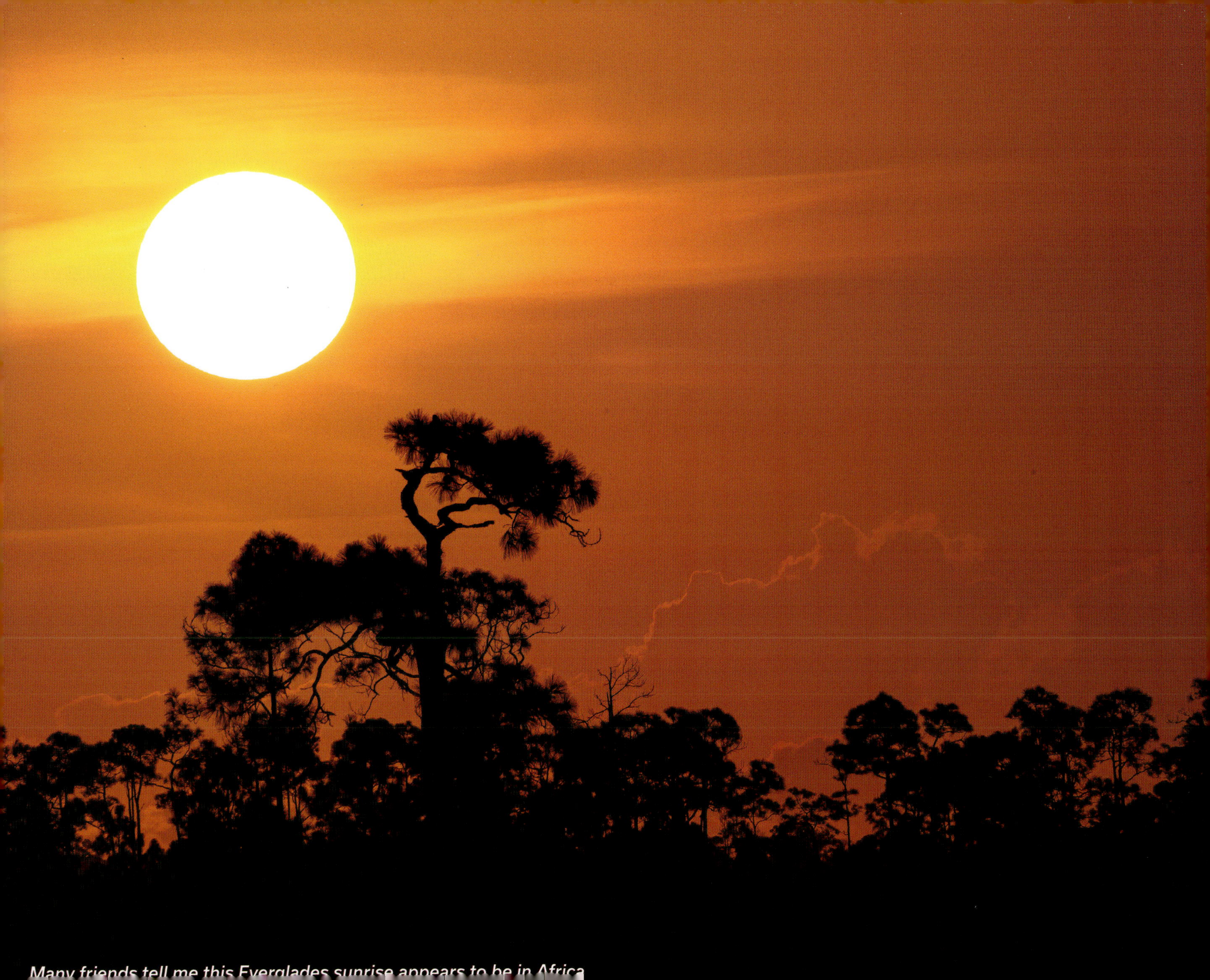

Many friends tell me this Everglades sunrise appears to be in Africa

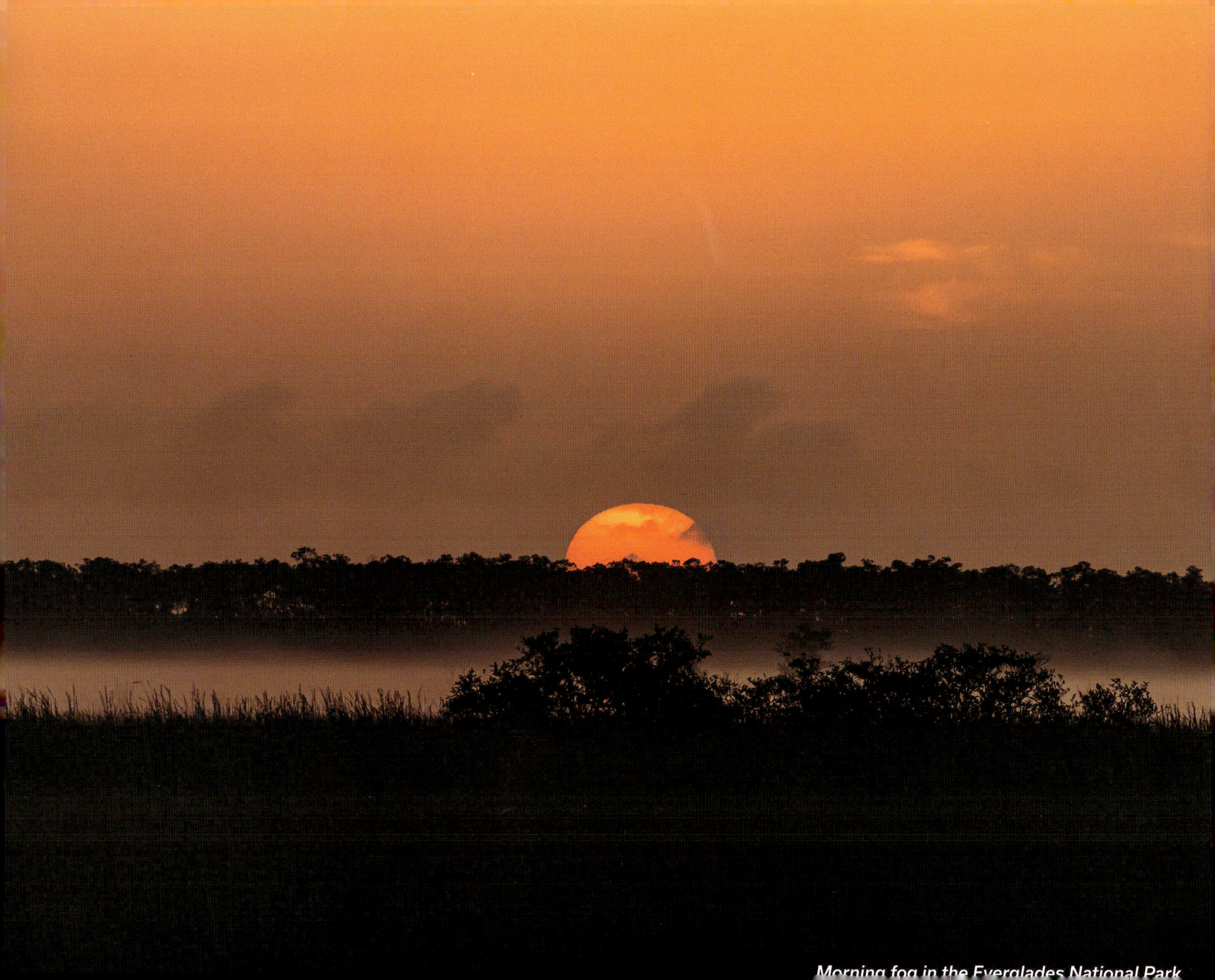

Morning fog in the Everglades National Park

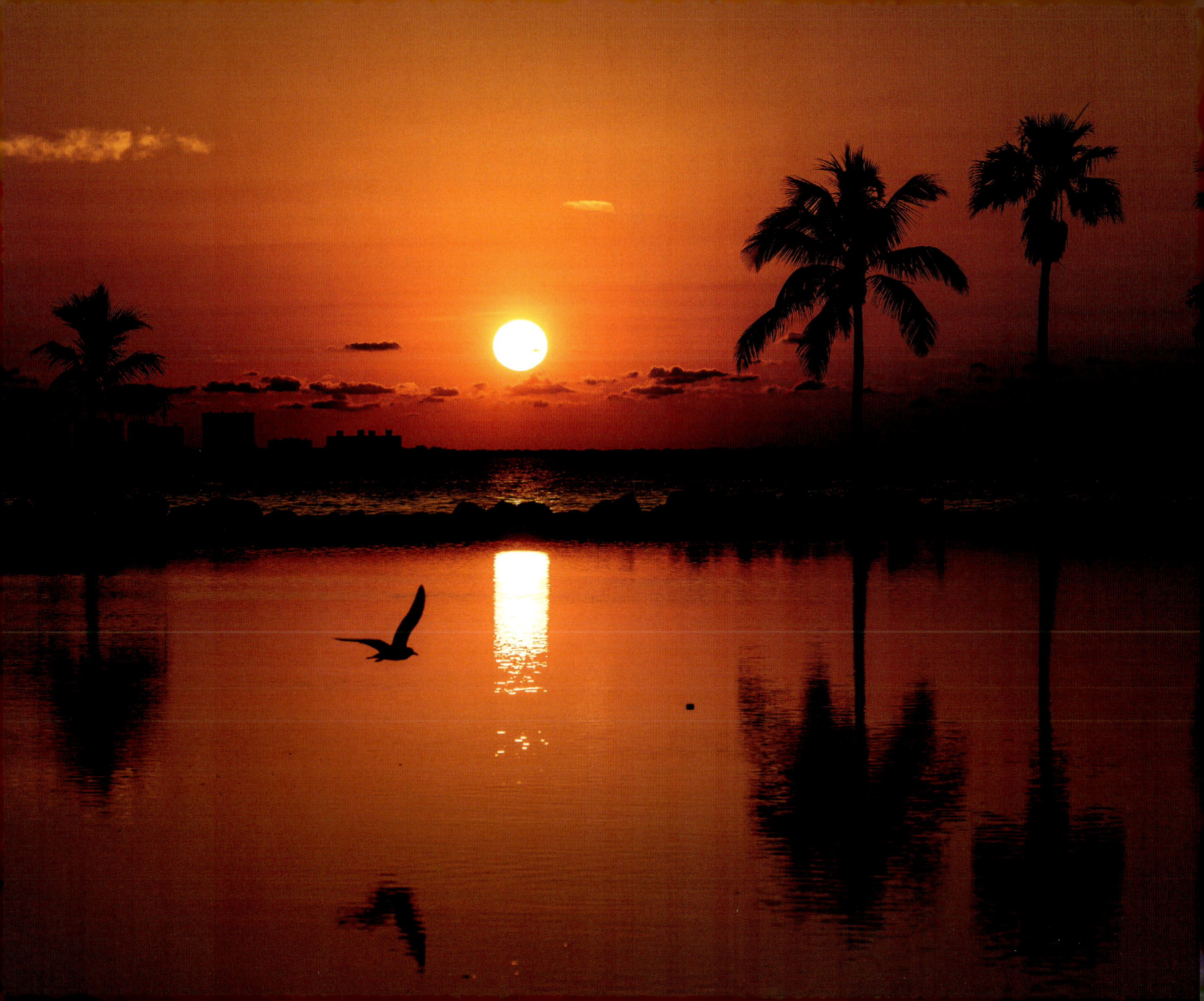

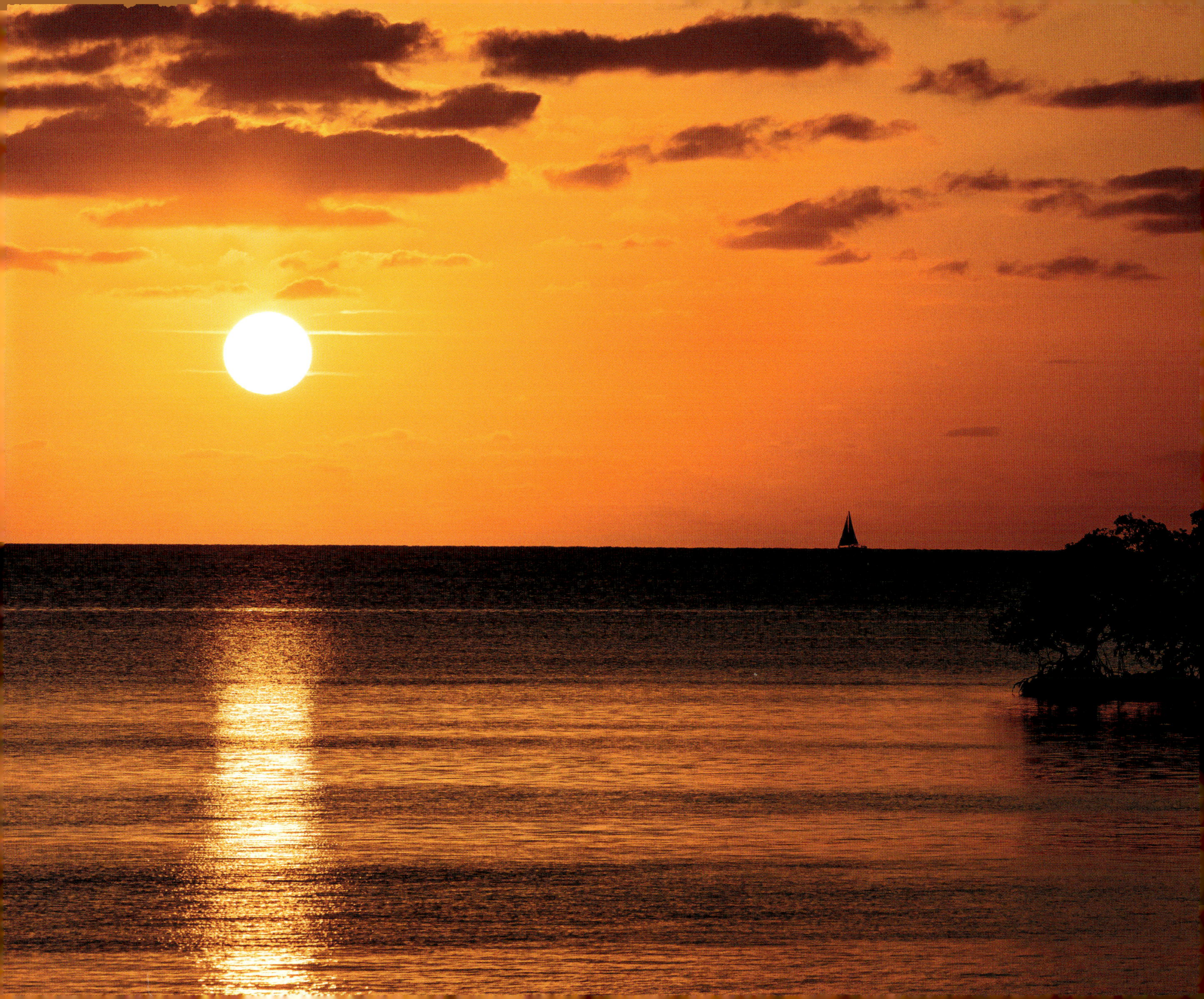

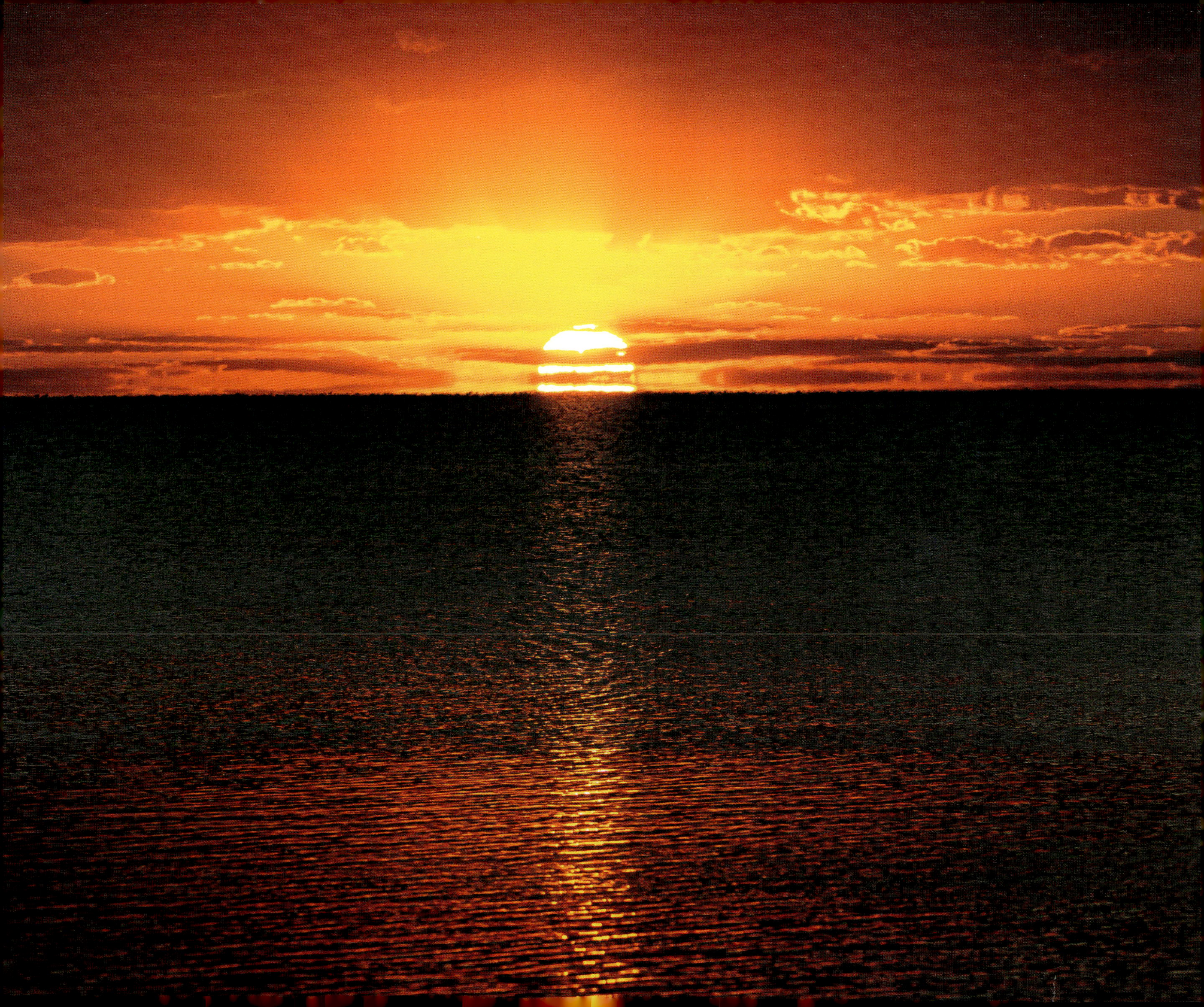

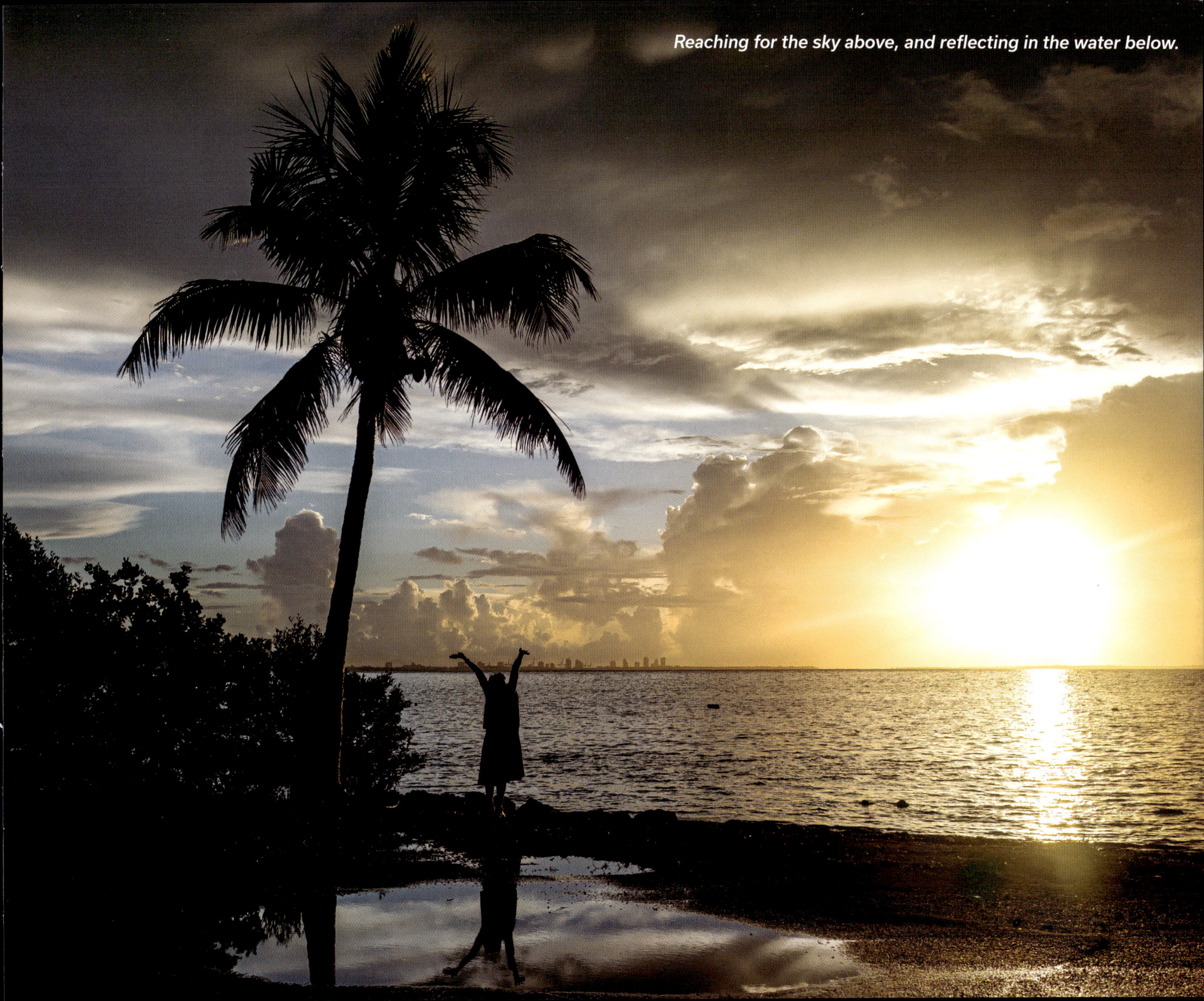

Reaching for the sky above, and reflecting in the water below.

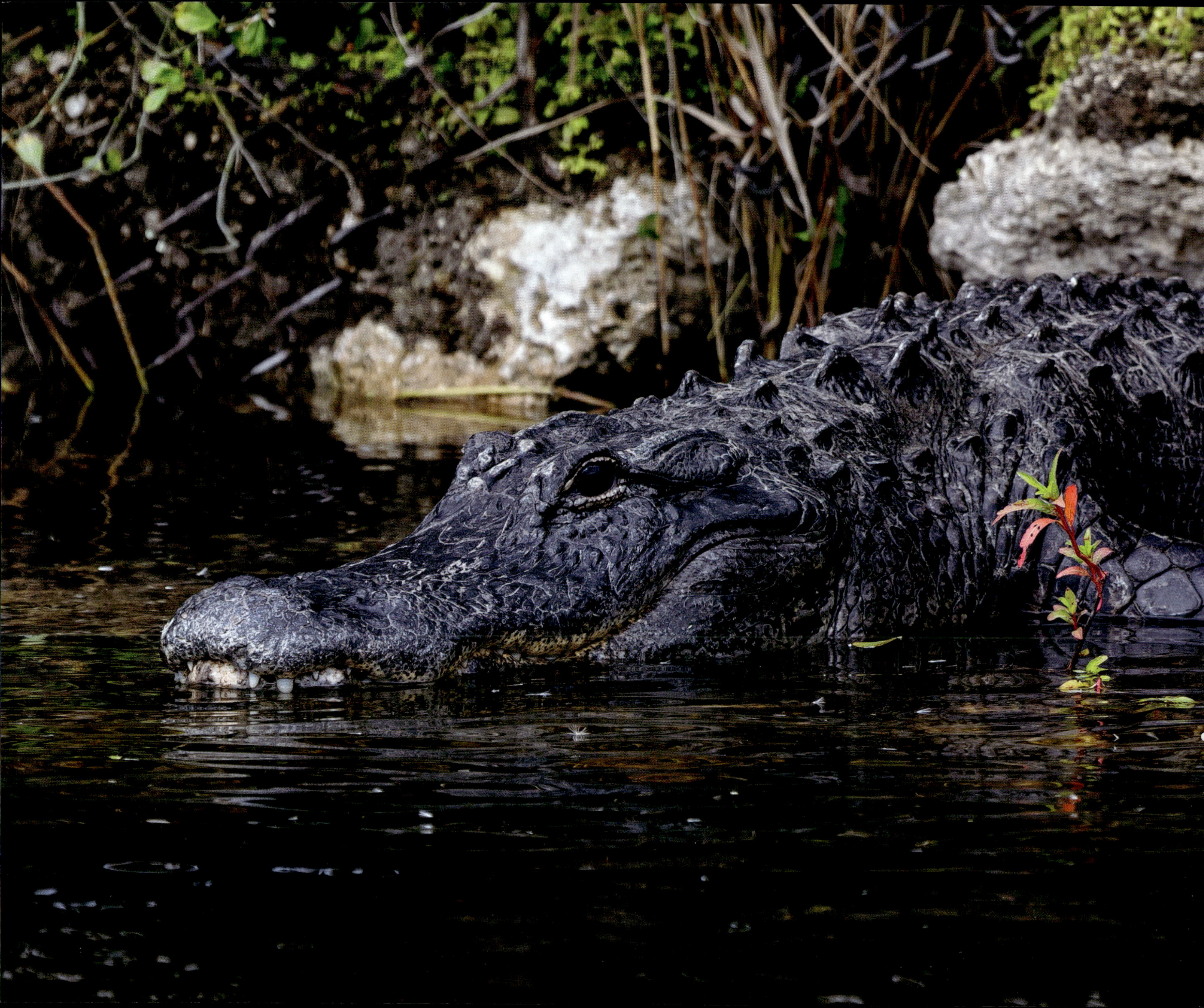

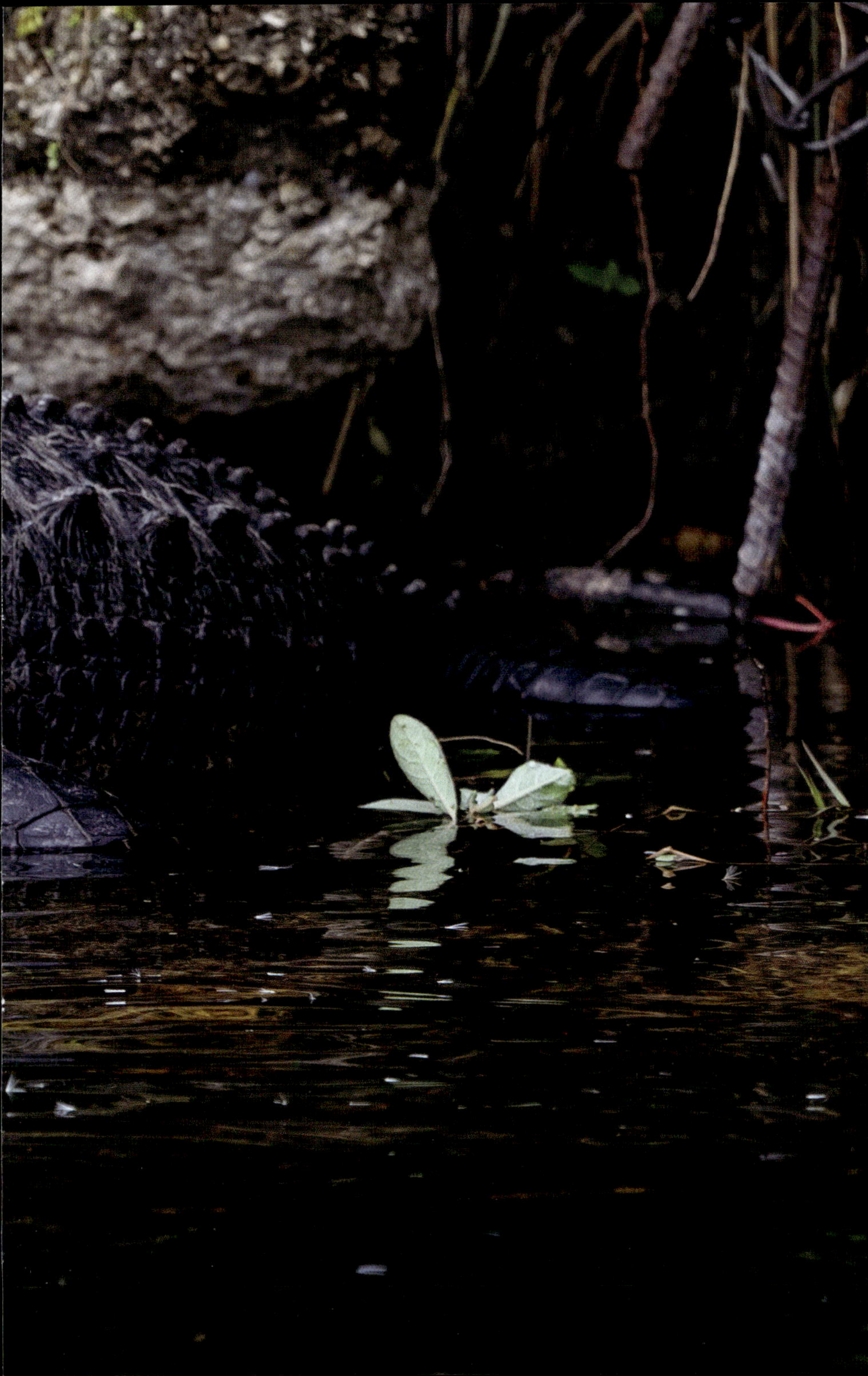

Florida Wildlife

Greeting the tropical sunrise every day is a menagerie of exotic birds and animals that I often photograph in strange and interesting settings and positions. We have cuddling owls, lovey-dovey alligators, smiling crocodiles, quizzical ibises, hungry ospreys, clumsy pelicans, and itchy shorebirds. Turns out the wildlife we see are often a lot like us, with similar quirks and issues, which should deepen our connections and steel our resolve to protect these treasures with all our might.

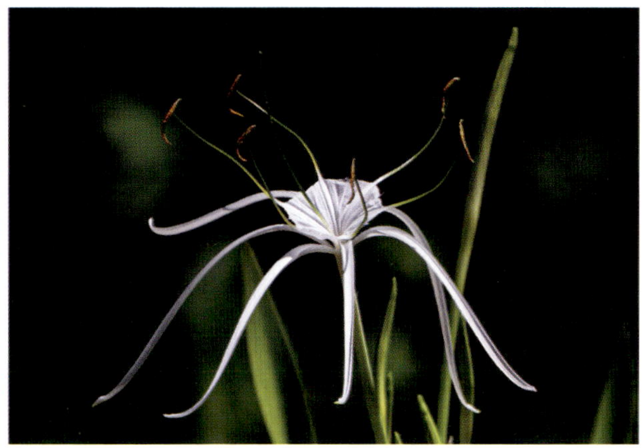

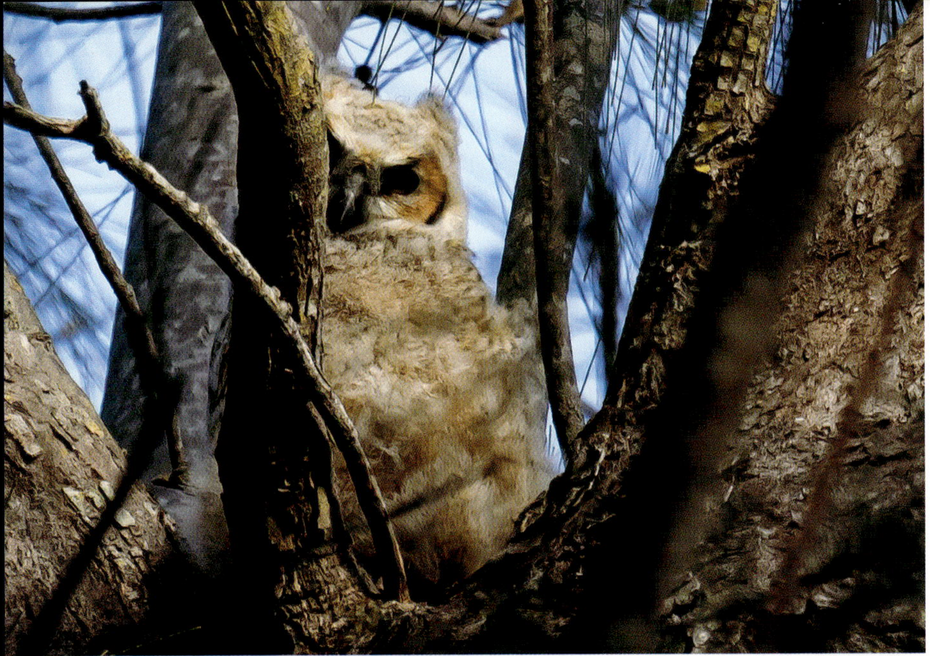

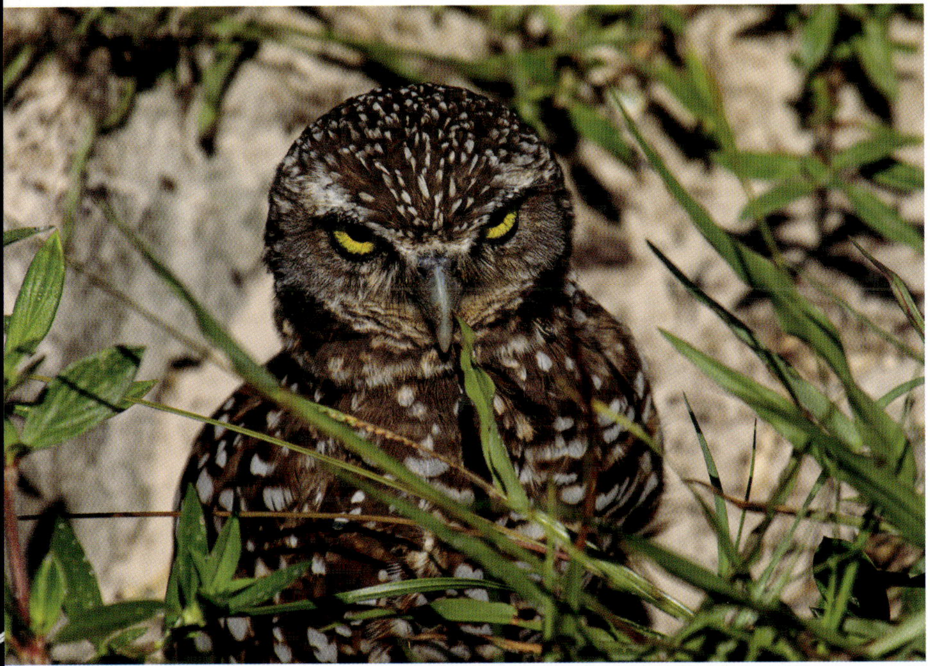

A shy baby great horned owl (top left) and two tiny burrowing owls with bold attitudes.

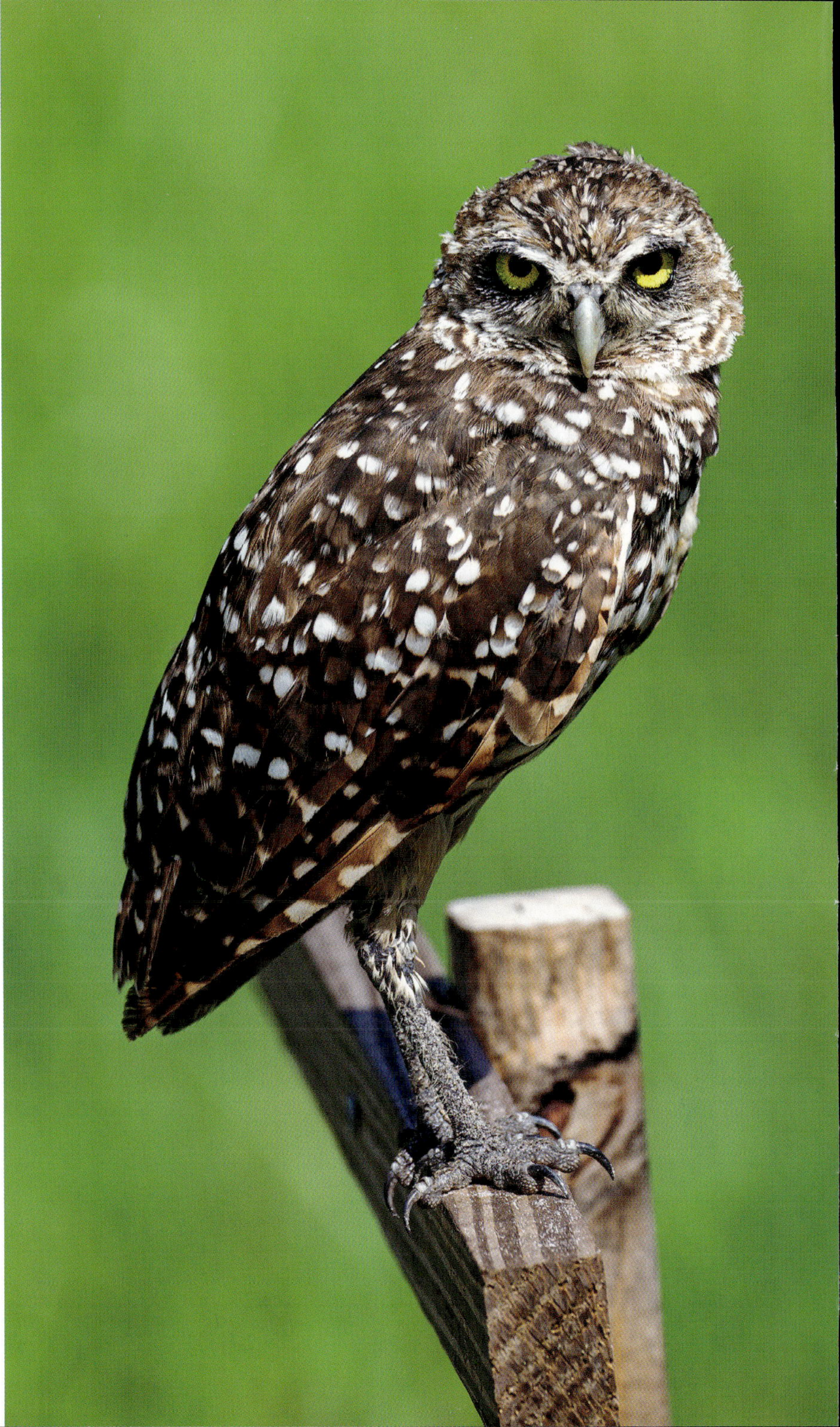

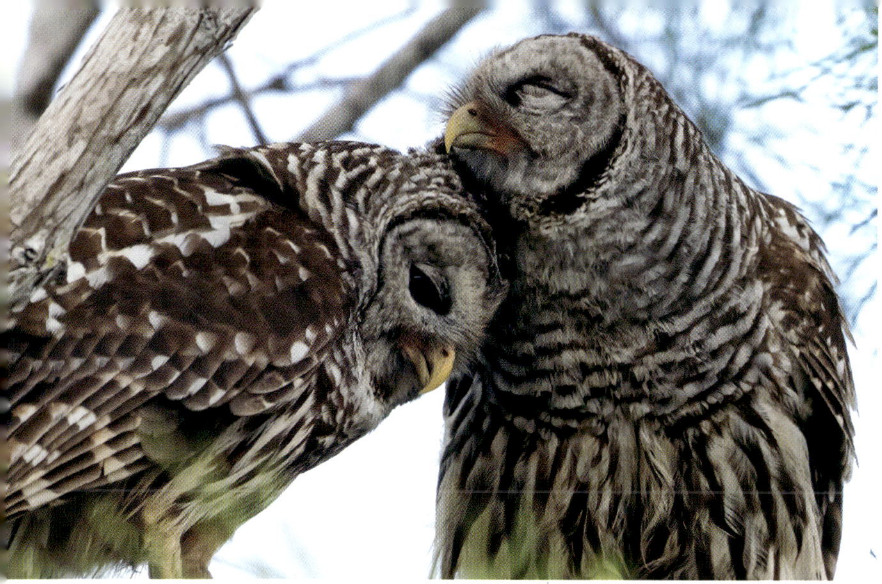
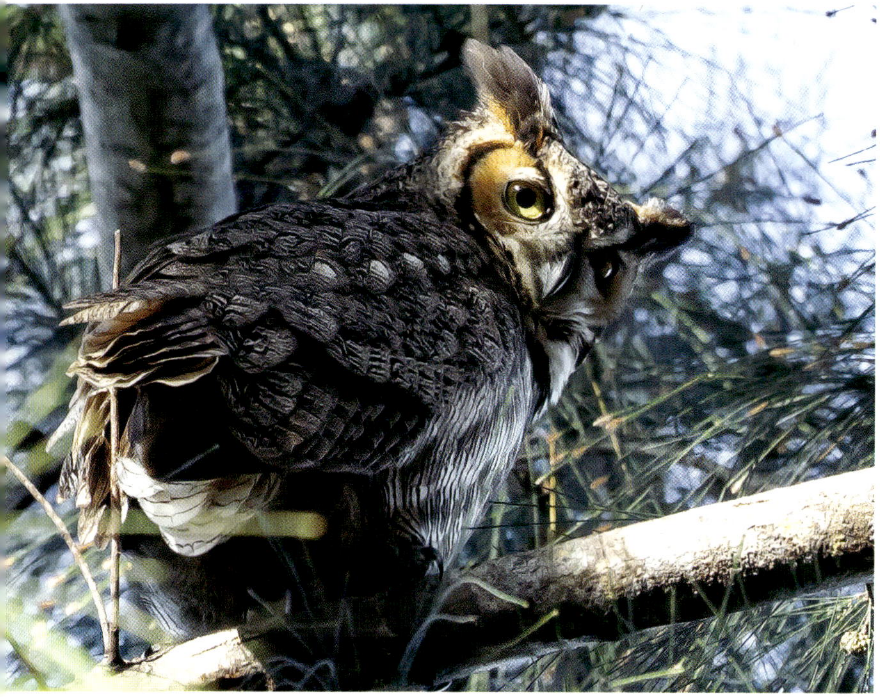
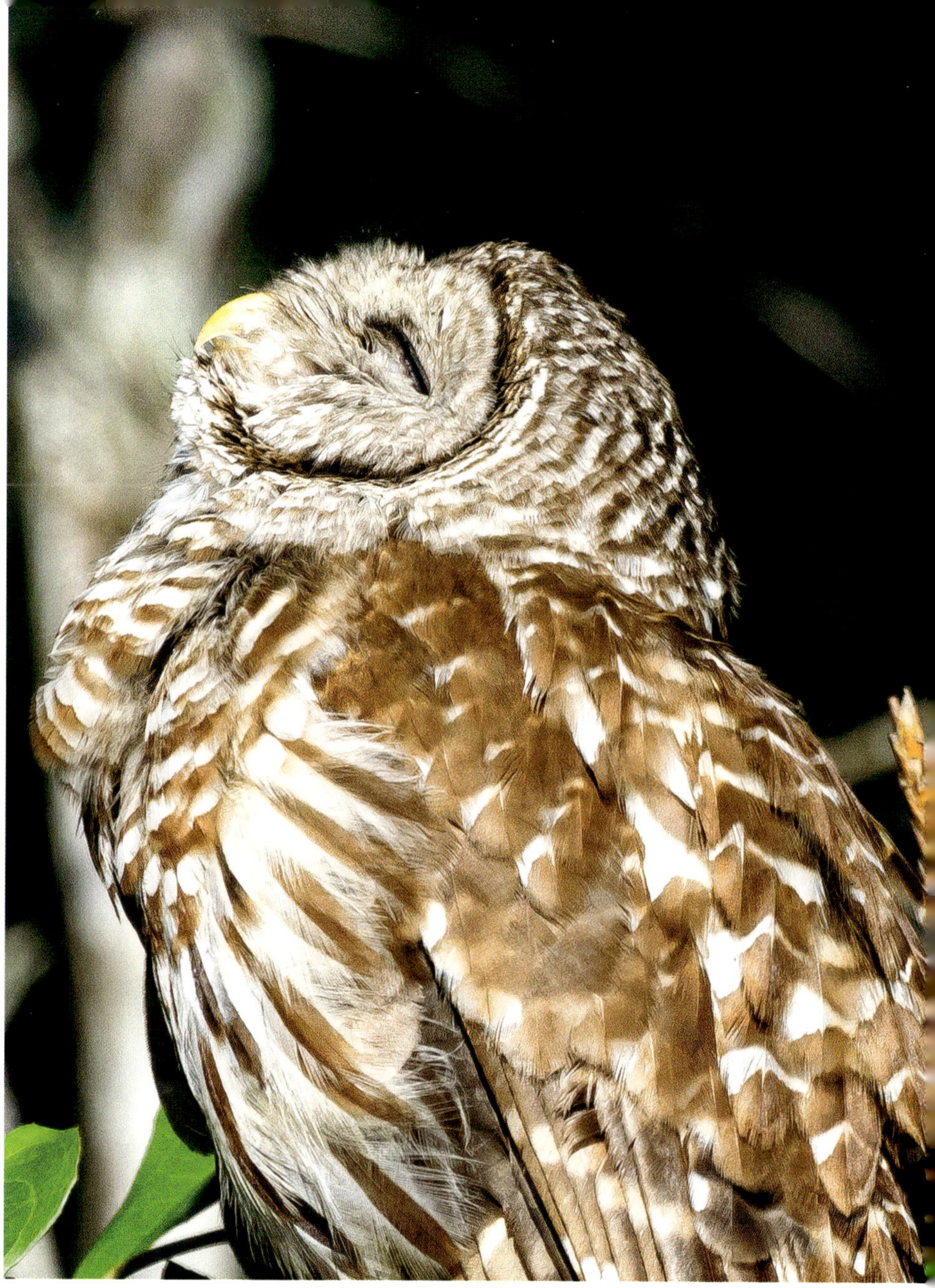

Cuddling and sunbathing barred owls that will sometimes dive-bomb wildlife photographers, and a most curious great horned owl.

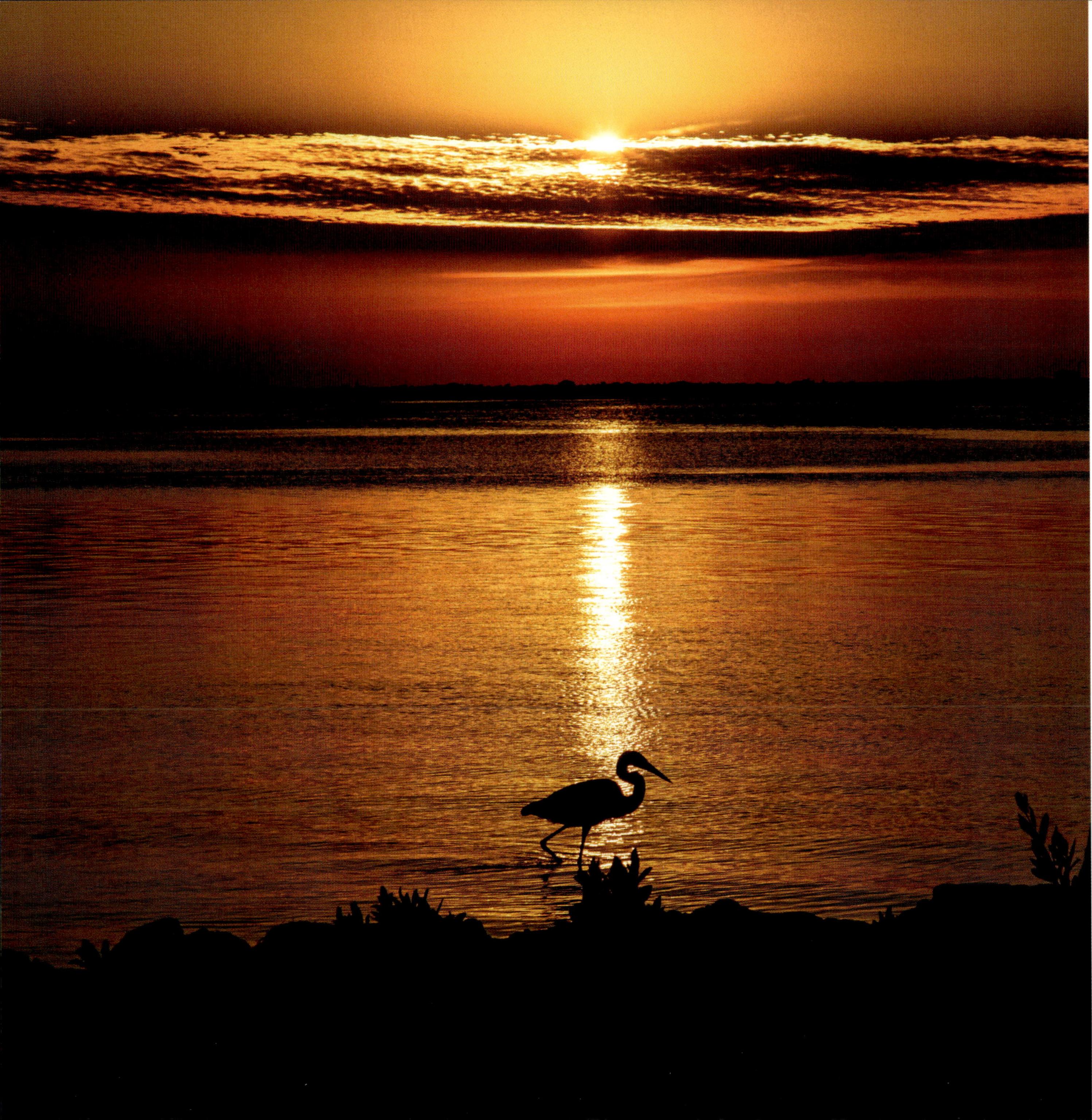
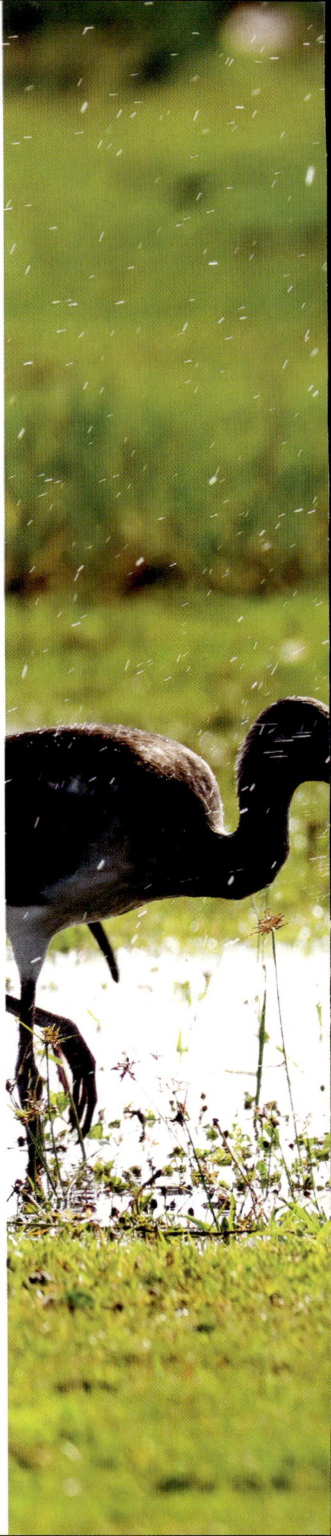

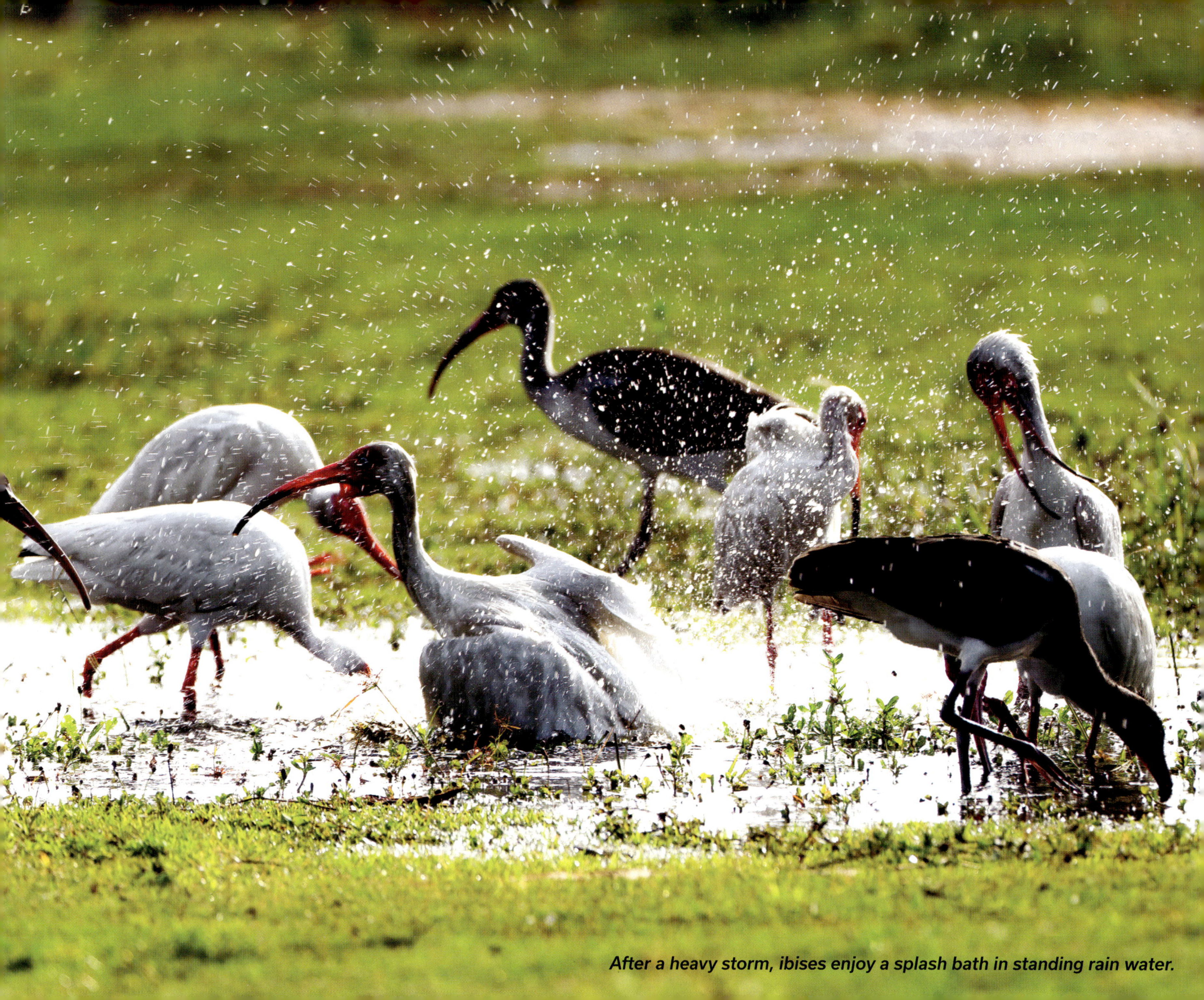

After a heavy storm, ibises enjoy a splash bath in standing rain water.

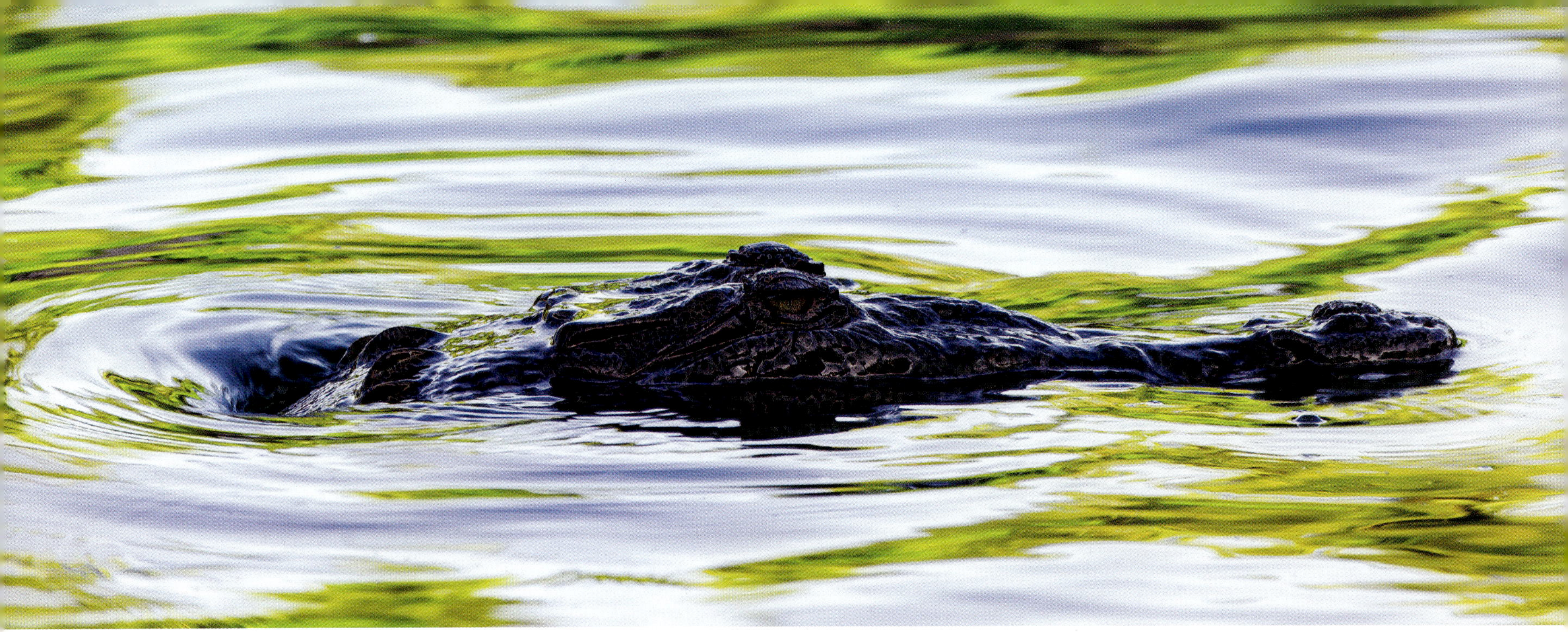

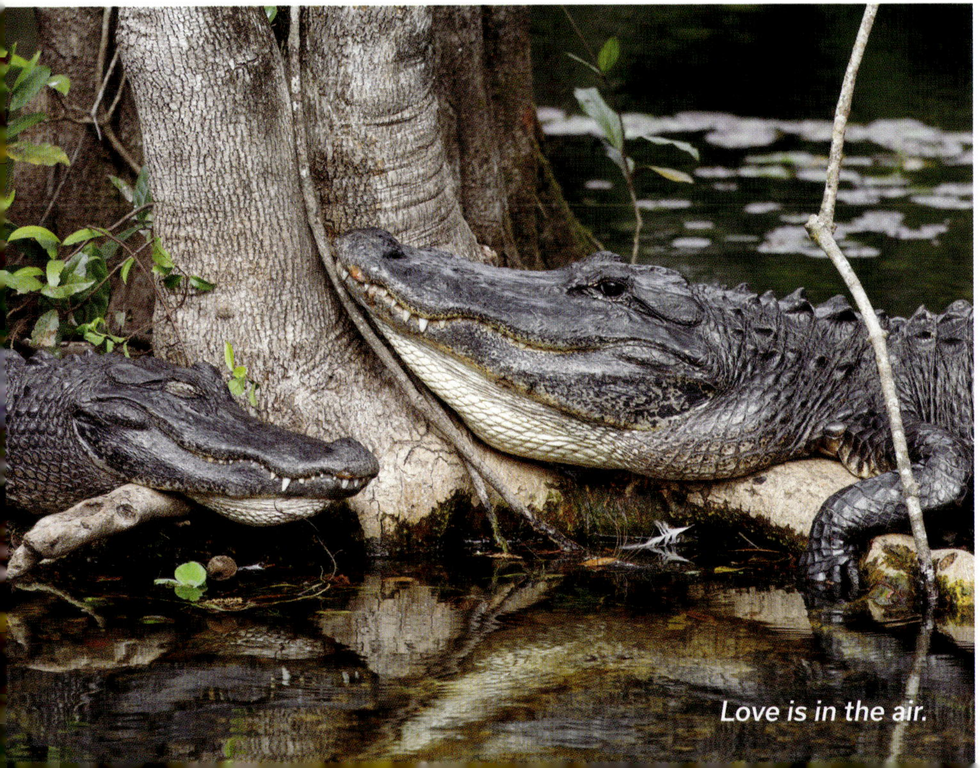

Love is in the air.

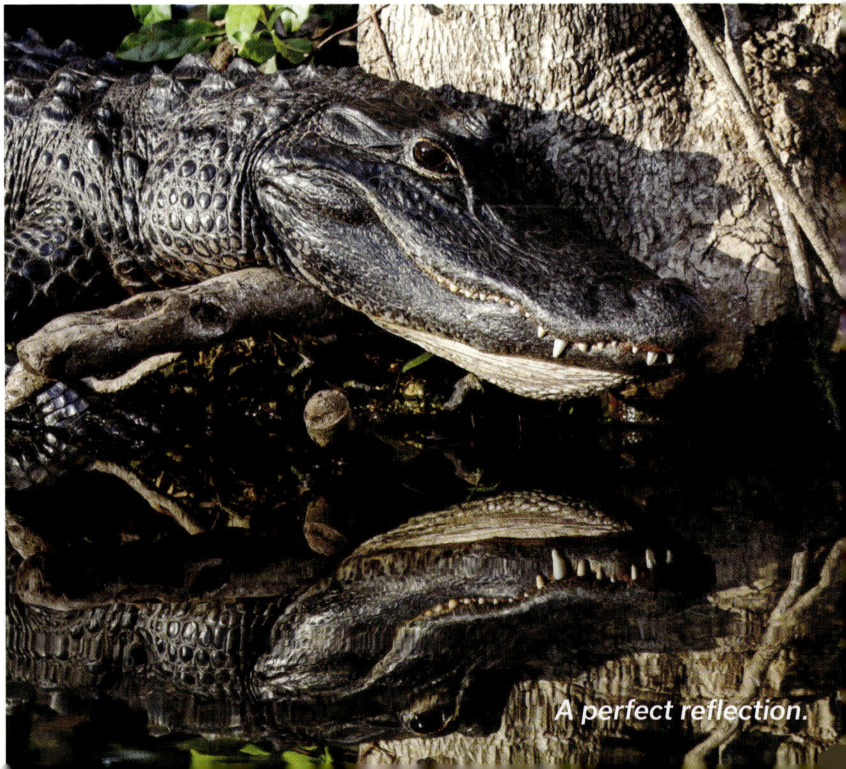

A perfect reflection.

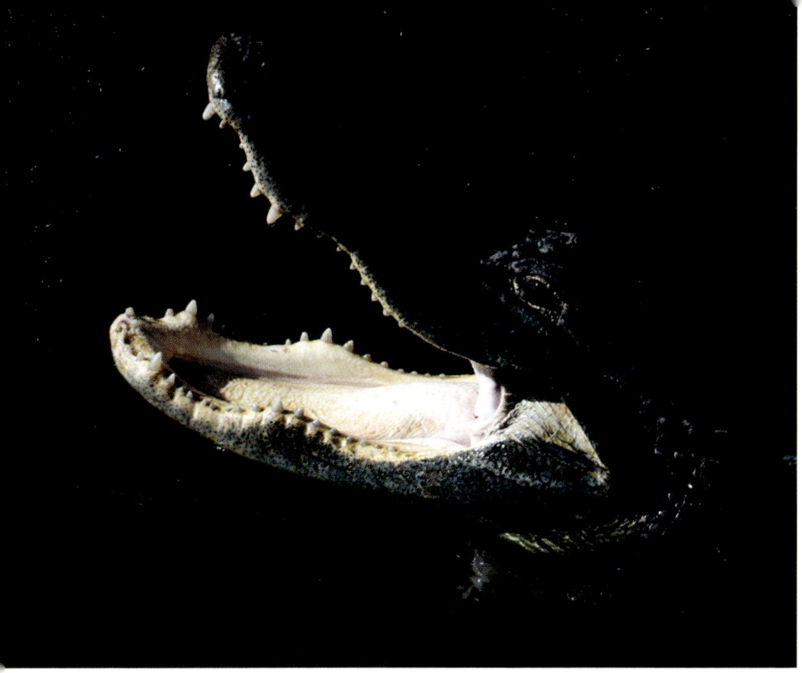

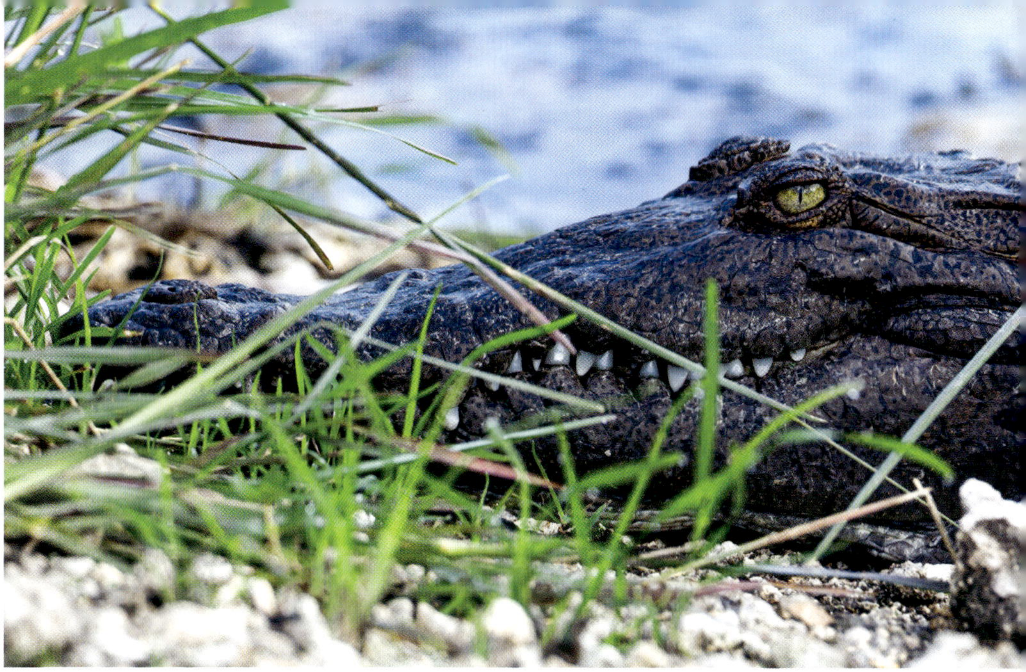

Crocodiles and alligators are among my favorite photo subjects. Thanks to a perfect beam of sunlight and an open mouth, I now have a formal gator portrait.

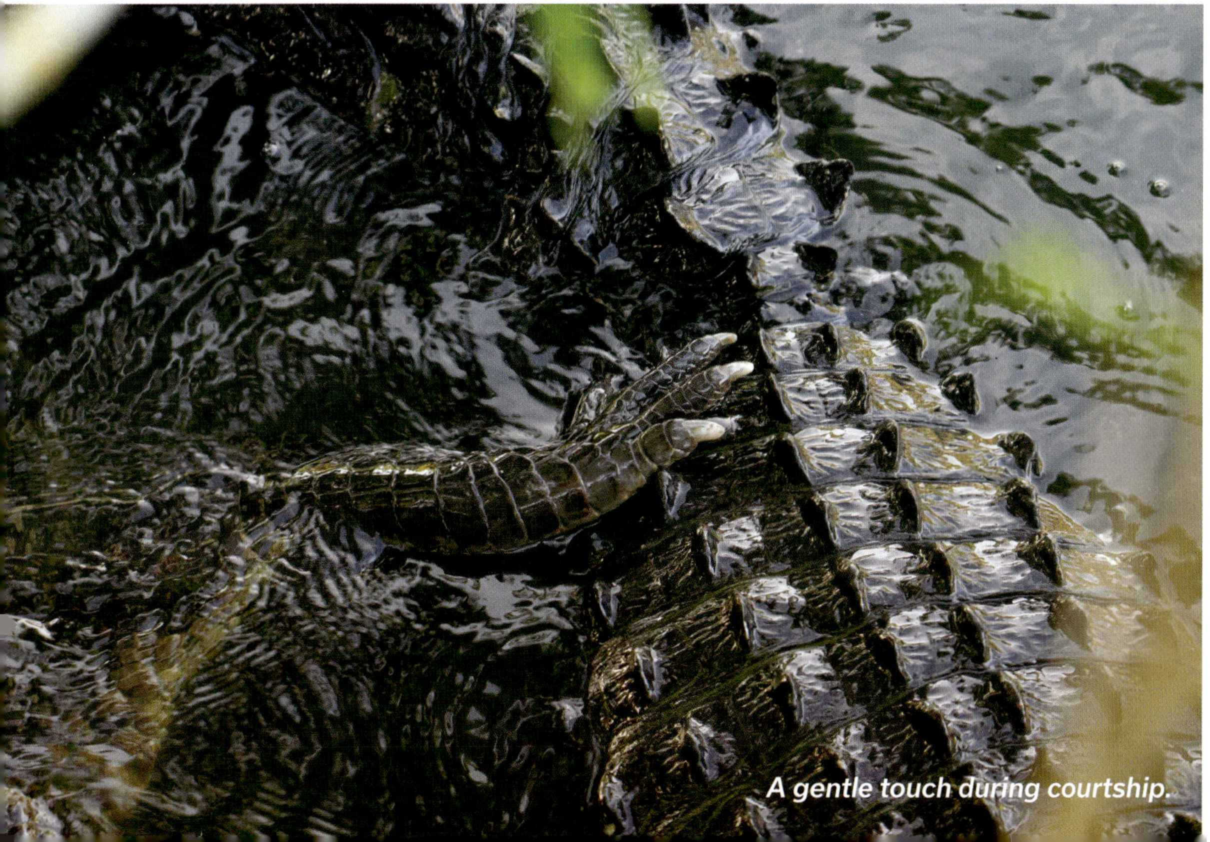

A gentle touch during courtship.

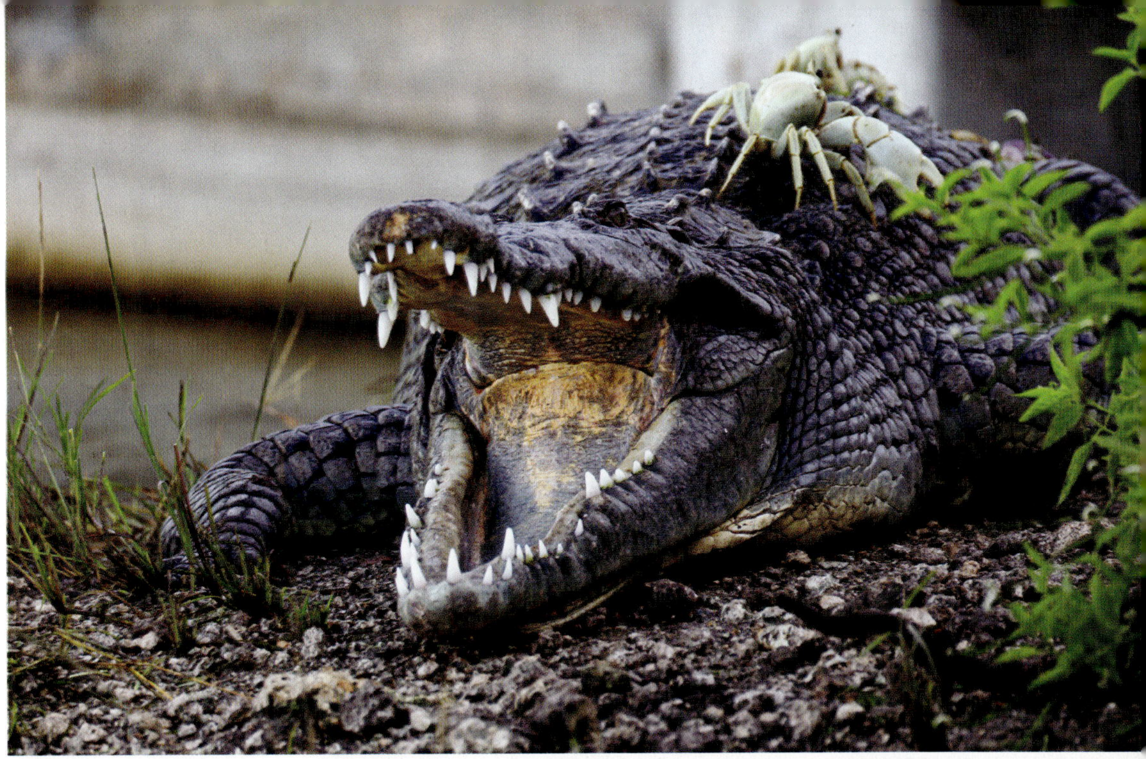

A crocodile putting up with a big crab on its head, and a male alligator growling and vibrating water off its back to attract females. It works.

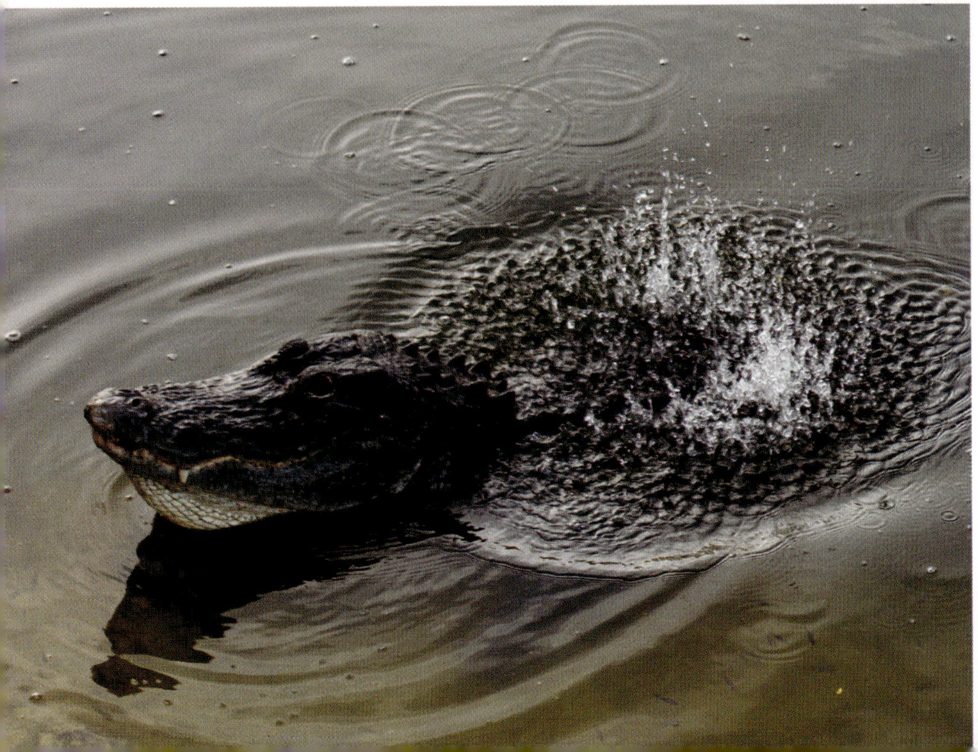

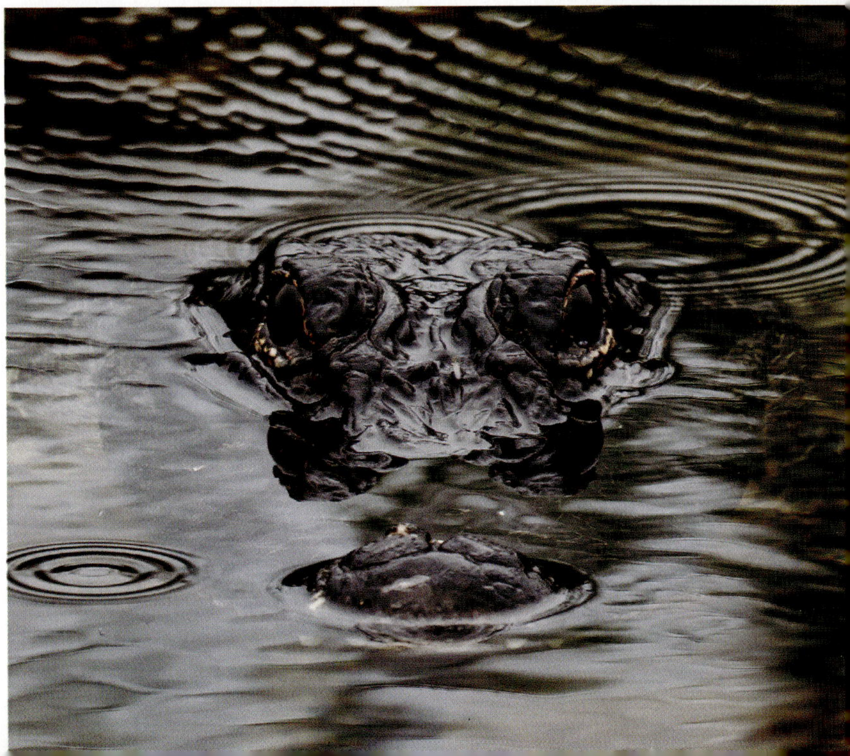

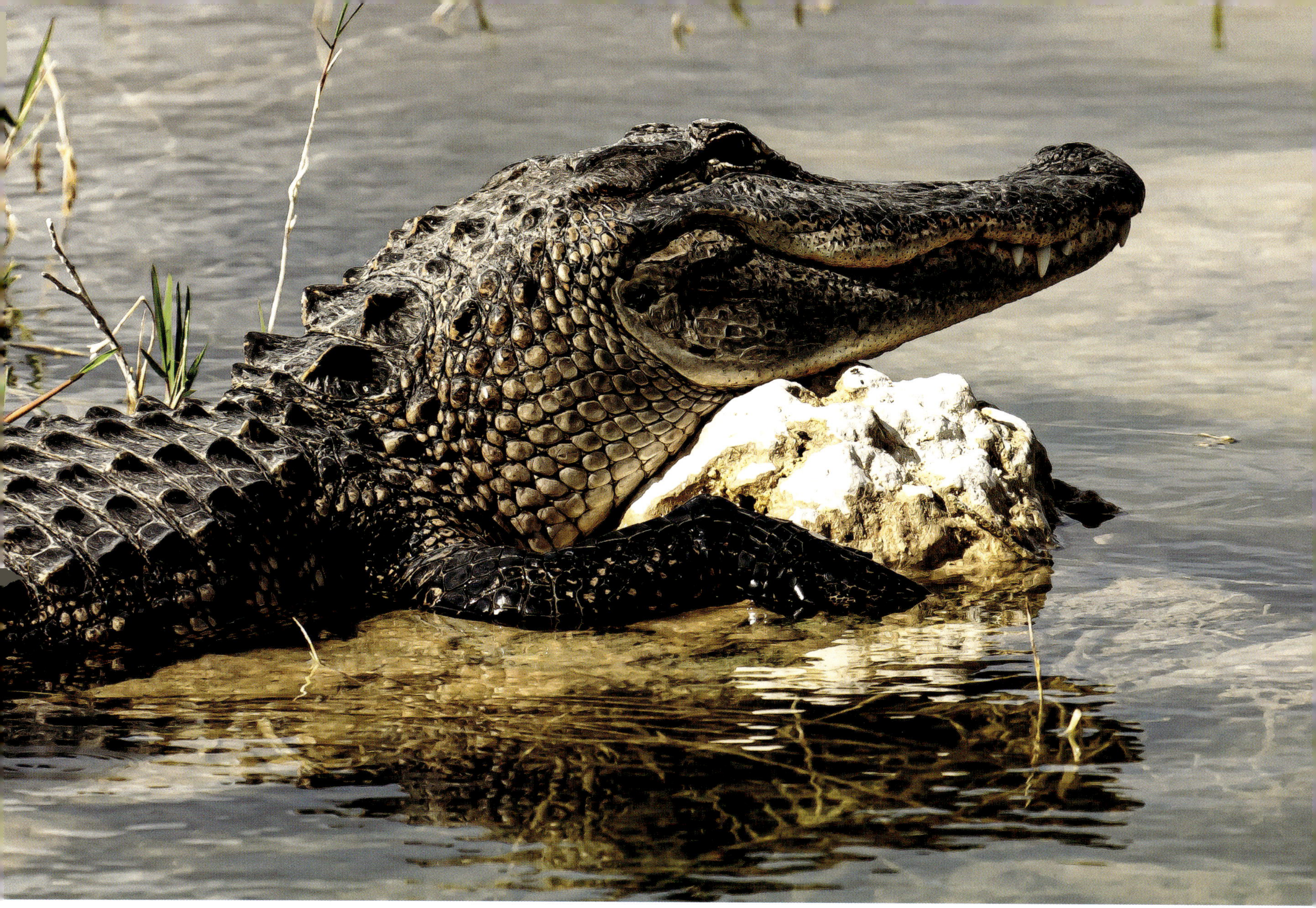

"You are my rock." A contented alligator basking in the sun.

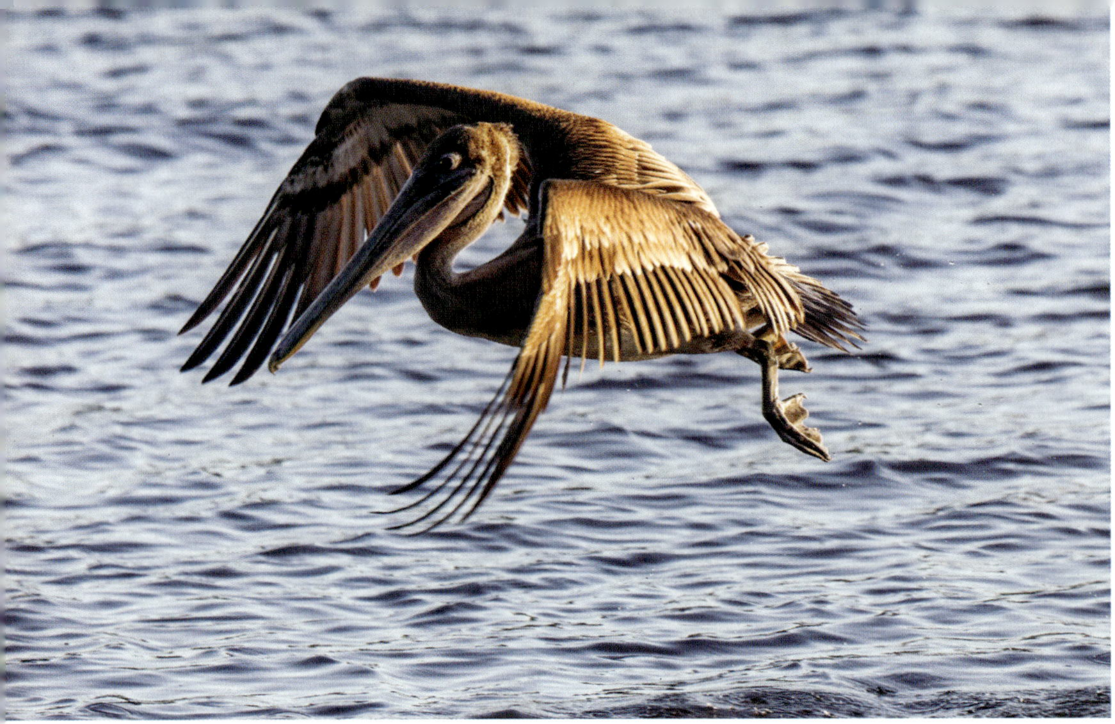

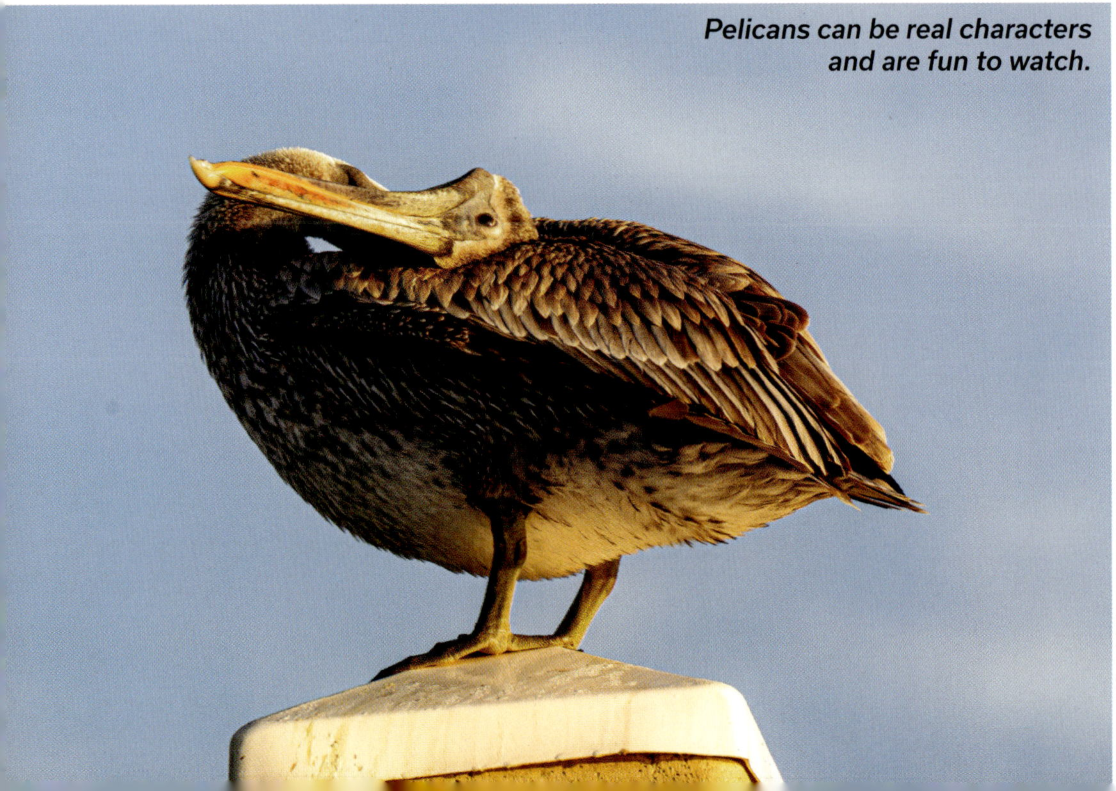

Pelicans can be real characters and are fun to watch.

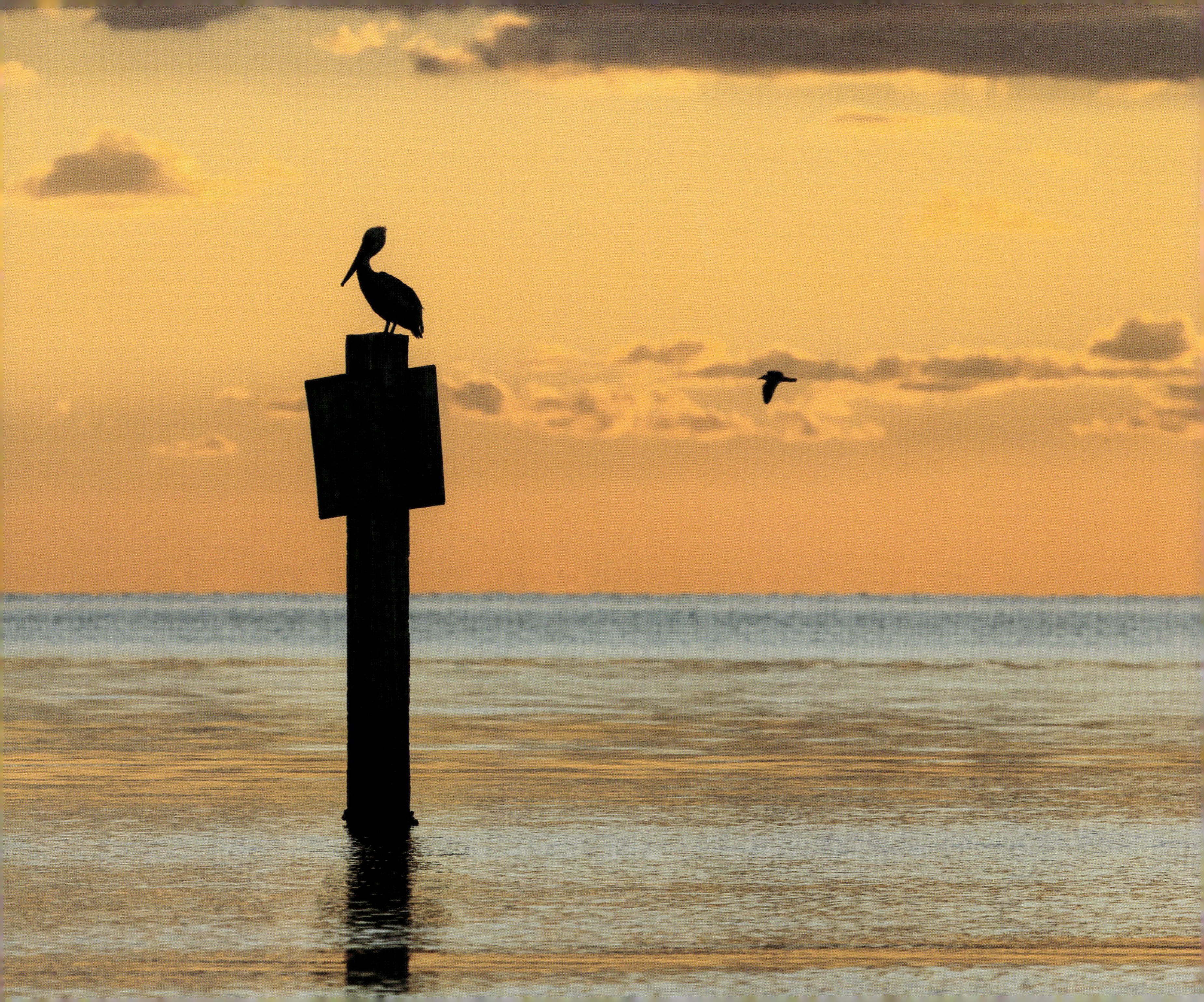

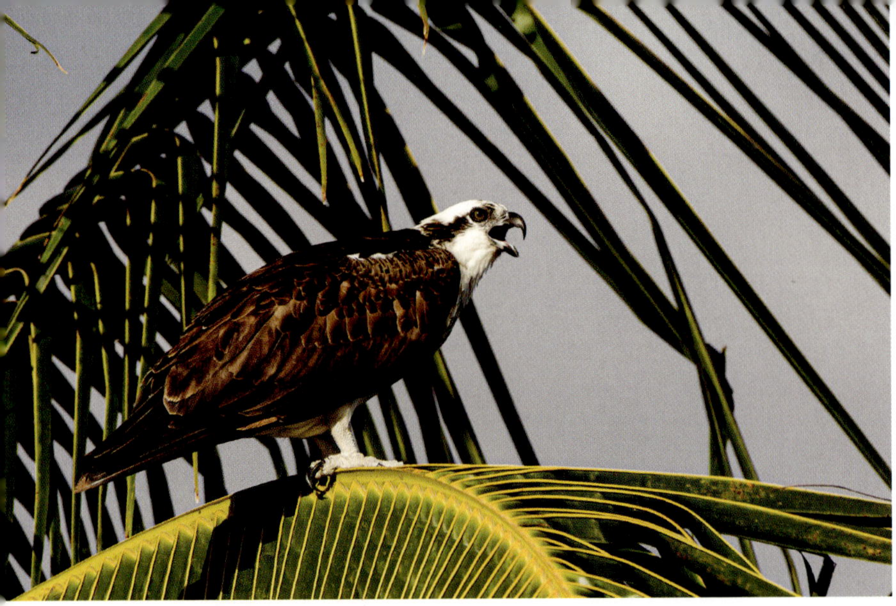

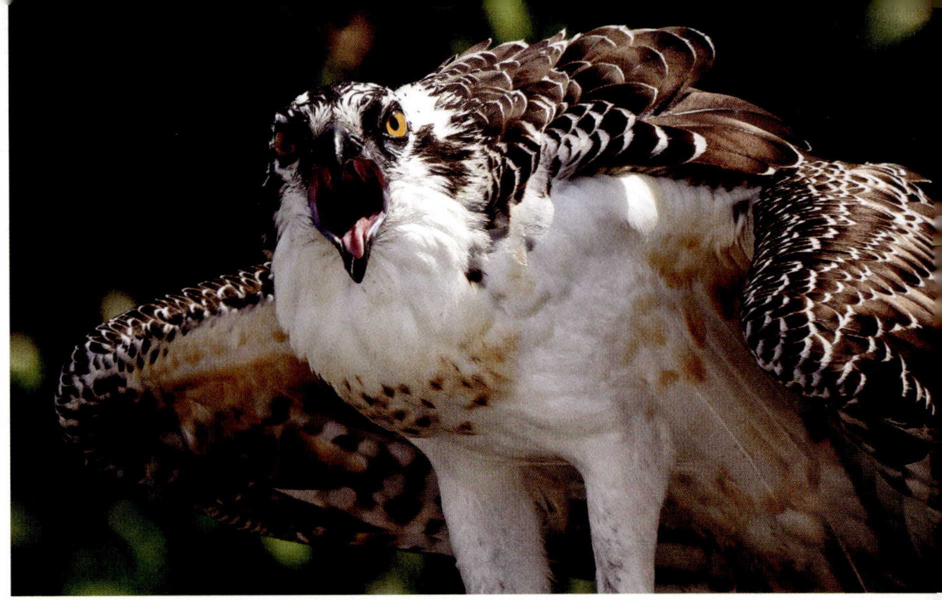

Whether a youngster or an attentive parent, ospreys always seem to have something to say.

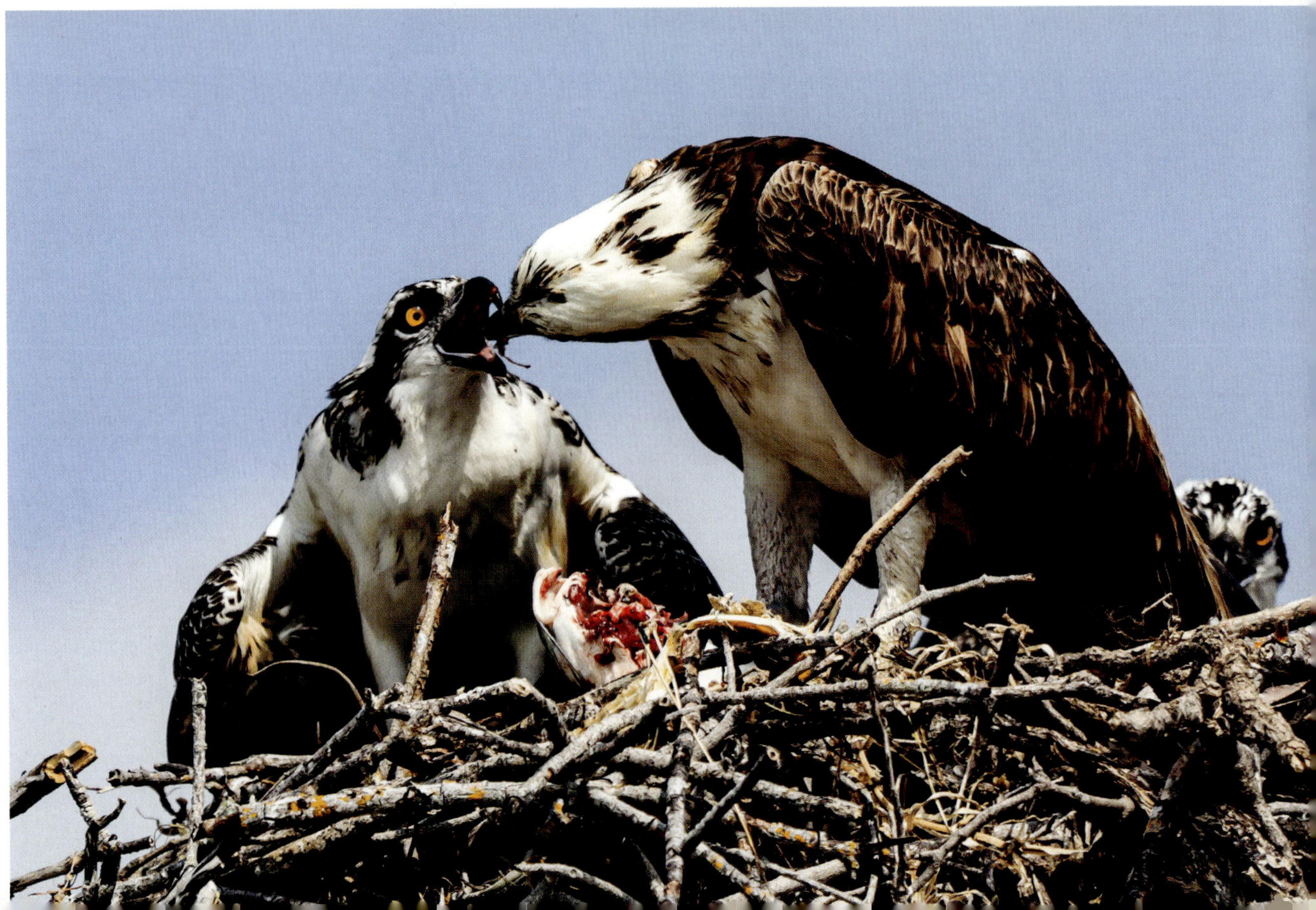

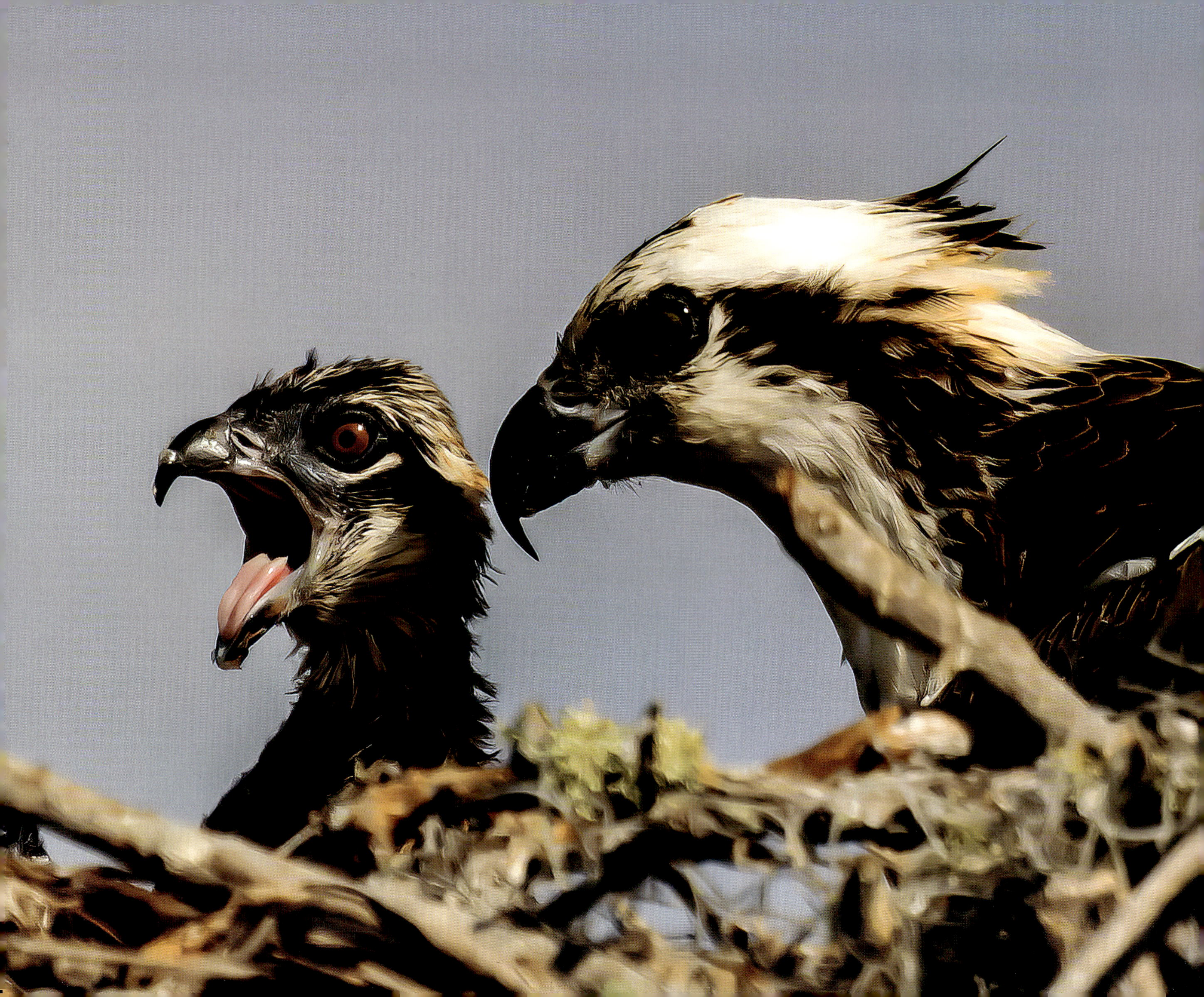

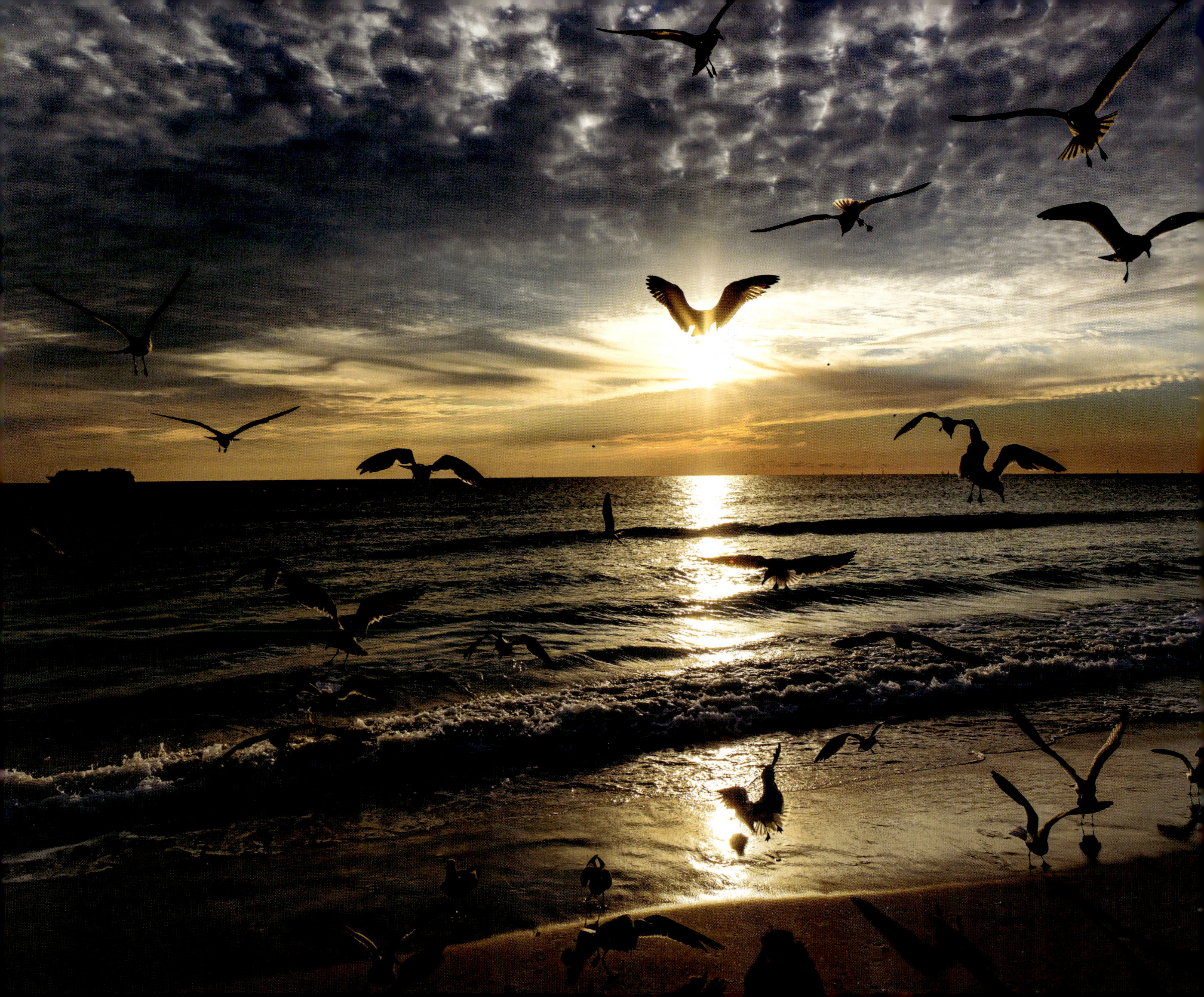

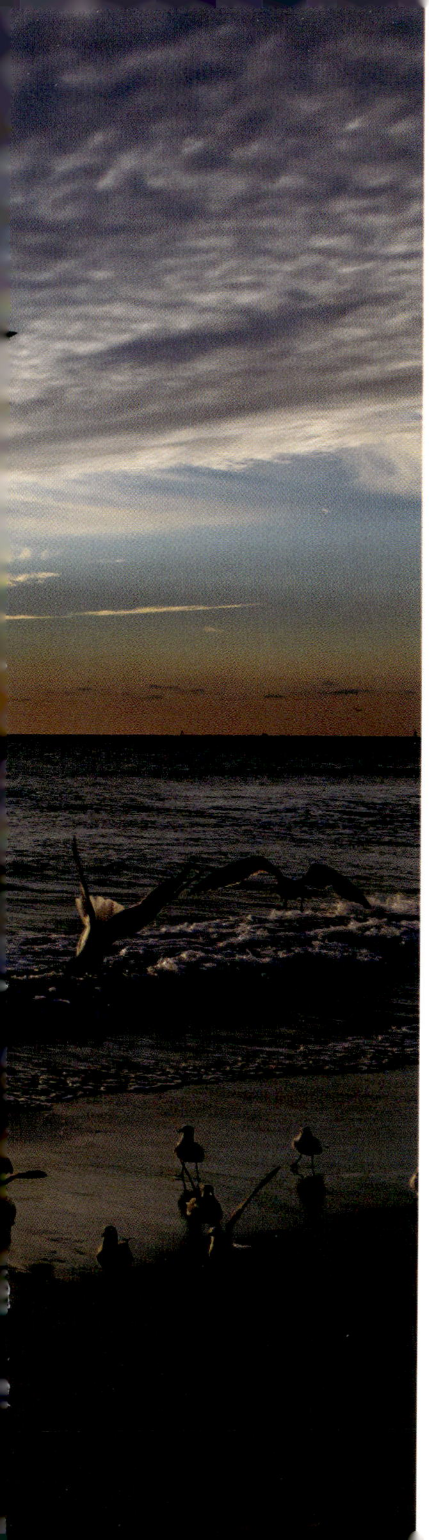

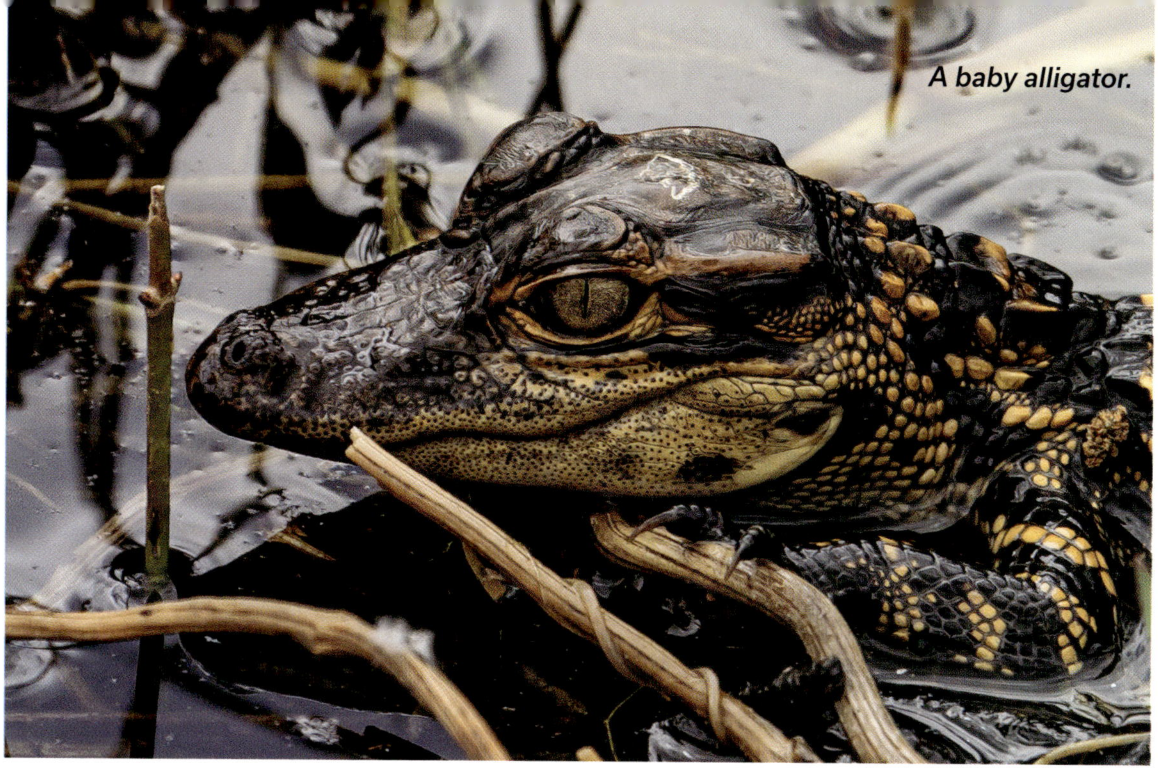

A baby alligator.

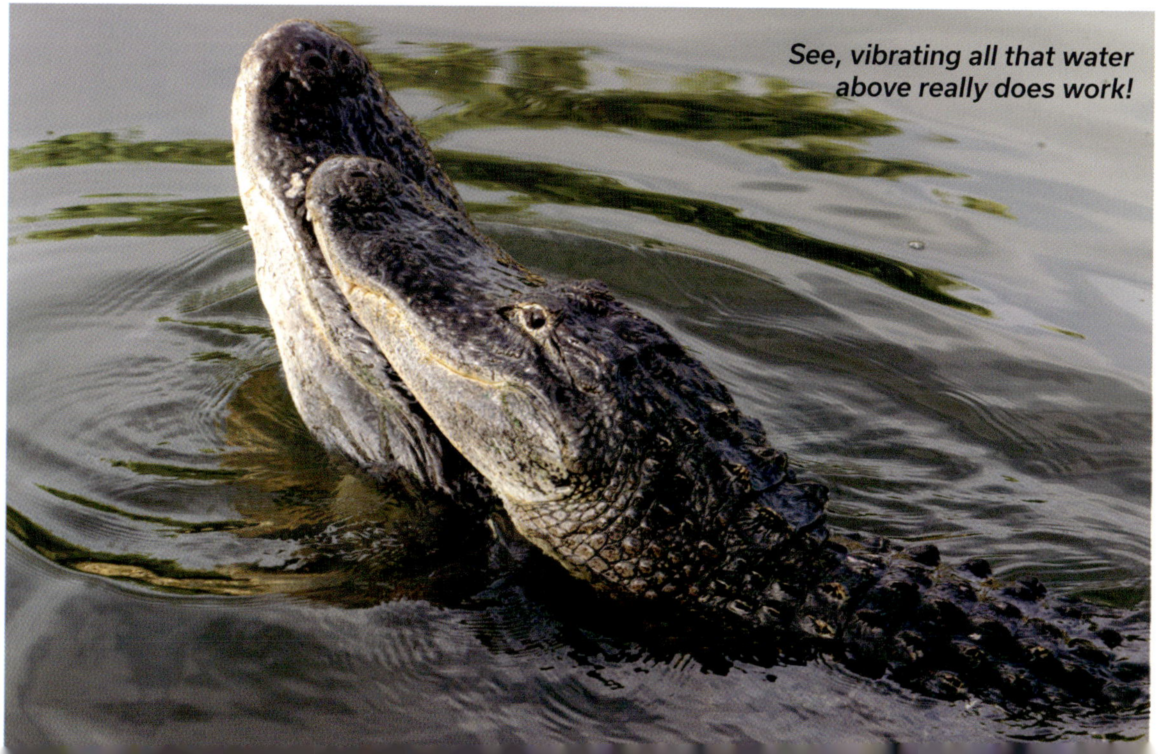

See, vibrating all that water above really does work!

I am curious about what this ibis is thinking? It seems skeptical.

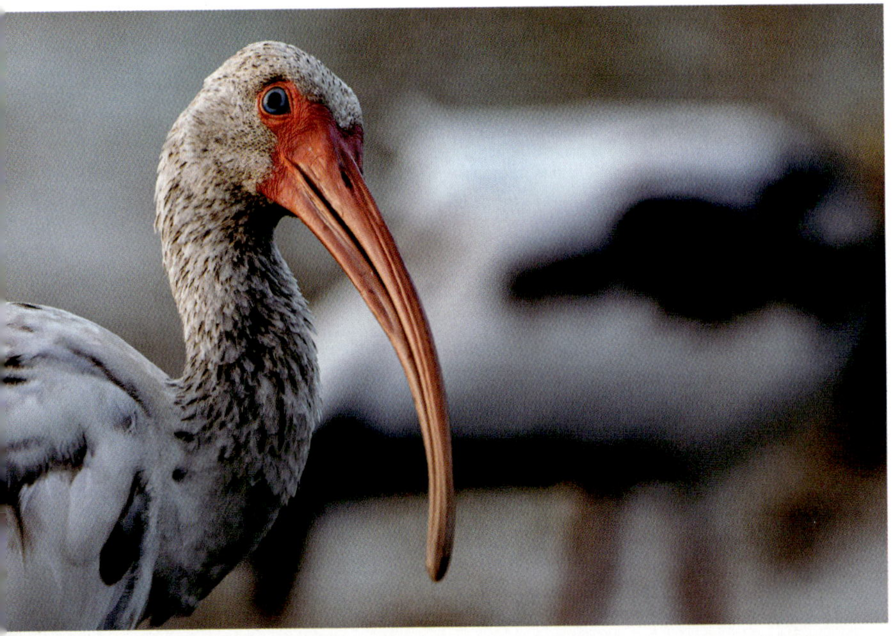

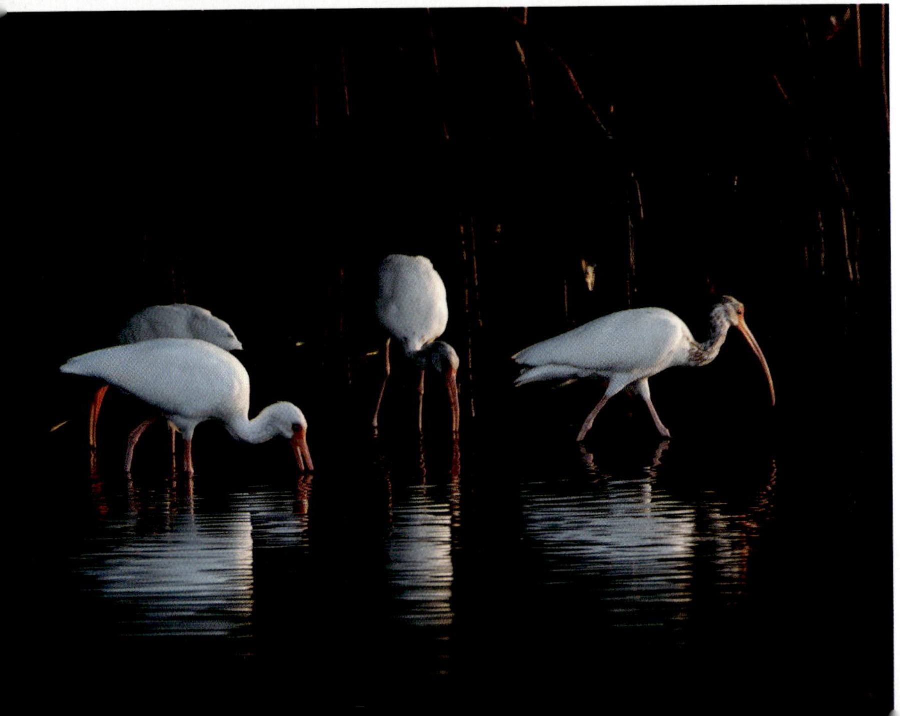

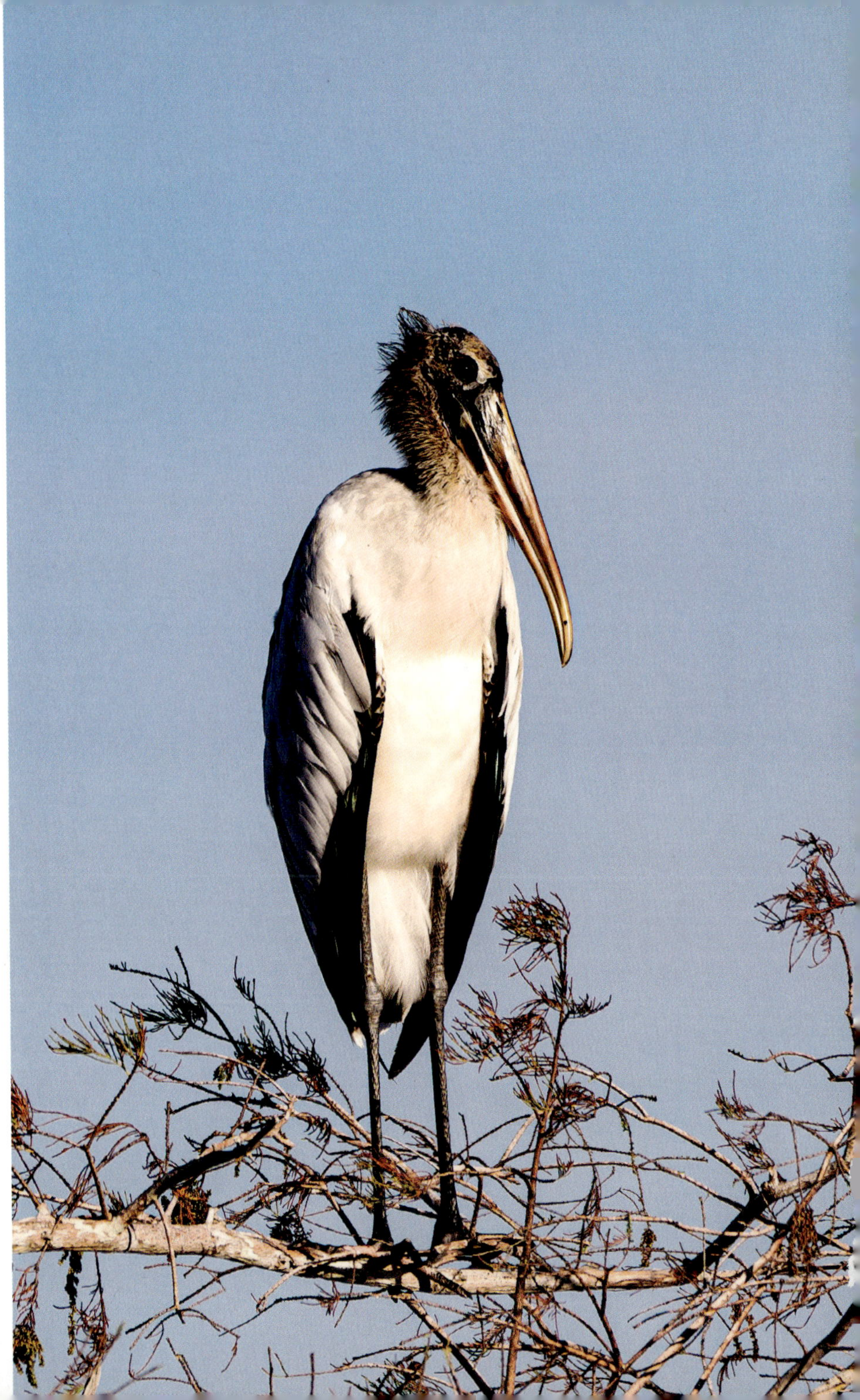

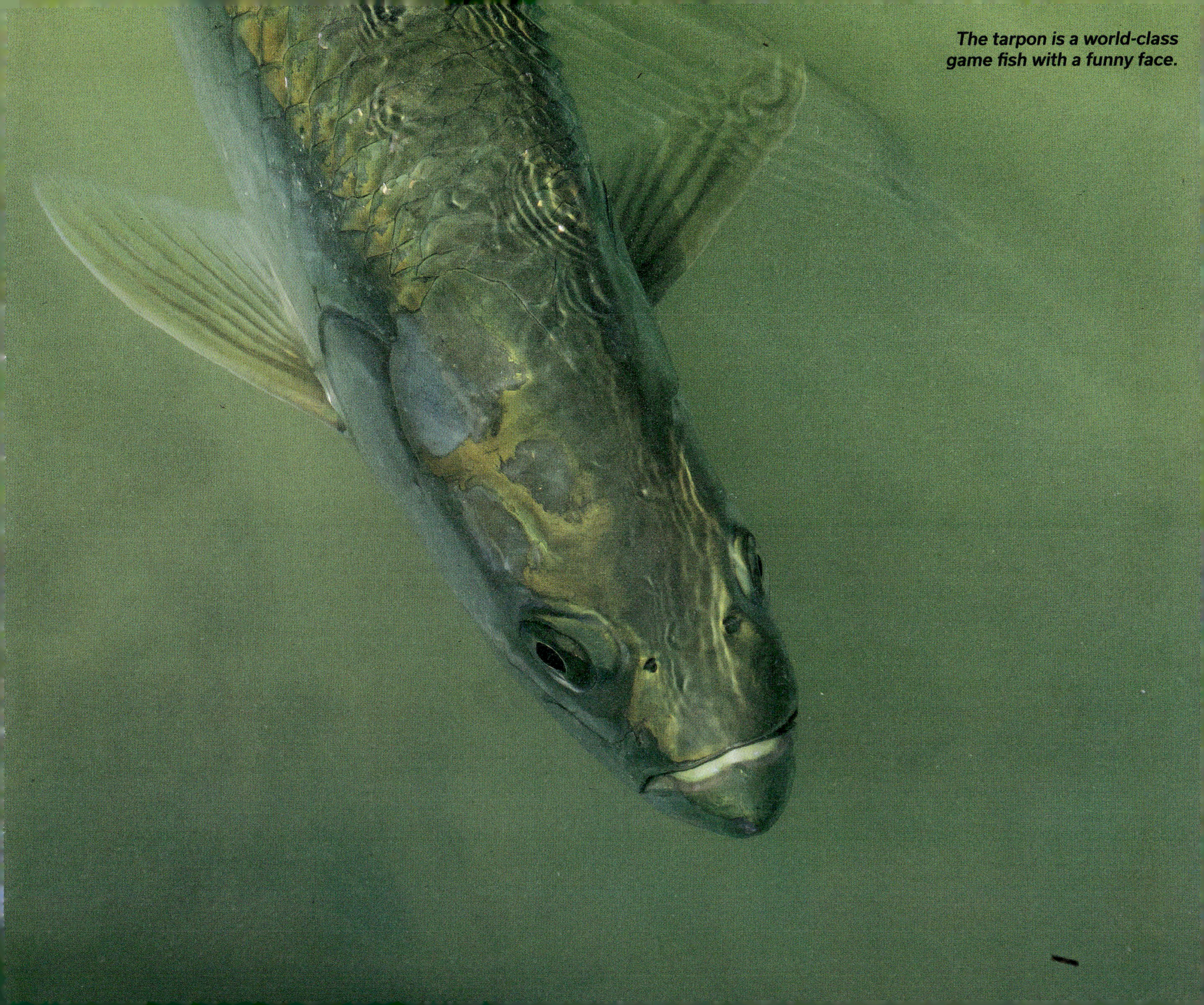

The tarpon is a world-class game fish with a funny face.

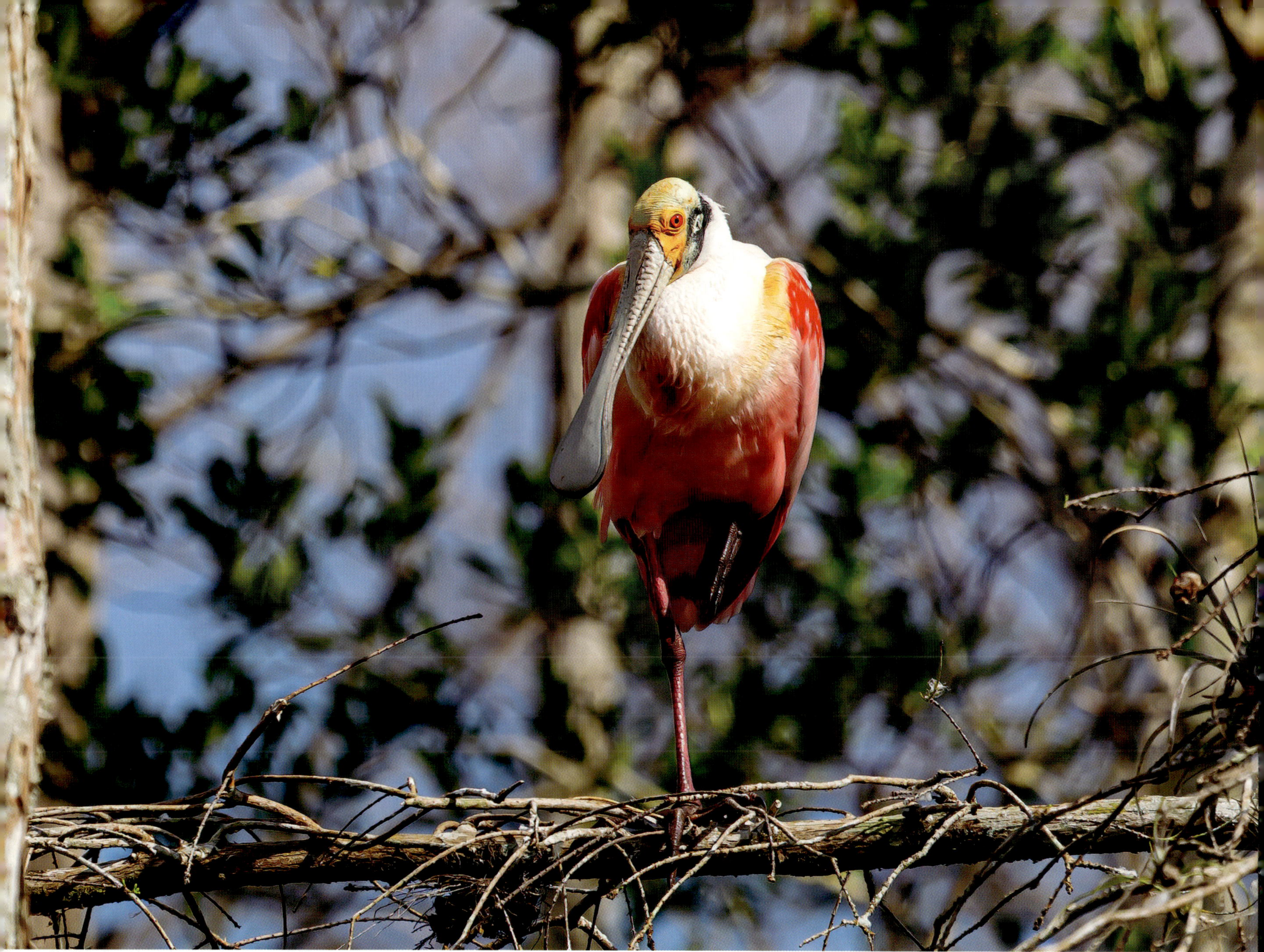

Roseate Spoonbills are among the most exotic and beautiful birds we have here.

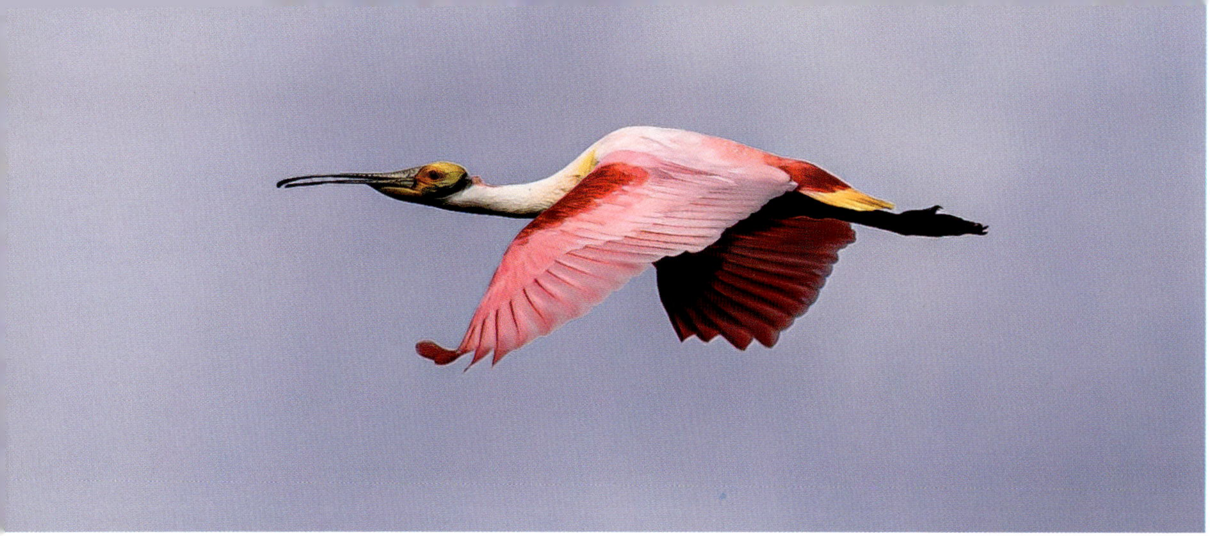

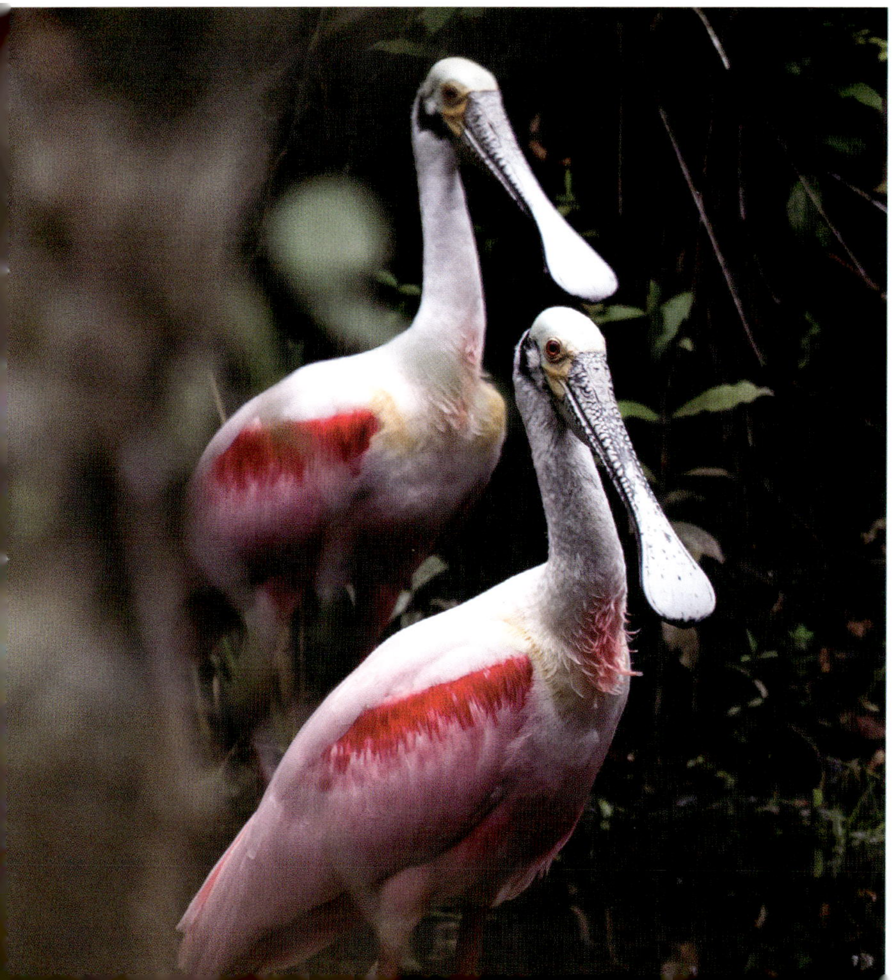

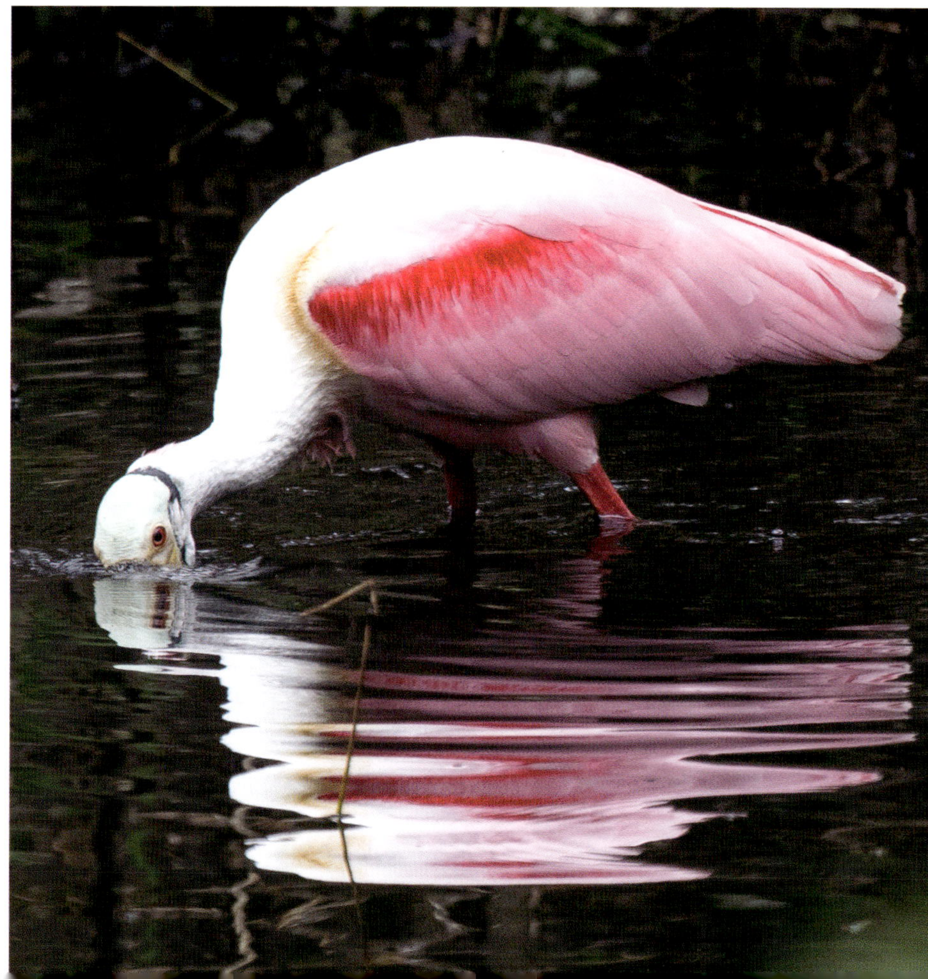

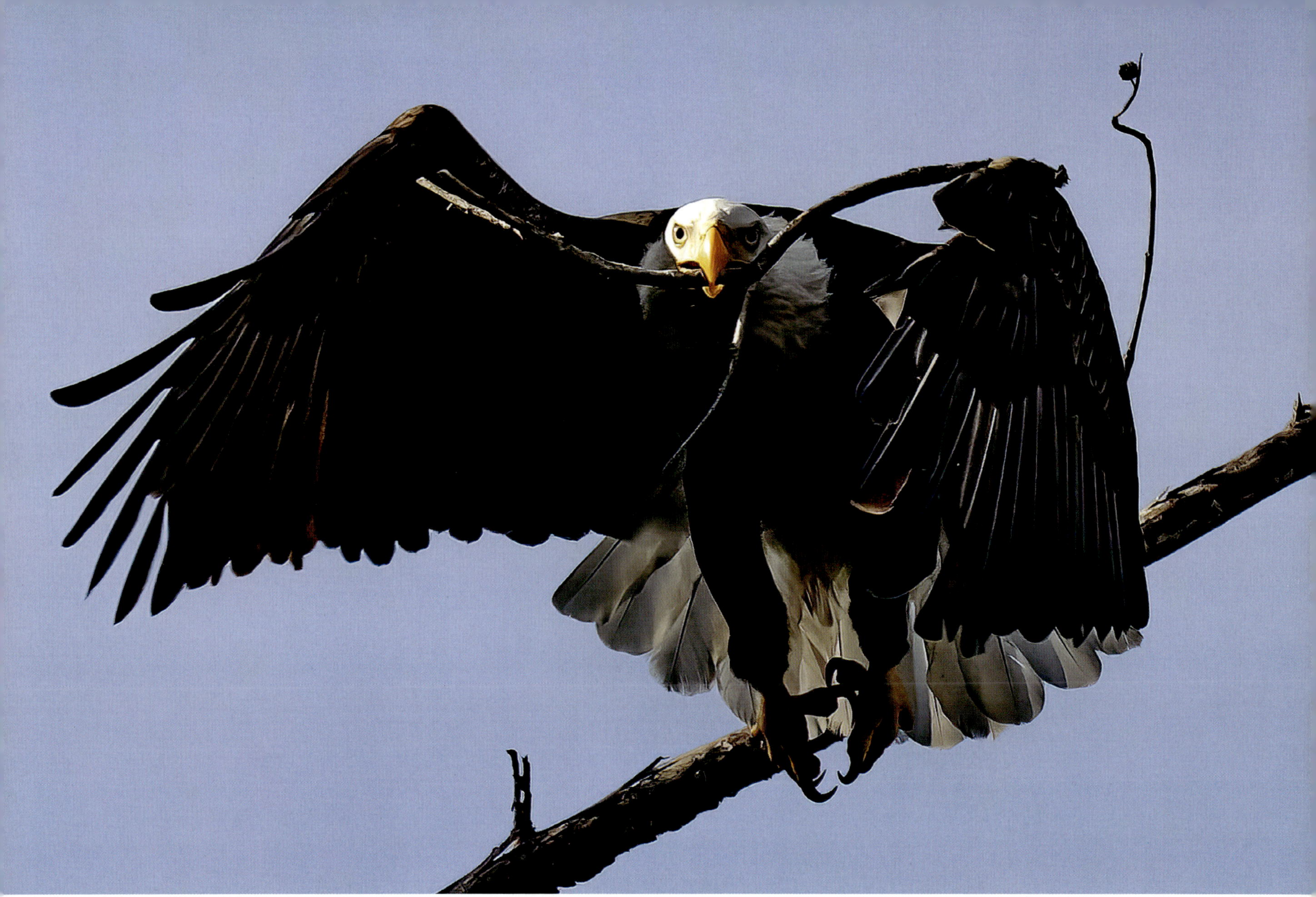

A bald eagle coming in hot with a big stick during nest-building season.

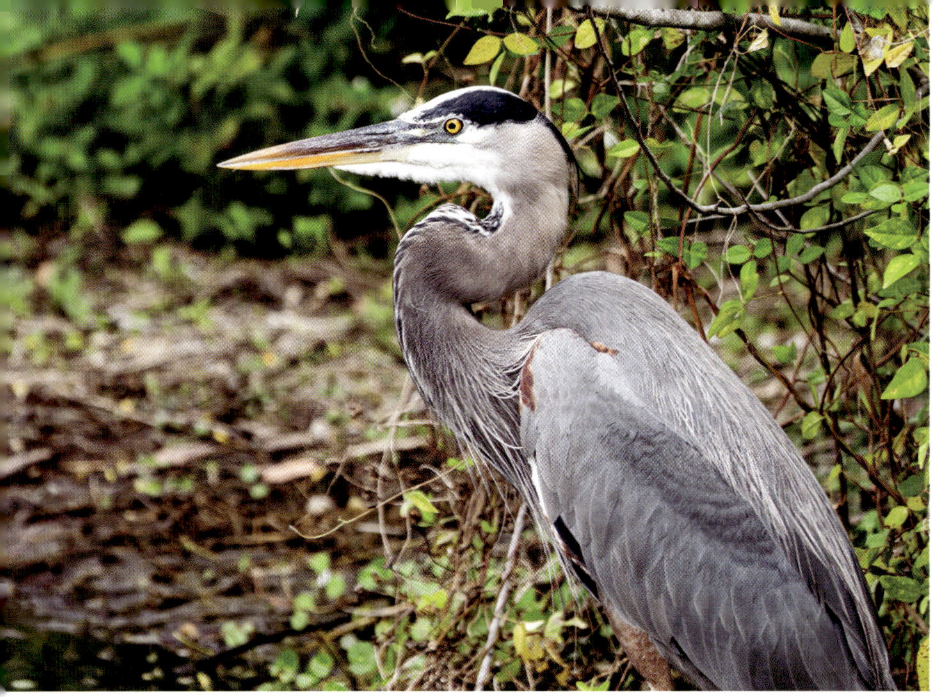
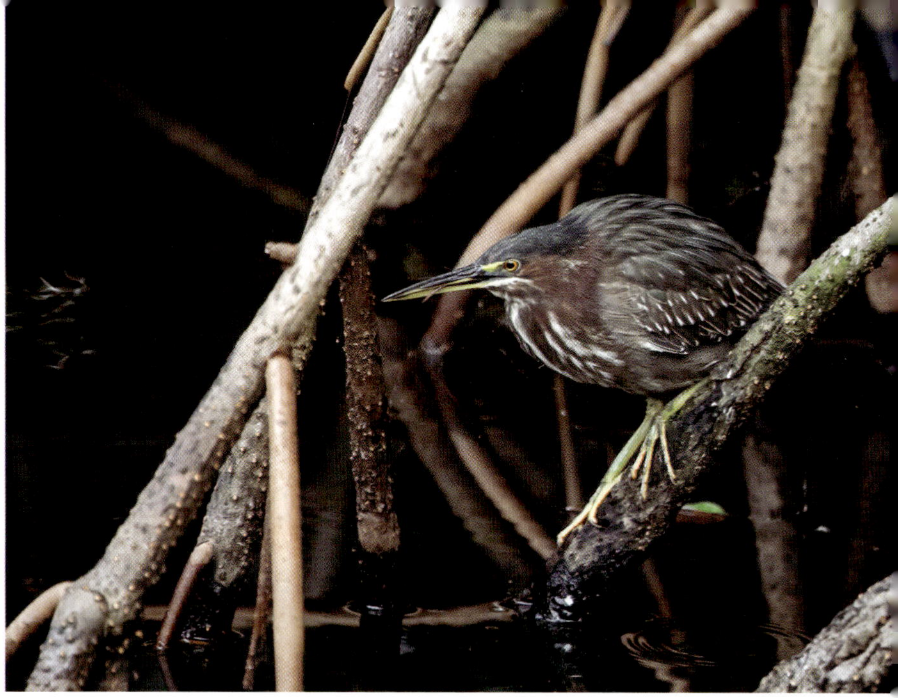
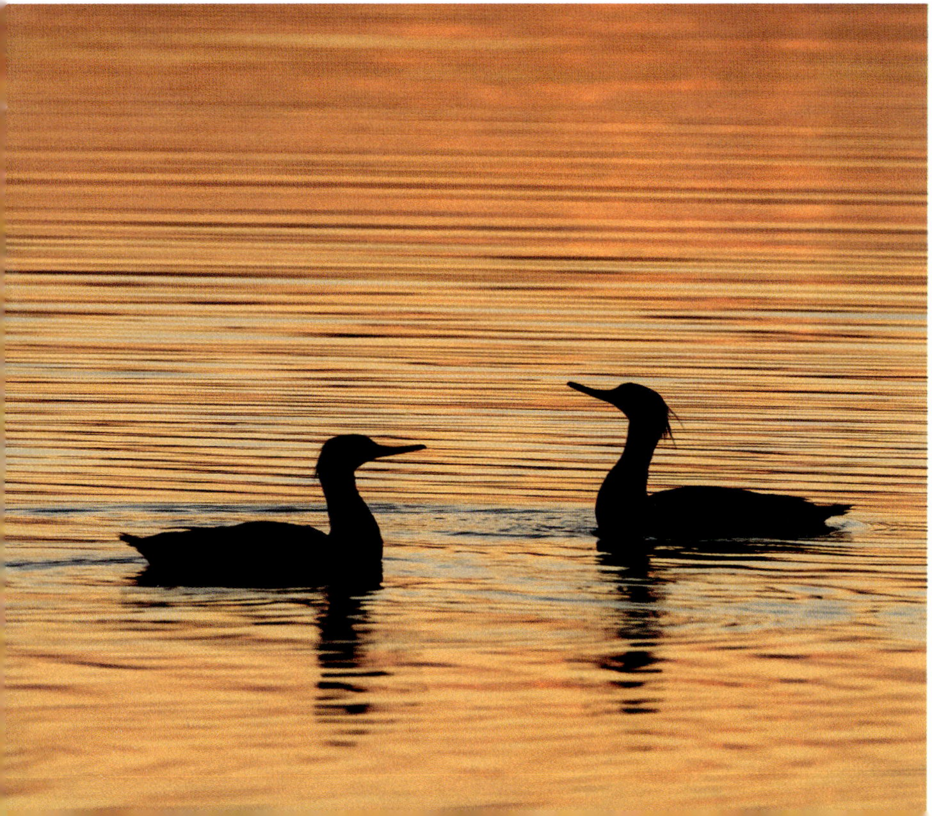
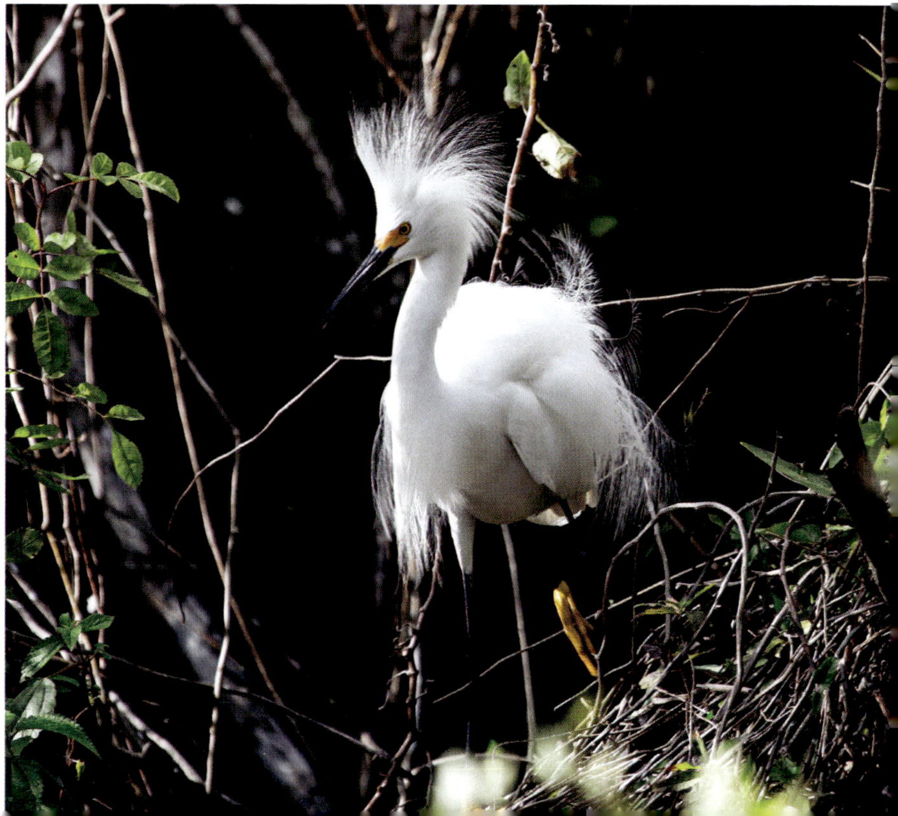

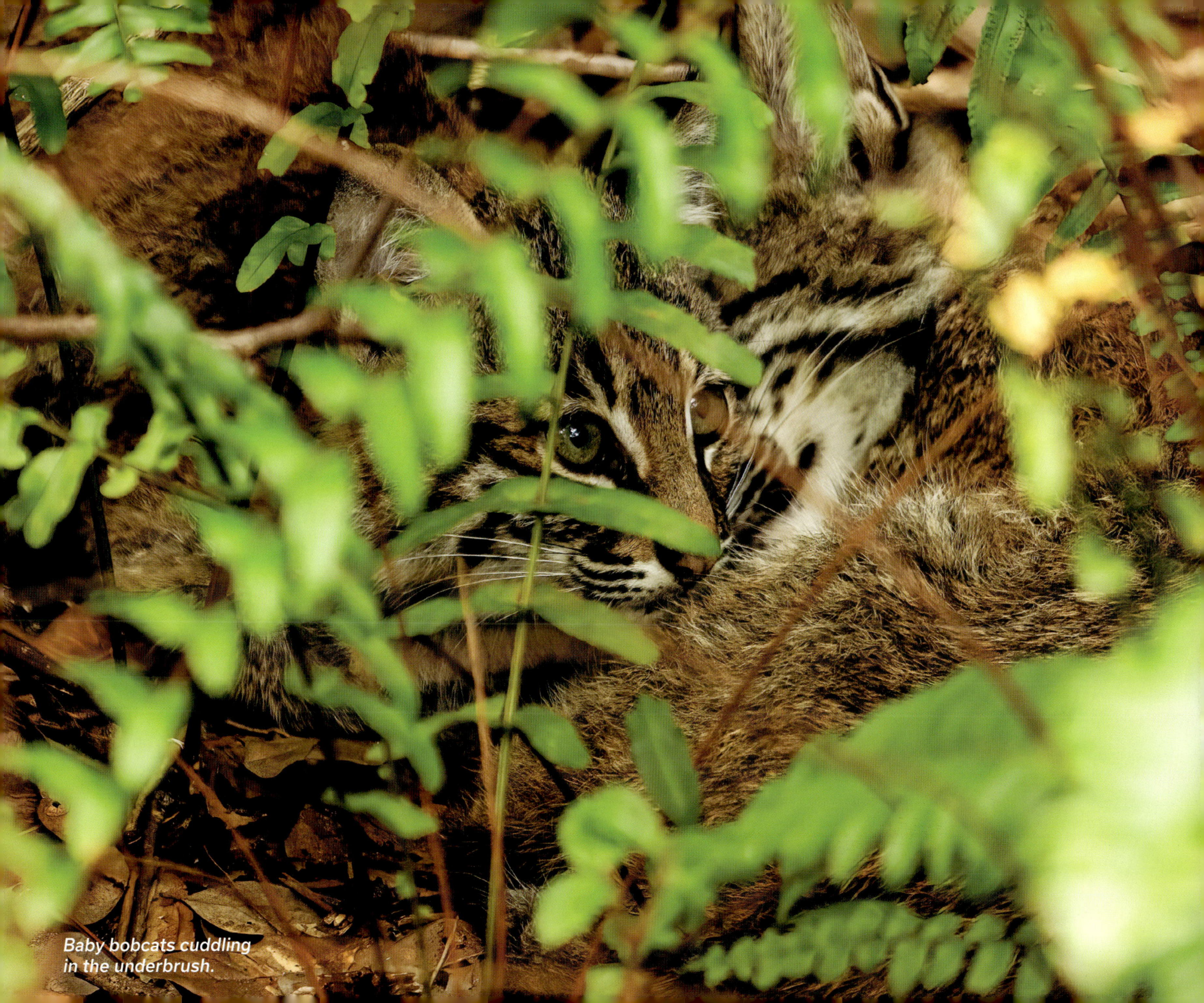

Baby bobcats cuddling in the underbrush.

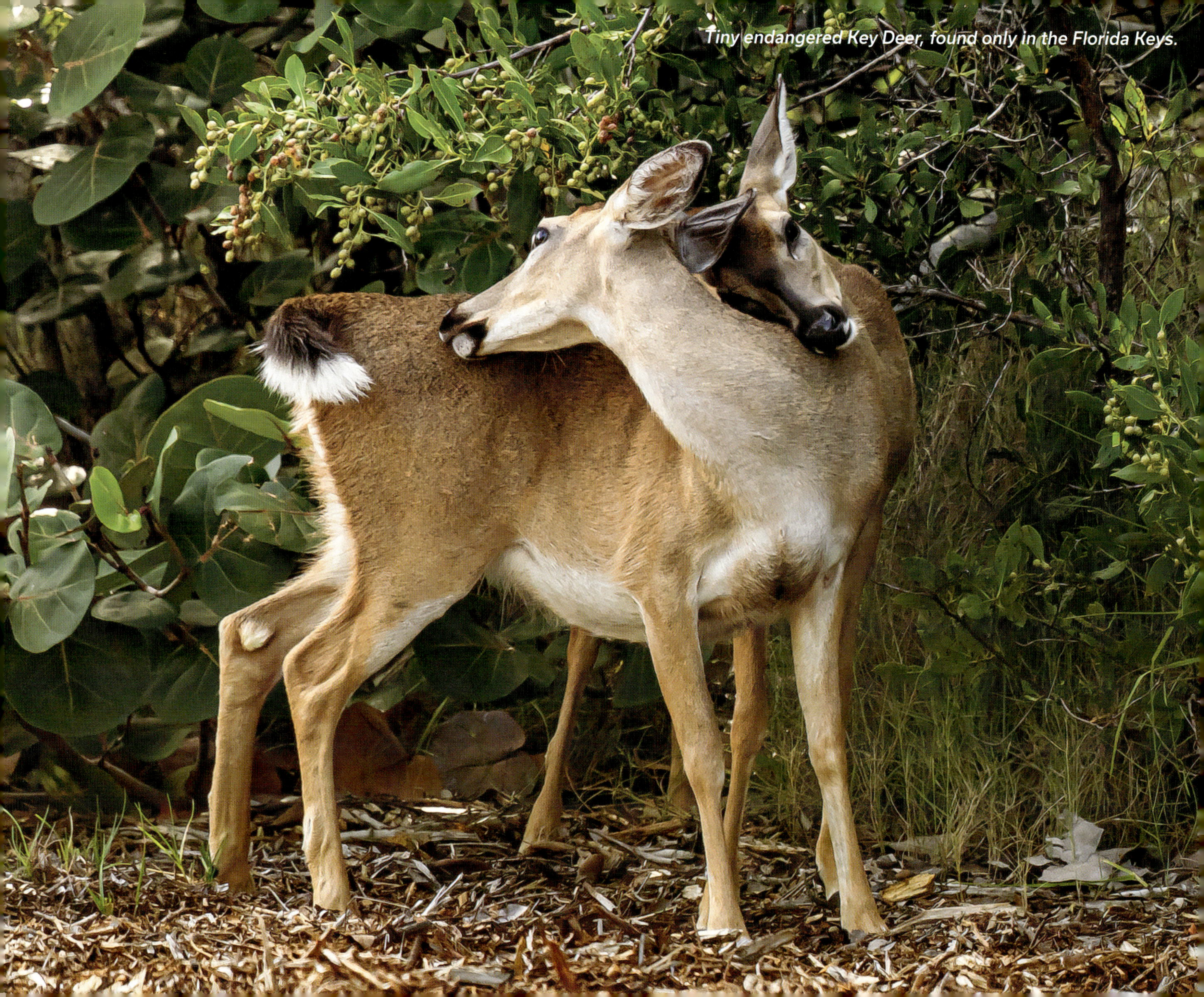

Tiny endangered Key Deer, found only in the Florida Keys.

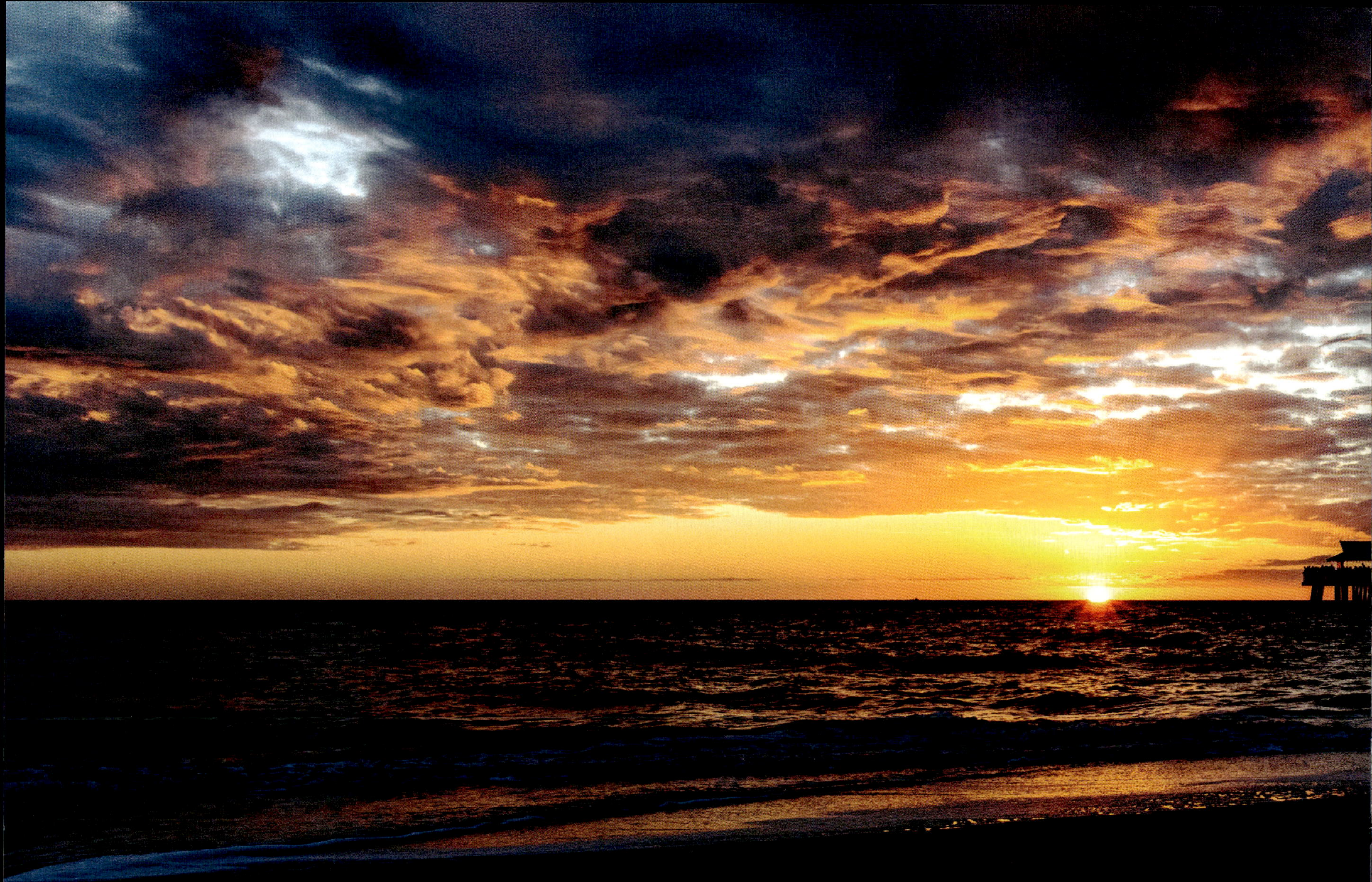

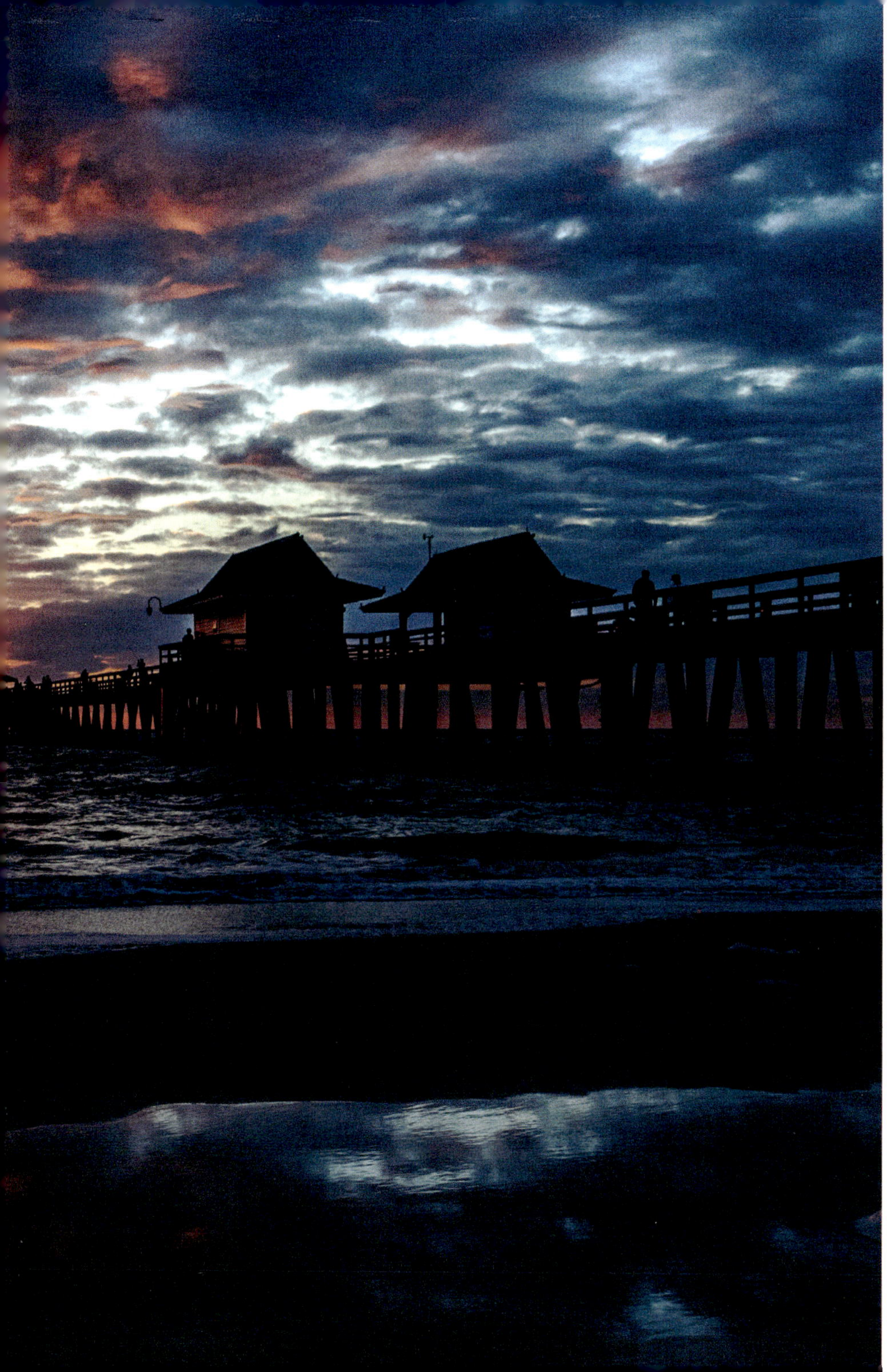

Sunset Glow as Day is Done

When you spend most of your time photographing sunrises, but make occasional late-afternoon trips to capture the sunset, you find yourself working in reverse order. The dramatic colors at the end of the day don't usually emerge until the sun has dropped close to the horizon. Once the sun disappears from view, the deepest and most brilliant colors of the evening will bloom into the sky until they, too, finally fade. Day is done now, and it's time for most of us to rest. In a matter of hours, the cycle will resume as the darkness of night once again melts away and new light emerges. We'll then celebrate "magic time" and our next new beginning.

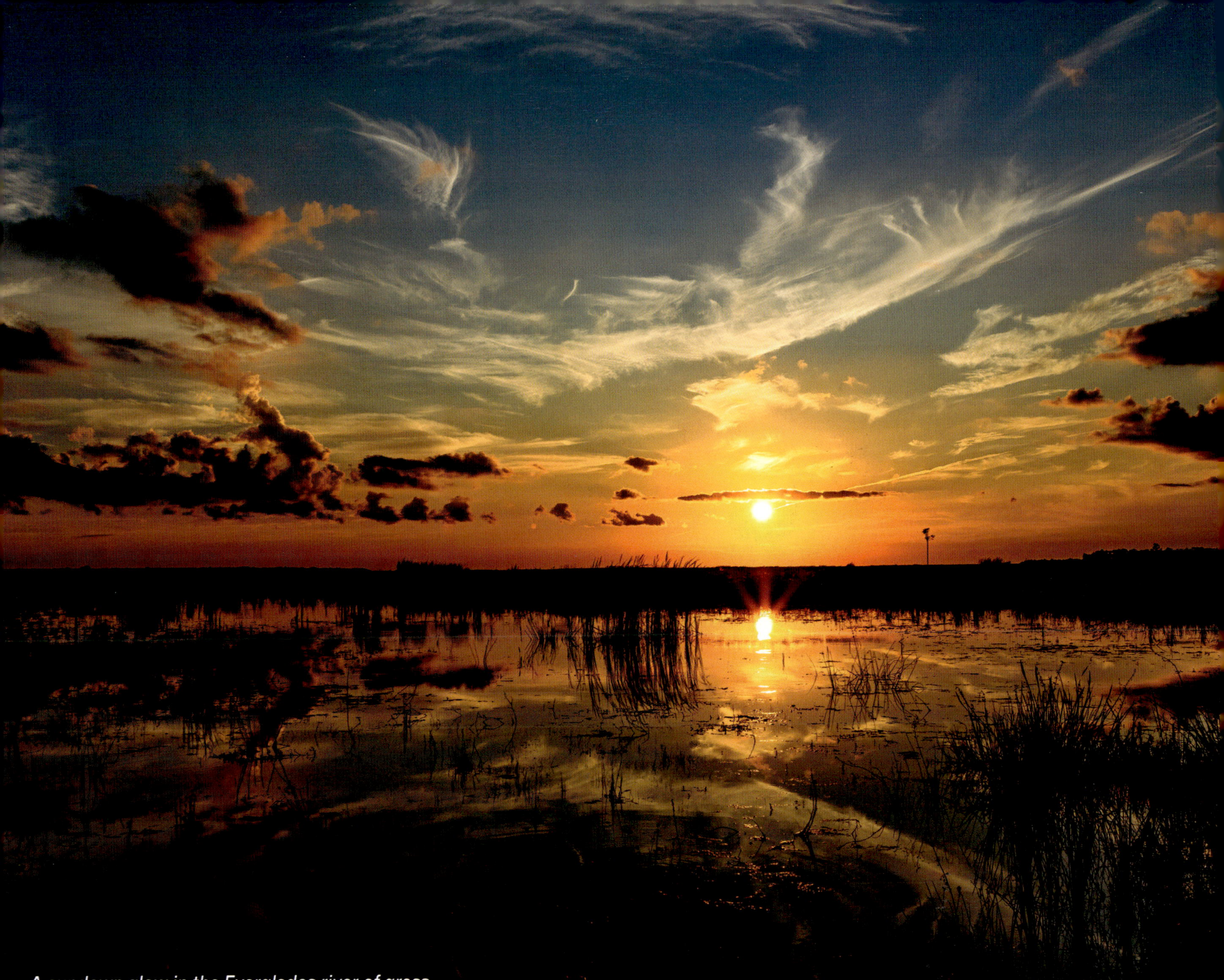

A sundown glow in the Everglades river of grass.

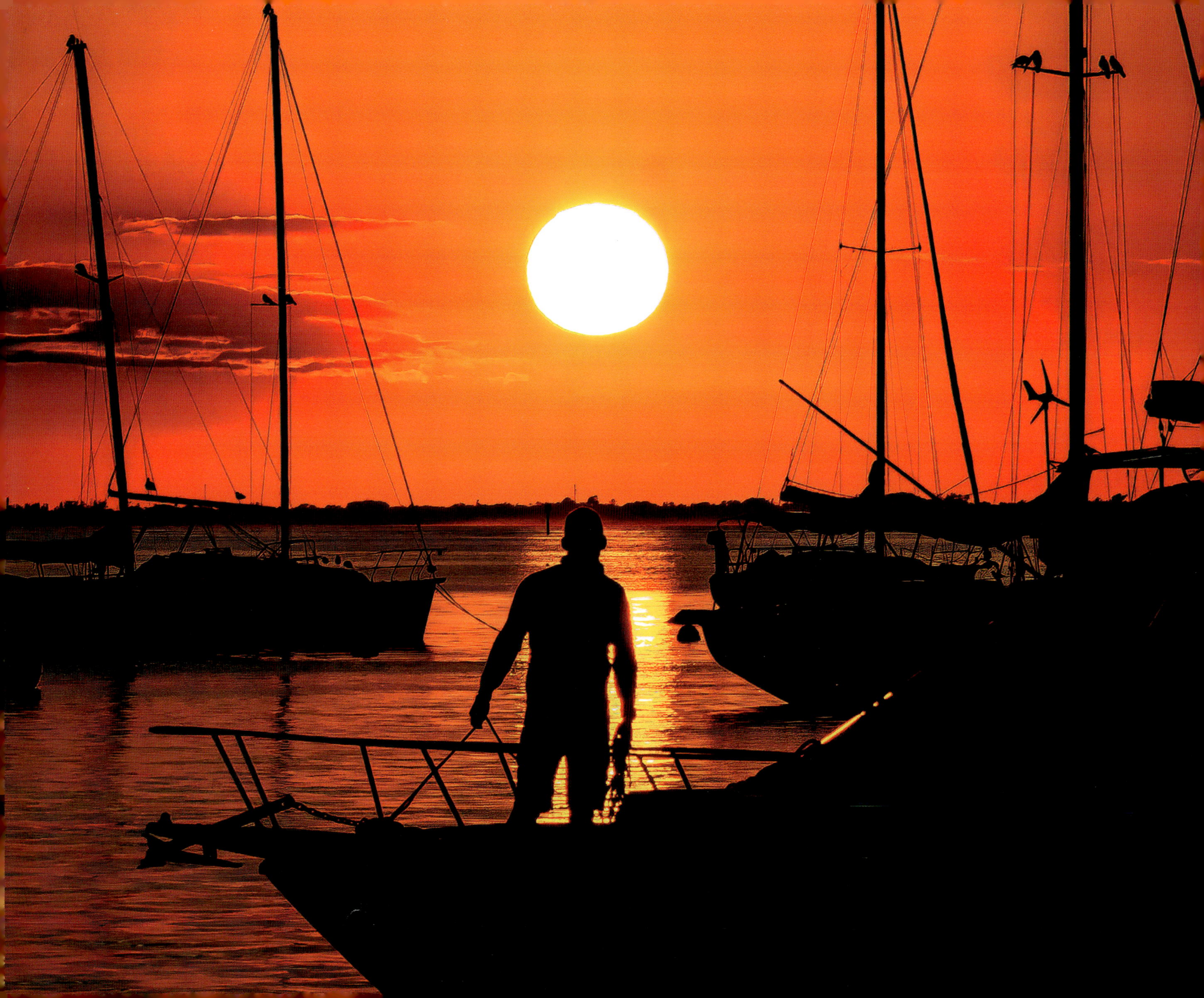

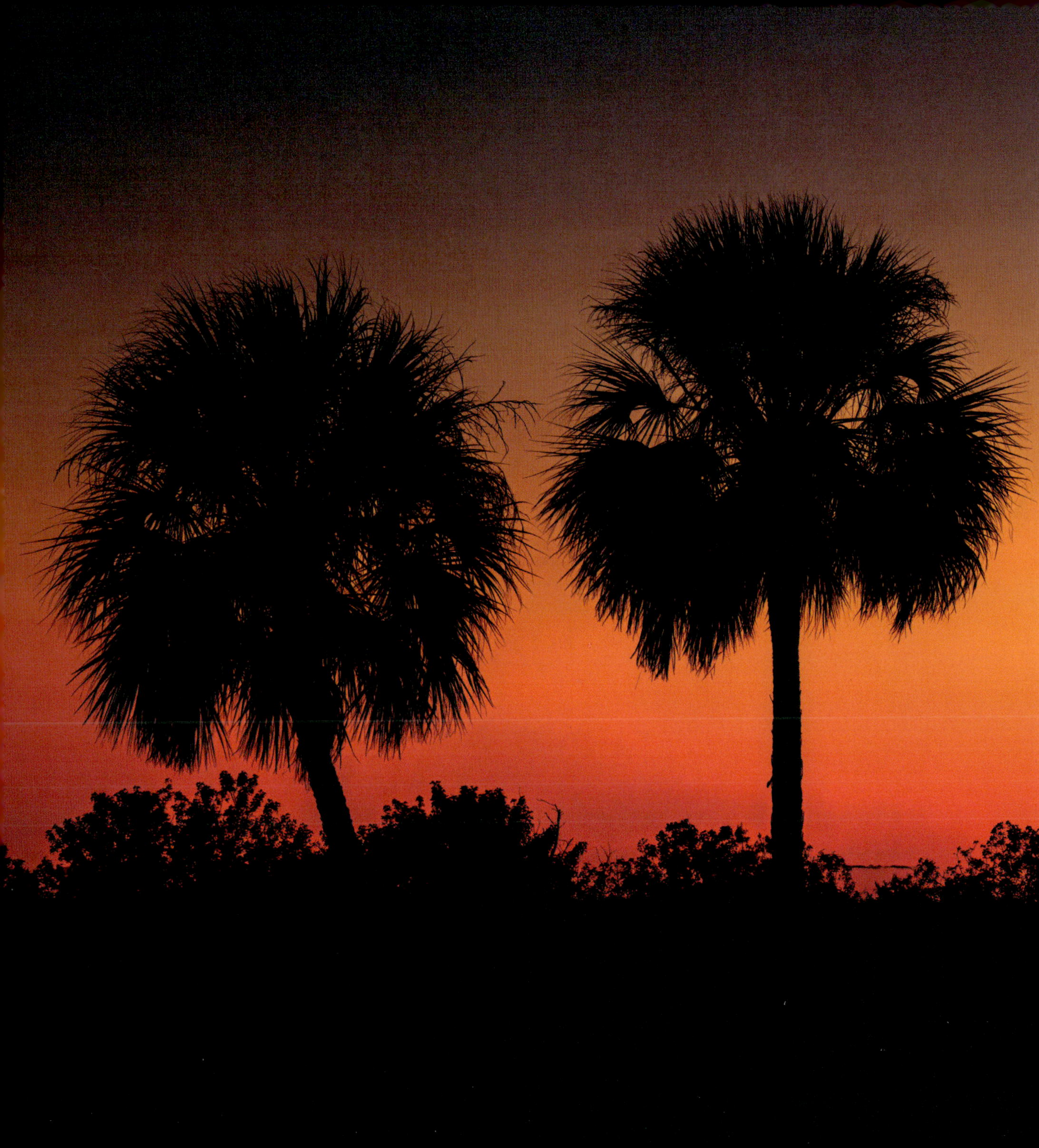

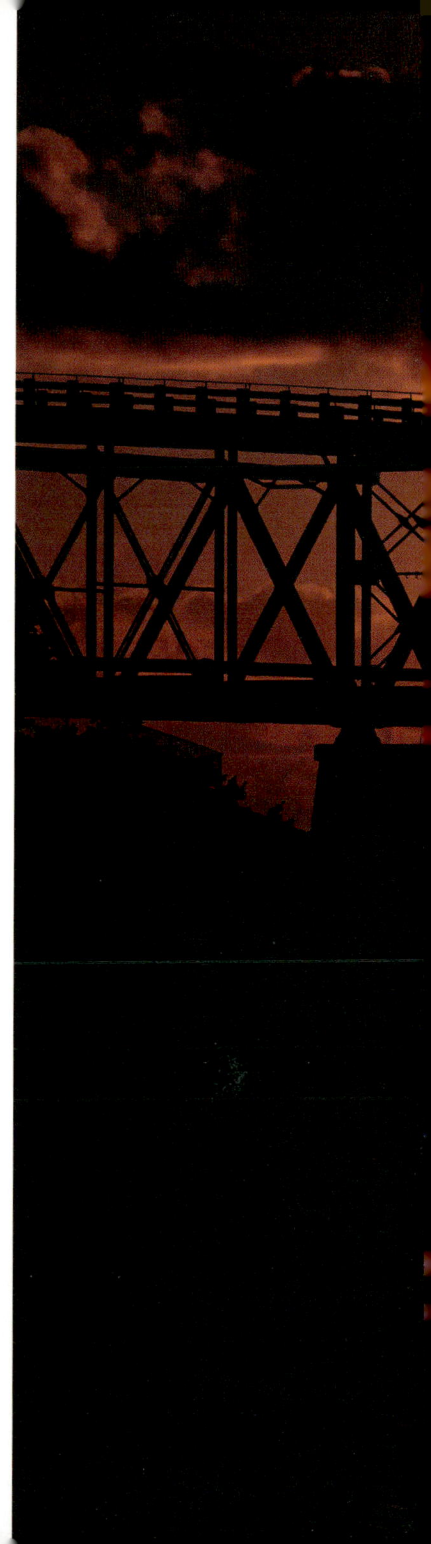

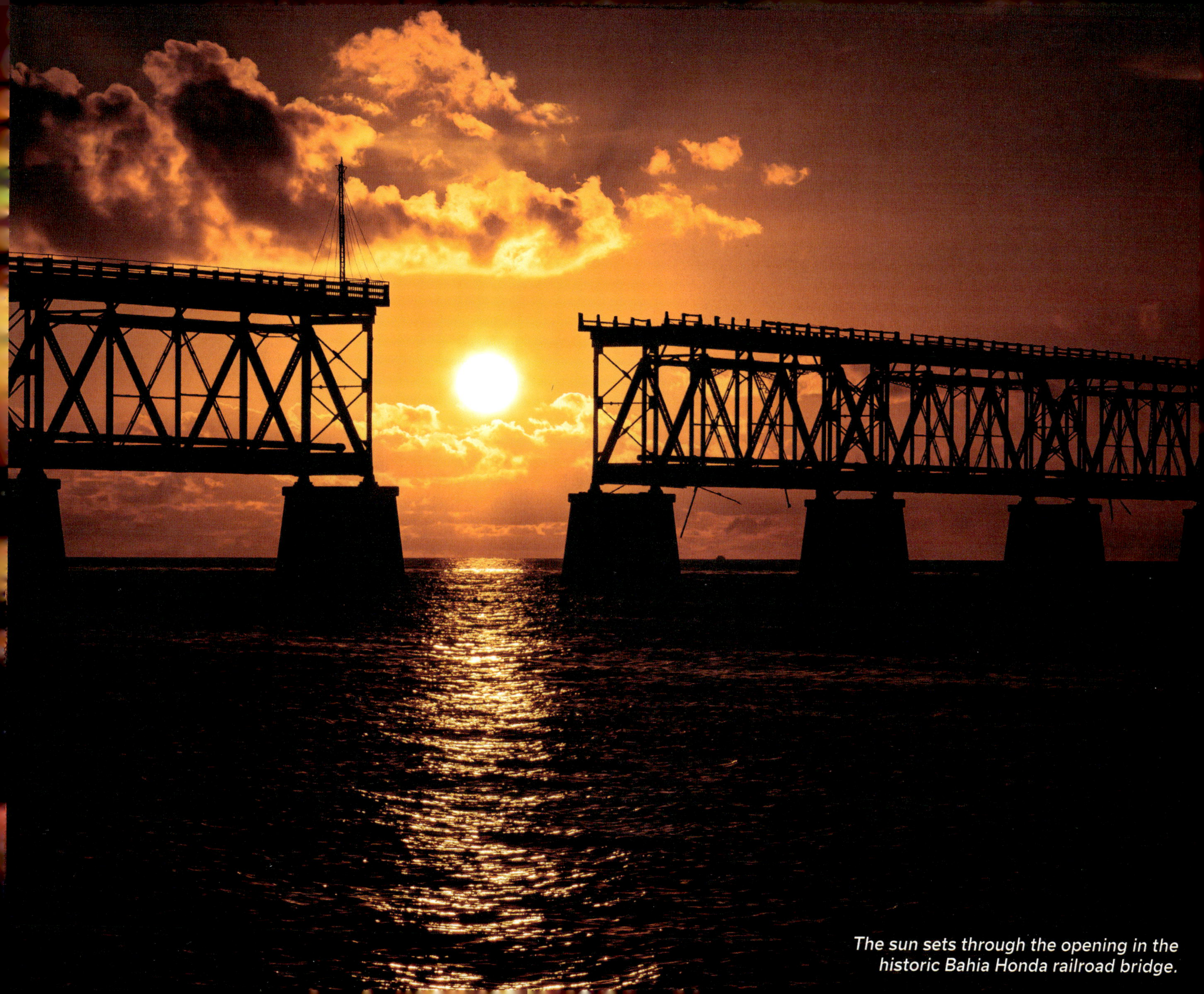

The sun sets through the opening in the historic Bahia Honda railroad bridge.

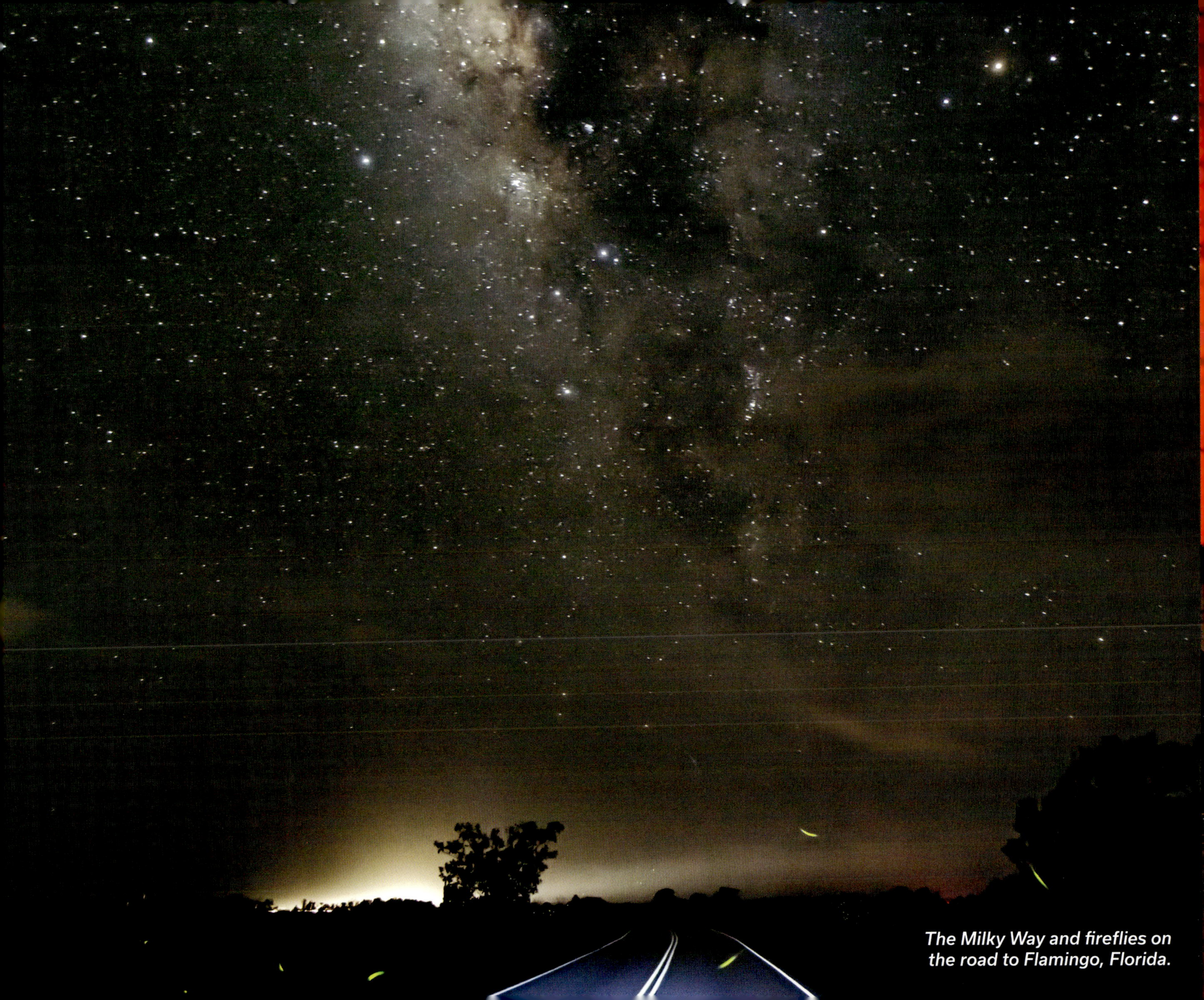

The Milky Way and fireflies on the road to Flamingo, Florida.

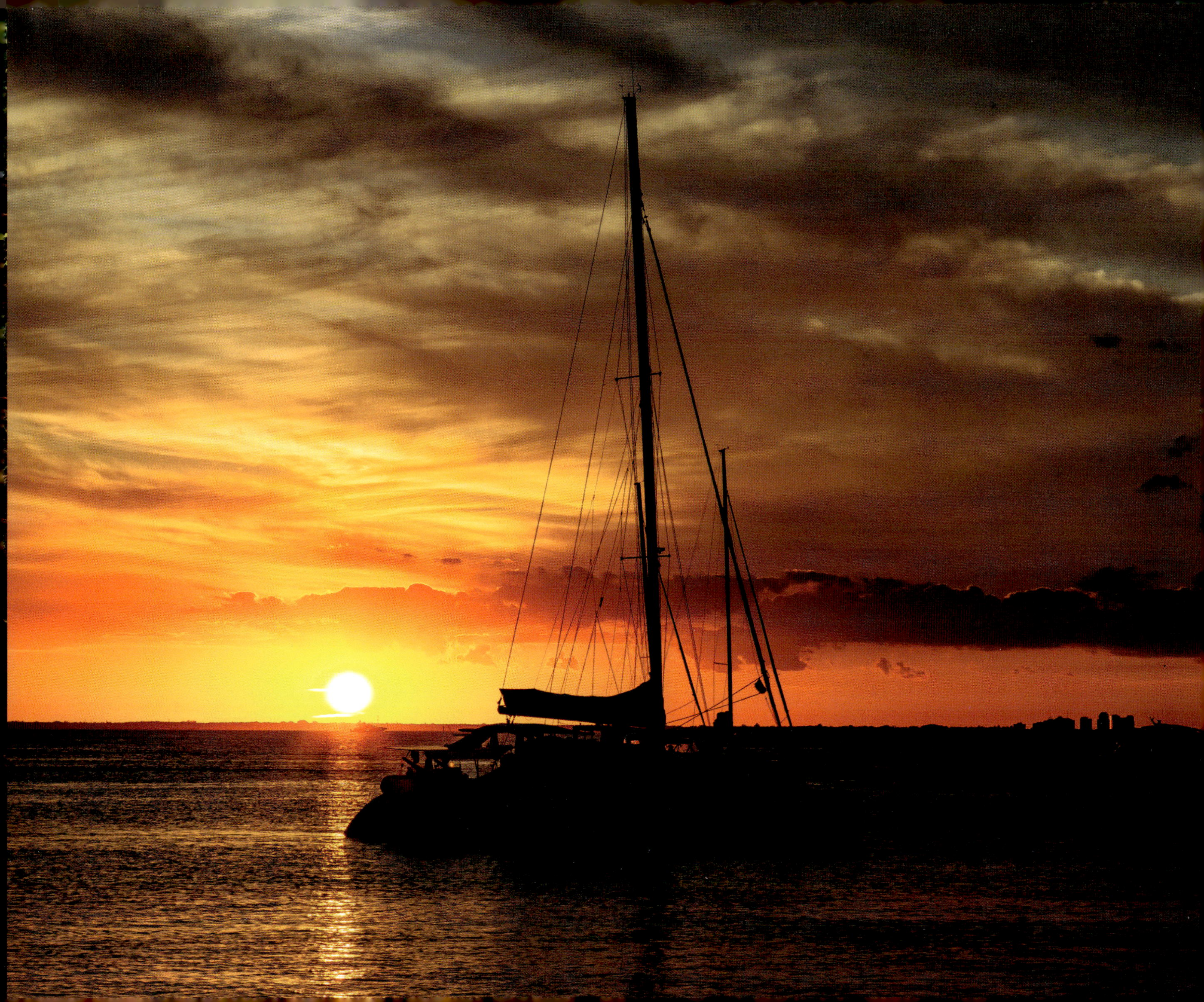

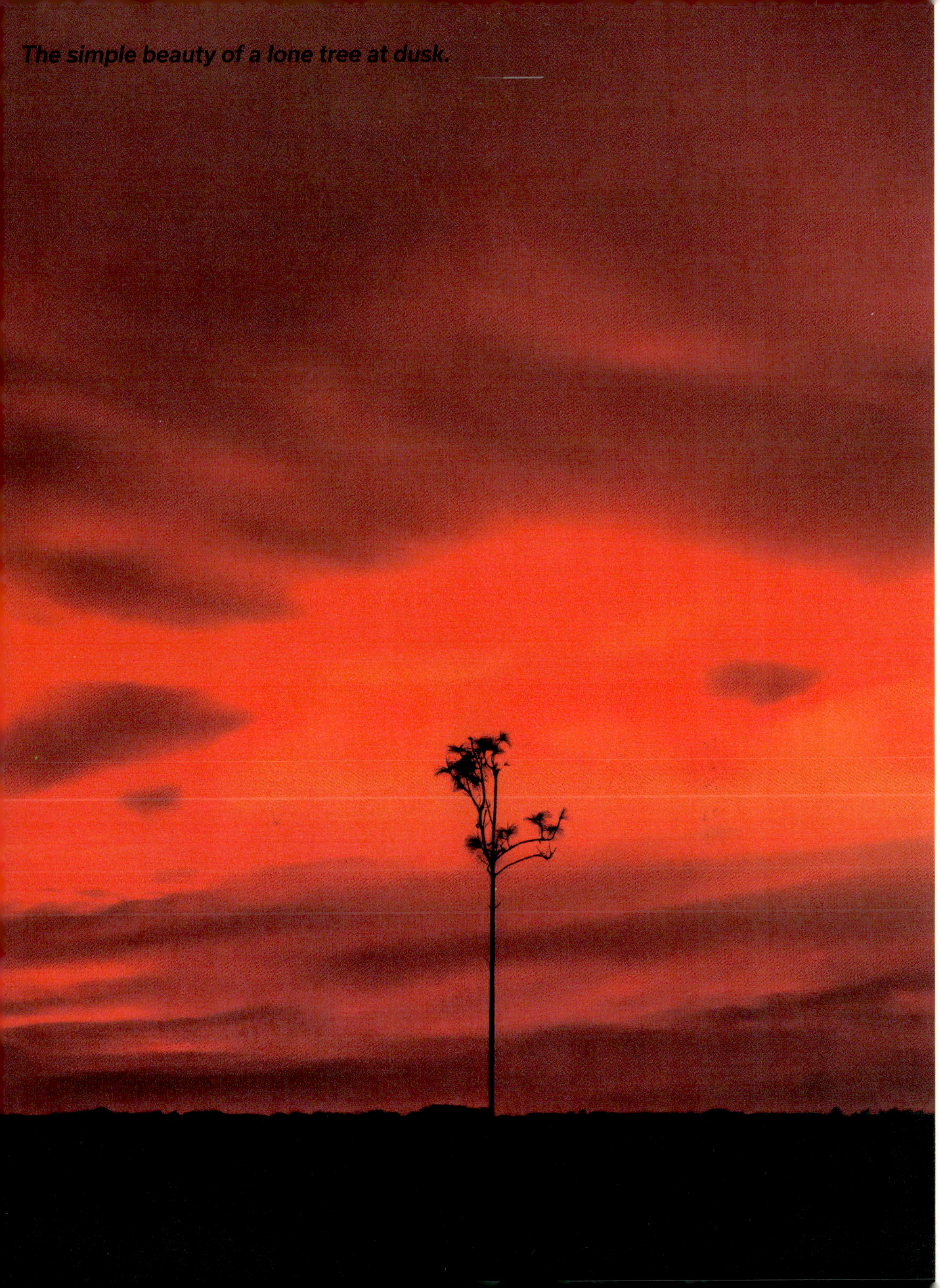

The simple beauty of a lone tree at dusk.

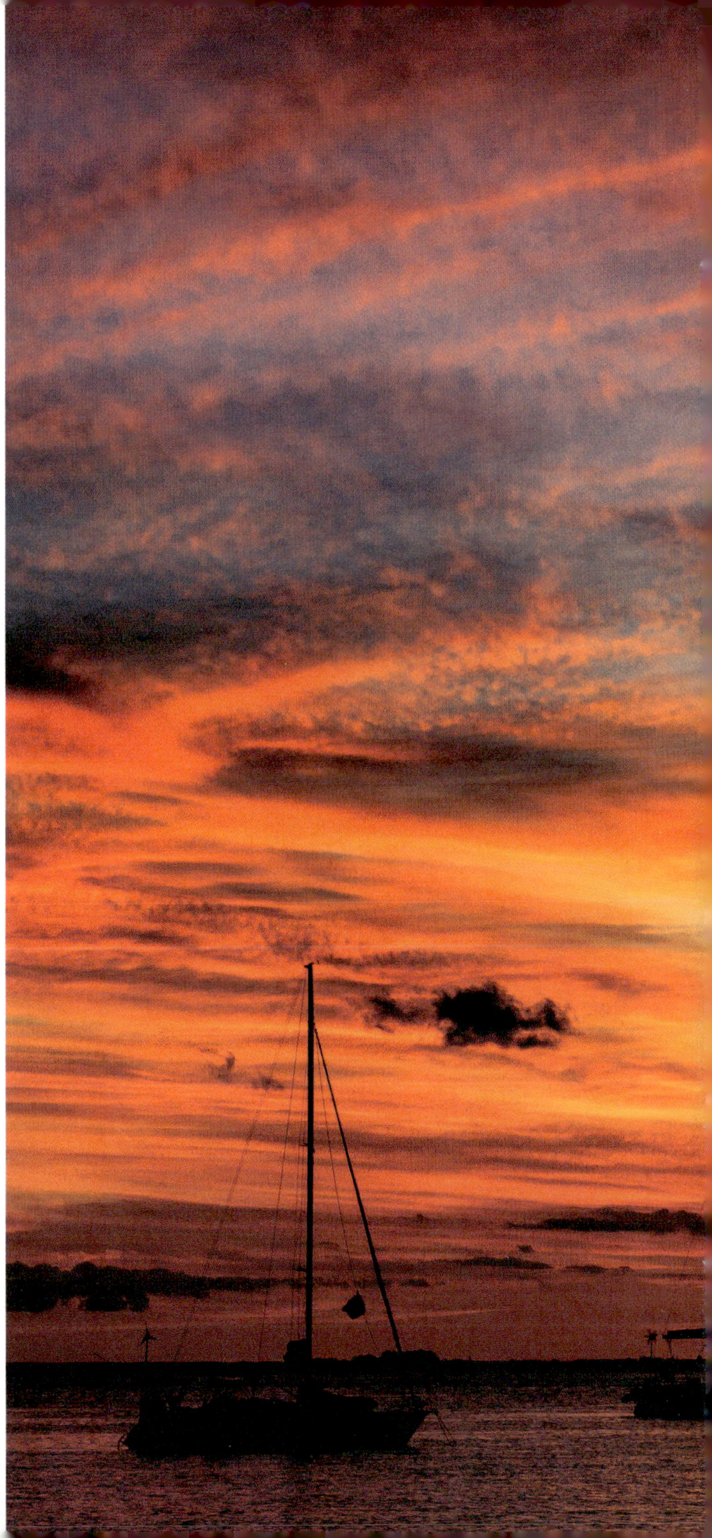

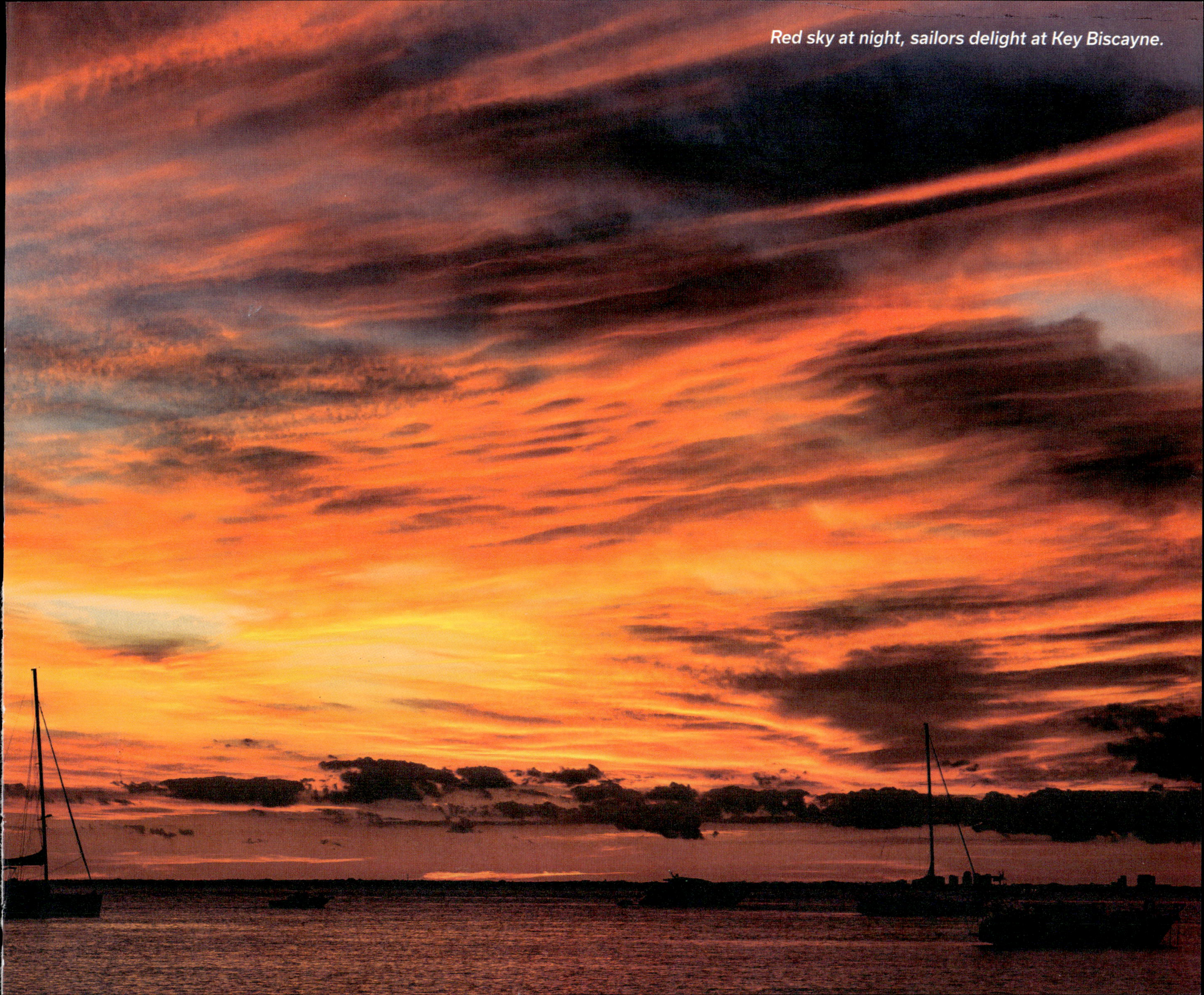

Red sky at night, sailors delight at Key Biscayne.

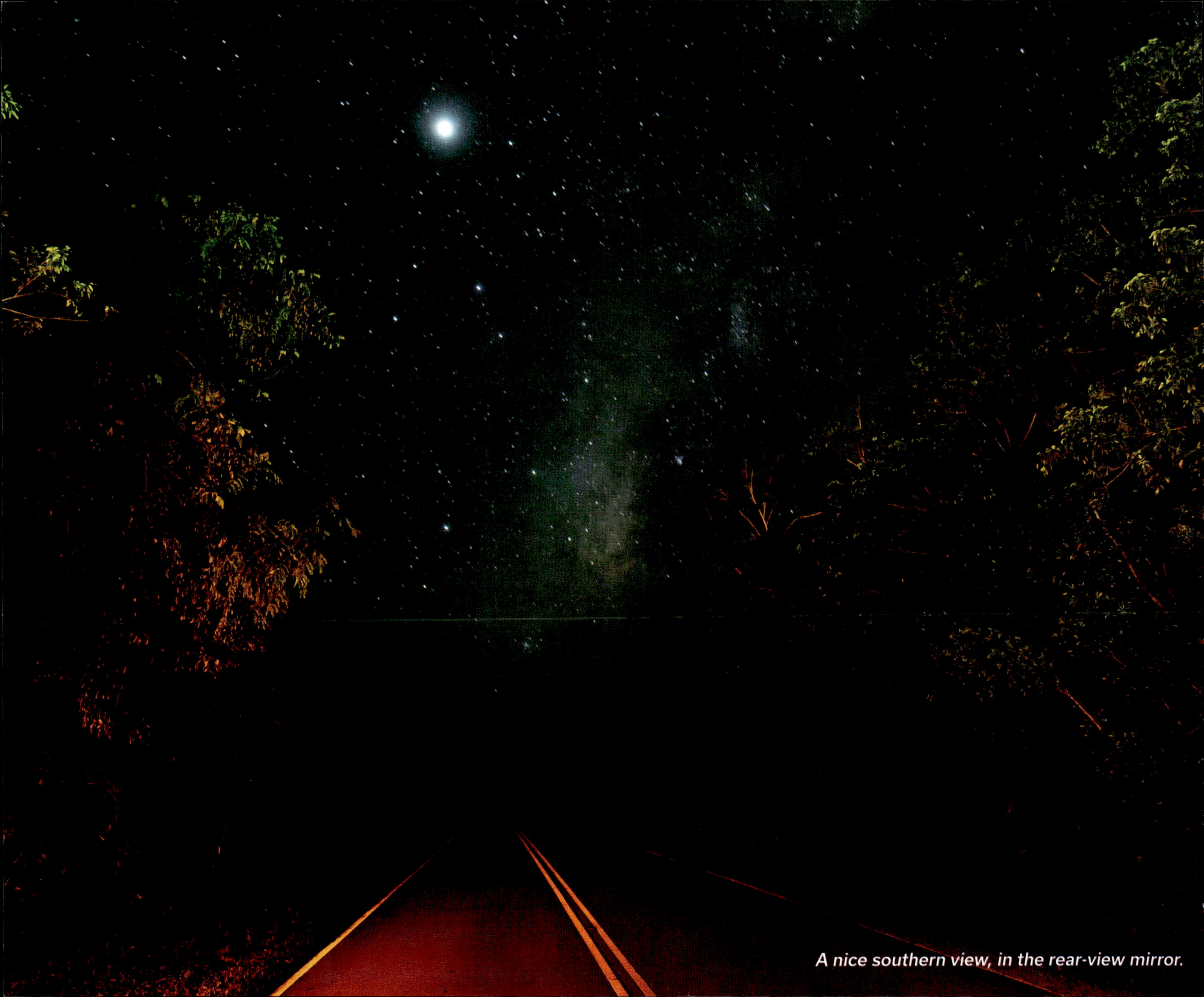

A nice southern view, in the rear-view mirror.

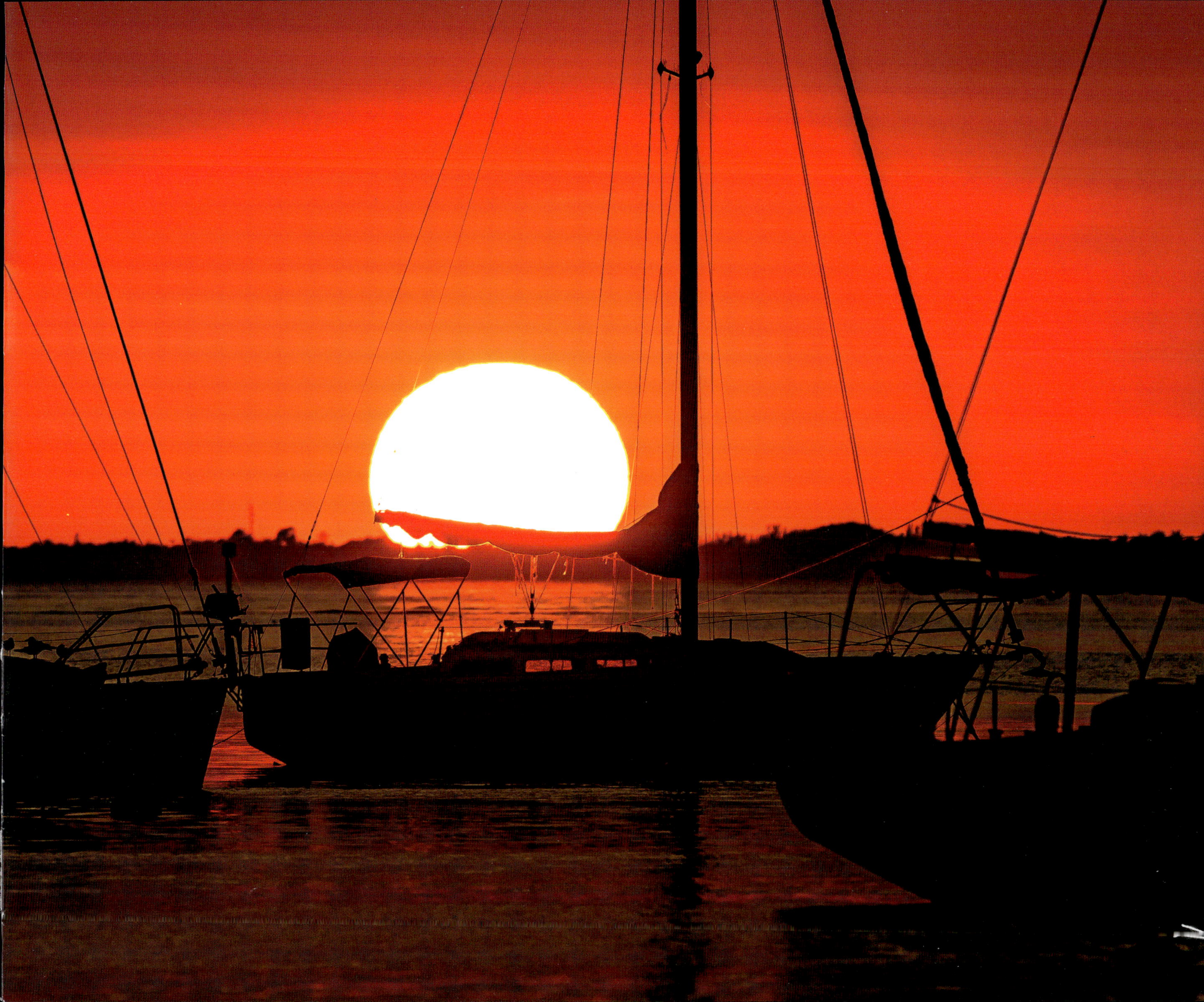

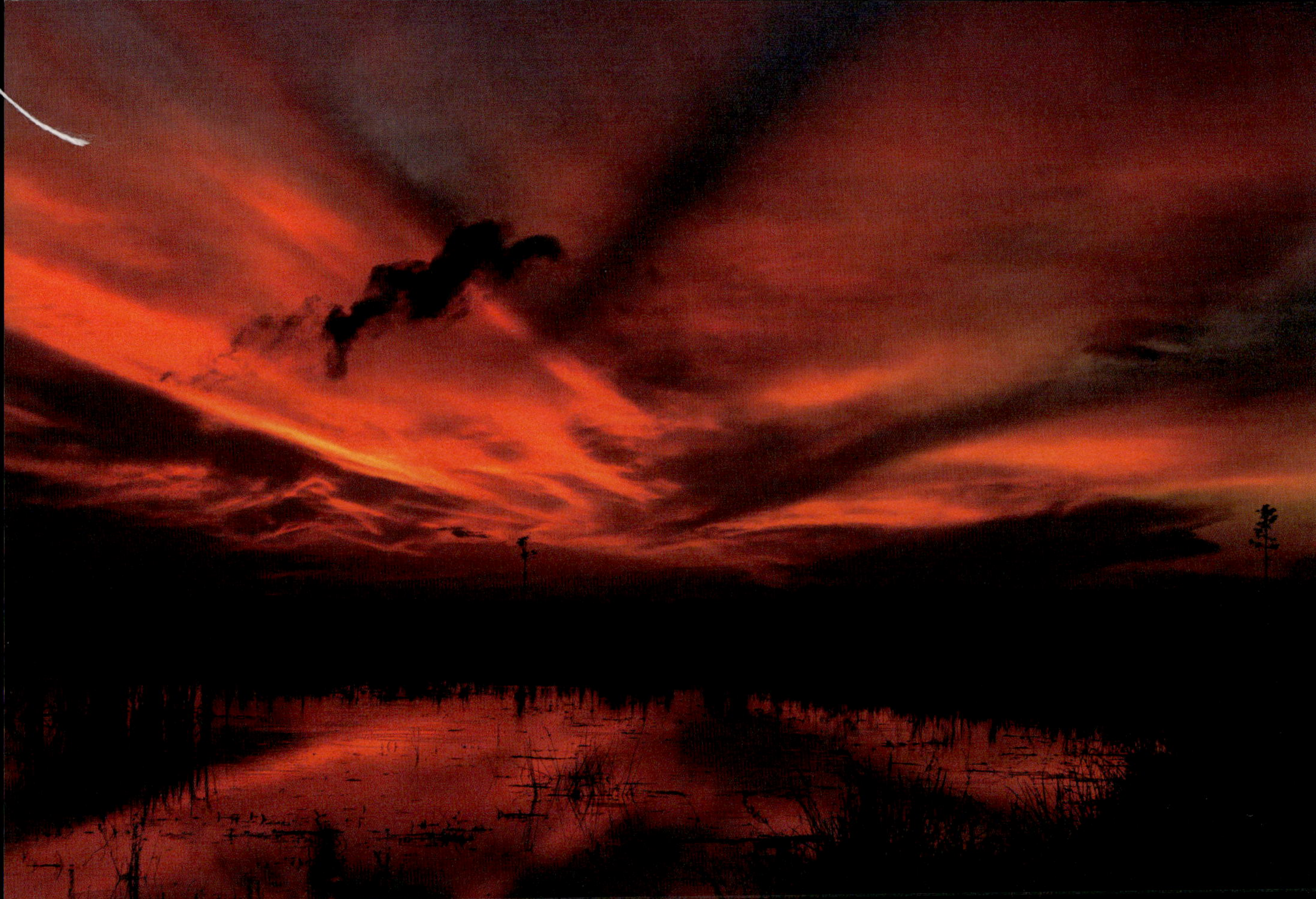

A fitting end to a good day here is a brilliant and reflective sunset in the Florida Everglades. Thank you for sharing my journey.

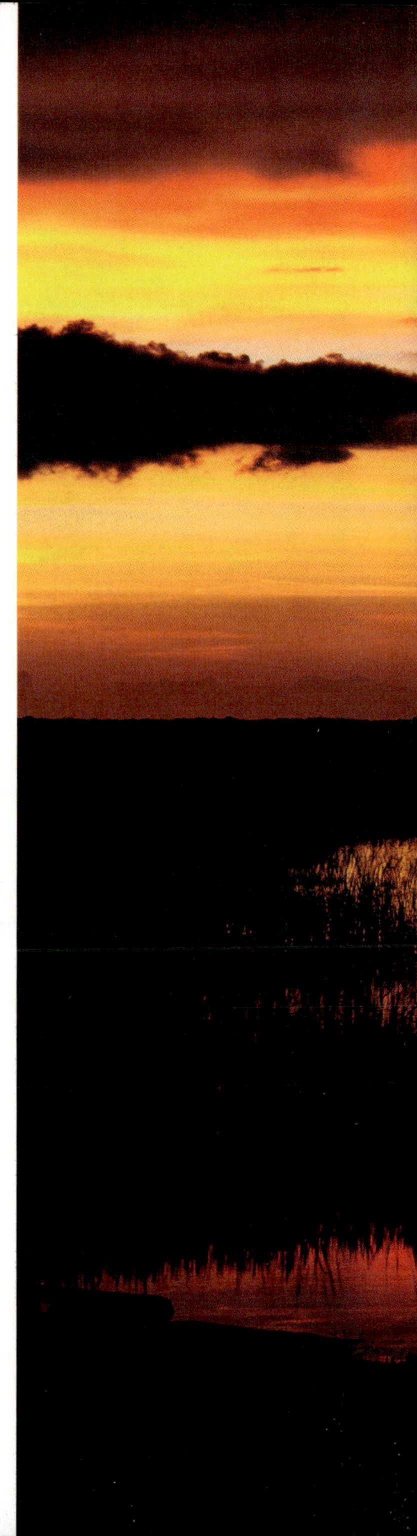

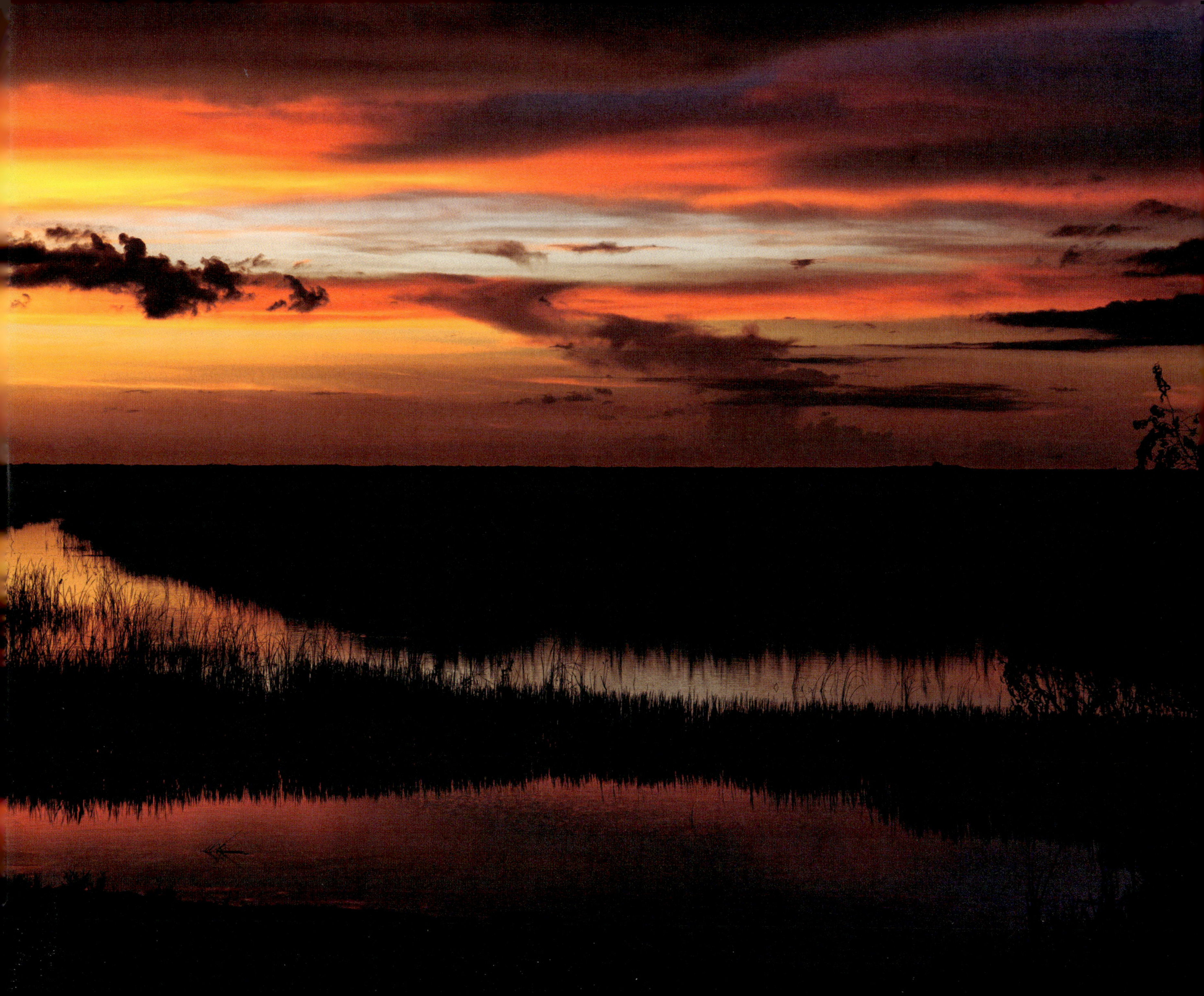

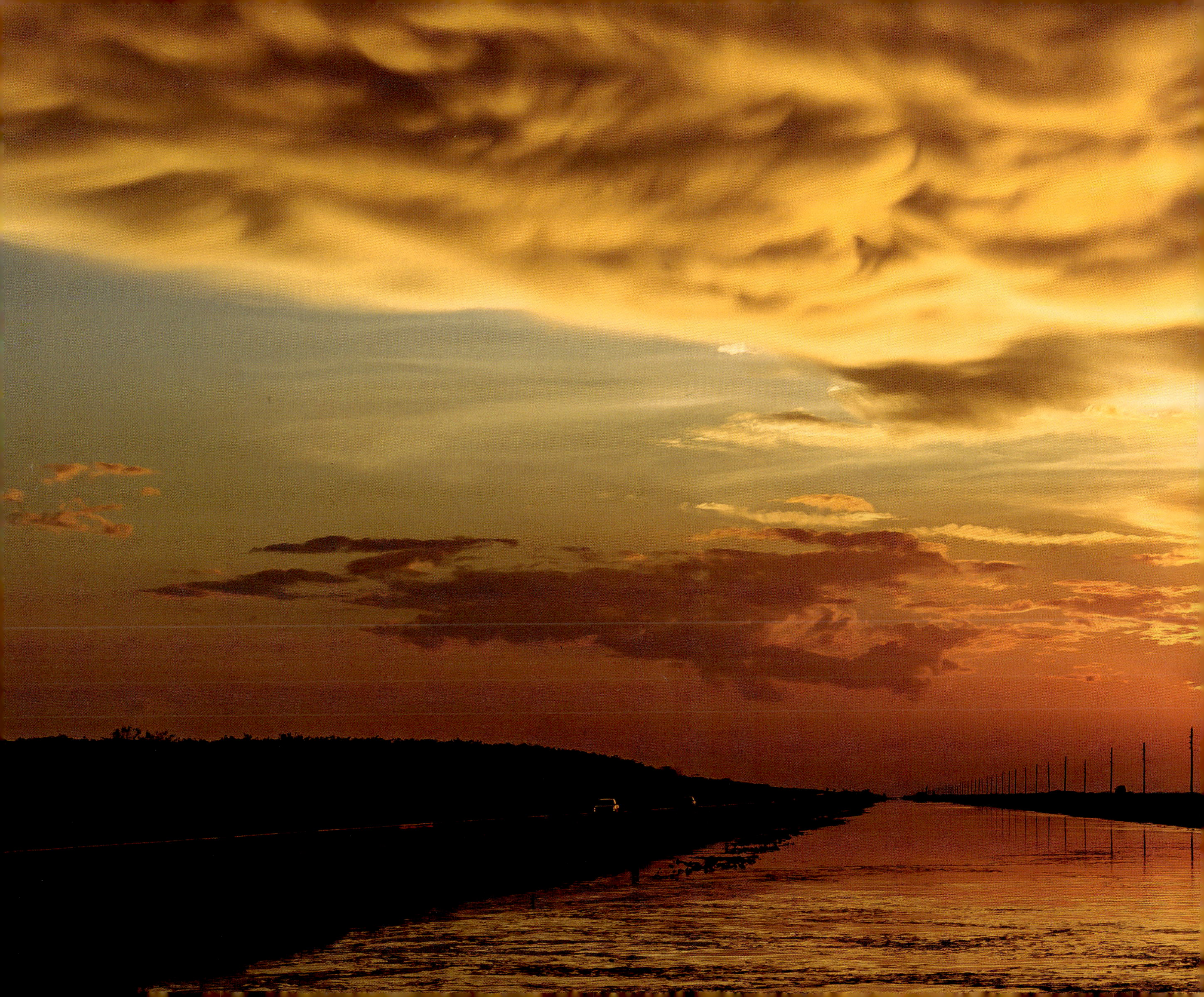

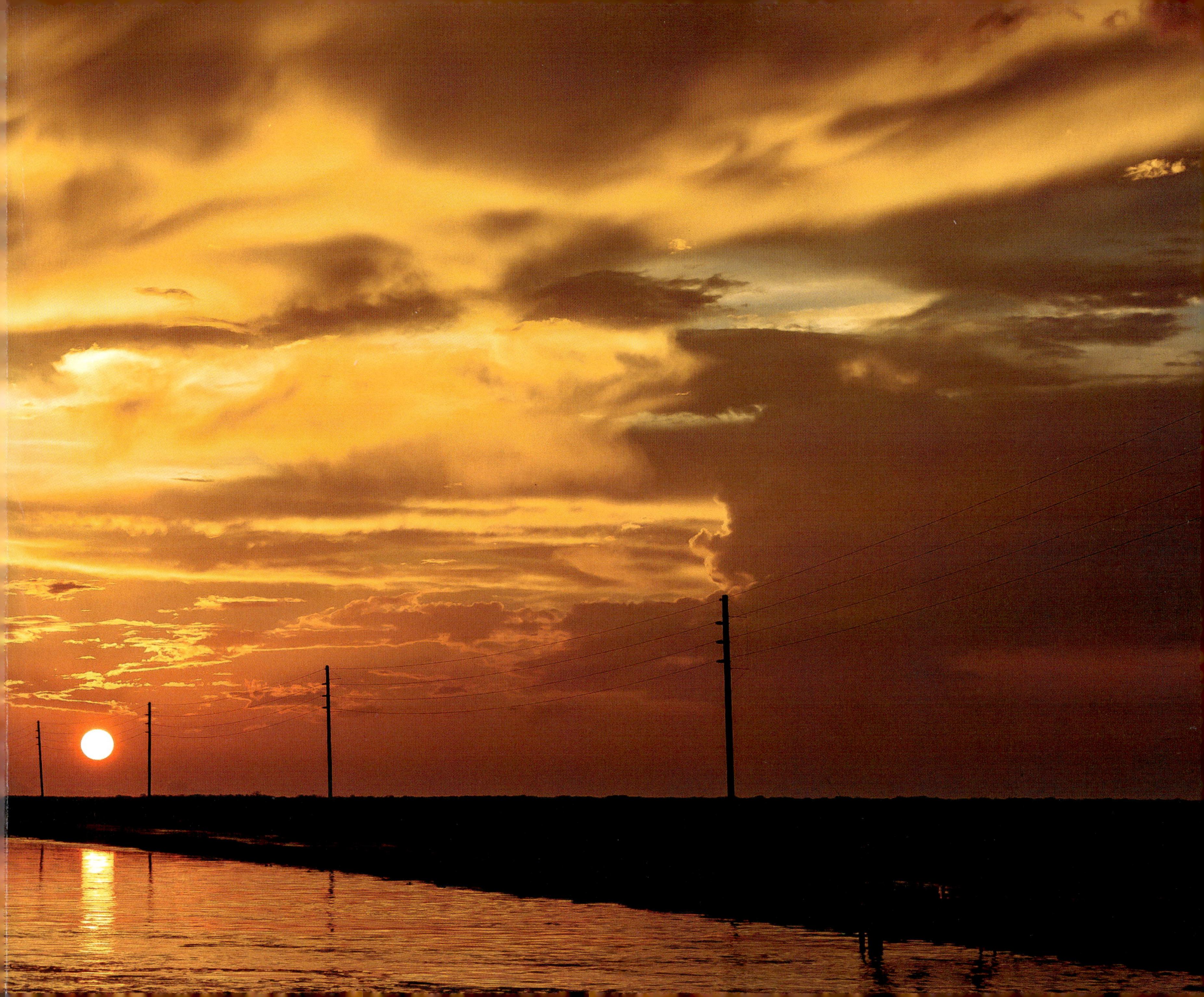

About the Author

Mark Potter is a 41-year veteran of television news and was a correspondent for ABC News, CNN, and NBC News. He has devoted his retirement to photographing Florida's sunrises, wildlife, and nature. He is a longtime resident of South Florida.

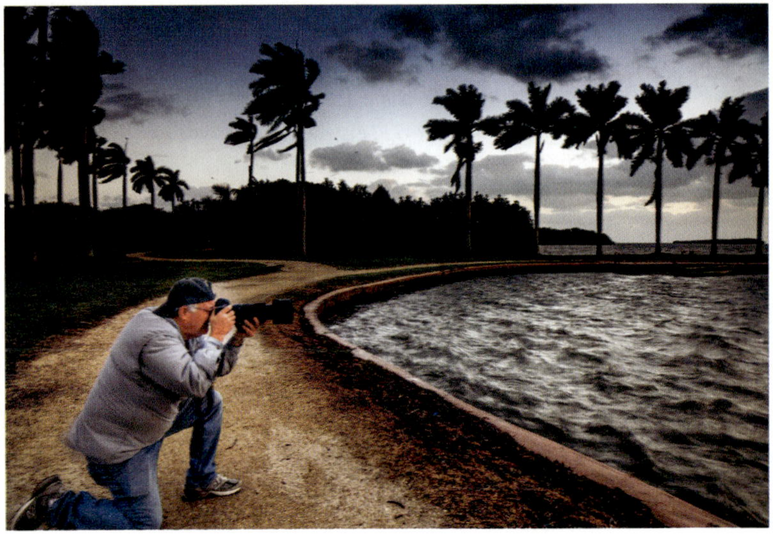

Credit: Jae Kim

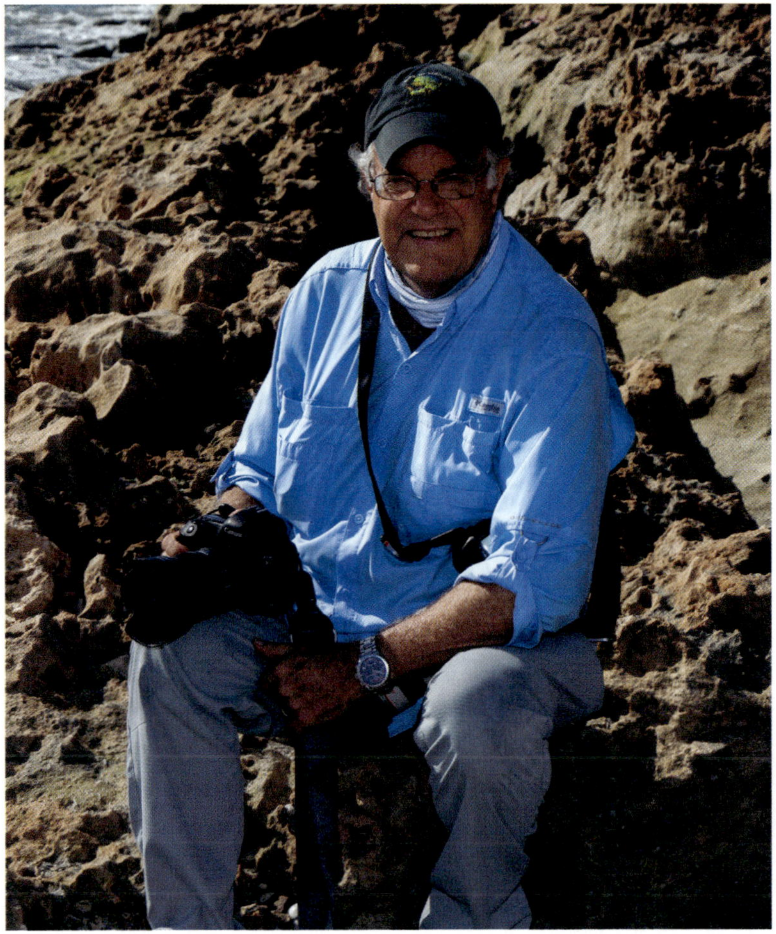

Credit: Lee Smith